D P T

Disclaimer

Most names have been changed; some situations have been adapted.

© Derek Peter Thornton 2024

Cover artwork: *'Self'* by DPT

The rights of Derek Peter Thornton to be identified as the author of this work have been asserted by him in accordance with the Copyright, Designs and Patents Act of 1988.

All rights reserved; no part of this publication may be reproduced, stored in a retrieval system, or transmitted in any form or by any means, electronic, mechanical, photocopying, recording or otherwise without the prior written consent of the publisher or a licence permitting copying in the UK issued by the Copyright Licensing Agency Ltd. www.cla.co.uk

ISBN 978-1-78792-052-1

Book design, layout and production management by Into Print
www.intoprint.net
+44 (0)1604 832149

*"True Alchemists do not change lead into gold,
They change the world into words."*

NIGREDO ALCHEMY

CONTENTS

Nigredo Alchemy **7**

Rubedo Blooded **47**

Albedo Cell **105**

Citrinitas Apocalypse **191**

Hex Paranoia **267**

Epilogue **343**

A Coda **375**

"What's in a name! That which we call a rose by any other name would smell as sweet;"

Juliet Capulet : Romeo and Juliet
Act 2 Sc 2 by William Shakespeare

Nigredo Alchemy

WHEN he was a baby

… he was said, by his mother, to sleep a lot.

One day, he looked up out of his 1960's pram and there, staring down on him, was his gleeful mother's face smiling; and next to her aura of pleasure was his Great Auntie Ruby.

She too was smiling.

He saw Ruby was beautiful and attractive. Her hair of raven black and her eyes of a dark deep sombre shade which shone with the delight of viewing, with the darkness of life and also a sense of wonder and a special delight in what she could see, what she was looking down on, and he remembers her face, the face of his 'Nana's' sister, smiling with the joy as she leant forward, slightly; as the child must have gestured, sensing of a wonderful structure, along with his mother, brought a type of communication, which seemed telepathic, being able to be heard in the air of voices, the surrounding silence, which they all experienced. Ruby knew the child needed to feel her nearer, to see her recognise him and D to like what he saw, as he would never forget it, her or them.

THERE…

…was always a black cloud over his head.

Him. The Butterfly; the Beautiful One. Im – *"That's 'im over there!"* Imbolc!? D, a title, *me?* Theoderik Peter Thornton?; Theodoric an Ostragoth!?; Who sacked Rome as a leader amongst men. DT, Decca Dent Peters, Depth, Druid; Thorn Pendragon!? Prince Mordred?; The bastard illegitimate son of Rex Arcturus and Queen witch; Morgana!? 'Symbol' hanging about the aether. Imbolc Thorn, a magic name.

Way back then, when all things were fought out in war and the Venus of antiquity was raped.

*

There is a family picture of him on his father's knee in a park. He is three years old. His hair is white in the light of the sun. He is young and fragile with a sensitive aura of delicacy, harmony, with a standard seated situation, safe and secure in his father's realm. Whereby, he may frown like the clown who is insulted for being and *not* being, what some may think he is? Even himself.

He would not agree and freely hopes the dharma of the world would collect the ultimate truth and relax the intentions of worldly massacre with soft, nurturing brilliance as to connect with the compatibility of the whole. Not 'it'; but *Godliness*.

*

There is a picture of him, aged twelve, with his younger brothers and sister. One day, they are playing in the front garden of the house at Laudanum Road; his sister is thinking about Narnia. She is seven years younger than he is. G is even younger, a babe, and J is one year younger than D.

He was there.

The photograph was taken.

He knew where he was, looking internally; introvert – *seeing*.

D was in his school uniform, a maroon-coloured uniform, which, after school, he would usually climb out of, to get into his 'civvies'.

But on this spoken day, he didn't.

D kept it on. He wore his Christmas slippers and knew he had a haircut to beat all haircuts in a "short back and sides, and plenty off the top!" styled thing.

He was sad.

He was sad and he could see.

He could see, Louise was with another boy somewhere and they were kissing. They were dressed in the latest craze, and had plenty of time to make their acquaintance.

He knew who he was.

D saw it. It made him sad.

His sister called them all over to have a photograph taken with her; with her Narnia imagination.

D was High King Peter. J was Edmund. H was Susan and G was Lucy!?

As they mounted to the sight of famous stages, the capture of immortality, a remembrance for when one has forgotten, the stardom of all protagonists; never knowing who was behind the camera, J lay out on the grass near H with G's cowboy uniform on. He looked like a clown in the circus, with the small hat perching on the top of his head.

G muscled himself in, for a four-year-old. D was called over to finish the picture snap.

He reluctantly joined them. He shuffled over and stretched out his body across the back of all the other three. Older and in uniform, slippers and haircut, he felt done for. He felt unstacked, drooped to the pits of all daily arms, thus, he was 'cuckold!'.

They saw the picture, later, and D noticed a great black cloud above High King Peter's head.

It was there for all to see.

From that moment on, the dark side was watching D; forever!?

*

He was depressed. He was forlorn. Saddened by his loss, by his sheer losing streak, but he could not face it.

Then, he walked into a silence, which became his soldier, to fight the darkness manifest outside of him, for the sake of ruining his entire life's force.

It begins with a small mind cloud, something, he knows not what, and grows with the use of the brain with coupled enjoyment brought by imagination, music, solitary dances, familiar voices; and then it grows to enshroud your whole soul.

*

She was called Sarah. She was of blonde hair and had a small strawberry mark underneath her left eye.

It took D one evening to fall helplessly, hopelessly, in love with her.

He was at school, primary, when he felt it was time to choose a girlfriend from amongst his feline contemporaries.

Dreaming or not, so he did.

He say the number 7, and had a choice of such: Christine, Linda, Louise, Belinda, [he put her there to make it seem important, perhaps, full], and a few others.

Oh! and yes, *Sarah*.

*

Sarah Jane Milburn. Even her name seemed to slip off his tongue, to rest playfully in his libido, to sex up his loins, and to pucker his cheeks for the raising ability to muster a very nice, well-thought-out, *kiss*.

*

Sarah. Biblical. Meaning? He didn't know, then or now; perhaps, Sarah was a name of a young maid. A given title like Mary; Mother. Mother of Magdalene. Mags.

Sarah Jane. Still it rushed through his brain. For in those days pre-Jung, the mind was thought of as a principle 'to use', 'to resolve', with or about?

So, he was using the brain. In his head.

Sarah Jane. She was fair. She was nice. She was a girl. She was pretty; with a wild look which takes the self – the soul – back to the days of pagan rites, the midsummer days, frolicking in the rays of the sun, with straw hats on and cream-coloured garments, worth the soiling, worth the good looks of merriment and joy.

Gone were the days to fear. Gone the pitch of darkness. Horrid the mind of adults, who slander the nature and run amok amongst the pure, delightful, innocent; bordering on curiosity, which would lead all into temptation, in so fulfilling the desired flame which burns in the pits of the stomach, for it is the area from which the passion rises, like a Phoenix bird!

At last to set upon the notion to *be*; to feelings, to consider, at last, a sensation setting fire to the old and purifying the ancient!

*

Oh! How he danced!

He made the decision to choose.

Sarah Jane was his choice. Not because she was the fairest. But, because she lived but two doors away in the cul-de-sac where D lived.

D was not allowed to go out. He was not allowed to haunt the streets like the others. He could not see all the other girls, because they lived in other areas, which seemed to be too much of a problem, if he was to court and romance his fiancée.

Just two doors away! He could go outside in the garden and call for her! He did one better. He went around to see her. When his parents were not looking, he left the garden with a stealth; sneaky. He knocked on her door.

She answered. He asked her out. She asked him to wait. He did. It all smelt of fish.

She came into the cul-de-sac, *'the bottom of the bag'* [French]; she watched as he played and danced, just like William!; his hat on the brim, aside with plum. D made her smile, he made her grin. His mum watching in silhouette and shade within his house.

*

Then, Sarah Jane went in.
He never ever saw her again.
Although D could look out of the bow window in his brothers' bedroom, as she made out for school with her younger kin.

D stood, one time, early, before dawn, and watched her leave her home, looking up at the window. He watched her, their eyes meeting, his heart beating, as he sang, to the wind winter morn, *"My grandfather's clock was too tall for the shelf, so it lived 90 years on the floor / when it stopped short / never to go again / when the old man died!"*.

Why D sang that, and how, he didn't know, it was just something he heard one of his brothers singing in concert at his brothers' grammar school – it was the only bit he could remember.

All in all it was all a bit haunting.

*

But, one morning, D returned to see again what he had seen, and sang what he wanted to lament with. But, she did not appear.

She did not hear as D sang with a great big black cloud over his head, that's what it was in those days, a *great big massive* thing, slowly allowing his poetic tear to fall onto his clothes, there, mixing with the surface of the garment and there, dry. Forgotten, like the millions of tears ever cried before or after: *Sorrow*.

*

At school, D asked his friend: *"Have you seen Sarah?"*

"Yes," he said. *"She's gone to Australia."*

He came, matter of factly and all. He did not show any emotion. He stayed with it all. D gestured, as one does, being thankful for bad news and the blues it seemed to render.

His heart! His heart had gone with her!

His heart and soul had left for Australia! He placed the emphasis on it all. When inside, he yelled at the stupidity, the downright *cheek!* The tasking of all averages, about – who would believe? – out of all those local girls, you would choose a flighty one, one who didn't even tell you about her leaving, to journey right across the world into Aboriginal land and all the way into a place later to be known as, *Oceania*!

*

The scene was pitched. Sad the story of Dr Zhivago, the treatment of King Kong, the emancipation of Zorro in the hands of Don whatshisname! But *him*, little ol' D. Why? Why D?!

Why make the cloud bigger, meaner, nastier? Why turn it into a tornado or a zephyr, like his dad's first car?

Was it now a hurricane, like the snooker hero Alex on Pot Black?! Was it a whirlwind to come?! Or was it just a jester's fart?! A lark, in the noonday sun?!

It was a gust of wind. The precept of nimbus cumulus nimbus. A dirty black cloud over the horizon, over his head, over the doings and coming and goings of D.

That don't matter then, it don't matter now, now that it's gone, now that it's gone and managed to ruin his whole life!

But, then, he was young, naïve and gullible, right to the back teeth, the 'fairy teeth' under the pillow at night with the 10 pence piece. No wonder, it didn't take it, didn't give blessings to his wish! Didn't do this and didn't do that, when the world was moving on to change, and the world forgot about the ship setting sail for unknown lands with his bleeding heart!

He loved her. He said he did. He did. He knew he did. He gave her his heart! She took it gladly. She took it and took it with her! Why? She didn't even leave him an address! Where was she going? Where would she be? He could look for her! He would turn 16 and go and find her!

He would save the money to sail, fly to Australia and journey a long way to be with her; at last! Forever vowed.

Eternal!

*

He had got it wrong. He had been funny. He was awkward. He had been aloof, trying to hold love sacred in the life of air, of the aether of all time, not to arrogantly step all over its intentions, its gift of bearing, destiny, result! Lessons, experience, whatever … would be, would *have* to be understood and realised, as *for a purpose*, or a reasoning to be seen, later, later on in the development of true love, the fastened love, to engagement, to marriage, in rendition, promised, fulfilled and blessed by the organised law of love and the nature in being alive, loving and loved by.

He was set afloat, all at sea, and without crew, only D; he became seaworthy and an ocean mutant, a crab, a crap crab; D, the sailor of greater seas to be discovered, uncovered and circumnavigated about the cape, about the bay, about the starboard and about aft!

Aft! Nowt! He was washed up at the tender age of eight, shipwrecked and marooned.

And it was all his fault!

D shared the experience with no one. He turned from the window, many days later in vigilance, having had his 'short back and sides' reduced to a 'skinhead' crop, as his mum stood at the door and sighed to see such a forlorn sight as sad ol' D. He had lost.

"…ohhhhhh… *love,*" she said. And she was right. She knew. She cared. He must love! But how could he? His love had been taken to Australia! A long way away! And he felt empty; he felt the chasm in his belt, the abyss to be filled, the darkness laughing!

So he cried himself to sleep that night.

*

He dealt with it. He stole some money from his folks and felt really satisfied, resolved to his satisfaction, never realising, the dark cloud had seen him.

He went to school, primary, and Louise could not – and never did – understand his choice.

"Sarah Jane?! Who is she? She's an army girl! I am local! I am yours! You are mine!"

In her dark forbearance she shirked off the depth of rigour.

Then the headmaster called out his name!

He wanted to see D. There he was in assembly, there he was, the great lover, the betrayed and the thief! He felt big, small big! Having become a rogue, a louse, a free boy, one to be reckoned with, and *there!*, even the headmaster knew of his notoriety and fame.

Right in front of the woman who needs him. There, right in front of his love, lost, *Love's labour's lost!* He had none to give, but she had plenty, she would heal him, she was love personified, she was lust and passion and hope and *amour*! She! Woman! She, the fair one, the feline one, the giver and receiver of all comers!

He entered the headmaster's office to see the end of his life pass right before his eyes, and he didn't even have one, hadn't had one, was never to have one and was seen to be the devil in the eyes of the Christian good of England.

He was a fornicator! An adulterer! A blasphemer! And he was lost! He was lost and would never be found! He was sin incarnate! He was lust, deviant, a thief – but worse; D was a demon to be slain! A horned devil to be contained and brought to bear under the feet of Michael the Archangel of all glorious goodness, which is manifest in all men, in all women, the biblical whore! The assailant sinner of mankind, so's man can rule the world. [Of course it has nothing to do with the planet we are inhabiting.]

And he was to be punished!

"Either I do it or your father does," the headmaster said matter of factly, which seemed to be the order of the day. The way.

A choice, Hey! He's not so good on choices! He seems to always choose the wrong things based on availability or convenience. Never daring to step out of his comfort zone!? Never sure about being able to attend to such address, to such needs, wants and fulfilments.

So, he opts for simple, clear and precise needs to accommodate the public, the masses, the individual; maybe, he should be a politician, a public body politic adviser, on keeping with the stray of brain, the strain of autopsy, I don't know. I don't know, and the devil in him says,

"I don't fuckin' well care!"

"And anyway," he said, *"I choose my dad, because he is my friend and he would never hurt me."*

He said. To the big tall living adult human headmaster man.

The black cloud had been at work and someone had slandered his name; somewhere, somehow, D was the enemy, the enemy of the state, the public enemy of decency and up-righteousness. The way of things is to do your duty and to do it well, at your chosen career, to surmount to better things and help the country grow, economically, commercially, brilliantly according to the will of God, his son Jesus Christ and in the name of the Father, the Son and the Holy Ghost!

Don't give it up!

Don't sell yourself down the river! Let us abuse you for our own sakes! We must sacrifice you, we must be seen to burn you at the stake, for our own good, you cannot live! For our own sanity you most be destroyed. You are the invader, you are the immigrunt! You are the terrorist of social life and the community, and you must be put down! Destroyed! Sent back to hell from whence you came! Beelzebub! Belial! Lilith! Dragon! Beast! Satan or the infantile devils of *legion-us Har Megiddo!* [A place known and called Armageddon.]

*

D was a skinhead with 'Pathfinder' shoes. D was a giddy boy. D was a thief. D robbed the tombs of kings and dug up the remains of the mighty! D denigrated the soul of St Dunstan, of St Gregory, of St Gunthrop! He salivated the soul of saints and grew in fashion to be the purple pirate of prose poetry!

But, *a sinner of love*? Never!

Maybe the headmaster was kinky, maybe he fancied him? Maybe, he too had lost his heart to a beautiful one and she had run off with it; she had stolen his heart, his innocent pouch of love.

She didn't mean to. She did not know. Sadness was D's heart and sadness was the soul of his heavenly black cloud floating, languishing above his head.

What had he done to deserve such betrayal from his loved ones?

*

His father met him at the school barrier, scowling, seething, the heat rising from his jowls, his heart, his bowels. He looked as if the message, a telephone call, whatever it was, had placed in his mind a picture of wrong-doing; a cascade of images obviously ran about his adult mind, like the parallel stories assigned to Jesus, in the myopic trophy of godliness and passages of parables, inviting the seeker to enhance his insight and personal views on the solvent argument; of what it all could mean, what it meant, and *what it really means.*

The look on his face said it all.

*

D was to be punished. He was to feel the wrath of God, of his father, of the system and of the society into which he had been born, would live and work in and then die out of.

D waltzed down the side passage, thinking in his eight-year-old mind, that his dad would not hit him with a cane, he would not bend him over a table and strike him with a blunt instrument across the buttocks; as if there was the place, 'one' thought about all rational things, about the logic of life and worked out 1 plus 1 equals 2.

He would make D bleed for this.

D *had* stolen the five-pound note. He had shared it out between three other people. K, J and N had received a pound each although K, being his best friend, had been given two pounds. D kept a pound for himself, finding it a struggle to spend it in those days, the 60's.

He had seen the fiver intruding out of the floorboards one early evening, when his dad had been hoarding his well earned cash, and was banking it under the floorboards.

He must have thought D was not upstairs, on his bunk, as he left it open and all the wad of fivers in clear view of anybody who could, or would, cross the landing for whatever reason they would be there. D went to the toilet. That's when D saw them. D took one. Not from the top – lower down – and rushed back to his bunk with ideas of rich pickings, high living, important decisions and loads of sweets to eat!

D had felt the black cloud around him. Covering every move. It was like a blanket, keeping him unsafe, not warm, and enhanced the feelings of wrong, the feelings of 'shouldn't'; an ominous cloud floating about the scene as an energy, a chemistry, to belie the mistake, the opportunity to take someone's property. It seethed like the vibrations of a black panther, a jaguar.

It was growling; the eyes had seen the coming of the sin.

D put the fiver under his pillow and threw such thoughts in the bin.

The next day, he gave bits of it away, choosing the right people to spend it and there would be no comeback from anything, anyone. D just gave it to them. Shared it out.

*

Early evening there was a knock at the front door and two fathers stood at the threshold, complaining to his dad, that someone had given their sons a pound each and they had said it was his son.

His dad called him down from his bunk.

D went down and heard the accusation, to which D said it was not true. D lied. But it had put many things to bed and it all seemed 'no harm done' by using a white lie.

Or so he thought.

The dark figures standing on the threshold of his life, darkening my father's doorstep, figures out of a black cloud, proud and knowing the intention of trouble, the will of sin; majestic!

They had obviously gone up to school the next morning and reported their findings to the headmaster at primary.

So far, they didn't believe D and he was a thief and a liar.

*

So, D is seeing the seething flames coming out of the nostrils of his dad, as he was told to get into his car, into the back, where he kept his work tools, he wept on a sunny midday and then drove him home.

He shouted "GET UPSTAIRS!", which D did.

D heard him talking to his mother, raising his voice, then the sound of the cupboard door opening, then the ascending of the stairs, giving D time to know, he was about to be hit.

With something? He was about to have his person attacked. He was to be taught a lesson for his sins. D was shaking inside and the world rushed in front of his brain, fast it carried on, the world at large, as my father entered the bedroom and with his walking stick in his hand told him to GET OVER THE BED!

He did.

He hit D seven times on the buttocks and legs. His aim amiss due to anger, his temper was a weapon to use the stick like a surgeon's scalpel, extracting the cancer from the body, the dead skin from the wound, the sin from out of the soul!

D had had enough. Feeling the pain of anus retention. So he stood up, turned around and wanted to say, *I understand*; but he didn't let him.

He was too carried away, he was burning with the desire of a killer, the flames of a rogue dragon, the sight of the enemy coming over the hill in world wars, he looked as clear as he could see in the deep grey haze of violence and cracked D about the cranium, on the left side, with the over-used, very hot, walking stick.

*

D just felt the crack at the side of his head.

It must have been going 30 mph when it struck him right across the psyche, across the understanding of all souls. He had seen it there. He'd attacked it like the warding off of Korean warriors in the Korean war; his dad had been in around '53.

D fell and scrambled under the bed.

D went totally white. He said, as he lay on his hands for a pillow, "I sleep now …"

His dad dragged him out from under the bed. Stood him erect. Looked at the claiming of souls and left the room.

D lay on his bed soaked in tears. The blood soothed about his body. The internal bleeding made his body sore, stiff and angry. It all hurt.

D never did tell the truth. Even after the beating. He told his mother, "*I found it*", another white lie, but what harm could it do?

What harm did *he* do?

*

It had been my mother who had called his name, during the spat, as he struck him across the head, hearing it, feeling it, it all must have seemed too much, going too far and possibly a crime, a sin, a human killing.

The black cloud had won.

The black cloud gave D the arena to be sacrificed, to be slain, to be an object to which all male adults seemed to have the need to destroy. He had been a gladiator without his sword.

A lamb to the slaughter.

He would have a nightmare in his brain from then on, it was a machine, churning, moving around his head like the siren of an insanity; it woke him, it scared him, it churned and spun on for years, a massive noise, at night, inside himself. Something or someone had gone.

*

D was sensitive. D was fragile. D was not soft, but poetic.

D was hurt. D was destroyed as a boy. D was abused, from then on in. D was used and tossed out into the world, like the carcass of a chicken, turned out for the slaughter.

D did not realise. D did not come to terms with his human development. He was marked. He was tainted. He was bruised and battered. He looked for salvation and he found it in life. Woman. In the throes of sex and love-making.

He managed to heal during his destroyed life.

The black cloud never left his side, never stopped floating above him. It was the cause of everything. It grew. It became a beast, a giant, a daemon and devil, the roar of hell, the crime of humanity; it changed, it stank, it haunted and followed his life.

Once attached to a sorrowful depression, in such dark melancholia, it never let him go.

*

It too became evolution. It too, fed off the imagination of a nation, of an art, off crime and horror, off killing and rape and human sodomy. It too, liked to see all those things.

It was called many things. It had many names, from being a black cloud of sorrow.

It was heinous.

It was evil.

It had no name.

It also looked for others.

*

Do you know how humiliating it was to step forward at secondary school dinners, and see who would want you at their table? Like being at a charity sale – *everybody looking at you.*

D would usually go home to Laudanum Road for lunch, away from the madding crowd, and those at school dinners would be eyeing each other up, to see what was what, or who was what for an hour in the playground, afterwards.

D on the other hand. Had to stay at home. Heinz soup, then, all the hour. Then be allowed to go back to school for the last 15 minutes.

No playground for him. They didn't miss him. He was sure.

Only, Louise must have wondered where he was? She would perhaps have liked to have seen him there?

This is the formation of his dark cloud above his head. This was cruelty beyond repair, only wild late nights and woman could heal this, perhaps even solve the riddle of melancholic darkness.

*

It came in the night. The mare to haunt all sleep! It would frighten the living daylights out of any boy's dream; sharp and cutting, it came, loud and vicious; it attacked the special side, the sensitive way, the fragile stance one has on a planet where all people learn to toughen up, harden up, even learn to kill; the mind changes, the prospects also, the world is a horrifyingly dangerous place, and the nature is too wild and devours its young.

There is none other than homo sapian which does. He was afraid …

It awoke the fear in vulnerable, naïve views on an inexperienced soul.

*

D drank in the army to rid himself of demons. He left the army, and drank himself to hell and back, hoping he had defeated his demons, all by himself.

He found love at the tender age of 19teen, and settled into the engaged bliss of good sex, good food, a house, a car, a life, a job and plenty of music to recognise the times past; the time with a saviour, *music*. Music had been there when he was a young teenager: The Ramones, Iggy Pop, Aerosmith, Springsteen and eventually, The Rolling Stones.

The Who was his first ever taste of rock opera.

It would take some doing, prising him away from the rock 'n' roll greats such as Jerry Lee Lewis, *'The Killer'*; Elvis Presley, *'The King'*, and the likes of Big Bopper and Little Richard.

Not forgetting, Bill Haley's *Rock Around The Clock*.

He worked and got up for work. He spent – *they* spent – and went out at the weekend.

They then made a baby with their young love making. She was fine, she was born on the 2nd of June; at 9 o'clock at night.

D was there. D saw the two heads. The heads of the ancient figures of birth. The god-given right to be a part of this universal adventure. There they were a head either end! It is an amazing sight to witness.

As his daughter was alright, they placed her in a hospital crib and D was the first person she ever focused on. With her little eye open, on her side, he said, *"Hey! You are okay!"*

You could see it in her eyes. The safety she felt, the security she felt and the true honest love which God and the Goddess had given them to have through their love for each other and their daughter's transmigration to become like them, part of them, made by them, *for* them.

Within two years, the black cloud covered his head, like a warm Russian hat, and the depression was so dark, so sad, so lost with melancholy's eccentric wishes, drove all his thoughts into groves and droves of elves, pixies and faeries with somnambulist figures, laying about drunk; Dionysus dancing with Bacchus, as they carried the sweating fat blubber of Silenus in on his palate throne, carried by nymphs, naked and clothed alike, with Nerieds, Ondines in the waters and poetic verse strewn for all to see in the ballet of the woodland forest glade.

D would fade. So, D left.

He walked away from his loving family and went to live in hiding, in lust, in the forest of ancient rites, into debauchery and drunkenness, lechery and sloth.

He was the faun of antiquity. D was a follower of Pan, the goat god. Being half naked and drunk. But, above his head and enshrouding him, was always the deep dark cloud which never left his side, his dreams, made his nightmares, and constructed a lie of a life for him to exist in with slumbering idolatry, illegal imagery and a hangover to allow the black cloud to bathe in the pain, the hurt, the hate and wash in the flow of the rivers of nausea.

*

Making love soothed everything.

The sensuality of rumps, the lumps, the curves and the swerves, made the world go around, for many nights and days, the stay of cost and counting courting hours towards the amalgamation of persuasion and performance in the dark arts of sexual penetration, seduction, slut, slovenly, dirt addressed, and pimp, the fortune was the prize, the prize was between her legs, the need was to be inside, at all times, in the hours of the dark nights, long and arduous, long the erection of excitement, popular pleasure, purposeful ecstasy, and a perfume mixture of lust, deviation, amorality sordid surrender and overcoming with the power of the phallus!

*

The celebration of all the dark demons, together found the place to party, to shriek with joy at the departing of honesty, amorality, value, so much as a virtue, in the stinking fellows of the blasting bellows, all fiend, looking nightmares, took humour, took jibes, sensed the line of sin run right into the veins of the evil one.

The black darkness hides many imaginative thoughts. Stores all the shadows made. Creates from the beating hearts of horror and loves to be, when the time it is to take away, whilst replacing the strength with insecurity, the power with vulnerability, the hurting with killing and the lost with a way to find a purpose in life by taking another soul, by bringing down the kindness to its knees and hear her beg for forgiveness, to turn from the scream, to shy away from all lawlessness.

Then the shadow, the shade, the silhouette has done.

*

Jesus defeated Satan, by taking all sin with him into Heaven and so, healing and forgiving, all of it. But, what was left were the *Legions*. The thoughts of many brains, bringing horror to the shelves of cobwebbed vintage vineyards, haunting cold damp dark graves, filled with all the possible four-legged creatures it could create, for the scared ability of evil, has a responsibility to make sure you learn, to know you would not, that you *could* not, go there, go over into there; that place, of gargoyles, leviathans, gorgons, black witches and uncanny elements none can bear.

The forbidden places. The long lost races of ancient peoples scared out of their civilisations, fallen. From what? By what?

That only allows darkness here.

In darkness there is danger.

Heal the darkness.

Clear the darkness of all responsibility to frighten the world. It would be a better place.

The flame needs sex. It needs fear. It has to be made to react to monsters, and it loves to be tricked by curiosity, the unknown, noise, sound, hearing or sight, of what is only put there by the black clouds of some of the greatest minds when they are melancholic, sad, lost; creating fiends out of the dark recesses, out of the shadow, from the plausibility and reality, it would never and should never exist. It does, and only for, if it wasn't needed by writers, Hollywood, bullies, murderers and stalkers.

The black cloud was only morose sadness. There are monsters out there!

*

His became a *god*. A demi-god. Demonetisation. The flighty of its wings came and went with noise. He knew. He heard the flapping, the strength, the lash of wide wingspans as it, she/he, flew to share, flew to ridicule, made out to flight, into the dark moon nights, flying, for no direction, flying into the chasm of dark matter.

What mattered, was that he was happily drunk, pissed, stoned, fucked or busy.

So, he made himself so.

He chased the 'pussy' and the 'pussy' found him.

That too became a chastity belt. The key to syphilis. To being a 'gonna 'ere'; his gonads ached with the pains of se x, the lust for the thrust to bang the bomb, to enter the temple of the whore of Babylon and fuck her, in her purple robe, whilst she fed on saints and sinners.

*

He loved with a good heart, He loved with a true heart. He was loyal, honest, steadfast and true.

He was the *pale rider* and so were you.

He found his failure in the tendency to need. He found his lust in the tendency to greed. He found his cross with the way he would bleed. He took his chances on the teacher of the dark arts, perhaps in there he would find the maker of clouds. The storms it will bring, the rain that would fall to drown out all our sorrows, the *tempest!*, he would raise, he would have to endure for the sake of exile, the sake of greed, to live amongst the faerie folk and wait for his chain, to enrapture and capture the true king of lands, fastened to the rocks, it would share his burdens, unleash his luck, take the thrashing, take the brunt, take the beatings, as the storms raise the sea! On the rocks, his heart is ripped from its breast! *"I will find my monster!, I will find my Caliban! I will find Caliburn! Caladbolg! Excalibur! and suffer! For the kingdom of Heaven!"*

So, he went and sat in a bar and drank the shelf.

*

Remembering the Auld Lang Syne, he sang in the local pub, one Xmas.

All his brothers and he, holding the arms across the chest and grasping the person's hand next to yours, up and down the movement, singing *"For old acquaintance be forgot!"*, looking round at the scene, when they were, past teenagers, going into men, his big brother with his friends, and all of them, about 25 people, singing away, so long ago, it seems, so many friends and family, so much to remember of the reasons why?; all was done or captured for the memory to hold it immortal!

There was no black cloud over his head that night; in't 'Gimcrack' closed down now?

What a *crack!* The beers and the songs and the singing, with friends, long gone, but on the night, the essence of joy on all the faces of people living; the drunkenness, the flare, the captured minutes and moments for time, in time, that was the place to be! That was the enemy!

My friend.

*

For a time it gave him reasons to fake illness. One time, he was very ill. Manchester United were in the European Cup, at Wembley against Benfica of Portugal. It was 1968.

He was allowed to lie on the settee, with his brothers in the chairs, wherever they could find, and together, his dad, let them all watch the match.

It was a sight to behold. He had not woken up from his deep melancholy sleep yet and seeing the footballers in royal blue and the way they played, made his mind capture the experience.

It was great. George Best, Bobby Charlton and the new kid, Brian Kidd, who at the age of 19teen played at Wembley, in the European Cup, and scored, the final goal to beat the Portuguese in white, with Eusébio, 4:1.

He had woken up to the world! He was healing! He was new! He was a Yorkshire boy, and to support a Manchester team of Lancashire would be sacrilege! So, he didn't. He *couldn't …!*

These times fought the enemy inside the dark recesses of his mind. In there, was the world at war, the blood, sweat and tears of many heroes and moments of sheer brilliance!

He let the mind free, to seek Jesus. He found him and passed his Religious Education test.

Grade 3, CSE. That's it, that's all he had, and when he left the secondary school to search for a job in the local paper, needing a skivvy or a labourer or a tea maker or just lucky enough to talk his way into a 'plum' pudding job.

He didn't. He got a job at Maynard's Wine Gums as a van boy.

As The Sensational Alex Harvey Band released *Vambo*!

The dark cloud met its match with music. Rock! The salvation of many yearnings, transparent youth! The ticket to ride and a battalion of drinking, drugging, womanising musicians, one could fear to meet, across the plains of battle, across the deluge of sin and universal pain.

They soothed it with music, and vice. Nice. He will do that too.

He did.

D was the long hair, with red 't' and jeans, BSkyB's and nowt else! He was invincible, invincibility, he was viler visible, predicative, valediction, kid. Young man.

*

D was in a pub at 14teen, drinking Yorkshire bitter, which was strong, bitter tasting and had a good 'head' on it.

The froth at the top.

He was on his fourth pint, when a man piped up, from where he was drinking and semi-socialising, as the amount of beer one could drink cut out all the chit-chat sometimes and allowed the beer to take its course. He looked over at D and asked, saying, *"Would you like a lift home!?"*

D knew him. He was Trevor the baker. D looked at him with blurry eyes. Having had enough, he said, *"Yeah. Okay."*

With that, D was in his car, driving home, Trevor looking for the turning which he seemed not to know. He said the turning, and he drove right past. D ended up at the local golf course. He drove straight in and made for the 18th hole. He got there and stopped the car. He said, as he leaned over to D, *"I fancy you."*

D noticed he had his hand on the lever, so the chair would tip back and he would be laying flat, as if the comfort of the chair was not enough for the early summer's evening view.

D said, *"I am not like that!"*, and jumped out of the car and walked home.

He told his big brother, but D said he didn't want him to do anything about it. Because, he had elbowed him in the face, swore at him, threatened him and left him with blood running down his nose.

Nothing was ever said or done to Trevor the baker in 1973.

*

The drugs he took to rid himself of the black tornado about his head, had been terrific.

He did acid tabs, marijuana, cocaine, speed and ecstasy. He did 'chase the dragon' once, no needles – it just gave him a headache.

Acid tabs for breakfast and marijuana all through the day; at night he would do speed or cocaine or ecstasy, whatever 'got him through the night' and drank loads, lots, every type of alcohol there is; was.

For 20 years, non stop.

If he were to take these new 'legal highs' today, he would simply be paranoid. Paranoid that the world was against him.

Take a drug, too much, don't want it, wish I hadn't! Those are the symptoms, this is the result. The psychology of my mind is *shot*!

He floats on a stream of death wishes and images of a thousand spiders, before he is all consumed with guilt, visitations, the devil and all the world looks strange, wrong, warped, alien, frightening, unfriendly, principle, it is against him, and he is the only earth-man there.

D sweats too much and needs to be consoled and calmed by a warm, loving hand over his forehead.

*

What does he know after all these years?

He knows: Who he is, well sort of. He knows that a chauffeur taking the wrong turn in Sarajevo, started World War 1. He knows confusion is tasking, until the time is right to settle with a clearer mind. He has been a supporter of many football teams, in association with, the 'Hammers', the, 'Blues', the 'Spurs', the 'Cottagers' and the 'Rangers', having seen into the game and all its opportunities.

He loves a good movie. A good film.

Perhaps the equivalent of many a book he has read, by authors such as: Miller, Kerouac, Dostoevsky and Hemingway, all alternative literature with a twist and a scorpion turn in its tale. Material which has challenged its era, generation, seeming to be quite tame up here in the 2000s, but he is sure the 2000 writings will look quite lame in the 3000 period of human consumption and taste.

*

He knows, the character of history can seem to share out the ultimate chimes of the way in which we have evolved, but, to the way we have seen war and sacrifice is the way we have eventually become, doubtful, in the comparison of conflict, when to die for us has been an honour, to show us our downfalls and our mistakes, when we naturally won't have to make the same mistakes again, in the 'Great Peacetime', and settlement for the human condition will go further into the unknown, due to facts already known, which leads us to the crowning glory of a space age.

He knows the spirits can interrupt the mind of living people.

Thinking they have a monopoly on the aether. That they, purgatorial limbos, are the inheritors of such, as the sky and invisible phenomenon.

He knows he is Druid of the new age order. A future thinker and sky worshipper.

*

He knows the natural herb marijuana should be made legal. It would be used by those who know the spirit, for the spirit of marijuana knows you. It has to be respected and thus it is not normally a 'white-man's' drug.

The knowledge of such gifts of the planet cannot be abused by a system and society which mixes their drink and have the most upsetting issues to deal with.

With the spirit of marijuana, it will show you, entice you, uplift you and keep you safe.

It cannot be used as a recreation, pastime substance; it is alive, it is a seer, a healer, a companion on the path of real truth and knowledge, not to be sidelined with the abuse of alcohol, with the abuse of self, and not with the outcome of leading to other drugs, sex and warfare.

It would lead to the highest spirit, in the heat, the heavens of the strongest of herb.

You would not have to do the likes of heroin, crack, smack or alcohol drinks.

D smoked resin for many a year there in England. But, the real spirit of marijuana is where it can grow, where it calls you, where you look for it and where it becomes your friend.

Lay down and smoke the 'erb man!

He don't touch drugs no more as *'is 'white-man's' brain gets paranoid.*

He knows he has just simply abused his brain, mind and cells of his thinking.

He knows if one dies on this planet not many people will know about it; if famous, okay, but loved ones and friends will pay their respects.

But, other people all over the world will not bat an eyelid. Sure.

I know that in books, a unicorn is depicted as a full-sized horse with an Alicorn, but, I think you'll find that the unicorn is a small full-sized horse, and only a maiden can approach the unicorn due to her purity and virginity.

He knows that crime will never cease due to need, greed and unrequited love.

To solve the programme of such things is to change the whole way the system and society of people are. It is not there at birth. It is something one grows with and takes upon oneself through all stanzas of life. What to do with life.
It has been upset, disrespected, abused!
D knows, it is no one's fault, but, one must take responsibility at adult age for what one can do.
Yes, the formula of love has been torn, hurt, abused in some way, as if the sense of an archetypal attack over antiquity which has been severed from the paradise in which the earth wishes to portray, in reflection of the terms and time of spiritual heaven.

*

He knows he loves Pablo Neruda the Chilean poet and Odd Nerdrum the Norwegian painter.
And not a lot of people know that.
He does believe the planet is sacred. And in a sacred place one must not touch, but *listen*.
When one can hear, then one is able to do what is right to light up a life. A life is a minuscule part of all living. So, to be ready for the evening's prayer, to warm the hearth, to eat well and talk about the gifts of earth and the amazing sights of chemical creation.
It is enough to see, hear and know.
D do know, it takes a lifetime to understand what one feels when older; it should be the feelings one has as a youngster, so that maybe the whole sense of righteousness and preparation for being summoned or departing from the creation paradox is and always will be the ultimate to be in, be for in an evolutionist lifespan.
He knows there is a before-life. An after-life is of one's making in life.
He knows the power of the 'power of the mind' is connected to the universe. It can conclude the questions about the after-life.
Where do we go and where have they gone?

*

It is to what you believe in life, is to where you can go or where you have prepared yourself to go. Nirvana, Avalon, Heaven, Holy Heaven, Hell! Purgatory! Limbo!

Why they exist and how they exist is unexplainable because words are not the expression for such places, it is at best feelings, emotions.

*

It is safe to have to say. But, one can look only from the depth of one's soul and see the confusion, the dilemma, the misunderstanding is stress, strife, struggle and hate.

The lovely blessing is to 'rest in peace'.

It has to be; we can. And the only way we can is *if we don't exist.*

In the place he sees, the beauty one is unable to catch whilst living on a solar planet.

Because of limitation? No, because freely, creation knows we are 'passing' through.

It does not accommodate for the uprooted. All else is an organic species and oceanic chemistry having to live by the solar power of a star. A burning heater, eternal till, immortal in, without such elements the planet would be dead. Silent. Inhabitable.

What more is there?

He knows we don't have to question. We question because of the way we seem to be?

He went to a holy place for an answer to his soul and once he was recognised for endeavouring to find out, he was given his understanding back, and it came like the torrent of all gigantic storms!

*

It taught him lessons, it made him crisis, it hurt his feelings and his heart, it tried to confuse his mind, and it saw he could cope with most confusion, only when he did not have anything else in his life which could or would be affected.

Job. Home. Family. Wife and Children.

He went to receive that what he had lost in the days of the black cloud, and the storm it brought him destroyed his life.

He is now retired from life. He lives a self designated exile. Solo, in solitude, solitary with his mind, body, spirit and psyche healing for the rest of his days.

He knows about love. It is the only arena we have to better all humanity.

He knows all problems will only be fixed when they rise out of humanity like the poison out of a bloody wound. It will move in time to be resolved, it writes history, but it belongs to the reasons of a human kind that makes us all today; troubled. Deep in the soul of us all. One. *'The Soul of Humanity'* is trying to heal. Trying to be free. Trying to understand, and trying to love everything.

He knows it does not because people control with power and the power is not to be controlled.

He knows he lived. He knows he loved. He knows he hurt. He knows he suffered. He knows it sought. He knows in sync. He was lost, but he was found.

Then he was annihilated by the powers of one.

To rebirth in a given lifetime would only be a game; the real thing, is to wake up all the sleeping demons of centuries, waiting for a moment to see the opportunity to destroy.

So he lived to be destroyed. He was.

He makes his peace with the earth's plane.

He has learnt his lesson of creation, evolution and spiritualism.

He rests his case, in peace.

*

Whilst in New York City, he was walking through St Mark's Place, in the East village, when seeing people milling about him, he heard a noise. He recognised the noise. It was the churning and turning of the noise he heard as a child, with the wheels turning grinding noises, which would wake him up and cause many juvenile nightmares.

He looked about and the noise was gone; out of his head. He had healed it, he had got rid of it.

He turned to see a young 'chick' walking towards him and as he looked at her, she looked back.

He watched as she manoeuvred past him, he followed her path and turned around, but when he looked again, she had gone.

Disappeared?

He looked everywhere, but she seemed to be gone.

His mind had emptied the nightmare and she was it.

He was told he would be destined to do something wrong.

It was the black cloud, sitting with him in Tex-Mex and Tapas, with margaritas and Cuban heels. It had persona and personality and made the world its friend.

*

D didn't know whether or not to trust himself. He trusted the weather, but did the climate need to trust him? After all, D was a menacing dirt dangerous black cloud, and maybe, there was rain, maybe, there could be storms, but whatever the outcome, he was shedding poetic tears and throwing tremendous tempers at the angry world at odds with him, at odds with Nerdrum, oddly enough for a poet, to capture the unrequited love for a 'passing through' organic uprooted man of humanity and humankind.

*

He would recommend, to all those looking for a way out of the 'norm', the system or just plain radical to read: Colin Wilson's *Outsider* and P.D. Ouspensky's *In Search of the Miraculous*.

For he knows the writer's job in life, is to right all wrongs.

Tranquillity is the feelings in life, one must sense in the whole of one's body.

He knows the best blow-job he ever received was from a man, the best 'shag', from a girl/woman who wanted his child, his DNA, his spirit in her offspring.

The best time he had made love was with M the Italian/American, who he married and had a very famous fling with in New York City, the year Lady Gaga was born: '86.

He has been kinky with most females, only it could be classed as a sign of boredom.

He knows he has had three prostitutes in one night. Prostitution should be made legal in this Cuntry, then all girls/women/men can be monitored, clean and safe in a brothel environment.

He begged for a 'shag' from a girl whilst his first fiancée was in labour in hospital with his first baby girl, whom we named after a call-girl from B, S.

Man is addicted to sex with the vagina. He will do anything to get it whilst his woman is in labour, going without, he feels inadequate, like Henry VIII.

One must heal and become Buddha. To seek the reference of solace is to change the routine and consequences of one's own destiny and fate.

*

The dark outcome is the black cloud, the rain will fall. Destiny is the moments in life which make up a destiny, which leads to fate!

No! To the Golden Gate and Alcatraz!

No! To a life of loving and caring about the truth of life and its lost knowledge from a beginning, which brings no end, finally, one can rest in peace, not pieces.

He don't need an autopsy! He needs to die a good death. Cremated. With a piece of piano music. His ashes scattered into the four winds, even, if there is a black cloud that day.

Gone.

His will and testimony.

*

Please.

*

He knows the world could be a better place if the mind of human life was right. We are too far in intellect to draw a humble picture, like van Gogh, to see humility in the everyday structure of the planetary affair.

We seek too much. We seem to know all about our history, but we seem to be searching for the 'missing link', when the missing link is *us*.

*

We search for the ultimate beginning through bacteria, and thrust forward in robotics to become the future.

The present is a recollection of incidents which partake in the isolated sequences which seem to be trodden affairs of the battle of Kingdoms, the heart.

A beating organ. It is the essence of aether imagery we should be searching. Mythology, Transmigration, Metamorphosis, Demonology, Symbolism, in the Occult is the opposite to God's reign, to the sense of the feelings in the Soul which brings the grounding of a love, which can pattern itself, with nature, with human bodies, with knowledge, we only have the engagement of sex down here. We are sex. She is tits and ass and man is a great prick!

The eternal formula for creation + evolution = sex; making love. Not war! Not slander or malice, and not the adult energy of sadomasochistic pain, which turns the psychology of the natural planet; diffident and warps.

We have torn the energy. We have hurt it. It is quiet, subdued and stinks. Smells of the intestines of a Hari-Kari radical's bowels.

Sniff the air. Hold in the oxygen. If we could see the invisible world it would look like an 'All day festival', for millions of years.

It is the dirt up your nostrils, which one has to clean out every morning. Make sure the 'bogey' has not flown onto your shirt or tie.

You would get the nickname at the office: 'bogey tie!'

I know that it is important to have a sense of humour, going through life. If you are too stiff or stoic, one can break, snap, stroke or attack.

Enough of learning the way of the world, the human condition, history, the planet, about himself.

*

D rids himself of the black cloud and ruined his life in the process.

Would he do it again? Would he be brought up in a dungeon? Would he become so panicked, so disillusioned, so distasteful, so insecure, and the depression become an energy?

No.

He would like to live the life he can live. But one has to find solace to do that.

He has and knows he can find the time to revise it all. Reflect and reminisce, nostalgia is the poet's tool and as he has said,

"I am the purple pirate of prose poetry. My spirit pseudonym is: Thorn Pen Dragon. And I should have been, although, I have become a wizard warrior galactic druid."

You can never change what a person will eventually become. You could kill them or hold them prisoner for a lifetime, but they would always be themselves, regardless of someone else.

*

They hurt him as a child, but they accused him of being a Satan. When his father dies, the truth will come out, as to what happened that day, what was said, to turn him so broken about D. He went on to break him down.

In goodness they used badness to quell badness, in doing so, they put his spirit in the hands of the darkness, the dormant sleeping demons, devils; they taught D to be a golden swordsman, whilst fighting to free himself.

D was left in both worlds to fend for himself and did. He reconciled the empty place he held for himself and became one, as the demon fighter, 'pug' or 'wart', a small childlike image of a golden cowl with a golden sword, only his nose was visible out of the hood, it was beautiful.

He then became what they had tried to destroy that day, and for many days after that.

He then used the spirit energy to cleanse and heal and rescue a beautiful woman from the destiny of sin and darkness which had entered her energy like the black mist of evil.

He gave her his love, his sword, his anger and his wrath, and freed her, so she could live a good life, with her three children, and he would have to live with the fact he sacrificed his long lost spirit for the good of another.

Okay, it was a woman, what man wouldn't? But he did it because he was crazy – and he could. He couldn't have her, the next best thing was to set her free, otherwise she would have been a French whore for the rest of her life and D would be 'gutted'; she would give herself to another and he would have to go without; forever!

He has. But she is well and motherly in her home country of France.

Half-time was three months in 2007.

Before it was seven years without and seven years after. But in those three months he saw it was like riding a horse; if you fall off, you get straight back on it!

He did have the destiny to heal the woman's sores, anyway.

*

It has come to this and that. He has changed the prospect of incarnation, rebirth, spirit telepathy, all possible with the outcome of seeking the phenomena of spirit energy, which was his own.

D searched in the knowledge of there being something 'amiss' in his life. Not a job or a wife, but the spirit one needs for life. He came to his own occult understanding of: Why?

He searched for the answer and got it. He saw it. He became *shaman*. He used the laws of all esoteric meditation and low and behold, 'Pug-wart' was presented to him.

Alive in a golden aura, 'in-tacked', with a shortage of D for 35 years and D without the part of him, which would have given him the reason to behold the representation of magic, wisdom, skill, talent and steadfastness.

They became one. D fell in love. She was a sinner. He healed her sin. His spirit was placed in the bin, like all abortions, he has lived without it for many years.

He was not quite used to it, for it brought the seething hell of negative energy, sent to waylay him, betray him, even have him killed, but they fought together as one, as himself and his son, he won.

But, D had to sacrifice for the good of the many and the few and woman.

The goddess would see he specialises in love.

Whilst the hordes of beasts and life livers hated D, he loved! He loved and overcame the torrent of turmoil and abuse, tantamount to suicide, murder, rape and falling down along way into Trinity: Virgin, Women, Mother.

He did ask Jesus on the Cross for forgiveness: *"I have sinned."* He did stroke gypsy rose; a Virgo's thigh on a bus one day; D loved it. He flashed her short skirt up and saw her small black brief knickers.

D was punished for such things.

He has never hurt no one. Sexual crime is abuse, hate, killing; murder, when it is brought to bear with children, woman, *anyone!*

D is healed from such things. He has his mind right. He is thankful and blessed that he isn't naturally like that. He has lived with many woman in his life and don't need paedophilia, ephebophilia, necrophilia or any kind of 'philia' to get by.

Philadelphia, *yes!* She was the best 'shag' he ever had, he told you about her.

The black cloud tried to devour his goodness, kindness, willingness, skill and turn him into a victim of a social disease and scaremongering. A crime for all eternity, but he knew he was too good for that to be him. He is who *'He'* is. Not anyone else. Not you. Not her. Not a soul stealer or a tyrannical power hungry lecherous despot!

He is a son of God.

As him and his Mum and Dad.

*

He has done and experienced most things in life.

The only things he has never done are: murder someone, have sex with someone underage, been a good father or supported Arsenal football team.

Not bad going for a man who lost his psyche, his interest, a load of woman and 'found himself', then went on to lose himself for the love of a woman's love.

Then he fell far, then he fell into the land of oblivion where across the waters on the shore of purgatory sighs the energies of limbo, moaning and groaning, like the poem of Dante said,

"Lo and behold! The children of sorrow!"

*

He loved and lost. He rose and faulted. He healed and found peace, quiet and silence amongst the many straying soul energy of indifference, irreligious, non-political and not baptised in the name of Christ.

His job is to reconcile them with crossing the rivers to Heaven where Christ has forgiven them, brought to his attention by him and his higher Spirits, and they may enter the heavenly Avalon, and return through the portal, not mortal, but, a preferred glimpse into the doings, comings and goings of all mortal conditioned coils.

*

Everyone in life has hated him, loved him, teased him, betrayed him. Talked about him, hurt him, misunderstood him, chastised him, made fun out of him, copied him, disrespected him, respected him, cast him aside, allowed him to lead, brought him to justice, brought him to bear, fucked him, tucked him in, kissed him, held him, had him, lent him out, brought him gifts, loved his tips, his lips, his poetry, his acting, everybody has laughed along with him, played him, seen the potential in him, not seen the potential in him, joked with him, poked fun at him, let him down, brought him up, picked him up, thrown him down, called him names, gave him names, a nickname, a close-knit name, a whispered spirit name, he'll claim, they claim, they charm him, they alarm him, they goat him, they choke him, he has sought them, they have bought him, they can harm him, he can harm them, they ignore him, don't know him, forgo him or he can forgive them, forget him, he don't forget them, need him, bleed him, feed him and shower him with joy, love, excess; vice, he loves nature, they love mice, he wants the planet to give, not to take, human life takes and does not give, unless it is to children in need of love from other human beings. People hard done by the system and way, who's to say, what goes and what does not?

The book is written: The Bible! *Nah!*

We must tender the day. For all days. The day is light, the night is dark. Live by the life of a living planet, then we would be far into research about the way of things and the way to simply be would involve no plastics, no blood, no vicious cycle, no neighbourhood. No dreams turning to nightmares, no jurisdiction of the faith, no poison palates, no early graves.

Just an arena of love, a word, an explanation, in terms, $L = OVe$ squared.

A partner, love.

Solitary love.

See the goodness in all species.

In man the most. For he has been shown to be the servant of destroying the female planet.

Like the misunderstanding of the feminine.

Masculine is brute forced energy, feminine is an art.

Together they are a brute forced art!

Take from the planet surface, there will be a recompense. Nature needs a symmetrical balance, as above, below. As birth, death. As give, take. As take, give.

*

Nature is many dark brooding clouds on the horizon. The metaphors for metaphysical fortune is to walk upon the earth, then leave. Do not take her riches, dig soil for her gifts.

Inside the centre of the planet earth is a female dragon guarding all the treasures.

How does he know? D don't. You prove that there isn't.

*

The glowing light of the sphere of nature's creation is an orb, so small, so precious, so beautiful, the awe of every living creature on the planet would be aghast to see, to feel, to hold or to represent the meeting of the universal solar heart of human dignity.

All would suddenly say; *"What have we done?"*

The bright shining orb would heal. All would be well. All would be okay!

Slowly, we come to terms with feathers and the ancient ancestral turtle.

We are born! We are re-birthed! We are renewed!

And D can love without danger. Without fear. Without us!

*

He is a new age solar king wizard warrior galactic druid. A Capricorn /Aquarius. *Kaprian.*

He is Thorn Pen Dragon. He is a wounded healer.

His home is the planet Taurus. Here, the earth. He is a grand trine earth earth earth wolf.

His universal signature is: Taurus; fixed feminine earth. Here.

So leave! All those who harm, hurt or damage the planet and all the living hearts on this planet, you must leave!

Stay, all those who protect, respect and love the Planet Earth and the living species which live upon it.

Don't hide behind those who you kill. Those you blame. Those things you hurt or harm, just because you are brutal, savage or inhuman.

Go yourself! Now! Stop 'tarring us with the same brush!'

And leave the rainbow children here in the experience that is called and known as *"Life on Earth."*

You never find the time to bring up your children right! Now you know why.

The black cloud is nowhere to be seen. He has a glad heart in his soul.

God is the all and everything. We feel, hear, see, touch and sense.

D is very unfit. He has been sat in a wheelchair for five years, smoking and eating.

He tried to commit silly suicide. But, *It* didn't work. Good. He can see it all now.

He is not made of much, but maybe, something?

He could have been an entertainer! He was asked at school, during his black cloud days, when the rains came, but few and far between, some days a storm of thunder, his dad would say:

"It was Thor in the heavens, with his hammer!"; D thought he was a natural when it came to mythology and the Norse gods of Valhalla.

*

Later, he was to read the *'Edda'*; read Gilgamesh, Tao te Ching, as Lao Tzu would remark,

"Leaders, do exist, they are not to be seen.".

Some of the Bible: *Revelations* five times, the *Popol Vuh, Beowulf,* and some of the dear old sad prose poems from the slaves of the Saxons crying because they wanted to go home.

The Story of O, by Paula Reage. Poems of Ovid, Dante and Virgil. *"Bury my heart at Wounded knee."* A "manifest destiny" they called it!

When the careers officer, at school, asked him, "What would you like to become?" – loaded question – I'm sure, that's what he said, "An entertainer." Being at school. So he said, "That is something you do at the weekend!" Weekend!? amateur! What about RADA or the Old Vic or something? In those days, they perhaps could bundle him off to drama school.

*

D got sent to the headmaster, instead, he should have said: "actor".
He was then asked, *"What else would you like to do, … as a job?"*
D said, *"Butcher! I could be an entertaining butcher!"*
"'Anything else?" he said.
D didn't have much left in him, to say, he wanted to be a travelling artist, tramping all over the land!
"No matter where I go or who I met, I shall make art wherever I go!"
The careers officer looked at D's black cloud, right above his head. Wrote something down and ushered him out of the door.
D didn't go to the headmaster, he told a white lie because of his black cloud.
D managed to get a job as a van boy after leaving school. They sacked him, unfairly, so he went and joined the army. Infantry. The 1st Battalion the Duke of Wellington's Regiment of Yorkshire. But that's another story.
He took his black cloud into heaven there!

*

In the Army, D met Diane. She was a quartermaster's daughter. Who he dated, she asked him out.
He was made ready by the 'lads' in Barracks, a velvet green jacket, his pants, someone's pair of shoes and a borrowed turtle neck, turned him out smart and accompanied by two consorts in the persona of Private Wade and Private Kenny; who did very well, he attended the date.
She arrived at the nominated place, in a low cut black dress and they both addressed the ritual of meeting, then took their drinks to sit down at a table.
The night went well, and they saw each other for a full year, until she had to leave, because her father was leaving the army.
For the next 365 days of the year she would attend to his sexual urge. She was born in Kowloon, Hong Kong, as she was a petite Irish girl, looking the more like a Geisha.
She would make him ejaculate by giving him the 'chinese wrist', as he was to call it.
She became so frustrated, many years later, as they were together, she

straddled across him, ripped open her white dress and relieved herself, he was the tender age. Now, he could not work out what all the fuss was about!?

He was never inclined to enter into coitus, and he knew 'It' all had something to do with his black cloud.

His damaged mind, his understanding, his commitment, the whole idea of using the phallus for such reasons was beyond his intentions, his capability, and worse, he didn't have the balls to do it!

He was too … *far gone?*

D was lost in a world of darkness. Clouds of mist covered the growth of his libido. Gathering moss! One has to do it. Otherwise, you are not like the others. You remain righteous, holy, perhaps sacred enough to wait for a one true love! Perhaps, one wished to live with unicorns!

But, to be in love and fuck!

Well, his mind did not let him. He was freely chaste. Celibate without reason.

Once Diane had done it. So did he!

D never stopped, committed, for 25 years non stop!

*

"I am sacred, but in the wrong world!"

One needs to be a human being, to form the spirit intended, otherwise, how can 'one' grow inside yourself, being able to let the spirit go one day?

He had to be the way the human world likes it to be.

To be him, would 'D' believe in the sacred ground of love, reaching for the height of immortal consciousness, leading him into his world, wherein, the spirit will flourish, nourish, and be respected?

"Yes, I have. I wait for my transmigration. I may have been born a psychic. If so, I would not have travelled to the busiest places to 'hear'."

They can become a psychic's nightmare. Too many lost, blinded souls.

D would have used it well, at least to better the intention of purpose. He knows it is 'easier said than done', in most cases, but, they destroyed his gift.

He has no use for it now.

He feels the rest is in the time he has to hear, see, the notions of a poet, the knowledge, as close to, a Neo-age Druid. Which in part gives him a feeling of being wanted. Needed by a familiar energy, to which he will return, retire and die for.

"*I bless them be. Blessed be us.*"

*

His grandmother did séance. She did not like what she saw. She was jealous, she was Scorpion. She made them think he was wrong, something was wrong, he needed to be extracted from his gift of sight, hearing and speech.

"*Talk properly!*" they would say. "*See the everyday occurrence, and act accordingly!*"

"*Hear my voice, the noise, the row, the turmoil, and you shall be here!*"

"*Extract the devil from him!*", D bet they said, he believed they implied. It was just a sad little black cloud above his head.

"*Into your hands go I!?*"

Not without a say in the way he could be, should be, might have been.

But, he lives the ordinary, normal life, one needs to find in the safe and secure world it can bring for adepts.

* * *

[Reflection: Nov 2023]

This is what happened … ?

He met a woman. A witch. Christine 'Woo' Harris. Glastonbury. A notorious woman who was connected to dark ways; as others had seen and realised. She cursed D and his ways.

Hexed. Wretched; an ugly crone who fell in love with D. Not just able to torment him, demented him, hurt him and bring him sorrow; she also fell in love with him and wanted to be his! 'It' commenced with hate, then looked to his charm and love, to seek a survival and everlasting requiem with forgiveness and a human understanding for mortal passion and unconditional love. 'It' cowled itself and wore a netted burka for a lack of viewing.

Then, it could not be lifted till he bettered his ways and life.

Although he wasn't too bad; there was potential and room to manoeuvre.

With her evil witch perceptions; he was to be damned!?

All to be lifted with a journey into the great dark depths of his life. Twenty years! It would take him to understand the simple terms to relinquish and redeem. Then destroy the possession within him in the terms set out by simplicity based on the need to refrain from addiction and ambition, so being able to lift off the hex which ruined his life and made him what he already was. Fine. Thanks.

Bitch! What could she have done or been, to be the way she was?

It ruined his life, lifestyle and life-force. To cure the hex? Goodness and virtue?

Next? It made him hate woman. He hated life and everything he had loved in life seemed to be tarnished and purged with a sense of unfamiliar taste or truth or respect and admiration. All gone. Hurt. Beyond abomination!

All was to be left to his imagination and not a blood-moon-queen.

As his connections having been experienced led to such as Valhalla!

She may have left, but, it is what she left him with – *nothing*.

The most popular of associations with the ancient rudiments of blood incestuous moon trouble towards her service and slavery.

The witch woman Woo was with child! As she walked towards him. And still she wanted him?

Destiny brings it all together, to see it off; and death; to see rebirth occur, which makes them both better people? – not his idea of enlightenment, as it makes him worse, to die, this the last vestiges to live again, psychologically scarred for the rest of his days.

One went to learn about love and faith.

Only to be tortured and murdered alive.

*

Rubedo Blooded

"Virtutis fortuna comes."
"Fortune comes with virtue."

                              The Duke of Wellington's Regimental Motto

STANDING in the dole…

queue in 1976, was like standing – in a dole queue. Or being recruited for the army in the second world war, having to queue up for bread in the USSR, although he wouldn't know what that was like, it was a welfare state, to help the country get to its feet again, then, it seemed to be a place to get free money, for doing nothing, but, losing your dignity or pride, queuing up for a future soup kitchen, seems to be charitable, but what sense of asking, please or thank you is worth the true meaning of 'to give', with an unconditional love attached to it all, with seconds coming with a smiling face on a beautiful young lady, who gives you her time, but in the outside reality of society, would not blink or bat an eyelid your way if you needed it.

Eddie 'the spoons' was in front of him, and he was small of stature, but big of heart, when filled with 'Thunderbird' or fire water!

He was full of booze, and playing his two spoons on his thigh-lap, a tune not unknown, but unheard of in the realms of easy listening. He was a good old boy, with dirty grey hair, a dirty jacket, slacks and shoes, and he smelt of shit, a bit, thou he was known to smell of booze, to cover the shit.

He smiled with his broken denture teeth and winked with his blurred eye, as if to say, *'How's about this hey! money for nothing and your tricks for free!'*

He itched for his turn up at the counter, he turned with his itch at the sight of the young boy behind him, fresh from the sacking, fresh from the system, fresh with a fresh smile and smell, and Eddie was his peer, Eddie the experienced one, the one with advice, the one to show him the ropes and to one day hang himself with it! The one, the only! Eddie 'the spoons'!

The young redundant behind him in the factory of sorrow was D.

He was a good-looking lad, with longish hair and a slight spotty face, he hung in his gait like the statue of punk, like Jimmy Dean pissed off, like Marlon Brando without any cotton buds in his mouth.

He was tallish with a dress sense of rebels. T-shirt, jeans, pointed 'brothel creepers' and a beaten leather jacket, been bought like that, worn and slightly torn, to fit in with his image of rebellion, revolution and punk stance.

He had blue eyes and slightly fresh in his face and underpants, he waited to be counted, to be freely paid, to lose the dignity he had built up from scratch, to finally let go of pride which got him into trouble with authority and headmasters, his parents or youth club leaders, he felt the naked stream of all the essence of armour roll down his face with his sweat, in his bowels the turmoil squeezed on his intestines and his bladder yearned for alcohol, he dropped off the heavy burden of responsibility to himself, his character, his personality, his charm, young wisdom, a poetic ending to a 17-year-old reign, in the metropolis of wages and pride, with good looks, which all the girls appeal to, as the job fits well and the jacket works, invested with a hum or a slight enlightenment as to romance, a charming man, a survivor over the state, the concrete bricks and mortar, the conformity, disillusion brought about by labour or skivvying for pittance.

*

He held freedom in his hands, his heart and worst of all he was going to lose it, right after Eddie 'the spoons', and he felt he had to find a way of getting through that moment, that future, with never a thought for himself, he lied about his destiny, he talked about his dreams, and he never felt more insecure, at that time in life, that date, that age and that dole queue, waiting for a handout, to be offered with the largest vibration belonging to guilt that could ever be assigned to the religion of sin or more; a disgrace to the kingdom of England.

With the jester at bay, the funniest way, he took the money and left.

The sound of shuffling feet, or a fart into the heat, a burp from food or beer, a sloppy kiss or a dress in bits, the world shrank, to a place in disappearance, avoided, until the day breathed oxygen into his face, and D went to the off licence with Eddie 'the spoons' and bought a quart bottle of whisky and some beers.

They sat on a bench and drank them, all, as one, he wondered about his future, his life, his work, his job, as he sank into drunkenness and played about with his heart, as Eddie 'the spoons' played a jig with his instrument.

The night came and the moon seemed the only light in his life.

*

D got a job sometime later at a Chinese laundry. He started at some awful time and putting the linen into the massive tubs of boiling washing machines, he soon got very hot, very sick and very bored, so he went to the toilet for a long shit. He had only been in there less than a minute, when a knocking came at the door, it was a Chinese foreman shouting something in Mandarin, and with bits of pigeon English, he could hear, *"… get back! Now! Get back! Work! …"*

He looked at his self, at his feet with the trousers rolled about his ankles with black socks on, he looked into his temper, his anger and impatience, he looked deeper into his life, the crap and the shit so far, so he wiped his ass, and went back to the boiling tubs of hotel linen, and thought, *stuff it!*, and walked out.

It was a very hot July day, and he was perspiring perfusion with tears, pore sweat and nerves of temperament bringing the sickness of labour into his throat.

He walked home, and entering the back garden, he saw his mother sitting at the patio table looking at him, when he noticed the child's small swimming pool in front of him, so on saying, 'hello mum', he fell head first into the half filled pool.

He felt the concrete underneath, he felt the warmish water about his being, and he felt the relief of cooling down, the membranes of his task leaving his possession and laying there in the manner of bathing, he got up and went in to the house to get changed. His mother said nothing, but he could feel her looking at the body he had left behind in the pool. She must have tutted her tongue and got up to get her son a nice cool drink.

*

Sitting in a pub with a pint of bitter, D overheard voices of friends from school talking. One of the boys, from the year below him, was talking about his dad being in the army.

D looked at his beer, around the room, at the boys, at his situation and said, *"Can you get a driving licence in the army?"*

The boys looked over at D who was well known to them, they all knew he was a good lad, but could be a bit crazy, saying, *"Yeah D, you can!"*

D took a mouthful of bitter and thought about it. He looked at his whereabouts and thought he didn't want to be in the same place all his life, and he wanted to get away from his dad, and the way he had been brought up was no better than a tyke, he wanted to be better, to be someone who made a difference to himself and not having to be a written destiny in the face of life, the dice it could throw for you. He wanted to be in charge of his life, his way and throw the dice himself.

He got up and walked out.

In the high street was an army careers office, so he went to sign up.

It was closed.

He was going to leave, when a uniformed soldier came along with keys and opened the front door.

*

It let him in, and he went in, straight up to the front desk and said, *"I want to be in the army."*

The soldier, with three stripes, replied, *"Of course, any particular skill?"*

"Yes," said D, *"I want to get a driving licence."*

"That would be the RCT. The Royal Corps of Transport." The Sergeant took out a piece of paper and started to read from it. It was about age, training, and choice of skill.

After he had read the papers, he asked D his age.

"Seventeen."

"Okay," came the Sergeant, who was writing details down, *"you will have to take this home and get it signed by a parent, as you are underage, and we need the consent of one of your parents."*

D took it home.

At the time of social upheaval and growing pains, adolescent sex and gangs of skinheads and boot boys, new mods and rockers, he looked at the sheet of paper and went downstairs, into the kitchen and handed over the A4 to his father, who said, *"What's this?"* not looking at it, but looking at his life and what was for tea that night.

It was something that would change his life forever.

*

Having gone to the barracks to commence training, the authority there told Private DT that he could go away and return in two weeks time as the rest of the forming platoon was still compiling.

So he did.

He went and had a bacon sandwich by himself in the local 'greasy Ada's' opposite.

He remembered as a boy when having gone to church one Sunday with his vast family, he returned and immediately ran up the stairs to get rid of the 'brylcreem' hair, the stiff collared white 'Van Heusen' shirt, the tie, that seemed to cave in during the day and attack his larynx and start to strangle him, his serf suit, a 'plain Jane' and felt like the cloths of an Anchorite or a Benedictine monk would wear, his shoes, the late great 'Pathfinders', with animal tracks on the souls of the shoe, for when one might get lost especially down the 'snikkit'.

Just as he felt free in his 'birthday suit', there was a call from downstairs for everybody to congregate on the back lawn and have their photograph taken as a family.

D soon learned the meaning of dressing quickly, for parade or exercise, or a call out for the streets of Belfast, he threw on his clothes and looking in the mirror, combed his hair; the hair, being parted on the right. He parted it on the left. He ran down for the 'shoot' and feeling the tug of his shoulders rise to the skies, the picture was taken and nothing was said.

He saw the picture later, after processing, and low and behold, he was totally different from the rest.

The rest smart and smiling, smartly donned in their suits, and the hair parted from the right. D's hair was from the left, although, he knew if the camera had seen him, it would have shown the hair to be parted correctly and the rest were wrong.

But, alas, the case in question was not resolved, and the feeling of dread, sorrow, fear and a little bit of loathing dramatic in his face forever captured in the day of change and the day he realised he was born wrong, somewhere wrong, to the wrong lot, to the wrong song and the song could be only sung by the Negro slaves.

The sergeant, who was to be his initiator, made the private wonder about his life.

All dressed up like a smart soldier, with a welcoming haircut and the shiny boots, the faded camouflaged uniform with the bright red stripes depicting his rank and status as a recruiting NCO.

D thought about the recruiting NCO family life, about, perhaps, his wife, living in the army house, so given and so called; D drifted into the thoughts of John Bull, the army boy who had threatened him, one summer, he was going to shoot him from his bedroom window with a 22 rifle. The pellets being able to penetrate the glass and smack D right in the eyeball!

D hid in his room, below the windowsill, now and again popped his head up to see if he could see 'big' John Bull with his 22 rifle. It was nerve-racking, the tremendous thrill of adrenaline running through his blood veins made him want big John Bull to do it!

He didn't and the world was a sadder place for it.

Why? He probably couldn't be arse't.

At that point of dream state, the recruiting NCO looked at Private DT and smiled. The smile was forlorn, creamy, but it made him homesick for his mother and father, his family and that fucking photograph, but Private DT knew, one day the feeling of up-bringing would leave him and all would be fine in the near future, as he turned from boy to man and the hairs grew on his chest, the tattoos amounted and the experience of sex was no news to him.

He left Colchester as an Infantry man. Having to do 18 weeks training just outside his home city.

The 'Elvis' haircut, the one Elvis had when he joined up, the awkward boots, the fucking 'putties', a throwback from the ancient days of jungle warfare, as the 'putty' kept snake bites off, the fucking 'putties', which had to be correct, as in rhythm and timing to arrive at the end of the 'putty' ankle, with it being able to be folded, thus tidied away, looking immaculate and postponing any necessary feelings about the army being, not in jungle warfare in Burma!, no fucking snakes in Ireland and making one look like they were just out to hit the fucking Somme!

Bring on the NI boots; high tops!

The training commenced and all was not well, as A Platoon was assigned four Corporals from other Regiments: Cpl. Babbitt, Norris,

Nodes and Leather. One QLR, Kings Own, QLR and Kings, respectively.

A Drill Sergeant: Sgt. Garnet; one PWO, Prince of Wales own Regiment.

And an Officer: Lieutenant/Mr. Hudson, 1st Battalion The Kings Own Borders.

Private DT would not find out his regiment until he neared the end of training.

The training began at 6 o'clock am, went through a very cold winter, and finished at the last post, making soldiers out of some of them, and men out of the boys.

Private DT was joined by: 'Scouter' Perry, Gary 'Emma' Keele, Steve Moonstone, Billy 'sniper' Kant, Frankie Stirling, Gus Rhodes, and a host of other celebrities trying out for the change in life from social waster or loser, criminal or rebel, they all sensed an onslaught of orders, authority, punishment, the biggest slander of all, when, all stood to attention, in front of the official NCO, they were all told, blasted with the name, to which they were associated, to which they would have to claim, any escape from, through, abseiling, an escape or aviation, a time in the 'slammer', or at best, 'jankers' for insubordination or crying on duty. The name given was TROGLODITE! *"The lowest form of human being on the planet!"*

*

The test of time was change, the ability to adapt, define and overcome.

The shooting range was cold and the targets unmoveable. The trenches dug without a night of warm, hot warfare, but nothing, nowhere, not even a sign of a 'Chinaman' coming through the bush.

Sleeping in the dugout mud and piss, to piss oneself was handy, as the warmth of the urine rolling down the combat trouser leg was comforting, nice and best of all *gratifying.*

The days in and days out, the coming and going, the nights on duty till 11pm bulling the floors and correcting one's locker, the clothes having to be a certain width and height as to fit the criteria of the non-commissioned officer's measuring stick; if not, then the whole lot would be tossed about the barrack room and the punishment could be painstakingly difficult, to say the least.

D thought about the world outside, how they performed, what the incentive was, at an age of teenage reason, he wondered about the 'birds' in the nightclubs, the beers drank in the bar, the comfortable nights watching television on settees and the family dog, the music listened to, and did anybody know what A Platoon was doing? Short-haired and cleanly amassed, to show off the discipline of manhood, for the trend of a function which would call you out at two in the morning and have you running back in, to change into a particular dress, which was at times so chaotic, somebody stopped, lay under his bed, as the orders were being called; he took a breather, only to run back out with the same dress he was wearing when he disappeared for a turn, without being noticed by any of the barking, *pissed off* Corporals.

D laughed at the wholesome characters doing their thing in the face of bullshit and adversity.

As time went on and the seasons changed, Private DT became 18 years old.

On his birthday the platoon went on exercise, somewhere in the 'bloody' winter cold.

He was ordered to have a shave in the snow. He shaved in the snow in front of all the rest of the platoon. Whilst the razor crossed the young 'zits' on his face, the blood mingled with the bright white delightful British snow. They were all ordered to sing *Happy Birthday* to him, as he winced at the tugging of his chin. Happy Birthday D!

The target ranges had to be ordered in such a way as there were live bullets about! D hated the idea of having to lie down in the freezing cold and fire off some sulphur stinking killer cartridges. He avoided the shoot as best he could, by standing about the barrel fire and keeping his hands warm, with others who had fired and were very happy with their score.

D took a stroll one day and ended up looking at a loaded Browning pistol on a table. He looked about him. No one was about. So he lifted the gun up and fired off the six rounds in it, at a stupid target, one of those guys that never moved or bled and seemed to always be carrying his rifle just for the shake of being shot.

Private DT went up to the target and looked at the bastard's face, his body, his rifle. Not one bullet had hit the target!? He looked and thought about the effect he must have made for the bastards in the bush behind the target, who being fired upon, must have run for their lives!

He lay the pistol down and went for a solo piss in a bush.

Private DT was told by Mr Hudson that he was to be 'back squadded' if he didn't do well on the CO's test. The Commanding Officer's test at the end of the 18 weeks needed to be valued.

D asked what 'back squadding' was.

"You will have to do the training all over again with a new platoon and trogs."

*

So, the day came for the Commanding Officer's test, and Private DT was up for it!

He ran the mile and came third; he did the obstacle course without a sweat; he called the measurements of the target out on the general purpose machine gun; he received for his pains a 98% on the jungle walk, to which the Corporal in charge told him a story. About the reason why no one receives a 100% – *ever!* The reason was, when a soldier approached the weapon on the ground to go on and face the 'bloody' targets on the jungle walk, they would always pick it up and check the magazine for bullets, off they would go into the walk and the targets would shoot up and the soldier would shoot them down. The final assault was a 'click' on the SLR, thus the soldier would have to take cover, and throw his grenade at the target, shouting *'Grenade!'*

"You," he said to Private DT, *"was very good, you did everything right, and it is commendable that I gave you 98%, because no one I know has ever received higher. But,"* and there was a slight pause, *"you are dead."*

D looked at the friendly Corporal and wondered what he meant.

"Now," the NCO said, *"when a soldier picks up the rifle at the beginning, like so,"* he showed D as to what, raising the rifle high had meant, *"what you find you have done is … blow yourself up! There is a trip wire attached to explosives, as a raised SLR triggers. You should slide it out. Like so."* He then proceeded to demonstrate the ideal movement he was relating to, and with a great big smile on his face, said, *"Well done!"*

D was dead and his wrist was cut, slit by a renegade piece of glass, there on the grass, as he fell to cover, he hit the only place the glass wished to be, to score the blood of war in the mind of a monkey, and the smell of blood, the taste was sweet.

D was a dead pistol punk and he came fourth in the platoon, out of 54 soldiers. He passed out and so did Lieutenant Hudson.

No one said anything, not a sound, not a jibe or a rasp of disrespect, everyone was happy, they had 'passed out' and as D went back to the list on the notice board for about the fifth time, Corporal Leather came through the door of the barrack and with his 21 lbs rucksack full of sand, with his army training brow sweating, said, *"Ah! There he is!"*

Corporal Leather was training for the SAS regiment and knew a 'bastard' when he saw one.

*

Private DT walked into the room which was full of officers waiting to give out a private's regiment. They looked at the specimen in front of them and asked, *"Which regiment would you like to be in?"*

D thought about it, and not too long. He had gone from a HGV driver to a troglodyte in a mere four months, so he didn't waste any time, in case he wasn't given anything; he said, *"Sir, I would like to be in the 1st Battalion the Duke of Wellington's, please, SIR!"*

"Very well," came the voice of an officer. *"The Duke of Wellington's it is."*

The 'Dukes' were stationed in Germany, NATO and were getting ready to go to Northern Ireland for a four-month tour of duty. Unbeknown to Private DT; 1 DWR.

*

The sense and notion of travelling to Germany was not to visit other countries or meet other friends, but to die.

The thoughts in the mini-van as it trundled along an autobahn, through the similar countryside to which we had taken off from, seemed to be like looking into the future and seeing the horizon of the sea where the clouds meet the excitement of beaches.

The best moment, D thought, was as a child, when mama opened an ice-cream and he waited for it. He seemed to be looking into the void of limbo, a comfortable place of wild unicorns and gnomes snacking by the oak tree trunk, looking at the make-believer, as the ice-cream arrived opened and the wait was over, the cloud dispersed and the bubble burst to travel back to the reality land of ominous smells and funny faces.

Private DT sensed something wrong to come.

He looked at his 'oppos' and they seemed to be okay, apart from

Frankie Stirling, who said, *"it will be alright"* in his telepathic sympathy.

D did not register the fear, the sent beleaguered mounting, a proportioned disillusion of a future state, to which there was no freedom, no turning back.

He sped on. The minibus arrived at the regiment barracks.

*

D walked into his billet, the room where he would share with five other people a single bed, a locker and a bedside table. He saw three men playing cards and walked straight up to them and said, *"Hello"*.

They did not move, they did not look up. They didn't answer, with manner, friendly, banter or introduction, but carried on playing cards.

The atmosphere was gambling, the sense of smell was a bygone era of trouble, they seemed to be planning their next move. They did, and Private Ponce Mitchell, Terry Sharp and 'Owl' Cheetah, got up and attacked Private DT.

They took him by the body and threw him on his bed. They hit him and taunted him and Ponce, the one with the large moustache, a veteran air, began to hurt DT's genitalia. He squeezed a testicle, until it ruptured and broke and in the mind set of the time, he seemed to say, *"You will not have her!"*

Who?! … who did he mean? They left him suffering on his bed, he had tears in his eyes and the pain of the testicle seemed to have ridden through his stomach and ached his very being. He was totally at a loss, as to why they had been so cruel, so aggressive, so unruly and dangerous.

It was all a mystery, which over the first days would come to light, as D met other soldiers, who told him about Ponce and his gang, about the 'Green-back' rapes and the fact that Ponce Mitchell was a killer already; having opened fire in Northern Ireland, shooting someone and killing him.

A 'Green-back' was a new recruit, just out of training. They would take him up to the 'company club' in the attic, take his clothes off and holding him down, they would polish his scrotum, balls and cock with polish.

Imagine, a red raw, polished penis, covered in black substance, bleeding *fast* and hurting like a bad foreskin operation.

They needed to be reported, and it was Private DT, who, slamming his 'tabs' in front of the Sergeant Major, told him of the goings on, told him about his attack and listened as the company Sergeant Major said he would look into it.

Nothing happened after they were reported, but the injury had set D back and he felt alone for the first time in his life, it wouldn't be the last, but he was new to an army regiment and everybody 'knew the score'; he seemed to have been ostracised for his procedure.

Then he met Mees and Lee. They were two mice … *No!*, they were two Private Soldiers called Shaun Mees and Robert Lee. They were ordinary boys from Sheffield, but they saw that D needed a friend, so they invited him to go into town and have a coffee; perhaps, make friends with those two friendly mice, who seemed to be astute soldiers, they knew Ponce and his gang, for being 'bastards' and they saw to it that no one committed suicide on their watch.

They were funny. They went and had a coffee, then did some normal shopping, then walked about the German town as tourists; looking at the architecture, statues and people who inhabited the streets.

They stood in front of a statue of King Wilhelm the second, who on a horse, was regal and larger than life. As they both took in turns taking photographs of each other, then D, D with a local native, an old boy who placed his hat on DT's head and together they joined arm in arm, as they both laughed. The funny old boy from Germany, was a good old boy, like any good old boy anywhere all over the world, so where has racism, bigotry, slander and insult of races come from?; they did not know, it was not there that day, and everyone had a great genuine wholesome time.

As the evening pulled in with a blanket of dark cloth, they looked at D, Mees and Lee; they asked, *"Well? Are you alright now?"*

"Yes," said D.

"Well," they replied, as if together, *"you can go now."* They both shifted their eyes in the direction of the town bars.

"Okay," D said, *"and thank you for all you have done."*

"t's nothing," S said. *"Anytime."* They both stood and watched as D walked into the night, saw a bar he liked, looked back at his two hero mice, and entered.

They stood for a while, looked at each other, smiling, then they too went back to barracks, to get ready for parade in the morning, happy in knowing, happy in showing, a life how to live, how to survive and laugh whilst the pain subsides and the laughter lines are the only wrinkles in the make-up of a soldier.

D looked up after thinking about those two, and there at the bar was Ponce, Terry and 'Owl'.

They were drunk, and D sauntered up to the bar, as they watched, ordered a beer, in English, and seeing a person sitting at the bar, seemed to side with that.

The person at the bar looked at D and said, *"My name is Jackson Cranleigh Elwood! How do you do!?"*

D replied to the friendly, welcoming soldier sat at the bar, *"I'm okay, My name is D."*

They both looked at their drinks, they both looked over at Ponce and gang, and together they defended their territory, together they showed, they could fight and would, but the glance was enough to know, they both had free time to enjoy the pleasure of drinking and L, as he came to be known, said, *"Do you want a 'Schnapps?"*, with a slight German lilt.

"Yes!" came D, and together they decided to get drunk, good and proper, with no difficulty, violence, anger or drinking antics suiting a lair of hyaenas, like the blood-soaked hands of tarnished souls, hurting from the pain of hate and aggression.

It was the last D saw of the 'genuine wholesome time', for the rest of his life. Sober.

*

They, together went about the town, the *Dancing Star* was a favourite night club, which they would never be out of.

Every night, about seven or eight in the evening, after drinks in other bars, they would enter and party the night away.

The German girls would run the bar. The 'squaddies' would drink and fight, dance, collapse, spew up or simply have a great night, into the morning. As soon as one bar closed another would open, on the hangover's *'reaper-barn'*. From one bar to the next, up the street and down, about seven bars all told, all owned by one man?

D and his friend L would be smashed, trashed and blathered by the mornings end, soaked in alcohol, soaked in extreme feelings and music, punk, rock, pop, anything to dance to, or be influenced by, or shit-faced, fucked, the very nature of oblivion was disrespected, the very nature of human living was annihilated.

Come the fall, come the spring, the excitement was too much for the air, the soil, the spit and sawdust on the German floor. The bars smelt of piss and vomit, plus there was a special tang to the essence, to name and shame, to insult, to walk within forever in immortality, was this tang, this taste, a mixture of all; mucus, bile, sick, sweat, sperm, germs, every feeling brought to bear by being in excrement. It was the pits and the shit pit hit the nostril senses with trigger happy remorse, perfume of demons, the bear pit of Elizabethan times.

Private D and Private L pissed it all up and wasted it all on the sheer delight of anarchy without the investment, without the T-shirt, in hell, but sheer bliss, to kiss the devil's arse, then bring the beauty of love to the fore and pore, bleed the ills of infancy, teenager, right out of the fucking window … hence, whisky, gin, Pernod, vodka, peach Schnapps and loads of beer, arrests, puke lays, fights and beatings, lost and found, hilarious song and blasphemy, the true verse of apocalypse, then up in the morning at six for parade, trim, smart, turned out, shaven, polished and alert.

D would cross the barrack square, enter the doctor's clinic and sign in SICK.

*

One time, they were walking past a music shop. The shop was closed and all the lights were off.

It being late evening. D walked up to the glass door and with his notion of feeling nicely drunk, kicked it in. The glass smashed as they waited for the burglar alarm. No burglar alarm! So they walked away, hid some streets down, then seeing no one had turned up, went back to the shop and raided it.

They took three electric guitars. A Gibson, a bass and some other type.

They called a cab and jumped into the back seat. They were taken to the barracks where they strung the gits and collapsed on their pits.

Sometime, they decided to play them. They sat down and played them. L on Bass and D had the Gibson.

They looked at each other as they tinkled about, then D managed to play a Rolling Stones riff on the Gibson. To which L watched, listened and joined in playing.

After a while, they got good and played the song, *Satisfaction,* by the Rolling Stones. Then they got bored and walked away from stardom, talent, money and groupies, for the rest of their lives.

They woke up and formed the band. The band was called, 'Joker', and it was a joke, it was purposely meant to 'not be', a failure, a band with no talent or performance, the real true punks; they were the real true punks, with distaste, bad breath, shit attitudes and no idea how to play.

*

The briefing was Northern Ireland, as D ran to the 'bogs' and threw up pure purple liquid.

He had been drinking Pernod Blacks all night.

The lesson was to learn the streets, the people, members of the Irish Republican Army, the terms and signs, streets and cars.

It was time for the war, no more peace, no more messing about with smart parades and bullshit, but, time for self-awareness, self-hygiene, self-proclaimed, a self-belief and most of all a self-respecting soldier of peace and war. To turn out, smart, alert, trimmed and knowing.

And sober.

During training for NI, he went to Tin city. Where he loved to patrol the mock streets, then go inside for debriefing, watching himself on video. He would look like an actor. He would do things to make his moves on the screen look like an actor. He loved it!

One day, whilst on patrol on the mock streets of Tin city, he was asked to house search, a particular house, and on entrance, in the kitchen, the mannequin, used for suspect dummies, was a female one, naked with a frying pan obtruding from her vagina area.

D approached the suspect, and looking at the situation, burst out laughing, as did the rest of the patrol, as did the officers watching on the CCTV; just about everybody laughed for ages, what seemed till the end of the war. They laughed, and the contagion was tantamount to upsetting the locals and finding the whole idea of talking to a woman with a frying pan up her 'snatch' was too much for anyone, as the whole patrol broke down and in debriefing, they all laughed all over again, this time at the expense of a great comic actor called DT, who knew he had been rumbled, but loved every minute of it.

No one did rush in that day and spray them with bullets, after being distracted by the sight of the frying pan, no harm done and the Oscar went to her.

*

The Creggan, Londonderry, was a very large council estate. It sounded like a mythical beast, which killed the village and was feared, until a warrior brave enough, was found to slay it.

It wasn't. But it was full of I.R.A terrorists.

The camp was at the top of a hill, overlooking the estate. The helicopters flew over ex-'No Go' areas and the *Pigs'* armoured vehicles would slam to a halt, the soldiers pile out and take up positions to patrol the area.

"WELCOME TO FREE DERRY", but they were not. As the first sound into the daylight air was the sound of an Armalite shooting off at the clouds, the birds, the blue sky, the universe, God!, where it landed, where it hit, where she bled, the immense Trojan of defence, breathing the anarchy of rebel War, necking the turtles' breath, the intimate guile in maximum triumph, pleasured by seekers and the muckers and paramilitary, blackened out to view the world in contempt with sheer bravado, needing a fix, to cure the pain of eternal damnation and the parliament of papal basher, queer slashers, maxima meritocrats and termagants, out and alive with stretching desire to fire the gun at the first British 'bum', which thought or thinks it owns Christendom. Don't!

And do.

Private DT's 'brick' jumped over a fence, into a woman's garden, and so did the rest of the regiment.

The 'brick', a format of four soldiers, on either side of the street. A 'Brick' Commander: Corporal 'Duke' Lawrence. A second in command, just in case the Commander got shot: Private Nick Adams. A 'Mugger', Terrorist recognition, that was D, and a 'Tail-end Charlie', someone who walked backwards and covered the rear: Private Neville Dykes, a Gypsy boy with indigenous connections, waiting to die and be *incarnated as an Indian aboriginal shaman.*

*

One day, a day like any other day, which was possible, except for the fact, we live by the Julian calender, and every day is different due to date. Strange how they got it right, perhaps nailed the coffin down with the terms of control and understanding, to represent the peak of human optometry impugn.

The briefing officer spoke out. *"Tonight, we shoot to kill!"*

He meant it too. Yeats Edger was loose and on the run from shooting a soldier. He was a known I.R.A terrorist, who lived on the Creggan estate and was known to visit his mother and have a full breakfast before going about his business and opprobrium.

As terrorist recognition, a 'mugger', so called, D sprang into action! *As tonight of all nights / there's gonna be a fight!*

They patrolled the estate looking for him, here and there, searching this and that, but no sign of Yeats Edger.

The patrol, code name 21Charlie, walked about a busy part of the Creggan. Private DT looked up at a window. The man at the window looked at him. The man, then seeing the display of aggression, coming from the heat of D, drew his woman in front of himself and hid behind her. Private DT looked and then, went the colour white. If the shade of white is classified as a colour, then he felt a pang of betrayal.

He would lift his SLR, a self-loading rifle and aim at the man, then in recognising Yeats, would pull the trigger and fire! The 7.62 bullet would leave the aperture and in velocity, fly towards the expected target, hitting him in the face, exiting out the back of his head. The man would be at the same time, drawing his woman in front of him, as the bullet hit her and entered her face, exiting out the back of her head!

Private DT would be arrested, after the shooting. It would then be found, the target was not the designated one and D would be found guilty of murder, going to prison for the rest of his days.

That's why he white'ed.

That's why he didn't shoot.

He moved along sheepish. He moved nearer the end of the night, without an incident and thanked the Lord for his discretion at the given moment of improvised spontaneity.

Nothing to report on debriefing and the two egg sandwiches he had after, at the grill, were absolutely brilliant! Just right. He loved the constant grill, cracked the eggs, 'sunny-side' up and tasting the essence of a good old egg 'sarnie', made him tired and ready for his four-hour 'kip'.

Another day, if it was at all possible for another day to be totally different, as to be recognised as a certain date, and given season, to be consequently replicable.

*

Private DT was assigned to another company for a developed patrol to recognise another known terrorist. He jumped in the 'pig' – armoured vehicle – and sped off to his destination.

The 'pig' was carrying three men, a Corporal called 'Frog' Egar, who had been shot and blown up in NI, but seemed to survive, and with his multiple scars would be seen to be patrolling the streets again looking for his 'white whale' and the calling of the harpooning tribe. Another 'bod', plus the main man – D.

As the 'pig' rolled into the new area, D looked out of the slit at the back of the armoured vehicle to classify his whereabouts. Unbeknown to him, having been playing with his mates [they were throwing 'half chats', half bricks, which were the same size as the slit at the back of a 'pig', at a target on the wall], a young Irish lad, about 13 had the synchronisation to be turning with a half brick in his hand as the eyes of D looked out on an unknown, unsuspecting world.

They met, they clashed. As the boy, seeing the 'pig' rummage by, 'chucked' the 'chat' and it entered the slit, *perfect!* It hit Private DT full in the face. The blood strewed down his chin, as the 'pig' sped on and Corporal Egar looked over at the sight of D, bloody and hurting with his face in his hands, and said, *"Good job it wasn't a bullet!"*

Point taken. Riding a 'pig' usually meant wearing a helmet, just in case of such unfortunate mishaps. But D had thought better, looking all like the star being taken to his coveted job, a hero looking for a destiny, a soldier of fortune looking out for that moment of bravery, which earns him his colours, his flanking ritual of acceptance, a medal of valiant regard.

On entering the base camp of his destination, D was rushed to the sick bay.

The doctor was a good man, as doctors usually are, but this one seemed to understand the situation very well and for his pains, D received terms of prising the wound a little bit more to make it look like he had really taken a knock, so the compensation for the accident in the act of war, would be sufficient to fit the trial and tribulations caused by making Private DT's face look like a brick had just hit him, better still, a foundation piece of concrete, lifted by a big man and deposited on the fizog of the 'ugly mugger', as D was called, when he went in for briefing, shown the target and also brought out into the daylight with his bandaged ego and detrimental heroic pride.

The days and times passed with observation posts, patrols, r & r [rest and reassurance], many deep nights sleep, for a short while, then 'up and at 'em', many times looking for Edger or some of his paramilitary brothers, who having set up a shoot, or a planting of a bomb, the war commenced, as Private DT got older and survived his first tour of suburban Ulster.

*

The days back at the regiment barracks allowed for settlement of skill and investment into a future in the destiny of a career.

The German weather was seemingly the same as England, with its four seasons, plus the feeling of a country healing from the legend and legacy of Nazis, being the worst time on the planet for human life, to have to go through, especially because the awareness of human conflict and pain were made more unbearable to the intended, the persecuted and society civilisations, making the world a horror pit of hate, bigotry, greed and murder, the general way of life, as all the people ever born before the sense of peace were the victims of war, which brings everlasting peace.

One such place after a day of soldiering, D would get drunk with friends and strangers within the regiment, then invite everybody back to his billet room to join what he called and was to be known as *The Crying Club*.

D would take them all back, drunk, pissed, fucked, in a mood for drinking and listening to the saddest music on the planet.

He would use Barbara Streisand as his catalyst. The music soaring into the heavens about love and romance, the plus side of a poetic heart, missing out on the world, as a soldier, someone who may die in his duty, to be laid out in a coffin and flown home, only to be received by their local family and taken back home to be ceremonially discharged with distinction, a sense of fellowship of bravery, a hero to the locals, who knew him as a child, at school, through his teething years and spotty days of teenage angst and music.

So, the growing soldiers of *The Crying Club* would start the tears falling down their cheeks.

The tears of love pouring over their lips and faces, onto 'who knows where?'; somewhere the tears burst, a crescendo of brilliant sorrow, morose remorse and a final farewell to all who knew them.

They cried, as the crying grew louder and the stop-taps were released, for a full term of hurting sorrowful pain, the tears joined forces with the vocals of uplifting fear, a sense of terms to come in a war to be fought, a life to be won and everything on the face of a girl, beautiful to miss, to remember and miss, like the tone of a sonnet, a stanza, an ode, to joy, to moments remembered to be able to keep, as keepsakes of momentous periods of frozen expectation holding lovers in suspended animation for the rest of universal infinite eternal time.

The music roared with galactic voices, as *The Crying Club* was complete.

Everybody, the hardest there, the rebel, the stoic soldier, the strict instructed believer, tears flushed, tears crossed the plains of living into dry-eyed deserts, for hurt, violence, pain and murderous clans indifferent to the difference of life, a special place in God's name, a hope for the salvation of the indignity of being useless, a flickering phenomenon, a beauty destroyed by power politics, kings and queens, horrible parents, shit paid jobs, isolated religions, transsexual – transvestism, homosexual lesbian -bi-transsexualism – asexual infidelity, Concepción's heterosexuality.

They could not cry; no more.

The tears dried up.

The thoughts of death, of dicing with murder or being shot, the abuse of life, the abuse of childhood, the loss of lass, the wife who betrayed, the bastard who spoilt your life, who hated you for breathing, had all gone into the dust, into the clouds of doubt, the biology of aether dreams, to be burnt in the mire of flaming tears, drowned out and sank by the law of sorrow, sank to the ocean base with waves of transuranic turmoil, released pain, unmagnified images of hollow souls, sailing the vast ocean of conclusion, could be soothed, solvent by the charming voice of a goddess ringing true.

The beer sank deep into the drunk tank and the feeling of freedom helped the soldier carry on his duty for king and queen, for his own salvation based in a world of brutal savagery.

*

The night a stripper came to the barracks.

All or most of the single soldiers were there. Shouting and jeering on the sense of the coming naked woman for all to see and view with whatever thoughts occurred to the minds of a soldier, loving woman, women's bodies, the vice of life is the variation of woman's bottoms.

She came on stage, not a beauty, but a seeming careless girl with German ways and contortionist rhythms. The crowd went wild. The chanting and cheering brought the house down as the music and her taking her clothes off were the ecstasy of sight!

Private Steve Hughes stood up and threw an ashtray at her. It hit her, and Private DT, who was situated at the front, stood up and told him to pack it in, shout he was sorry or he would be very sorry in the morning!

The night was a great big piss up and the stripper survived the onslaught of squaddies screaming out obscenity, needing a feline fix and basically having a lovely evening with the company of whores. The evening was a great success.

At 4 o'clock in the morning, Private DT was awoken and ordered to dress. He was being arrested and was marched to the barrack prison by two regimental policemen.

He was cast into a cell. Left to sleep off his boozy stinking alcoholic stench till the morning, early he was woken by his Company Sergeant Major Jackson.

With his notebook in hand, SM Jackson entered the cell. Closing the cell door, he looked at the morning Private DT.

The sight was frightening. For them both. SM Jackson then said,

"*You have been arrested for the murder of Private Hughes!*"

"*What!?*"

"*You argued with him last night, went to his bed later on in the morning and reaching for an iron leg attached to the bed, you detached the leg, and commenced to hit Private Hughes in the face with it. He was found unconscious, with blood everywhere, taken to hospital where his last words were DT… Have you anything to say?"* came SM Jackson, who was looking at his notes. He raised his head and revealed that his face was one which had the characteristics of two big jowls floating from his cheeks down over his chin, which made his mouth look like a dachshund hunting his kill.

Private DT was stunned. He moved about the cell feeling trapped. He panicked in his heart and remembered the argument with Hughes.

"I didn't do it!" he said adamantly.

"Well, we have the proof," replied SM Jackson, who after this received the nickname 'Jowls' after meeting with fate.

As SM 'Jowls' Jackson left the cell, he didn't look at the accused, but left a sense of fear for the bedevilment of facts laid out before the mind of D, who sat on the bed with his heavy head in his hands; with a slight gesture of bewilderment and trepidation, he began to cry onto the palms of his hands. Through his fingers, the tears dripped onto the cell room floor.

*

Hours passed.

The sound of the barrack jail could be heard awakening into action – the shouting of orders and the voice of taunt with malice intent on abusing the arrested soldier for his failure to be a soldier of worth, promise and duty.

The morning came and went, like the feathers of a bird seeming to take flight, only for D the weight of gravity, his hangover, the possibility of being guilty without parole, gave him a feeling of being buried alive with the weight of a soiled earth upon his life-force, bruising and turning the daylight hours into eternal night without light, without prayer, to hell, to meet a maker, a faker, someone who set him up to subconsciously blackout and commit a sin, a bloody act of violence on a sleeping soul who would not know what had hit him and would never ever see the light of day again.

Then the door of the cell opened.

It was SM 'Jowls' Jackson.

He said, in no uncertain terms, *"You may go. You are not to be charged.*

You will report to the Regimental Sergeant Major, where he will speak to you on this matter." He paused, then he looked at the rough beleaguered face of a spotty-skinned animal and said, gesturing with his arm and finger, *"Get out of my sight!"*

Private DT did. Fast.

He went to see the RSM.

The RSM said, as D stood to attention, now he could relax, with the look of a late 70's punk and a bad breath to prove it.

"Private Hughes awoke from his coma and told the police who it was. It was not you he named."

Private DT asked politely, *"Sir, if I may be bold, who was it?"*

"Private Firth was mentioned," insisted the RSM. *"He went to Private Hughes' bed-space and 'bed-legged' him many times in the face. That is all you need to know."*

"Right, Sir!" said a very happy and relieved soldier.

"You are dismissed! Get back to your duty!" came the order from the accomplished high ranking NCO Soldier, who had taken one look at the monstrosity in front of him, thought about all the scruffy punks out in civilisation, without a job, or future, whom music had given them some sort of home to go to, seeing it in his established disciplined office, in the name of a great big hungover moron-like member of *The Clash*. It made him nauseous. He had to apologise.

Private DT turned on his heels and marched out of the RSM's office, hit the corridor and ran; he ran as fast as he could, straight out onto the barrack square flying like a bird, he had seen in his devastation, he sped across the sacred tarmac, straight over to the NAAFI for a celebration with his living, loving mates, to run into the night, through the day and eternally for evermore. Amen!

*

The regiment, *The Dukes*, had a football tournament in which D played for 'Charlie' company, 8 Platoon, shirt number 6; left half, in the mid-field.

Staff Sergeant Bob Peace wanted him in the team, so Private DT accepted.

The final was against the Drums Platoon, who played in yellow. 8 Platoon played in all royal blue.

D borrowed a pair of boots from a friend, polished them well, screw-in studs; a black pair of unmarked football boots, in which he felt like he was wearing velvet felt.

The game was good, average, the score grew to a winning advantage for 8 Platoon.

Frankie Stirling the centre forward for the blues, had the ball in the penalty area, D followed him up and shouted for the ball. He received it, trapped it, with the motion of his boot feeling like a ballet shoe, he struck the ball.

It traversed around the defenders squabbling in the area, heading for the top right hand corner of the goal. The goalkeeper lunged for it, the ball went straight into the area were no goalkeeper could have stopped it. Right at the axis of post, bar, right angle and velocity, travelling at a pace to drown out the roar of the supporters, the weather, the deep moans of the opposition, the planes flying overhead, the voices in the world, the fart from fat bastard, the burp from pissed up shit fuck; all the noises of an insane world came to a halt, as the ball hit the back of the net and the world paid homage to a piece of footballing genius!

Private DT, Number 6 for the blues, turned, looking at the dust of bodies strewn in delight on the sidelines, signalled his pleasure and joy, by hitting the air with his fist and telling vanity to *fuck off!* The world to stick that up its anus! And ran to his position, where Staff Bob said, *"Nice cross!"*

They laughed, and finished the game with a 6:2 win.

That very night D got pissed out of his head with the rest of the party. In the morning he couldn't get out of bed. They put it down to fatigue and he spent two days in hospital getting some well earned sleep.

He awoke during the time and the duty nurse told him that his Sergeant Major had been to see him. He had seen D was asleep, so he just stood and watched him for a while.

D thought about the sight of SM 'Jowls' Jackson standing, looking over the football hero, like something out of an American film. Touching.

With pride, D went back to his well earned sleep.

*

All and everything averages out in the end.

The harmony is reassured, as the balance is set right.

All destiny is fixed, all experience is personal, when we veer off the beaten path, we must be ready for the strangest difference, to face an ultimatum of consequences, only the fate takes its course and all participants pay the price of endeavour, of ambition, of a past riddled with loopholes only for the future to catch up to itself. One is going on sixteen, but is 92, by the time one catches up with an abused childhood, one faces death, complete and wholesome enough to warrant a good life. We think we know what we are doing. We wing it and hope for the best. We worry, and the outcome is simple and tried. We concern ourselves with a goodwill, which is present in time of need, when the world is a torturous place, best stay out of it, when the world is criminal, best not get caught, when all the laws and rules are breached and abused, one should be ready to defend the free will of choice, and slay the bastards who want to grind you down.

*

The day arrived when the regiment had a sports day. Private DT was in the 4 x 400m relay team for C Company. The race was in German weather of reason-ability. The favourites for the race came from A Company, who had two regimental runners in their team.

The race began with Corporal Scottsdale, who smoked and ran a winner on the first lap of the track; he handed over to Private DT, who set off running like an unrehearsed rabbit.

The wind in his lungs, the movement of his thighs, the swing of his arms and the urgency with which he moved through the first 100 metres, then onto the top 200 metres, had him leading on the corner of the 300-metre mark. The opposition was nowhere to be seen. Then out of the blue came someone, who decided to run inside of D. D knew he was on the inside lane, so the only place the runner could be, was on the high jump sandpit!

D gestured with his arms, to signal the 'cheat' by one of the A Company runners, but to no avail, as the race was on. No one heard his shouts, no one watched as the opponent ran across the sandpit, so, together they met the 100 metres.

Now, D had not trained for this. He was picked and so he ran. As they hit the 100 metres the wind changed course, right into their faces. The track became a never-ending road, moving further and further away. As the A Company runner came on strong, D started to wobble. His legs started to jelly. His whole motion was taken away from him, as if he was in the hands of the Olympic gods. He strived to control his notion of emotion and devotion to his team; he looked to the handover, changed his baton into his right hand, and the hand of God moved his little body on to the finishing line like he was destined to be glorious. They both hit the handover together, as the days of abuse and self inflicted pain came rushing to his heart, to his throat, as the the nausea of a thousand drinking sessions ran straight out of his life into the bear pit and shit the load out with gold medallions shining in the sun for the eyes to be blinded.

The handover had been a success, he could slow down the motion and hope for the best, as the handover was to a soldier who was short, a good goalkeeper, but could he run?! NO!

He seemed to relax as the track swallowed him up and the regimental runner from A Company was cutting up the track. He was Parcel Lewis, a regimental rugby union player as well as a runner, his thighs were the size of a human torso. He was big, he was fast and he was out there on the 300m mark as soon as he ran towards his final destination, handing the baton over to his other regimental rugby and runner, John Johnson. He did, and C Company were coming in last. The baton was handed over to C Company's last runner, who was Steve Grossman.

Now Steve Grossman was fast. He tucked in and shot over the 100, the 200 and on the 300 had caught up with Johnson. The rest of the race was moved into that arena called 'insignificant', as Grossman and Johnson hit the last 100 metres. They were neck and neck.

Now, if Steve Grossman had been given the baton first, he would have pissed the race! He would have run the fucking marathon for the Olympic gods for a thousand years; if only! *If only!*

They sped down the track towards the jeering and cheering regiment. This was the heroes' track. The Olympiad Grade 1, the honoured souls of sport – not war – and they seemed to be coming in together. They were puffing at the air as the wind of change. The screams grew louder as they neared.

Then the world stopped!
In its tracks.
Stopped.

The motion of all triggered use of human cry and endeavour seemed to fade into instant rays of glorious sunbeams. The sun was there, the sun came out, the sun lay on their heads the triumph of winners, the speed of Grossman, the lead of Johnson. The laurel crowns sat on their heads as the air came back, filled their lungs, to finish the ultimate race of athletes.

The line was crossed. The head of Johnson reached with protruding essence for it. Grossman leaned back, as if someone had put a hand there and stopped him in that minuscule of a second.

To join in the finish, to win fairly together, as black and white brothers. To show the world, to show the nation, to stick two fingers up at Hitler and show: Jesse Owens was right! The world don't need murder of brotherhood, not war, not defiance, not blood and gravestones, only remembrance!, love, friendship and endeavour with a fast sprint to the finish in power and command of all the days in the history of the world, saying, *Well Done!*, and it was!

Johnson and A Company won that day. D spewed up, out on the field. But the day was won by all. No one could judge the finish that day.

The sun shone as the awards for such greatness were given out. Nice statues of an athlete.

D passed them by, going back to barracks and thought about the 'one that got away'.

What a day. What a way to end the sun's majesty. Alas, Steve Grossman deserved better.

It was time for the regiment to do a tour of Northern Ireland again.

*

There he was on Falls Road, Belfast.

Based at the army camp; Howard Street Mill. Four months tour, with call sign; 82 Charlie, as a 'Mugger' again.

The 'Tour' was going fine, what with internment having an effect on the I.R.A. Bobby Sands interned in Long Kesh, H Block; The Maze Prison.

Like others being charged with being an illegal organisation, raids at 4 o'clock in the morning, catching them by surprise and prising them all out of their beds, into a cell bed, where some decided to 'hunger strike', on which Bobby Sands went all the way and died.

Many a time, on the 'Falls' looking for other members of a terrorist organisation, such as the I.N.L.A.: The Irish National Liberation Army. Full of 'cowboy' shooters and young men looking to make a name for themselves.

Two such boys crossed the path of 82's Charlie's *'Mugger'*.

They raided a public house. A Saturday night. They cordoned off the pub, and 82 went in with Private DT leading the way. He walked straight up to two lads sat at a table at the far end of the room and asked both of them their names. They answered.

"My name is Mickey Mouse," said one, a blonde with 70's sideburns with a look of great attitude and spirit.

"My name is Donald Duck," came the other, who was of black complexion and shady teeth, both looking like they needed a good wash, a shave; and sure they were good looking in their tanktops, flares, 'Doc' boots and Ben Sherman shirts, but they had no respect for the British Army. D replied, *"You're Mickey Mouse. And you're Donald Duck, well, I'm Goofy!"*, and he smiled with his two incisors missing.

They looked at each other and winked, the smiles on their faces were smirks, a grimace of saliva seeming to dictate the broad stem of their lips, after lifting their pints and taking a great gulp, looked into the eyesight of an Armalite, and fired the trigger.

The mood of the two, the mood of the room, the mood of D, the feelings of death biting at the breath of contention, as the blood seeped out of the corners of his mouth, tasting vile, a crisp smash turning his body into air, as the floatation seemed to be otherworldly; D cried in the corner of his eye, the tear splashed over the grounds of all graveyards, the weeping sound of the lost dead mourned into the light for redemption and forgiveness in times of the 'Troubles'.

*

Hollow the return to reality and relativity was, as the two Irish soldiers commenced drinking, D turned and walked away, as the bar was busy, faces unknown, the look of the barkeeper as he turned his sight on Mickey and Donald. Goofy signalled to leave the pub. As the 'brick' of 82 Charlie turned to exit, D was thinking about the film written by Stephen King called *Stand By Me*, when one of the boys says, *"If Mickey Mouse was a mouse, and Donald Duck was a duck, what the fuck was Goofy?!"*

Pluto was a dog, so what in the name was Goofy?

It was a young British soldier just doing his job for queen and country, who had been pointed out as on the list of killings for the snipers of an illegal organisation.

They were members of the I.N.L.A. But they could not be brought to justice without first-hand evidence. Being caught red-handed, that seemed to be the problem.

*

The day when the Commanding Officer of the Regiment came out on the streets and walked down the middle of Denmark Street with other officers and NCO milling about him, like full-on bodyguards for the President of the United States.

82 Charlie were out and patrolling behind the savage audacity of the oppressors illegal in the foreign lands of a Catholic island, who fought for the right to be free from tyranny, the houses of English parliament and the blood on the streets and hands of teenagers ready to die for Ireland.

The 'Divis Complex' was right behind them, as they turned to march up the desolate street of *'something rotten in the heart of Denmark'*.

The 'Divis' was a known sniper point, for the shooters to fire at their target, then get out of there fast, moving from flat to flat, as the sympathisers were many and the aim of the deception was to flummox the squaddies into great frustration and blame, as the doors would be kicked down, the flats searched and found amongst the masses of Catholic paraphernalia were secret passageways made deliberately for escapees.

D looked through his infrared sight and made out the complex in its complexity and flats until he stopped at a barrel of an Armalite at a window ledge.

He didn't know the procedure for firing at such a sight, he wasn't sure what he saw, he didn't see it, he wanted to open his magazine out on the place, all twenty rounds flying at bricks, as the sound of large bangs hissed about the harmony of synchronisation, changing the world in another place, as the energy set off for foreign lands, entering the minds of disillusioned punks or angered children. *But he didn't.*

He set off across the path of Denmark Street, and ran into the sightline of the Commanding Officer. He turned and slowly ran back. What effect it must have had. To see the soldier run across, cover the target would put the sniper into a new frame of mind. To run back across the line of sight, would frustrate, an all ready incompetent terrorist, who wants the kill for promotion, prestige and money, instead of a 1,000 for the officer, he would probably receive 50 quid for the 'buckshee'. So, he needed to see it done when the feeling of *destiny's doing* was rife.

It worked. D lined up his sight and it was gone.

The Commanding Officer turned to his entourage and asked, *"Who is that soldier?"*

They replied, *"Private DT, Sir!"*

The soldier being noted was in line for a promotion to Lance Corporal and The Queen's Commendation for Bravery: The Queen's Gallantry Medal.

Private DT was to see neither of those delights offered by Her Majesty's Armed Forces.

*

"Fortune comes with virtue" was the motto of the Duke of Wellington's Regiment.

Private DT was and had been brave. His fortune, well, that seemed to be on the cards.

He sat in the chapel talking to the sense of oxygen in the air, in the atmosphere, looking at the gold and ornament of the house of God. He knew of Jesus. He knew he was a friend to everyone alive. He felt the love for the sacrament, being heard to his thoughts, listened to and answered, as the fear and worry was the sense of death prevailing over all soldiers. To be able to stop such inevitable ends, seemed to warrant hope, avoidance, forgiveness, only the silence, the terms to which he had had to see for himself, the depth of dilemma brought him to his senses and made him change his mind; too late, too long, too gone, too involved with war and its outcome, with the enemy having your name on a bullet. In the fate of darkness receiving his soul and making ready for a newcomer, a soldier of fortune, an inherent dichotomy of morbid glory. He heard the story of his choice in his head, his view of funeral turnout, the music played, the union of his body empty in the casket, born by sympathy and sorrow on to the local church, to be able to tell the world he chose to die, early, to make his defiance known, to bring the zenith of his disrespect for the disrespecting hordes who destroyed his life before he alone could live it.

He heard the reverberating tremor of the Holy Ghost tremendous in theory and honour, seeming to hold pleasure in the living hand of harmony, joy, unconditional love and ecstasy, to which D had never known and never would and above all never be able to change his feelings from the day it all presented itself, as he had drained his body and will, he had drank his soul down the river, he had wished for nothing more than what he knew best, he could receive and supply to his dregs of a smarting life, given idolised chances into 'make do' and 'count your blessings' politic.

He smelt a rat and the rat was: two good-looking boys of the I.N.L.A. would see to his suicide, played out on the streets for the romance of nostalgic afternoons, always remembering the blood, the tears, the triumph in angels, devils, forgotten for the lot moves, forgotten for the times change, for they don't remember and could not help but forget, about someone you do not know, anyone who was not in your heart, something which had to be done because he wanted it done, he wanted to create his own destiny and fall in the face of adversity, proven loser, proven devil of hell, proven idiot with a brave streak for insanity, a crazy legacy, a drunken rock 'n' roll lifestyle, which caved into quarries and quarrels with terrorists and angry young men with the exact same philosophy as most:

'The future is what you make it, and so is your death, for the past is theirs.'

*

The streets were hot and heavy, cold and freezing to the bone, which ever it was. To set the scene was a feeling of autumnal bliss, as the leaves fell from the trees in golden, yellow, ochre hue, seeming to die in the face of life, leaving the harmony of summer behind as the flux of bereavement sought honesty in the face of rude dead drills, motioning the collapse of life, the swing of nature, to breathe no more the oxygen giving synthesis, heaving large graves, coffins leaden with old crones, loved by relatives, addicted to life, stringing out the commitment like a die-hard waiting for England to win the world cup again.

The birds made a noise for grains of food, the atmosphere changed into a rider of sheer death, riding through the fields of corn, taking out the majestic sun with clouds as big as cities, dirt cities, as half dead people in dirt cities crammed the side path, looked up to the heavens, giving hearts for past Indian summers, needing an explanation in nature, such as: 'You have to die to be reborn, afresh and new, to see the world with a child's eye, innocent and pure, like the glory of new paint for the walls of the internal house.'

As all houses are personal graves waiting for a gravestone and a dead body.

*

D hit the streets with the rest of C Company. They danced down to the hub, they drilled into the space, as the shoppers stopped to spit, vomit, at the sight of army might.

He walked along the street towards and through 'The Divis'.

On the other side of the coin. He told Donald to *"fuck off!"*, as he handled the Armalite and took it to the window. Donald said, *"It's not fair, it's his turn!"*

They argued into the hour, where the booze and cigarettes flew out and into their gaping, serried, mammoth gobs, which seemed to be chewing, chewing gum all the time, the beer and cigs were consumed. *"You're serious!"* exclaimed Don, looking like the emancipated prick he was.

"Yea!" shouted Mickey, *"I am deadly serious! If you know what I mean!"*

They both laughed, as the masks of Mickey Mouse and Donald Duck sat on their heads.

"You're pissed!" replied Don, who knew because he was too, *"you won't hit a fucking ting!"*

"Fuck off!" shouted Mick, *"I'll wait for the knob and cut his head in two bits!"*

"I'll do it!" replied Don, who had sat down and was falling asleep, nodding off, slowly, his eyes shut, his eyes opened like pea holes, the caesium of conjunctivitis spreading over his eyelids and nose, onto his mouth, till he gave over to slumber, a nauseating drag of a snoring kip, given out by leprechauns to take the piss and laugh at the way Don

breathed through his nightmare teeth.

"*You'll fucking do nowt,*" whispered Mick, "*you fucking shit-bag cunt! I will wait, soon, you'll see, he'll come smirking about that corner and look me in the eyes, I'll fire into the sight of his target hopes, deep and deeper down, I'll shoot out his eye. Split his brain in half and kill the fucker, if I'm not Robin fucking Hood!*"

Mick looked over at Don.

"*Sleep you ponce! Dream of fucking leprechauns and I will be unicorn for the cause, a principle of war.*"

As Private DT looked up at the 'Divis' through his 'night-sight', Mick took a shot.

The shot hit D in the shoulder and it knocked him to the floor. The blood was pouring, as Mick kicked Don, as they both ran out of the 'sniper' flat, grasping at jackets, beer and breath.

D sensed the feeling of pain. He looked like a very ugly and awkward mess, with the face of undistinguishable breathtaking, a heathen aura, seeming to be so far away, he gestured with his rifle, out to a place in a desert, he seemed distant, laughing … the heat … a boiling seething turmoil of bitter sting, a dead bullet sang songs in his heart, lifting the skin, the muscle, the blood streamed hot and nasty into the lonely road … as he lost the focus of life, the sight of man-made ornaments, the bliss of noise, the silence of scent …!

He woke up from his sleep, with a removed sphere of sound, a fear gurgle … awake, D was soaking in the hot dreams of death.

*

The corridors of power were busy. The frame of the organisation in the disciplined regime of a legal force was 'second to none'.

The bodies of voluntary soldiers doing their time and 'getting some in' was a sight to behold.

The letters home, the two beers a day rations, the lack of sleep or the full day off, the inspection of weapons, cleaning or equipment, was nothing to do with the length of hair to be allowed, longer than usual, longer, so the officers were seen to grow hair over their ears and collar.

D had a plan which he shared with L. He would grow his hair at the back and go to the Army barbers, who would be asked to lift up the long strands to shave underneath, to make it look like short-back and sides when placed up, away, in a beret. L had a 'Mohican', so he would not be checked for a haircut.

On parade, they both seemed to be adhering to the law of length, when it was noticed, L's 'Mohawk' was over his collar, so he was checked.

"Get your haircut! Elwood!" The 'Mohican' being the shortest of haircuts which crossed the scalp like the bridge over the cranium. Still it was hilarious!

D on the other hand was also checked. Asked to remove his beret, he was found to have a decent mop top on his Beatles mania, so once checked, *"GET YOUR FUCKING HAIRCUT, T!"*

He did and the large lanky strip, which looked long when combed out for the civvies girls to admire, was cropped and what was left was the shortest back and sides ever seen, left to the winter neck, the abuse of others, who had a comfortable fringe; last of all that indecent feeling of ridiculousness, which always crossed the mind of a human being first, without the bullshit of army policy and a freedom to be, not prove, not impress, not enhance, but seek the time of loose morals, values, virtue and never have to worry again about the sense of dress being scruffy, holey, with a dirt big hole in the crutch, where the ruptured ball could hang, free of charge, amidst in air, soaking in the oxygen, seeming to be the biggest rebellion of any statement, since the cock of Jim Morrison was seen as offensive and the punk era had an icon worth invigilating.

The time was rife and the days of boarding school seemed over.

Private DT was walking along the corridor, ready to go out on patrol and recognise more terrorists, when a clerk from the office walked avast him and said, *"You getting out!"*

Of course! He was! He had done his three years, from 17 to 20. He was now a *man*. Not a teenager, looking for a career, a peer, a life's learning curve for the future, a future which from the land of the rich and poor, a poverty belonging to 'no future', when he was in the position to be cutting short his City and Guilds in terrorist recognition. He thought for a fine moment about all potential and knew what he most do.

He got out.

He always wanted to, during the days of hating it, he remembered, with a venom, even when he trained in Tin city and went on to the real thing in Northern Ireland, he was forgetful of his decision, but it would never leave his heart, added to the 'smell of a rat' in Belfast, he thought he would not be very good as a soldier with one arm, or hold his future wife and child without it.

He was offered promotion, a home, an army house for his future bride, the Regiment were going to Gibraltar for three years, where he would play football for the regiment, train all day, playing Number 6; left half, mid-field.

It all sounded too good. But, he turned it all down, because he could never talk to anybody about going out on patrol, knowing something was wrong, he might be shot, he'd had a dream about it, he would have stayed in, if he was not due to get out halfway through a tour of Belfast.

A conundrum dilemma inducing a failure all round, when in fact he was a success story in the armed forces. His report used the word 'exemplary' to express his duty in the army.

'Exemplary'; *'An example to others'*; *'Very good'*.

For his work in war not peace.

He left Howard Street Mill late at night, with others, in a Land-Rover. The night was mild in configuration, as the night owl was sweet, the stench of Belfast long gone with the sea wind, the bright amber lights, lighting up the place, showed itself to D, as he climbed the hill out of the city, the Land-Rover seeming to hold in gear, as the stretch of the silence went into the thoughts of the gone in the night, the words spoken on the lips of harpies, *'Goodbye D'*.

D searched in his brain for a reply; it came: *'goodbye'*.

*

At the barracks back in Hungover, Germany, Private DT was asleep in his bunk, when the door brushed open and Sergeant Major Leatherdale walked straight in, up to the bunk and shouted at the person well asleep in it.

"Where is the tape recorder?" He stared with his eyes on the top of his nose like a bird of prey.

D awoke and seemed to have heard him far off in his daydreaming imagination, he pointed to the locker.

"It's in there, Sir," he said, hoping he would find it and leave.

He did find it. He then switched it on.

The words on it were:

"*… My name is Mickey Mouse"*, in a very brogue Irish accent, which seemed to be very foreign in the acoustics of Germany and English soldiers.

Sergeant Major Leatherdale then stopped the tape, forwarded a little, then played it again.

It then said, "... *and my name is Donald Duck.*"

On hearing that and switching it off, Sergeant Major Leatherdale turned and said in his uniformed manner ... *"Fuck!"* [which rhymed with *"Duck"*].

He left and D heard the echo of the words again, the accents, the time and place.

Yeah, he had forgotten to hand in his portable tape recorder, which he used for his terrorist tracking, by turning it on in his flack jacket and taping those he spoke to.

He went back to sleep. The echo of the Sergeant Major's boots, the laughter in the pits of both their stomachs, the last order he would hear, the SM knowing he was not a future soldier, made the feeling of not been wanted a lot more intense, the feeling of all foreign senses, in voice, movement, touch, moment, hearing, taste and fragile sensitivity, made D realise he might have made the right decision after-all.

He was left alone in the world after three years. He slept.

*

He got out at Bulford, Wiltshire.

Across the way was the neolithic monument: Stonehenge.

He felt it. It seemed to hold his attention and with a glimpse of senses bequeathed to mysticism, he felt very happy and looked forward to 'civvy street' and the opportunities it could, should, would or might bring him.

He would never be an HGV driver though. He had been listed on a driving cadre whilst in the army. The reason for joining up was to get a driver's licence. The cadre had arrived at the point of time when D and L were in 'peace time'. Which meant they were constantly pissed, getting into trouble, being disciplined for it, having a good time at the age of 19, whilst the machine turned, L and D yearned for freedom! A freedom they couldn't find, and they knew why!

Private DT had climbed into the driver's seat of a Land-Rover and sat listening to the instructor tell him the first procedures. He had got as far as turning the engine on, when he stopped what he was saying, looked into D's bloodshot eyes, smelt his breath and saw to his astonishment Private DT was still drunk, first thing in the morning. The instructor bawked, as he adamantly told Private DT to get out of the Land-Rover! D did, he was thrown off the cadre. So much for driving, a driving licence, the reason why he joined the army, or an HGV, which he so wanted.

He left the Army an alcoholic, without a stitch to his name, so he headed for the sea-side with a pack on his back. A real vagabond bound for stardom and freedom, bound for the road which leads to gold, to riches untold, to fun and frolic, to sunbeams and sunsets, to love and loving, to women and drugs, to beaches and bathers, to the deckchairs and long hair, to short jeans and hairy legs, to earrings and tattoos, to rum and bum and shun the scum, to blues and wine and fine to dine, to gypsy nights and tights in flight, to morning sleeps, peeps and beeps!, to the glory of freedom looked for, upon in so many ways, in the days of the soldier looking for a way out, of this mess, of the world, off the earth, as far away from all the orders and cordons and heavy nights with early dawning, the trip to knowledge through experience was possible, not to stay in life, the way one should be, the way one is liked to be, but to change and change for oneself, the health of self and no bloody dust on the shelf would stop him, hinder him or devalue him.

So, he bought some fish and chips, an 8-pack of lager and went and sat, looking out at the Atlantic ocean, on home soil, on home turf, the mighty 'Blighty', and he was ready for the next stage of his life, which had begun with the phrenological word *Exemplary*.

* * *

The world was his oyster. At the age of 21, he was ready to become invincible, all for the world to see and enlighten, a focus based on the freedom of hearts and minds, to find the elixir of life, the 'Philosopher's stone', hear it drop, the sound, a sound so mild, so natural, the world could not hear it. For the noise, the insecurities of generations, the public affair with capitalistic consumerisms, seemed to D a giant with one eye, a Cyclops, who ate the flesh of people, when it was his turn, the giant shouted, *"WHO IS IT?"*. D answered, *"I am nobody!"*

The giant then left him alone, as how can one eat no one?

He didn't care. He didn't understand really, but the thought of ignorance in the world seemed to be the blanket under which all was slumbering, not just for the world at large, but to improve one's self seemed to be the responsible thing to do.

So he went to the public library.

The books, the rows of books, the subjects and information was overwhelming. He heard the words in his head, as he sat at a table in the library.

He had to have a meaning, a purpose in this world. Some reason to be alive!

Why? What for? and, *where are the answers?!*

He saw a book on the table, reached over to it, slid it across the surface of the table and looked at the title of the book. It read, *The Classics of Greek and Roman Mythology*.

He opened the book and read the first word, which led to the next and so on, until he was immersed in the classic stories of Ancient Greece, the stories passed on through generations, until that day he was reading about them. Achilles, Agamemnon, Aphrodite, Hercules, Oedipus Rex, Medusa, Ajax and so on, until it read into Roman myth, with the stories of Kronos and his wife, Rhea. Zeus, the philanthropist, who seduced woman disguised as a swan, and on, to the end of the informative mythological outcome, spelling out the past, to be present, for the journey would always be connected to the relativity of history, to be repeated or to be played out in another time, like the present, like a hero out of the pages of ancient representations; archetypes and symbolic, seeming to add up to the world of adversity and audacity, seeming to inspire a hero sat at the table of a modern world, looking for the answer to his precept journey, of honour and his galactic energy for the secrets of the world, the undiscovered plateaus, the dreams, to awaken the prophecies of antiquity and stand to hold the world on one's shoulders like Atlas, a giant with strength, with great desire to help the world in its beaten path to glory or written stories of manifest destiny or progress, which seems always to deter the planet, only to help the human on it, the inside of consciousness, the subconsciousness, with a duplicate for metaphysics and truth, a seeker of lies to fight the principles of greed, and finally put to rest the best of the senses of the sex of war.

A librarian came up to him and asked him if he would like to go for a coffee.

It was Sheridan Bernadette. He said *"Yes."*

And that was it. He sat opposite a beautiful woman, who saw the hero in him.

*

They made love. They made mad passionate love. They fell in love and then she dropped a clanger.

She told him; she was a call girl, a street walker, if you like. The world's first profession; a prostitute. She said it matter of factly and it broke his sensitive fragile heart.

They had talked about his heroism in the army and he wore the green and purple 'campaign medal' on his chest as they made enduring compulsive love-sex.

Yes, he had put it through the skin on his chest, on a deep phosphorescent high, on drugs and sex. Yes, it hurt and yes, she soothed it, but *this!* This was the bee's knees of fascistic slaughter of ya bloody daughter! This brought tears to the hardest man, this was the sexist weapon the world was scared of, why men went to war, why women don't! Why they give and take away, they are the portal to creation, then they leave the blame and responsibility to savage man, who has about as much idea how to run this place as the apes in the jungle trees!

He was sick, he vomited right there and she cleaned up his puke, like a spook out of hell.

*

He didn't want to be her pimp. He was her pimp, but to be a good pimp one would have to know the ropes. He looked and dressed like a pimp. Dinners for Arabs and perverts and other pimps.

In the gambling dens, the street firepits, the bed orgies and bits and always spare 'tottie'; spare, going for a song, a groupie for the pimps, double-faced tosser who loved his work, the wife and the strife of the sadomasochist's knife point, to hold and be bold, to death do us part, and where's the party and booze for the organised pimp show, the blow by blow, the intrinsic bullshit which brought white coke and rum, the orthodoxy of graphic choice?

She, Sheri, was good and in great demand. The punters paid out for a nice big Gemini ass!

D just sat back and watched as the world turned white and smite bright in the morning light when everybody had to face the dawn of day. She left and he went away.

*

He sat on a bench somewhere and contemplated his future? He realised he had been through an experience to change his outlook, so he got himself a real job.

He started work as a civil servant for Her Majesty's Royal Marines, in the Sergeant's Mess.

The term 'Mess' meant a place of clean-cut controlled environment for the use of respect and admiration for the serving force of Her Majesty's Royal Marine Commandos.

He was a steward, a flunky, an overnamed waiter, but it paid well and brought many fringe benefits and perks.

He was introduced to his shift staff, as the morning shift was 6 till 2 and the evening shift was 2 till 8.

There was the Head Steward; Pierce Coates who was 60 then and an old boot at it. What 'it' was was another matter, as Pierce seemed capable of dressing himself, smoking every minute of the day, and ordering his staff beneath him about.

He loved women and found the time to serve the Commandos with a plodding tripping flair which could only be appreciated by a friend or a comrade in the words of Marx, seemingly Karl not Groucho, whom Pierce seemed to have the width and whereabouts of.

*

There was Andrea Andrews, a nice man who could be summoned up with the words belonging to a gardener who grows his own roses for the sake of his own grave plot.

Oh! and JB; one John Butterfat, a Private Walker of Dads' Army to Pierce Coates; Capt Mainwaring.

In getting it, 'the spiv' in war, was the skivver with the 'tab' in the corner of his mouth, boasting about his birthplace and drinking his full of beer. Always one on the go.

Then there was D. A young recruit, who had long hair and an earring. A moustache and a sex life to envy; the pearl of sunbathing with a thong–stringed beaut.

The meals came and went. They jumped to the job. As the white shirt and bow tie, black trousers with black shoes were regimental enough.

The overseeing boss was a Brougham Youngstown who liked to drink, order the staff about and play carpet bowls when all the commandos were on leave.

His 'oppo' and help at the running of the 'Mess' was a 'Bustard' Brownian, who liked to drink, order the staff about with the orders of Brougham, and play darts or carpet bowls when the commandos were on exercise, at war or on leave.

The intention eventually dawned on D was to finish the serving, then get to the snooker room to play a few frames of snooker. Sometimes they would play darts between them and because D wasn't very good at darts, they all nicknamed him 'Deadly'.

The head chef was Rains Daly, a very big Scotsman with a temper of a very big Scotsman, who was good and qualified at his job, was a very good darts player, left-handed, loved his beer, and had a sense of humour, which could make the likes of Dante and Virgil laugh.

On his left, was the assistant chef Moresby. A man with a 'quiff' from the sixties on his head and insecurity which brought the tears and embarrassment of red cheeks to his face every time he wished to play the sturdy notions of a full committed life.

They played snooker too, Rains would hit the ball at a 100 miles per hour and the bloody injured thing would go down.

Moresby was quiet and lifted the cue, as if his life depended on it, with his wife as the bet of the outcome of the winner in the game.

They both loved a pint, or two.

The meals were straightforward enough. Smash and beans, you know, fish, chips and peas or beans, carrots or gravy, with pie or sausages or chicken in a sauce and in the terms of all chefs, what the fuck would stewards know about what we do?

Vis-à-vis bah! The stewards were washed up heroes, drunk with the light, as the terms of being civil kept the troops happy.

*

So the days passed in the shade of grace with a feeling of being useful or helpful, when the social need of a finality breed sanctions the floor one can walk upon, only to be liked and thanked for the dishing up of character, personality and a good plate full of English grub.

The other shift comprised Pete Dunham, Roy Stilton and the great Lennon Foxed; a Marxist and man of the trade unions, who supplicated, that no man should work for no less than enough to warrant a blessed thanks and a social conclave of wife appreciation.

In the dish-washing room was 'Glass eye' David and Edward 'Eddie' Edwards.

On the acid sink, for burning all the metal to be clean was an ex sea-captain called Pete Hyacinth, ex merchant, loved his pipe, peace and quiet and rumbled around like an active volcano on heat.

It was intensively boring work hours and paid for the blood, sweat and tears of a lost life, finishing up with a smoke, a drink and a rummage of trouble packed up with the wife!

Not quite right for Deadly, but he was thankful for the time he had to play snooker and drink till the beer shone out of his ass!

The two other chefs were Tony Bernardo and Sid Prestwick who were from Italy and Blackpool respectively. Tony was sluggish and Sid, cross-eyed. Tony smoked as he cooked, the drips of his nose sliding into the concoction, and Sid was a moaner, who moaned about the lost days of Stanley Matthews and Bat Lighthouse, when Blackpool was great and not just a den of iniquity.

The star of the show was a the janitor; a good old boy, famous to the face of the universe on Pete Piquancy, a sailor, who knew the sea, was a bit landlubber, had a cheeky sense of humour, was respected and loved by everyone who ever met him. He was famous in the archetypical of mankind, for even the woman loved his way and heart, seeming to have a cigar in his mouth at all times, loved to see the influence of character shine in the souls of all the boys who trod the path of redemption right into the arms of the maker, the ferryman of St Elmo's, didn't matter much to Pete, all was well, so long as the world knew its place.

Not forgetting Les Dunham, a dishwasher; Pete's brother, was a fisherman by trade, had hands like the hands of a barbarian warlord or William Wallace, had five kids with his Mrs and loved his beer, darts, snooker, Pete Piquancy, carpet bowls and a fucking good laugh!

Her Majesty's Sergeants' Mess.

All of them were over 60 years old. Semi-retired and life-worn.

Civil servants to a passion. Apart from the Dunhams and Deadly.

Brougham and Bustard were in their prime; 50 something?

In those days, age was not wise, it was for dying with.

The troubles the great wars must have brought … !? It showed, but they hung to their true character and didn't budge an inch when it came to perverted insufficient deficiencies presently presenting itself in the guise of love and sex for all the generations to come.

Apart from Deadly, who was a 'piss-head' with the IQ of a sexual deviant, searching for his next fix, the 'pussy', the width and breadth of all penetration, with the comforts of love and clandestine happiness of pleasure.

He was young and so was the 'pussy'.

Punk had been and gone and the 'new romantic' re-birthed the soul of a nation looking for a fix for the next twist in the tail of brethren horror or multitude illness flamed by the overindulgence of erotica.

The re-verb in our protagonist's head, *'Hope I die, before I get old!'* meant it loud and clear and who the hell wrote it?! Well, blame the society we live in and not the individual's ignorance, please.

"Hope I die! … Sid!," shouted Deadly, pissed up and full of joy, for the shift went well and the money rolled in and the neon lights were bright and she was gorgeous and beautiful to *beholden*!

"Get your fucking knickers off!", he heard them all say, he heard the words in his brain, which one day would be a mind. Mind you, what he did and didn't do; mind, was up to you! *You Geordie fucking cunt!*

*

First thing on a morning Pierce would shout, *"Deadly! The cruets!"*

Whilst D lay on the changing room settee, nursing a hangover.

The cruets – to all those ignorant enough to know – are the vessels in which Joseph of Arimathea brought over the blood and sweat of Christ on the cross over to England for the safekeeping away from the hostile hands of those who had condemned him. Somerset was the landscape to which uncle Joseph pierced his staff into the ground and founded the protection of the grail. In the hands of English folk, to be able to fight evil with the righteousness of forgiveness and might.

No! In fact, it was that the salt and pepper pots needed filling before breakfast.

*

Breakfast is when you break the fasting of night-time slumber, not so much a religion, but a necessary reason to reimburse the strength and will of a living body.

Apart from a great big fucking hangover which deteriorates the body, tires the mind and deliberately sets the tongue to dehydration and nausea.

Deadly moaned and groaned to his task, fulfilling the need to laugh off his vomit encased throat, as JB tackled the morning lay out, looking like a good old stale morning beer.

They were ready and the sergeants to higher-ranking NCOs filed in.

*

One morning, early, a duty sergeant rushed into the Mess demanding a bottle of milk!

D suggested, *"A bit early Sir!"*

"Yes," came the duty commando, *"there is a war on!"*

"Where?!" asked Deadly, who was getting a fresh bottle of milk from the kitchen refrigerator.

"The Falklands!" came the answer, the rep-lie of a very urgent need, to leave with the bottle of milk and also get to task, as to the needs of the intention of fighting one.

D thought, he thought for a split second, as to the daylight hour and pushing on through the great big hangover scenario, said after him, *"Where's that? Scotland?!"*

No answer. No digression. Where the fuck was Falklands?!

The war was in South America. Argentina to be precise. The Falkland islands belonged to the offshore delights of mainland Argentina, but the Brits lived on there, and they weren't moving, with their double decker buses and red post boxes, they had a right to roost, and the people were lively Brits sharing the island of Falklands and St Georgia with the nearby infestation of snow and polar bears of the South Pole; Antarctica.

So, the Argy invaded and tried to take over the island, because someone had gone to St Georgia and tried to sell some 'rag and bone', but were sent away, so they went to the Junta, the dictators of Argy at the time and complained. Well, that was it! They decided to invade.

Without talking to Prime Minister Thatcher about it!

So the original 26 Commandos from the Sergeants' Mess where Deadly worked were sent home via Uruguay.

Seen on TV with their hands above their heads being marched sorrowfully away, to be sent home without any dinner!

So, when they arrived back, the Mess fed them. They ate and rushed on back to take the island back for the Brits who lived there.

Deadly thought about why it was that a Task Force was sent to South America to fight their way back in, when all Thatcher had to do was go herself in a private plane and give the Junta a great big bollocking! That would have worked.

Less cost, less life, and surely through dialogue or dialect the day could have been settled over a cup of tea and a Briton? *No?!*

He thought tenderly, as he supped his ninth pint and pissed up against the wall.

He staggered home and fell into bed. He slept and woke to hear of the sinking of the Belgrano.

Then the Goose Green bit, then he realised, that he must have been the fifth person to hear of the war in the country.

First, the invasion. Then, contact the barracks from whence they come. Then, contact the Defence Secretary, who would wake up Thatcher, who'd call the troops out for battle – thus the duty Sergeant rushed into the Mess and screamed there was a war on in the Orkneys!

It was D who served him his milk.

A living memory forever to tell his grandchildren.

*

It was time in the summer for the 'Grand Summer Ball'. Just to change the subject.

The summer ball meant flying fish. A dish to go beyond the realms of skill and wishful thinking. The time to show the Mess what Daly, Moresby, Bernardo and Prestwick could do.

Apart from shout and scream to move the fear of the kitchen along, brush one's quiff till it looked like a toupee, dribble the snot from one's Italian nose into the carbonation, and be cross-eyed when looking at the cue ball when trying to play snooker.

The tarpaulins were raised and all was set for the display of large rainbow trout flying through the air, set on a tripod frame, to make it look effective.

Four, either end of the tarpaulin and Mess diner.

Rains managed to finish his first and set it up with ease. Everybody clapped and jeered. Then it was Moresby the quiff, who struggled to save his face from turning bright red and misdoing made the rainbow trout even more colourful. Then Sid, who, cross-eyed, walked in the opposite direction till he was sent in the right direction, only to be shown the frame to which he could mount his trout. Then, Tony Bernado, who was well equipped in skill and snot to make it, but he had one other failing besides a runny nose. He never tied his shoe laces up.

For a chef perhaps one should wear mules or flip-flops, but Tony seemed not to give a fuck, so he motioned towards his frame. Everybody stopped what they were doing, as he headed straight towards disaster due to the shoe laces hanging about his feet like the hangman's noose at Tyburn.

Everybody cringed, didn't look, couldn't look, looked cross-eyed, turned away and whistled, went to the bar for a glass of water, as it wasn't opening time yet, thought about sex, did all they could to avoid the inevitable.

So, one step, then another and right in front of Tony was a guide rope, so to avoid his laces he navigated the situation like the fall of Rome, he then tripped over the rope, the tarpaulin rattled, the sky went dim, the flying fish went flying and the rainbow was spread out in the sky. The whole world laughed to see such fun and the fucking place erupted with sheer disgrace, sympathy, irony, humour, disillusion and felt the drink take over the rhythm of the veins and make the heart grow weaker. He tripped and fell head over heels over toes, over laces, over his snotty Roman nose, and in flutter wept, in flight growled his apology, his accent turned from passion to dog Latin, right in front of the whole staff, who pissed themselves with joy. It was ridiculous to behold, but destiny has a strange way of teaching the onlooker a great lesson when it comes to untidy, messy, Mess chefs!

*

One last genuine laugh, has to be when Tony Bernado had a moped bike, and on the back of the saddle was a backpack. He took a bag of potatoes and put them in there.

Rains Daly said, *"watch"*, so they all did.

The next day Tony came storming in with what looked like a plate of mashed potatoes.

He said, in his awful pidgin English accent, *"Who has do this?!"*

Everybody looked at each other, and finally head chef Daly spoke up.

"I did," he said.

What he had done is to go outside, open the backpack, take out the bag of potatoes and replace them with a plate of already cooked, mashed potato. So when Tony got home, he opened the backpack and there were his potatoes, mashed, steaming slightly, with the air of surprise.

They all laughed.

Tony stormed off, wiping his nose for fear of tears and a great big snot flowing out of his nostril like the flowing river which leads to a waterfall, leaving the banks of the stream silently to meander gushing to the ocean sound.

Those days were nearly over for D.

*

Pierce retired and two days later, having worked all his life, up and died. D learnt from such stigma, he said goodbye to all the crew and played his last game against Pete Dunham.

Dunham was left-handed, and could make a decent break of 20, if he put his mind to it.

D played a good game and his wild shots seemed to run safe instead of being left on for the opponent to take total advantage and so win the frame.

D ended up on the colours.

He watched as he downed the yellow. Then the green, with a screw shot, then the brown with a back spin, plenty of bottom right-hand side. Then the blue, an easy blue which put him on the pink, which is really called the salmon, which he potted nice and followed through to end up straight on the black.

D chalked his cue, looked at the pocket, then the angle, got down to play the shot, to make a nice 27 break to win the match. As he flowed back in the grip of his wrist, the palm of his hand guided it through his fingers, the bridge to which he used was natural, all seeming to be the final bow, on his curtain call of a career as a steward.

He tiger-eyed the black and placed the cue dead centre of the cue ball, when Les Dunham walked into the snooker room and – moving the door and closing the door, then looking over the situation to see what was happening – made Deadly fluff the shot!

It went somewhere, over the bloody cushion, bounced out to the angle of beyond and ran faster down the table like the break off of a one-handed pool player!

Les said, with a sense of irony, for they were hot on irony there, *"Deadly!"*

Yes, he missed. Yes, he missed his chance. Yes, it was fitting that the moment of sheer genius was abound, someone disturbed the bloody lot. Mindless of fact or fiction, friction or rubbing of the chalk on the 'v' of your thumb and index finger, was bloody well inconvenient.

They laughed the brothers Dunham and Deadly, but he wept inside for failure to complete his destiny with some kind of panache or style or charisma or brilliance, which could develop his mind into being the snooker player he wanted to be, and he knew deep down he would get bored, as he got bored of most things available on this natural planet.

They all hugged and said goodbye.

They played well in those years and together they had some great games.

Friendship was forged over that table and that was only a break of 20, but it would have to do.

* * *

D went through the middle earth and got a job at a private golf club, as a barman.

He worked from 11am to 11pm for £45 a week. It was not enough. He did try to come to terms with the season of Rolls Royces and second car 'Jags', which rolled up to the clubhouse for a double whisky in a crystal glass, then *home James!*, to the wife and luxurious penthouse suite reality, having driven home over the limit.

It allowed D plenty of time to ponder, look yonder, surmise, procrastinate and also the feeling of understanding the sense of time, was due to the passing of hours, from when to open the bar, when to serve the small few, who attended for a ritual slink, then to wait for the odd drop-in, thus to close, weary, tired, exhausted and lost as to the outside world and a minimal grip on reality when it came to last orders.

The place cheered up at the weekend, when the club was used by members, doing the 18 holes and snorting whisky around the green, arriving back at the clubhouse, where D in his white socks, would serve you with plumb attrition and confidence. He also wore a suit with Spanish shoes. In his lapel jacket pocket sat a placed coloured handkerchief to symbolise his style.

He waited for the place to empty. The fruit-machine was on. It gave out a £100 jackpot! He walked up to the front, leaned into the back, and with a set of keys opened the back of the fruit-machine. He touched a lever, and the fruit-machine paid out a £100. He collected his winnings, added them to his poor wages and nobody knew the wiser, as someone had won it! He saw them do it. Can't remember their names?

D left, he'd had enough of conservative hypocrisy and went out into the night, with a revenge to conquer the day and holy circumference the night-time dance of death's darkness. He left the world of work behind. He left the system to pay for itself. He left the conforming capitalistic deterministically falsehood for his bed.

The golf club gave a picture to the police of D, but they did not find him, he was long gone, he was only in trouble for absconding with the bar keys.

He paid for a room and climbed into the 'sack'. Got up, had a shower and went to the local pub.

He would dream of his life full on with army duties and weapons and times and war ethic. He sweated out the syndromes of the phoenix demons, he healed the first quarter of his life and never looked back, as he strove forward with a new heart, an open heart, an open mind and a habit for drinking, because he liked to.

He went to sleep for two years. His dreams mingled with horrific nightmares and visions.

*

A profound resentment osculated about his head – no need for conversation, no need for friends to hear the end, no one would be there when his world collapsed around him and the feelings of vulnerability turned to triumphant minimalistic palindromic irony based on naïve art, words from the mind, captured images about the creation of life and how to explain it with totem and taboo.

The freedom to be was only allowed in the senses of the imagination. And in the imagination all could be resolved. Having seen the cause of all hate, the despise of fellow humans, the destruction of humanity through everyday ignorance and blasphemy, he turned to passive delight, to the opposite of being, in his parents, his responsibility, and torched the impetus of spiritual torture, hearing the words over and over in his head, when in bed, when drunk, when dead, when the world went running for money, running for fame and ambition, running for the essence of present skill, worth, understanding, effort, duration, education, a curriculum of pure lies to confuse the people, the individual, the freedom fighter, only to lay down the law with justice and judgement could the world feel safe with the torment of 'white trash' insufficiency and crime.

The words, void of self education and self awareness, seemed to echo in the corridors of morphogenesis. I had to have a meaning, a purpose, some reason to be alive? Why? What for? And, *where are the answers?!*

Over and over, the whispered sound, the edge of verbalisation, the terms of disquiet, roamed the phrenology of muscle matter, a cranium solution to problems, pain, all returned to the mind, the brain, a muscle seemly in charge of the soul, a massive choice to equate, find a solution, an answer to, to all prophecies and history's backdrop for the present's sheer foolery, pathetic rules, dishonourable breath, a remembrance of details forgotten, in the transience of travesty, the pains of planetary disease, a survival bringing less adversity with more paper money one had.

What a bunch of knobheads, he thought.

The world rushed on by as he slept. Turned awake, felt the cream of nature's hibernation and reaching for the comfortable meditative position, fell to deep, honey unmoderated bamboozles.

*

His life was half drunk/half sleep. The rest did not matter. That was for the bourgeois and the fascistic frame worker, for show and power, a worthless point in the eye of the mountains, seas and gorges; caverns of ancient hand paintings, sending the future a true message of female worship, the vulva, the young, the gift of life stood against the 21st century's use of kit, a man-made equipment, full of availability, for the leisure and recreation generations, having won the war, it was time to celebrate the poverty of sin, the welfare of shit-states, a combination of non-availability in the pages of ancient works, ancient bibles, triggered maledictions with grounding yearns for riches, bigger pitches, butterfly stitches, itchy britches and a magnificent champion of the energy and skills to kill the animal kingdom, the past of war, the books resurfaced through the phoenix of Nazis, a populism given to leaders, fat bastards and rich ambitious takers, reapers, child molesters; if you don't do what is good, then bad will not happen.

It's okay as that would all be understood in the future. Time changes the true sense of equation.

The answer is coming! It will be solved. It is all God's work. Stop it! God's work.

Darwin was wrong. You cannot separate the evolution of species from God. *They are the same bloodless thing!*

*

D walked about in a poet's shirt, long hair, earring, baggy drawstring pants, high Russian boots and a terracotta overcoat, long, down past his knees, with a collar to keep out the winter snow, the barking rain and the Scandinavian wind.

He haunted the library. Reading the Classics. Then, the bastards! Cameos. Dostoevsky, Lobachevsky, Tchaikovsky, Dosimetry, Vladivostok, Stanislavsky, Astrophysics, Gogol, Henry Miller's *'Black Spring'* and *'Tropic of Cancer'*, D.H. Lawrencium's; Cunt!, Oscar Wilde, Comte de Meadowlark – all obsessive works of fiction based on fact based on autobiographical experience. Cankerous, Burrows, Hemingway, Joyce, Ginseng and all the writers with existential problems, the world could and would not deal with, iconoclastic god, whore bitch, rum and coke, slid and a poke, the world was to seize the day, to make it pay, to let it slide, leave it all behind and let go, die on the wing of a dinosaur, spit at the sun and watch it sizzle!

But, please ... the great god of antiquity in Dionysus, Bacchus, Silences, the hunchback satyr, the akimbo nymph, the tortured breast, Quarreller of Brest – Jean Genet, the violent homosexual, the psychobabble of Sartre, Sake' soliloquy and tendency to shock, damaged the page with a rock and vomited in the hand of the beholder.

The healing was illness, to be reborn in the tools of words. Calm, could be worse, could last forever, when the death is uncertain and one does not want to die. To cry and reach for the comfort of a stranger when one hates human life. To be shy when all you want to do is shout. Shout out!

"You fucking bunch of bastard typhus, cleaved from the same bastard generation, takers who had no father, who hated the sense of feeling, the upper-crust felt, the lust and break down, pornography with a loaf of bread to slice apart with a sabre sword, to bring down those beneath so they could look almighty and great and good in the community of worth and status, thus God watched as they killed in his name, the blood poured into the hearth of the goddess and she became ill with violence, stress, war, turmoil and horror, as children's buggery in the playground of filth and sin, the blemish of a modern day present became the holocaust of a future! Ghat on the protozoic!"

*

In tears, the conscientious objector passivated. The tender rose crescendoed the imagine, as the cream suit ruffled with the dust, dirt and sunshine, *"he stylised the bandanna"*.

Weakly, he lay down to rid himself of dizziness.

He would awake. See the light of day, look out to the cumulus mediocre clouds and know his situation. As his whereabouts seemed lacking responsibility. Lacking in arrangement, timespan, routine, commitment, so, he knew there was no tax. No tax paid for street lights at night, the social forces in police and fire brigade, the council tax for ground and living plots, a service of all services hoped for in charity and Samaritan goodwill.

He knew the NHS had to be paid for, as they did a great job and everybody at some time in their life gets injured or hurt; *'so don't get hurt!'*, he thought; just be careful and have no need to attend the A&E

reception. He didn't need the armed forces for war. He didn't need to feel safe from 'thugs' and violent sons and daughters. He didn't need to be lit up to see the streets at night, and to have to pay for a place to live on the destined planet in creation was a paradoxical blasphemy based on human rights and humanity as a given consequence with being.

The need to eat was an overindulgence of umbilical pains, a solar plexus to join the reality of earth's evolution, to devour, to have to eat another, the rhythms of a being, a food for the order.

Imagine the hunger being cannibalistic, infertility monomaniacal starvation inflationary with staving the empty orgasmic void, which in nature has to be quelled, a hungry child waiting to be loved in a world filled with unloving kinds, seemed to be the opposite of the speciality of self, contained, responsible and top form for the survival and adaptation of a universal planetary environmental manifestation.

What to do? What to become? What's on offer? To the individual or unity. What has one to do to become a 'should' or a 'could' or budding brilliant force to be reckoned with, to be respected for, or still, a saviour of the situation of a human condition? Human condition! Ha! Laugh!

It's a beautiful manifestation of the god-given right to *be*.

*

Do as is right, in the name of all, do not fall to the wrong, but fight to maintain the goodness for greatness for human consciousness.

So, D sat down to an old 1800 typewriter he found up in the attic, whilst exploring, and wanted to write. To write. That's what he did. He wrote. He looked at the A4, then at the type, then at his mind, his brain in his head and saw the thoughts wrangling about and around his soul, about his heart, in his knowledgeable experience, in his destiny, his fate, the sense of 'not knowing' was the habit, a curb, to which he desired to see, to find, to write and imaginatively create a novel idea, a story about the make-believe world of magic and mystic adventure.

He saw his terracotta overcoat and climbed out from beneath its skin. He saw the sweat of his fear for life. The insecurity to watch, talk, say or listen. He knew the characteristic of personality's requirement and wrote about the parallel need to be. Be the best shoes, the best looking, be the best clothed, the best dancer, *the best!* The best master, the best lover, be something, be ambitious about what you do. So he wrote about failures and losers in a world of vanity. He wrote about someone else and about something else. An alter-ego which altered nothing.

The cruel world of Dickensian hate, betrayal and horror. Be natural about the need to develop, destiny will do the rest, so long as one's fate is not as black a hate.

*

The bohemian existential iconoclastic drop-out classified, self-designated within the holy masses, only to spend many nights awake, for the candlelight shone in defiance of all progress, ideas and civilisation to be the only rebellion, bright enough to lay claim to existence, a pure speck in the cosmos and never to be able to live like the tribe of modernists do, in luxury mansions, family and values, lost on the poor, virtue found in the poor and moral tendency to be hypocritical and forgiven blasphemy.

Night after day-light sleep, if not capable of begging up the 'coffer', then it seemed only right to be drunk with the words of creative migrative works of the unholy banished. Banned. Banned from reading, when the world was ready; red.

Later, before the time, the conclusion of devil's work and words, then it would be the future to concern the present with an insight to pornographic images, moments of sexual deviance, moralistic collapse, virtuous voices singing the songs of fallen angels and less value for the coming of a second messiah or the right to be called precious or divine, as the world created by society's voted leaders, is, were or was, one to be built on Sodom or Gomorrah, Babel, Babylon, sand and soft soils of souls.

The naked bodies rived in the steam of beds. The heaving of throats, as the sound of letting go, of orgasmic sighs, seemed to make pain pleasurable, seemed to hold the beholder in chains as the freedom of losing seemed to hurt the more and better, as the strength caused through the ambivalence, the apathy and empathy for flesh, the taste, the scent, all seeming paradisical in a tidal wave of ecstasy, momentous to the desired craft, sensory to all takers and wanton for all revolutionist fighters, leading the sordid, through to the promised, the lands of heaven, a shout to the glory of kind and a thank you note for the creator. Thanks!, and I shall come again! I shall love the feeling of addiction to love, to love love and love the lover who gives us telling tales of after birth, before birth and during sex, let us pray and be thankful, for we are blessed, we are divine and in us is love, sex, need, want and to give what is needed!

She was good on a cumulus clouded day light hour.

He looked at the ceiling, his arm above his head making room for her in his single bed. She lay with her whole body, nice and plump, voluptuous for the the beggar-man to be charmed with alms, she too looked at the ceiling, thinking about the feeling which is lost, never to be captured, never quite to be expressed, talked about to others with a greater feeling of experience through drama. She said, *"Do you want to go to America?"*

D answered, *"No, not really. I have never thought about it."*

"Well," said Kate. *"I have an application for a summer camp there. I don't want to go, I can't go.*

I am living with a University Lecturer who has me and another student in his flat. I love him and I can't leave him. I don't know what he would do? Marry her, or something ... I have to stay and watch the situation ... he loves me, I'm sure ... If only he would say.

She is okay, but I was the first, the first choice, she was the second wife and he seems to be doting on her more than me, that's why I am with you ... do you want to go instead?"

D did not answer as he had fallen asleep.

When he awoke, the application was on his bed, for him to see and read.

He read and went.

But first he had to see the man.

He got on his bike and rode to see him. Well, it wasn't his bike, he borrowed it from his friend who was married and seemed to encourage spontaneity of the venture, whilst crying in his 'two up two down', three young kids, a mortgage with a wife and rumbles of tendency to nag; life.

The bike took him to the application man, who signed it and warned D of the trip to London to get a visa, then his meeting in the big hall, as an organisation period for the flight to America.

He was to land in Scranton, Pennsylvania, *The United States of America.*

*

"Oh, full of scorpions is my mind, dear wife!"

Macbeth: Act 3, Sc 2
William Shakespeare

Albedo Cell

TAKING *a walk* …

… about the States. The sounds of crickets and bullfrogs made the place a lot different to the local colloquial sound of England's cricket bat crack and the silence of toads.

Without the nettles, overgrown, dandelions, daffodils, daisies and wild lilies, seeming to haunt the soul of an old world boy, it seemed refreshing to warrant delight, when the sound and taste of America seemed bigger, louder, honest and tortured, in the sense of pure relief, when the nature could not be captured by senses, but only by the invisible self, which some call the spirit, the soul of a life-force, which can recognise the doing of right or wrong, the playing of nature in its own front garden and everybody's holy preponderance towards the gift of water being the treasure of life, and life was not cheap in the nimbus stratus clouds of an Amish worship or the pilgrims' placing, the Indians' last stand or of a new world contaminated.

*

The sun shone around the planet and the states took the brunt of a daylight strength, presumably honourable, thanksgiving, reverend, popular, with a consumerist's flavour in architectural ambivalence, justified by race, colour and creed, to soften the sheer blood of ancestral genocidal annihilations.

The feelings already adapted to new surroundings for D. So, he changed his name to Decca and took the surname; Peters.

Decca Peters was at liberty to spit in a spittoon, to chew the cud or 'bubbly' gum. He went out, into Scranton, into a hardware shop and bought an NYC baseball cap, the New York Yankees blue with white lettering and a pair of white, with the black NIKE strip, ankle-length training shoes.

As always with his jeans and T-shirt he was Americanised, as well as forthright about his appearance being explained unless you thought he only wore a baseball cap with NIKE trainers on his feet.

He smoked KKK; Marlboro, and wore dark sunglasses. He felt at last like Jimmy Dean's attitude and Marlon Brando's brusque tones and command. And his happiness was genuine freedom based on anti-responsibility and the American dream, whatever that was [better, he thought than a British nightmare].

Not forgetting that life was made to do for others. That all responsible actions paved the way for others. For all good there is a bad. The more one is good in action the more there is a bad reaction somewhere else, synchronism absolved in acid drops and symbolical liquid.

Life teaches lessons to be learnt, and time arrives in age to know. Life is about knowing and one has to reach a good old age to release the wisdom into and around the barren rocks of a society deaf, dumb and blind to the beliefs of a life.

Happiness is comfort and willing to bear the affairs of life in knowing, to share, takes skill and awareness of human indignity.

*

He got a job in the kitchen, with other students working as waiters and waitresses. An ancestor of the Cherokee Indians; Blade General Clarence, told him he would be a 'veg' chef. Decca said he wanted to be a dishwasher. Blade told him in a mild manner, his 'hero' was a dishwasher, but, he wanted him to work with the chefs, who were to run the kitchen, and they all came from the Ozark plateau, Arkansas.

The 'Hillbillies' with their beards and dungarees, with pretty nieces in summer short skirts and bare legs, liken to showing off their underwear in the outdoor cornfields. Well, they were nothing like that.

They were kind and strong and ran the running of the 'Kosher' Jewish meals good and well, and Jackson the head-chef, had a beard and a small Jewish face, but he knew he would never have handed Jesus over to the authorities, not in a million years!

There was Blade and his good virgin cooking wife, Jana, who loved to bake with the main ingredient, love, and to share all her cakes with the kids in the camp, and she took to Decca like he was hers, as she was a virgin mother, and she doted on his every move, which to Decca felt like the negative dark streak of being watched by English knob-heads, but he soon got used to it, what with the feeling of positivity, her caring nature and a willingness to listen Decca out.

Then, Rocky and Rubinstein, who were gay. As flash as a five-bob note! They were the epitome of 'Hillbillies', but held hands, kissed, and winked when they were to retire and cuddle up in the sack together.

Blade, Jana, Jackson, Rocky and Rubinstein all worked in the kitchen and Decca was to become their friend and loyal 'veg' chef.

The girls were in abundance. The American girls were very similar to English girls, but the only difference was a seemingly open arranged attitude to the safety of, and, the trust of human dignity.

Sure, Decca didn't have any, but he soon saw that they could put up with the less of species, even knowing, they could have a 'fling' with an Englishman due to and because of his *lovely accent.*

*

Decca noticed that, so he spoke a lot and used it close, to the finesse of breath flowing in the direction of a good campfire fuck.

Then there was the 'groupie'.

Decca had been seen to sing with the summer camp band, who organised a concert for the kids, with all the singers singing songs of different artists, different years and entertaining the Jewish children.

Decca was told – he sang two songs – that he was surprisingly good! He knew it. He enjoyed the fracas, the fame, the ideology which stemmed the picture of greatness, lying on the sultan robes of inconsequential love, for the beauty of ballads, he twisted the rhyme, he hurt the soul, in doing the utmost fashion touch to all songs, in bliss he sang, in hope of a sad world he waited and hoped, and then he watched as the children adored, the essence of popstars, the boy hero, the mentor of millions, singing the tunes to find the cause of the universal language of aliens, from different tribes, the universe would verse the chemistry to create others, others not like us, but funnier, different, perhaps more sexy!

She sat at the back and watched, as he put the final touch to The Police's *Every breath you take / Every move you make / every cake you bake / every orgasm you fake / I'll be watching you!*

She wanted him. She wanted him for his genes. For the artistic cells of talent and artistic intention, she needed to child his clone, the son or daughter of his, so she made her move of 'groupie'. She was an assistant to the kids, a Philadelphia babe, 18, ready to do well with her intentions in life's choice. She touched him, looked him up and down and knew he was right for the task.

He shagged her. He shagged her on the stage, that night when the camp was in bed. They shagged together, she gave him her dark side, the known side, the intelligent choice of love with a respect for her friend, lover, sperm of her child, the fountain of union fed the beautiful loins of female dips and lips and tits and bits, in which he adored for a lifetime, in which he loved deeply, down in the pits of heaven, the joy of lust doubled with eternal love and the equation of freedom was sexual release, as he looked in her dark eyes and she looked into his, he said, *"Yes?"*, she said, *"YES!"* – so he did. He came in her vagina, vulva, clitoral womb, and she loved it all.

They finished together and they left apart.

Dark the night, with blue juxtaposition-al congest-us clouds.

They said goodnight; she said his name.

He did not know hers.

*

In the kitchen he had become a celebrity. The idea of donning a bandanna and filling a 'veg' bucket in up to three minutes was ludicrous, but made possible with skill, timing, concentration, a mind for therapeutic meditation on rhythm and the crazy tendency to 'show off' and do something in life seemingly mundane and turning the situation into a spectacle of outside interest and self-preserving ego massaging ability.

Decca would do such things; Blade, a half Cherokee, would howl with poetic justice for a world having abused a son of goodness and unbelievable protencial for famous moments in a spacial life form of stereotypes and followers of leaders who know of their shy vulnerability and fears.

Blade spun the yarn. He made the myth. He turned the whole of the kitchen into an ashram of sweaty Turkish bathers and Indian sweat lodges.

*

He loved Decca. He loved him like a brother. A father who was fair, sharing, honest and wanting to better the holy potential of a skilful man who carried an abused child, who was deep in a conscious cave crying, who was deep in darkness for any to see, and only Decca could rescue him, only Decca could love him and make him better, well, and heal the soul of his childhood and days of being a young boy, who depended on the parents for guidance and faith and unconditional love.

Decca drank a bottle of Jack Daniels whisky in the hot night of Pennsylvania. He sweated at the prospect of finding the sight of himself. He grew ill, he felt tired, he felt the surge of hate dwindle away his strength and attack his truth, as the night closed in sleep, the sleep brought the sight and the nightmare continued till he awoke in a camp hospital bed.

As he lay there half conscious, he heard a sound around him. He heard it, it sounded familiar, he thought it was the wings of a swan, flapping in the wind, as the anvil cumulonimbus clouds moved infinitely unprovoked above.

It wasn't the dead soul of a poet. It was the sound of a helicopter, out in the daylight sun, sounding familiar in the heat of a childhood summer's day, contrails in the sky, with lawnmowers and children playing and music in the far off background sounding out the present rhythm in guitar skills and riffs.

The helicopter sound carried on, farther and farther away, then back, closer, nearer to, like the busy sound of his mind as a child, the constant wheels churning and turning insanely in his head, regardless of his brain, his mind, it was a head with ultimate pain, which surpassed the nerve endings with pressure, to always gladly stress the uncomfortable hatred of a beaten body, screaming in lamentation for a saviour to free his bondage, to hug his soul and kiss his lips, to heal the tears and brush off the monsters of religion, who had tried to destroy his manifestation.

He sank in and out of sleep. Peeping and peering out at the light, the scent of the grass, the minute cricketing and bullfrog chorus, a harmony of untouched nature, which could state the freedom of power inherent in the earth's purpose, for, being untried, unresolved, chaotic, controlled breaches of majesty and focused troubles, always seeming to fight for the territory of might and tender to the following night in replenishment, a timescale, bound to change with an alluring loss of a nurturing sovereign love – children.

Blade came to see him. He stared at the sweaty face of his friend. He looked at the silence in the laying frame of change and offered his 'rape-seeds' to his god.

"*What's these?*" asked Decca, a quiet, silent voice suited to whispering and the Chinese.

"*Rapeseed,*" said Blade. "*It's good for feeding the soul.*"

"*It looks more like birdseed to me!*" rang out Decca, who looked closer at the seeds and might have been guilty of laughing at the lack of grapes or orange juice or bananas and maybe, for the worst accolade in the heathen book of visiting the ill and sick to bore them with hope, was flowers. Dead flowers; ripe but ready then to die, with the patient or with the death of friendship in need of replenishment and excitement at funerals, weddings and Pass-overs.

"*What are they?*"

"*Rape seeds,*" came the unconditional answer from the poet without bias or blasphemy considered in his virtue.

"*What a fine name for food for the soul!*" thought and said Decca, who took a mouth-full of the budgie nuts and fell asleep. The seeds bringing no joy, the sleep incessant on depriving the sleeper; life, and the hospital visitor a doctorate of hypnosis corpus.

The nurse fancied Decca. She was from Ithaca. Where-ever that was?

She was big and fat, although the fat was sexy to a fetish liking. She was jet black and beautiful, so the need to wish for perfection was out of the question, as she was very big, like she was voluptuous and all over voluptuous again.

*

She helped and liked to help. She never needed to be emotional, so she was an aloof large attractive nurse, who would be good for an injured rich film actor, perhaps, she knew the look she was looking for and in the man she would invite home, and she did.

She invited Decca to Ithaca, but he declined, after thinking about the sex with her, the fickle need to have to wake every day and watch as she bombed about with her great big huge ass, always attentive, always the caprice descent, based on reliance; the bed going with him, as he was idle and she was full of fat ideas and fat feasts of love and satisfaction for the masses.

He would fuck her and leave. Yeah. That sounds right. That's the way to live life.

*

The time of the summer was good. The Jewish children had a great time at summer camp.

One young Jewish boy was always eating honey. He was called 'Honey Bear', because he would try to get into the kitchen and steal a honey bear which he would squeeze into his mouth as the honey ran out of the top of the tube.

He was like Pooh the bear. He would be caught climbing through a window because he had got stuck. His little fat legs shaking in the midday sun as people would try to help him back. Pushing him forward, or trying to press his head back on through the small window where he had attempted to find some honey.

He could die, if he had too much. He was round, big for a young boy, and fat. With a great big smile on his face when he had had his honey rations.

All went well and the awards for good work were given out, one of the last nights they were all there.

The kitchen staff were all awarded a blue apron with their names on.

Decca had torn his trousers and was on his way to change them, when his name was called out. He rushed back just in time for the children and audience, having wondered where he was, to see him accept his award of a blue apron with the initials in white: DECCA.

They also saw the split in his breeches, it was right up the right leg, so it seemed he was showing off his thigh and hairy leg for all the females in the camp to see. They all whistled and jeered, as he accepted his gift, they all clapped and laughed as Decca put the apron on and the whole situation was amended.

The red embarrassment on the face of Decca, plus his joy of being accepted for his help, made him feel free from bias and indiscriminate buffoonery, to which he freely showed the love of his heart, the blood rushing to his unshaven face and the thanks for all the experience he had received from people with unconditional love for any sex, colour, creed or nationality.

It was America he was in. He could tell. The place was vibrant with acceptance and human dignity with which even the angry criminal would seek forgiveness and cry tears of his history's torment.

No one is made unequal in the eyes of the imperfection-al bloodline of modern day world national biological ideologies, with which a respect for creation's species of homespun rudiments stayed sacred and divine in the hearts of all.

'Honey Bear' didn't die and Decca Peters set off, at the end of the summer camp, to New York City.

*

The first feeling, the first steps into the 'Big Apple' was frightening for Decca Peters. He was after all a small town boy with big intentions. The towering high blocks of skyscrapers seemed to him to be like dinosaurs. The giant type. The Tyrannosaurus Rex! type.

And as he felt insufficient, looking down on the ground at his feet, a shame came over his brow. He saw in front of him and on the floor, purple painted feet which led somewhere, *where?* He did not know, but to be guided and shown around the place, seemed to be a good idea, so he followed the purple footsteps.

One by one they stepped along, as if the step was the average step of a person visiting New York, as it led past historical buildings and monuments on the island of Manhattan.

Until finally they led him to a small green yard of overgrowth and vegetation. It was a medium-sized allotment. Where people could go in the asphalt jungle of New York; wearing Wellington boots and doing some gardening, planting flowers, growing vegetables.

The last foot led to the gateway. Decca looked up and saw the rows of greenery and shrugged his shoulders, tutted and left the area.

Leading himself about this time, leading himself who knows where, but he would get there, he would feel out the place, the gut instinct would be strong and he would find his destiny there, amongst the city streets and neon lights, frightening nights and debauchery.

He knew he had arrived in the 'place that does not sleep'. But, he did, and he was tired, so he booked himself into a small hotel/bed and breakfast place, went into his bedroom and dived on the bed and fell exhausted; asleep.

He fell asleep and dreamt on Amsterdam Avenue, in Spanish Harlem; where the rundown hotel was situated. Quietly he slept as the Puerto Ricans lived out their fate.

Too late the Golden Gate, shown in his mind, leaving the Hudson River.

He had never been there before.

The cumulus pile clouds led him out to the Chinese restaurant where he ordered a plate of spicy noodles, which tasted of peanut butter, but he loved them, he devoured them and then he noticed he had chopsticks in his hand, using them well between index and thumb with the control of a Chinese veteran.

He smirked to himself, outwardly he was showing how impressed he was. Inside he was beaming with a full stomach and hipster pride.

He paid and left, leaving a tip and picking a mint on the way out.

He found a bar and ordered American beer. Then another, and after 6 or 7 Budweisers, he was joined by a very ugly woman.

She was a sight for sore eyes.

She was everything the American archetype would be. She was a caricature, she was large faced in all senses, she spoke a slang American voice, which seemed to remind Decca he was in New York City and they pronounced many things like it would show someone came from a State of facsimile.

They talked about the situation he was in, she was in. They talked about the future of the world bound due to the way things were and how it would accumulate and add up to the answer in closure with both having a seeming insight into metaphysical mathematics and philosophy.

Did they?

They drank and forgot about her face, his foreign deployment without plans or a public idea for direct ambition with a solution for monetary investment and, as she would tell him in a very broad NYC street accent, *"The rents are astronomical here!"* He believed her, determined to get on her good side and chat her up; he did and she invited him back to her apartment.

He thought about her face through a barrage of many alcoholic stupors. But his philosophy was, *'You don't go looking at the mantelpiece, whilst poking the fire!'* in a broad English accent.

*

They entered the apartment and dingy and dark they stumbled on the bed and fucked each other.

In the morning Decca left early, whilst she still slept, and went down to the East Village to possibly get himself a job. He walked into a restaurant and tried to sell himself off as a vegetable chef. No jobs were going, but they needed a barkeeper. He took it and sped off back to Laura's place, for that was the ugly woman's name, to tell her all about it.

She was home. She was snorting cocaine, as he entered. He sat down opposite her and ignoring her offer to partake, he spoke of his triumph at the restaurant called *Continent Diversity* on St Mark's Place, the Lower East Side.

She snorted a line and coming up to sniff, then pull up on her coke, she wiped the excess of her nose, closing the nostril to get to the better effect of the line of cocaine riding up her nose to the brain, where she could see the change and taste the smattering duty of the drug, and said, "Well done, you can stay here and pay rent if you want!"

Decca replied, "I would like to stay. If that's okay. I'll go to the hotel and pick up my things."

He left and went to get his things. He returned; she was asleep in her apartment in Spanish Harlem.

They slept together, they made love. They snorted coke, and drank beer. They had a party, as her caricatured face began to grow on Decca, as her personality was beautiful, and inside was a pretty woman, who could feel love and share her heart in moments, caring about the kingdom of humanity, animals, the environment, with a suggestion or two about how to change the problems and influences human beings have on the planet. She cared too much, she cried, and spoke of the shame which seemed to effect her every day, knowing how it was out of her hands, and the little bit she could do, care and sympathise, was not enough, but, the only way to deal with her personal feelings was to indulge her addictions in drugs, sex and working for Greenpeace, going about the island of Manhattan asking people to donate a certain amount for the dolphins being caught up in the nets, whilst fishing trawlers fished for tuna.

"You must join and help us," she put, as the beer and snorting sniffing was going well.

"I will, once I have settled in my job," said Decca, who seemed to feel the drug in his mind and body sending the flush of difference around his aura and seeming to change the world about him, with ecstasy, over indulgent love, moments of deep hypnotic thoughts with sights of fear joined with a ridicule and laughter joining hands with the future of paranoid ballets, schizophrenic time-spans, brain indulgent insights, talkative sentences, brought on by images flowing through his cerebral hemisphere, as the tongue pressed about the words, the words sounded hollow, and with ghostly distance, trailed away onto the landscape of voids and limbo haunted places. He knew if he could be heard, then someone or something would be listening, picking up the sound and following it to the outcome.

She asked in bed during afterglow, *"Do you have a middle name?"*

Some things could come to mind, anything could present itself and the skill to share was the freedom of speech which felt like the ultimate freedom searched for by civilisations since before Christ.

Decca answered, *"Dent, that's my middle name."*

"Is it?" she sounded shocked with the reaching thoughts of comfort and joy, feeling her heart wanting to know why the name was the name of the man she loved.

"Yes," he returned, *"Decca Dent Peters,"* he said with a pride and laughter, knowing who he was, why he knew the name and what it meant to him. *"My mother and father were Beatles fans and it was the Decca label they were on when they had me."* He carried on speaking with a large grin on his face, thinking about the most famous music band in the world, who were loved by the British as well as the Americans. It gave him an aspect of authority over his feeling of been connected to a landmark and historic phenomenon such as the boys from Liverpool who seemed to be the most famous people in the world, ever!

*

"Every decadent person always peters out!" he shouted, with his head on his pillow; she lifted hers and put her ugly senses, laughing in his face.

"Of course!" she realised, the rhythm and prognosis which had arisen in her sight, that his name was funny, a play on words, his parents had captured their son, as many parents do in such a natural way, that to name someone is never wrong, as if the name given to a newborn child was already established long before they lived in the suit of symbolic armour or carried the branding of initials, which balanced their forthright monopoly in attention or gave a glimpse into the world of myth and

family, when a name rings true, is heard by the ears of the universe and sits in the immortality of hopes and dreams of children looking up to their heroes, idols, peers or notorious criminals, set to trigger the mind at the flick of a switch, in history's path through the centuries.

"You ARE decadent!" she moved and laughed, as she attacked his body and drew down to perform fellatio.

She did, and he could not see her ugly face.

The days were full of cumulus radiator clouds all over the modern Amsterdam cathedral.

The name of New York City was originally New Amsterdam. The Dutch influence didn't show, but the Italians, Puerto Ricans, Irish and Jewish did. In NYC, you could receive any culture culinary.

Decca fed on the slice of pizza.

There was also Moroccan, Turkish, Korean, Polish, Greek and the odd fish and chips.

Finally, Decca faced the truth. He stayed out all night and went back to the apartment. Laura was totally out on her bed, strewn across the bedclothes, as if, having tried to undress, she had collapsed in a 'fucked up' heap, vomiting, the dried up remnants of spew over her half undressed body and all over the bedsheets and floor.

She awoke as he came in.

She ranted and raved about missing him and where had he been?!, who had he been with?! and why?! Why had he not come home … ? She ran on, as he turned to his inner flame, which had risen due to insult, on the basis; being owned by a very ugly drug-addicted bad fuck, made him shout at her.

"I HAVE FOUND SOMEONE ELSE! I WILL MOVE IN WITH HER TODAY! I WILL GET MY SHIT AND LEAVE!"

"YOU CAN'T," she shouted. "I HAVE HAD FOUR ABORTIONS! … AND I AM PREGNANT!"

"YOU BITCH!" he shouted, and struck her about the face. "I WILL LEAVE AND YOU CAN KILL THAT FOETUS TOO!"

"YOU BASTARD!" she spat, she screamed like a woman on her all fours, hair falling about her crazy face, the insanity reached its pitch as she picked up an ornament and hurled it at him.

It hit him and he cried. The injury adding to the injury which ran in his mind and his heart, the cage he found himself in was only escapable with sheer strength and determination to abort this place, to leave without trace, to consider no humanity, the karma of immediate action.

He left through the front door, rushed down the unpainted stairway and out into Spanish Harlem, running for his life, running to disappear, for she could never find him, she could never know, she could never tell … his mind adrenaline, like his thighs and feet, ran until the breath in his heart was pulling on his self-inflicted indulgence. Yes, he had met someone, yes he could live in the Lower East village, yes he could work and play and be an artist! Yes! But the woman he had met was a kept woman, who wore a wig and drank like a lush, she had inherited enough from her great aunt and lived the life of débutante in the village, like it was Beverley Hills!, like she was the broken heart on the boulevard of broken dreams.

The painted face, the dark mascaraed eyes showing pain, disillusion along the way of love. Lost, no love, picking up the nearest victim to fall for it, the money, the place, the trip.

She needed love and sex. He must give it, for his own room.

Decca got a new job. Better change from the *Continent Diversity*, Laura could find him there.

*

He got a job with a removal firm based in Manhattan called O'Reilly Brothers. It was a small firm run by two Irish brothers. Small jobs, but enough to do. It allowed him to see a lot more of the 'Big Apple'. The famous places and streets full of people, be it Wall Street, The Twin Towers, 42nd Street, Central Park with Park Avenue. Hell's Kitchen, Chelsea, Harlem and Spanish Harlem, where he would keep his head down just in case he was seen by 'you know who!'

So, he would get himself off to work, then return, have a shower and dress to entertain the broken heart of baby Jane.

She would demand the playful tactile approach from him, then they would venture down-town and hit the bars and restaurants of Greenwich Village. She would pay and he would be her resident gigolo.

He hated it, he seethed inside with malfunctioning fire! The blaze of a daze working soulfully on the opposite side of the normality of judgement and justice, seen to spare the rod, the cause and only the effect was his parole, his tears could be heard to cry in the recesses of the outermost climate in the most barbarian of hostile continents, with the spear of destiny been a snort of coke, a few more margaritas, a resting place for the wicked, as the dance seemed removed from gravity, the love, plastic with an operation to secure the vanity of ugly surgery, and he knew he was in the same cauldron, but it was full of frogs and toads and puppy dogs' tails, he knew of a heroin, not to inject and kill the spirit, but to save him from the crossroads of hectic and her hounds.

Was it the way to get ahead? She did. Was it a way to capitalise on a given situation? Was it a graveyard for the lost souls of limbo? Was it the demon of possession haunting the very conclaves of ancient relics, like the body of a zombie woman, who needs blood or love or just the power to kill or destroy with the nurturing kindness of an archetypal mother figure, to exist with some resemblance of life?

What happened to her and why? He never found out. He had lost his way. It was big! It was bigger than he was, it could swallow you up and spit you out with bagel bits on a frosty morning in the aftermath of Christmas fever.

The one headed of a gorgon's snake-filled charm represented money, fame, capitalistic acrimony and a dog eat dog world of power to the top and never drop, for fear of age or talent, as the famous actress would fall down the stairs drunk, found by her young lover, by the time he realised he genuinely cared about her and was sorry she was dead or had died.

The gigolo momentous was paying dividends, but the next move must be important to survive the torrent of karmic abuse one would receive after all those years of trying, she came into your life and you settled for that, she settled with you, and then came the knock at the door.

It did not matter in this climate. NYC could make you or break you and that's even before you realised where you were, what for and why!

It was time to leave and go and see the American Indian called Blade.

All is a manifest destiny, all is in the name of progress. All the trees on the plot of 40 acres to which Blade and Jana lived were deadwood trees. The Ozark plateau.

Blade burnt fires all day and she baked bread. They lived an idyllic life on the vine bushed, rickety bridge, Brahma cowed countryside, busy with insects, ticks and bees. They collected water from spring and swam 'skinny dipping' in the small streams heavy with the sound of rushing forth, the gurgle of ponds and fear of crocodiles or deep sea monsters.

Decca had caught a Greyhound bus to Little Rock, the birthplace of President Bill Clinton, he had waited for the connection to Eureka Springs in a small local café where farmers of the plough and tractor would stay off and have breakfast of grits and brownies. They seemed to wonder as to who he was, sat there all foreign, uncouth and dishevelled. All disorientated, plus jet-lagged and freezing, as the winters were *real* out there in Arkansas.

*

Decca ignored the piercing eyes and the spitting thoughts of bigotry, perhaps racism. He drank his coffee and got the bus.

He walked the rest of the way, up. Up towards 'Moonbeam' house, where Blade was seen to be loading the fire with wood and his aura in time and tune with the mighty Wakan Tanka.

He saw the figure coming towards him and immediately shouted, *"Decca! Me old friend!"*

They came together like brothers, who had fought in the American civil war, and one of them had been lost, perhaps dead, whilst the other made it home to start a new life.

They turned arm in arm as Jana came out to greet them, to see her men, the two men in her life who made up her charm, made her feel loved and made her see the reason for being on the planet was to help the two wild Indian renegades come to terms with the way of the world in its capitalistic modernisation consumerist greed.

They all hugged. They hugged for ages. 'Pheasant' the dog came out from under the house, looking and sniffing at the trousers of the wayfarer. The house. The house was made of wood. Waterproof wood. A stairway leading up to the front door and the rest of the ground floor mirroring with large windows.

You could see in and you could see out, all about the house. The upstairs was the same length and size as the ground floor and it too had windows, it was a glass-wooden shack. A shack taking us back to the days of prohibition and backwaters. But it was a palace built for a reservation of deadwood trees and harmonic peace. The sound resignation in the heap fructose being the bees and wildlife, allowed to roam the forest, with as much right as the plot of land being bought with the intentional investment of holiday homes and campsites.

Decca was home, and they made it feel so.

He sat and looked at the home of paradise. The bookshelves, filled with the works of some of the great writers, who came out of the landscapes with such fascination: Walt Whitman, Henry Longfellow, Henry Thoreau, Jack London, and the tall tales of Sitting Bull and Geronimo; The Little Big Horn, Wounded Knee, works on the Civil, Vietnam and Korean wars, all patching up the wounds of Hemingway, Kerouac, Ginsberg and Steinbeck.

The shelves heaved with power, pain and loaded guns fit to fight the enemy with which could take away the freedom of the American way.

The kitchen, heated and hot with baking and cooking. The pots and pans, the array of equipment on hand, hanging from hooks off the wall, to stir, shake or spin the home-made cakes, pies, sandwiches and poultry dishes.

The scent and smells of wooded bark, summer light, dark kind hearthstone nights, the studious insight into poetry and words, the baking of an earth set tight in the skulls of history, torn by time and healed by love, a love so unconditional and kind, vanity and factional beauty were the enemy.

Freedom, was being free from impression, condition, compromise and influence. It all seemed fresh, a token of bliss without the darkness of ignorance and it dawned on the sun-setting mind of Decca, as he glimpsed the hush; 'heaven is another state', separate from even the known universe. It is a human 'thing'. Which is more than the limbo of life; and why? It is free from hypocrisy, dichotomy of all opposites, *it is immaculate perfection*.

He slept that night in a clear hum of fabric stillness. Breathing the air of God. Taking the turn of slumber, sensing his clear dreams, leading the story and accepting the praise.

It was darkness about him with safe secure light brought by the earth's understanding of a representation to be. To be seen. To be one with love and cherish the calling of the primeval mother to the tasking of wills, to break the cord and set oneself free to live amongst the better and the needed, the safe and the wanted, the reason and purpose, to be in manifestation of bodily form, to see with the eyes of self, to feel with the hands of love and to move in a stealth, strong, determined and forthright into the direction of union, en masse, with matrimonial care for the enabled terrific deformity of the world struck down by evil days and ways.

*

The coming of the summer days joined enjoyed prancingly with such character and know-how, the caves dwelt deep to comfort water, the shade cool for overheated livestock, trees yawning in the bright lit strikes of beaming sunlight, as the wolf moved side by side like a ghost ready to prowl the parallel of destiny with running bears and stalking cougars.

By the time he awoke, and by the time he spoke, the days and nights had turned again into death's dark somnambulist wake, as the fall brought leaves seasonable to class an artistic majesty and the warm hearth always brought grins with beards, warm cups of tea in ballet with the rumbles of stomach for a meal to feast and bless for those who too had not a stitch to wear or hunger to bare.

Thanksgiving came and went and Decca was very thank-full.

He; told you about his sun.

They cannot tell us about heaven. They cannot send a message.

It is blissfully greatness, and to see how we are here on a planetary experience is awkward and silly, problematic and crass. In comparison with holy life in eternal exception.

No one has more dignity which rises above everything, than has the *human*. A dignity which sets them apart from creation, evolution and evil. Humanity's saviour, which feels purity of a heavenly grace.

*

Happiness would come and he would never quite feel safe and secure when it did. He could never be totally happy. He would wait for the next occurrence, the next dilemma, a problem set to arise from adversity and the life long journey of destiny in historical disharmony.

He left the Ozarks and pastures with Brahma cows shining up the dichotomy of sharing the difference and fitting into the scheme of things.

He walked to New Orleans, through the fog and the cotton fields, through Baton Rouge and the stormy nights of Cajun mumbo jumbo, bubbling for the fright in fear of the evil setting night, foreboding with dark angels flying through the air-filled sky, to nowhere and the abyss of howling demons shaking the foundation of voodoo blood and chickens' food.

Making the void in his life filled with limbo's dream of being, not being baptised in holy tap water and an unholy vagabond to the boring contraflow of Christendom's Jesuit discipline.

He thought, as he spoke the words out of this mouth to the elements seeming to be, *'Nothing good should come of this life – his destiny – had a dark side – which if he didn't face, then he would have to face up to some other time'*, better he thought, as he spoke out loud to the night air and the sleeping crocodiles and wild life wilder than he could ever imagine hidden in the long grassed bush there to his left and right, *'When it was safe enough or peace and love reigned in his life, than at war and dangerously subsidiary to society's factions. When and where? – he would have to journey to find out.'*

Sleep was deep in his Aquarius eyes as he passed a very dark ominous shack. The place seemed empty, with the wears of time and winds of nature had taken its toll on the outside porch and the old rocking chair, which looked like it had been there during before the Civil War or the Human Rights marches.

Decca walked up to the creaky front door and knocking on the first door, being iron meshed, he saw the other solid door begin to open.

It was a small Negro boy, who looked at the stranger at the door with his big black eyes, as if he had just seen a ghost, a ghost from the past, a spirit who had flown onto the porch, as was the reason for all the bad weather and the problems in the world. The boy said, he seemed to ask politely, with a command of his tongue which was older for his age, "Can I help you?"

*

Decca, looking at the real thing. *The Real American Negro*, the ancestor of the slaves who created the *Blues* music, through faith and belief in the Holy Father God looking down upon them and giving them the strength to overcome all the horrible hatred and racist abuse they would have to go through to become who they were. How they did it? Was beyond the comprehension of a simple white man, a man who had known bigotry and slander, but thought of it as ignorant useless bullshit, no good to no man and no good to humanity. *'Fuck 'em! They know not what they do!'*

They stared at each other as if recognising the history between them. Then they arose from the deepest of slumber, deep in the heart of slander. Decca answered, *"Can I have a glass of water please?"*

The boy, turned and shouted, *"Mama! A man wishes to have a glass of water."*

At that, in sight of the boy, in sight of Decca, a woman appeared out of her other room and walking towards them, seemed to be the epitome of Negro life, love and motherhood. She was dressed in a flowery summer dress, with the mixing colours of faded orange and turquoise flowers. Her legs were bare, as the black/brown sheen shone gold as it bounced off her calves onto the rotten wooden floor below to blind the rats at dinner beneath the base of the shack. She was bare footed and the souls of her feet seemed to be a lighter colour than the top of her toes and shown cartilage. She was serene in looks. A beauty to the rugged force of the raw and rough life one would have to lead in poverty and the poor, a standard of living one gets when one is happy with the simplicity of childrearing and lonely nights without the runaway father. Her hair was a nice relaxed dark black afro, which she seemed to love in respect of her mirror, which told the truth about the sexuality of her dying breed and the vice of the night, which could be fought in the light of the church, the gospel and the gospel according to. She glimpsed at the boy with the attention of a loving mother's eye, which always would love her offspring, and wondered as to who was at the porch door. She looked straight at the white-faced Decca, who was a Caucasian white, but his pigment had caught the sun in the days before, walking directly into it.

Decca looked into her eyes and saw the days of stress and strain betray her loneliness and peace which she seemed, to him, to have to wrestle with, and sleep with in the passing of a life, in the responsibility of human living, when the days stream along slow, the boredom is challenged with Bible pray and the Lord takes its toll on the cheeks of Christendom and walking, talking, present-day sinners.

The moment exploded and she spoke first. *"My son says you need a glass of water?"*

"Yes I do, Mah'm." Long and bittered out came the voice of Decca, which had the twist of twang to it, like an English actor playing an American personage.

"Son," she said, looking straight into Decca's sleepy, weak and hungry eyes, *"go and get this gentleman a glass of water!"*

The boy ran to do it. As he rang out for all the swampland cotton trees to hear, the voodoo spirit man leaning on the trunk of the tree watching outside, *"Yes Mama!"* he troubled.

The time it took for the boy to return is the time it took for Decca to show the woman that he was okay, that he wasn't there to harm or hurt them or slander their name all over the place! He was quiet and looked straight into the ideal of friendship with any colour, creed or race.

She smiled and waited with her head slightly down, not trodden, but intrigued as to why a man would be stood at her porch door late at night, just before bedtime and prays, asking for a god-given right for a glass of nature's gift to life and survival.

He sold his soul and she bought it.

The honour of the seconds passed as the boy returned, gave Decca the glass of water and watched as Decca gulped it down, fast and lushest enough for the sounds of ecstasy and flavour to resound in the throat of his thirst and bring to his heart the god-given right to life.

Decca finished the glass of water and offering it back to his audience, said, *"Thank you very much."* They looked at his politeness, and nodded their twin approval at his thankful heart and words which seemed never to be heard at the frame and front of their old porch, creaking into the language of the aspect of it never happening, but it had, and their world changed forever. For now on, they knew there was a someone somewhere who had the dignity and pride to be thankful for the simplest things in which God could gave to a capitalistic consumerist world bringing hatred, hot lust and the fires of hell!

The stunned peace and silence was broken only by the need to close the door, reflect and revive the sense to recompense dear true nature and the odd stranger who had darkened their door with the small light of love for all heroes of everyday nuance and pleasure, seeking compliance in offering, simply what one had; not having to refuse, when the terms were destructive, greedy or genocidal intentions. They all smiled and Decca turned as the glass stayed held in mamma's hand, a prayer lasting on her lips, the boy smiling at the white class of peace at last, and the night swallowed him up like the water drank with natural thanks and deep prayers for the world of forgiveness and gift.

The shadow moved away from the tree, satisfied and the lady closed the door. They went back to their given lives and Decca walked away onto the road into his destiny, perhaps his darker stratus fractured fate, which always manages to ruin someone's life.

*

Decca walked straight into New Orleans. The moon full in a dark blue cumulonimbus mamma's clouded sky, setting the sin picture for the feelings of Bourbon street and vampires from the catacombs of the living dead, who have lived for centuries and walk the earth as the next upbeat atonement to a sexy Goth with leathers and bright shining teeth.

The French quarter was sleeping, soundly with the echoing back sound of the evening's saxophone resounding over the periodic bayou, of the Mississippi river, flowing through the famous Quarter, which had produced, Louis 'Satchmo' Armstrong, voodoo, the riverboat gambling stud, Jambalaya, and the belle of the plantation, who had an affair with a Negro slave and gave birth to his daughter, who became the inherent owner of the estate, as the half-caste Patois.

The make believable world of belief in understudy, the apprentice, the Grand Wizard in a magic world of curio and Satan, herbs and deeper meaning of candles, lit to search out the spirits in the corner of the big stately home, which was half alive and half overgrown with hanging vines and drooping cypress trees, with the sense of mist turning to the heavier fog and making the groves disappear with the coming of the bogeyman, as the howling earth gives birth to a zombie city dancing in the effervescent moonlight to all jazz and alcoholic mysteries in witchcraft, necromancy, creatures living throughout the duration of changing presidents, popular culture and the honourable influence of mamma's soul food and segs on the souls of the dancers.

He lay down to wonder, in the lack of sight given to the limitation of clouds, down and deeper than the cumulations, which made the air eerie and the breathing non-existent, to find the reason for the palm of the hand over the mouth, was to see if the breath would affect the skin, as it felt the stream of air caress the sorrow lines of hard work and the palm readers' destiny line and life.

As he slept he had a dream. It took him through the canvas of abstract ideas and surrealist imagery out in the feedback of ghouls, ghosts, spooks and spectres. He saw the ruin of nature and the ruin of man's soul, he stood in the flaming landscape of a dream turning with ambivalence into a fully fledged nightmare with running fillies and steaming nostrils, as if the pigment of red blood was in the eyes and the heat seemed to come out of the bowels of the planet, as the shrieking, horrifying, blood thirsty necrophiliacs swarmed the horizon, joined by all sinners and witches high above on broomsticks looking for the puritanical persecutor, the justified blood of paranoia, misleading deception, hidden away, too frightened to be discovered and found evil, striking the nature of goodwill, turning it to the floor and keeping the feeling of love for the self-reliant, self-prospered, indoctrinated, a sorting of the sight to seek redemption and turn away from humanity, feeling the need to damage all quality and value with a stench of pits, so blind and rotten, the dirt is encased from sore flesh, reeks the atmosphere of allegiance, to beyond the grave, 'Wormwood' is the subconscious, developed to be insecure and psycho-pathological schizophrenically deluded and guilty of unrighteous sin.

He awoke with a start, so deep the nonsensical memory, he smelt shit and when he opened his eyes he was laid on grass with a lump of dog shit about him. He tried to focus and saw the mists retracting, as if the steam of the kettle was mixing with other elements to seek interception.

He managed to make out a statue, it was dark and rigor, it was still, but smiled a lip jaw smile, which changed the metal endearment of animism, to a simple stiff in a garden of dog dirt and damp dew droppings.

The smell made him vomit nothing, as he hadn't eaten since –? So, the bile was retching and painful, plus the statue of Louis Armstrong was still smiling, so Decca found the funny side of it and began to sing, *Oh what a beautiful morning / oh what a beautiful day / oh what a beautiful feeling / everything's going my way!*

He rushed out of Louis 'dog-shit' park and didn't look back.

He looked for a bakery, he looked for a dead body, he looked for the beggar and the busker, the early morning whore, he looked for the dirt forlorn streets offering a solo soul somatic, a dime, a nickel, a dollar or a quart. He would go on to find a quart and try his luck in the quarter with his American quart, but he threw it into a hustling tap dancing black boy's cap, who was good, even great, his friends thought and knew so too. Decca received a shouting *'Thank you!'* for his efforts, his intrigue; the charity of explicit sex in a glorious ballet with soul and concrete, battering the bounce and attacking the weak element of all Achilles heels.

In the evening Decca moved through the gambling crowd, the whores of whisky and card sharks with 'tricks'.

He looked at the old place, so new and shown to be sundown for the pity pouring of dusted silverware and designer clothing in panama hats, shirt and 'kipper' tie, loafer spats with tricolours and a pair of 'strides' held up with braces, held up; so the sucking of the cowslips joy could hold the codpiece a hand and relive the uttermost sanctions of being divine for the name of sexist's beauty vaginal pathos, giving rise to power and self-relief with benefits by all balustrade.

*

Cigar smoke seemed to inspire memory in the scenting of mist, the whores slept safe in knowing the night's 'tricks' were lucrative. The tourist rushed to ice-cream and trinket, to and through the heavy verges with cornerstone entertainment blocking the route to drink in a sleaze bar with Tom Waits making the atmosphere, the black baby woman looks determined to tell you, as all the heavy-belted Cajun caterer would envision, snake venom and chips, as trumpet solos rang out down the street, Decca did not hesitate to sign into a doss-house for the period of the Christmas to come.

He knew he was there for 'Fat Tuesday', but, 'Fats' was not ready and dressed to kill till Mardi Gras in March.

*

Alienist Orleans the only place where it is stylish to be dilapidated and forsaken, through the weather, the time past, gone and wept over like the rains over the Creole, wear, basic wear and tear of the eyes, sad with adversity and romantic piano music, with the hurricanes of hatred, and a worn torn war of rubbing, cleaning, shining and moving over as the metal wears with age, as the Earth cools down to a soaking of the sea, to juice the loins of river plates, social sun dryness and dehydration fear.

Having booked into the Ben Turpin doss-house, where he was given a bed Decca soon found the bed amongst many others. It was five days before Christmas day, so the place seemed eerily empty. He climbed on the top bunk and rested till falling into a deep enough sleep.

Not deep enough! He awoke to the noise below him. Someone had mounted the 'pit' and decided to snore, burp, fart, stink, you name it, he was it! 'It' was so annoying to Decca, that he completely awoke and looking around him noticed that all the beds were still mainly empty.

Whoever had charged themselves to book in and sleep, had chosen to *die!* Because no man could put up with the shit below Decca; no man would allow a pseudo-animal making so much disgusting noise to live, let alone the fact that 'it' had chosen to be below another instead of choosing one of the other 50 beds in the cross-eyed Ben Turpin's doss-house.

Ben Turpin was the funny looking comedian from Hollywood during the days of Chaplin, Keaton and Lloyd. He was so cross-eyed it hurt to look at him. It seemed to be beyond laughter, as if the method of seeing such a sight would make the feasting fit for humour, but alas, it just seemed desperately poor on behalf of the studio in Hollywood's arranged life of living in suitable conditions for the said product. He was also born in New Orleans. Poor thing.

But the bastard below was hankering for a belting, a beating around the fucking cross-eyed chops, which would be possible, until the 'thing' went on a farting escapade.

He farted and doffed! Cut one and let go! He forced and pleasured! Nipped and tucked! He, 'it', the 'thing' was a *bloody human disgrace*, but he was free to do it! He was alone in the Ben Turpin, all alone before Christmas day and 'it' had been celebrating with liquor and spice, fucking turkey sandwiches and all things nice, *on the first day of Xmas my true love sent to me,* a boffin gaffing in a farting tree! It stank and the depth of bowel gathering was similar to a sewerage joining the poop with air, as the former sprang from the recesses of the prostrate, with an influence of aroma, a scent in Turkish toilets, Brazilian hygiene and Indian shanty town squatting. It was a human disgrace, but none was there to judge or witness this crime of humanity.

Decca tried to sleep, but found the stench of Satan too much, as the sound of orifice betrayal was consistently heading for the first nostril available or the taste of the palate to dignify the texture, a value or a virtue of the god-given right to smell, belch or simulate the late great Ben Turpin's reason for the way he looked whilst 'cutting' a flatulent ass!

Decca got up and picking up his bag, stormed out of the Turpin doss-house and walked away in the snow-filled streets, quickly, with earnest and pomp; he never looked back or sideways, as he sped down the opening of the French Quarter and left the holidaymaking façade to Japanese tourists or dirty farting bastards who had no consideration at all for others!

*

Rushing out down the street and out to the Mississippi waterfront, Decca saw two men, having a drink, of alcohol, on a bench, looking out to sea, the boats, the smell of salt and sandy fish.

They looked at the figure walking towards them, and to them figured he was a lost soul on the scrounge for a 'buck' or a drink. They didn't have enough, just enough for themselves, so they were prepared to refuse his offer of 'having a swig', and enjoying his company.

Decca sidled up. They moved not, along the bench, nor to indicate a stranger was welcome amongst strangers in a strange world.

Decca looked at the two old Hoboken men, trying to raise a smile, as the smile was the best way for a friendly stranger to be accepted into the realm of the passive drunk, who felt the need to see the world through glazed eyes and the drunken recesses of a broken life.

They did not smile back. No. They did not want this smiling stranger to have a swig of their whisky bottle. They were adamant and he was already without knowing it, ostracised.

Decca spoke, he seemed to sense they would know the answer to his question. *"Can you tell me how to get out of here?"* he said, not seeming to share the naïve interest he had in not knowing where he was and not being able to work out which way he should go to get out of there.

They hesitated. One of the seemly experienced men, hugged the bottle tight to his belly, as the other, looked up to the sky, saw the reason why, looked at the water, turned to his friend who had the bottle secured, felt secure and said, *"You can get a freight train out of here!"*

A freight train. Well, Decca kind of worked out the look of a freight train and knew it was for carrying cargo not folk. So he asked, as politely as he could, as the bottle was checked and all was safe, *"What? Can I jump it?"* A nice question answered by the question, only the reason to know how and why one would jump a train, never mind a freight train, is only known by the ol' vagabond and his quest for Prohibition's workforce.

"Yes, you can!" said one of the tramps, the one holding the bottle of whisky safe. *"You can go anywhere! Just stand over that way there!"* He pointed to an area just out of the line of sight, seeming to trail away, as if it was the track for a train, noticing the bottle was one handed, the other man gestured to have it, so the one holding it, took a swig and handed it over to the the other, who cleaned the top with his sleeve and took a long swig.

Decca looked at the two men, eyed the bottle, being used to soothe the blues of an old boy, and with the eyes of a vagabond seeking adventurer, squint, as if handsome, showing the universe he was onto something and something big enough to experience, to share with his life the old ways of travel, for the man searching for work, for the Yankee dollar, he felt the blood of history surge about the place, around the corner and over his head, and there, where the bottle man had pointed, there was Woody Guthrie, there were the songs of Dylan and there was John Steinbeck and *The Grapes of Wrath*, in which the poverty of the poor was strong in will to be rich in heaven, when the time came.

Decca said, *"Thank you"*, and left the two drinkers to it. They seemed to squabble behind his back over the Jersey state line, but Decca didn't notice, as he was too busy looking for the place to wait and jump a freight train out of New Orleans to heaven knows where.

*

Decca Dent Peters walked down the line towards a shed, which probably had something to do with the train and its track, but what? It didn't matter. It was somewhere to hide from the driver of the freight train and then manage to skip up into a carriage.

The sun beamed down from up high, as the sweat on his brow was wet and salty like the liquid of the sea, drinkable, only if purified.

The clouds shone mighty in the cirrus of theatres, displaying tragedy and comedy in the same face, a face to behold with respect and fear, larger than life, the living force of nature, the universal garden of possibilities and logical facts, holding on to the answers which never present themselves unless mistakenly faltered upon.

It all seemed set for a merry-go-round of horror in the ghost train of scary spiders and unseen hands, bringing to bear the tablets of fate to hold in fear at the fiesta's gate.

He heard the train a' coming, he crouched down and waited, ready to spring at any time, like the lioness at her hunt, for the food, she would spring the bock and bring the cub the food to love and devour.

The train came in front of him; self and shed, instead, he hesitated and watched as the freight picked up mighty speed, he jumped, he jumped and sprang for his life's worth, holding, finger-tipped a ladder to one of the carriages!

As the train soothed along the track, Decca fell from the ladder, he fell backwards, he fell all over the place into a ditch. He felt his arm go! He felt his heart spring, he felt the mind dazzle the brain and ask for 'no pain', the pain came and the snap and break of a fragile skin and bone crashed the ground, solid and earthen, formidable and unforgiving, he felt the urge to scream to cry into the sky, he felt the need to bleed and lie down in the ditch for the death of dying was enough to know, he could never live as a crippling paralysed monster.

The freight train sped away, down and noise out of sight and hearing.

Decca lay in the ditch, he checked his whereabouts and bodily parts, as the sun shone on his pitch dilemma in the ditch which may have given him a stitch, he noticed, he had broken a fingernail. *Ow! that fucking hurt,* he said to himself. Not knowing the language of a thousand swear words had blistered the setting sun on its run to the other side of the world where the Australian could leather the storm with a skin of Aboriginal texture.

He sucked his index finger. Of all the fingernails to be broken. The others were in a position to be strengthened, but the index was alone, seemingly the most important finger to be used in the kingdom of all hands.

He knew he could bounce back. He knew he could do the 'jumping off a freight train' better.

So, he picked himself up and sludged to the outside of town, where he had noticed a bar, from where he could possibly get a drink of water.

He was parched.

He walked into the bar. A small Orleans drinking pitch, to which the barkeeper was a lady, lass, a denim strung out, hung over hussy, who had just the time to look up and carry on with washing the previous night's glasses.

A man was sat at the bar. He was dressed in fancy clothes. He seemed to be entertaining himself with a Japanese girl sat on his lap. He looked at the dishevelled spirit casually striding the barroom stool.

The man, in the smart attire, suit and shoes; out of a famous label?, seemed to find the need to watch Decca, as the Japanese girl, felt him here and felt him there, whilst he seemed to peer over whenever he could, through her hair, cleavage, under her armpit, he looked and stared, until Decca not seeming to receive any attention from the lady barkeep, said to the well-dressed man with his Japanese concubine, *"Tell me Mister, do I get a train out of here?"* Decca said it with the greatest of American air, that could possibly be tried, on the hair of a hare to be heir to the king of Tennessee, to which the man in his feathered cap said, and he spoke with assurance and certainty,

"Sure you can! Just walk a way's down the line, not too far and you will find the train runs at about five miles per hour."

He stared at the man in the Vietnam combat jacket, wearing no shirt, jeans and boots and an old rucksack for company, looking like a Simon and Garfunkel song, and carried on saying, to the faded, holed denim bitch behind the bar … "give the man a drink, on me!", as the man then shuffled the Japan off his lap whilst looking at the face of the old American icon, splattered on all the billboards, for the age of wisdom to spy, that she was getting old and wrinkled like the crow's foot on Sitting Bull's ass!

The bar-bird started to do just that. Watching as the liquid of the beer poured into the glass, at an angle and entered the regime commonly known as 'to be drunk!' She did not look up.

The man, the owner of the bar, the man, who with his land and his lot and his prayers and his holy ground, sounded the trumpet for the biggest deal of all, when he said, *"I'll be going, babe, but, watch that man over there."* He left, with the giddy jape.

Decca received the drink, the frothing beer, the ultimate in quenching the thirst of a lifetime's alcoholic-al nightmare, always never one. Always more, always never able to have a few and so go home and do, 'go about' something else.

So, Decca sat and looked at that there dear old beer and contemplated his exit.

Denise the denim babe with the crow feet face and Sitting Bull's ass, spied her shied and spat in his direction as a reciprocal of faith in knowing one's kind and not having to look behind when bending over or hanging up a picture for the coward assassin would be waiting to take its pick on the finger-lick of a trigger hot to trot the legend of a hero's hour and the history of the west, at best is Jesse James, Billy the kid and Butch Castrate and the Sundanese kid.

So, Decca stayed and drank his beer. He refreshed his parts and sucked and soaked his broken finger in the cooling hobbing beer. Expecting a miracle, he didn't, but he did expect to rise out of his seat, send the black eyes of the cod and peas to 'who do you please', and get the hell out of there, with the knack and reassurance of a pack of wolves or a vulture scaremongering for life, as the main reason to eat would be to drop in on death.

Accepted, he bowed out and went into the world knowing that there was someone somewhere who knew of his intention, his reason for being, and would remember the man sat at the bar, who needed to jump a freight to get the fucking hell out of hell.

'… five miles or less, no just there, the best …, there, let the train at 5mph, coming your way, slow as the day is long, and fast as the sun will die.'

He could shed a tear, he could cry, but he didn't. He felt good and the destiny of good-hood is right and fair and true on the side of the God-friendly brotherhood of faith, faith in the kingdom to come and faith in your child and maker of all senses!

The train rushed down the track. It seemed to pass, a passing passé, so Decca sprung and jumped, he hit the ladder on the side of a carriage, and swinging with his torso, he managed to lift himself and his life up onto the base of the rungs and so climb, stealthily up towards the caverned carriage opening and drop into a coalhole full of blackness and emptiness. A pit.

Inside the carriage it was black, dark with a smell of coal or dust, whatever it was it was empty, so, Decca rode half asleep, wrapped up in a sleeping bag, which he had managed to always bring with him. His rucksack was empty apart from the sleeping bag. He stood up in the clothes he had and always wore out a good pair of heavy boots.

He fell asleep. The sound of the train tracks out in the air seeming to rhythm with the drumming of an eternal beat to secure the holiday of all progress, to deliver and pass through the black hills, once the sacred spirit ground of the Sioux Indian.

The freight train unbeknown to its passenger was heading into mid-America towards Alabama and its forty thieves, its human rights days and a holy sanctuary for the black man's peace and power.

*

Decca awoke in the mid-night-light and sensed there was something very wrong. He looked over the top of the carriage and saw a light being carried along the side of the track, seeming to shine in and out of the other wheels and carriages, seeking, looking for something, perhaps someone.

Then it dawned on him. They mostly do this looking for vagabonds jumping the freights, for the city to city tramp, who rode on a free ride, which they had done so for a hundred years, and still the light flashed and a voice spoke, shouting along the track, undistinguishable to the ears of the freezing cold night, up, up on the peninsula hills, snow lay like blankets of frost, bitter to the skin of the fox and the ears of a brier rabbit or coyote.

Decca manoeuvred his weight and climbing over the empty carriage which would be seen in the flash-light to be, climbed onto one of the wheels of a vehicle cargo and wrapping his body about it became the wheel. The sleeping bag was dirty brown/green.

The light came, the voice ringed air with smoke and breath, seeming to flow out to the oxygen less, boiling the frozen and melting the tears of an aerodrome of frost.

*

It shone on the sleeping bag wheel. Decca had managed to cover every-part of himself, and he could hear the shuffling of the train security guard's feet, his slight ruffling of trousers, as his jeans seemed to gather the frost and brandish a solid rub against his walk. Defined, the light shone right through the bag; one move, one breath, one itch, one freak, thus then the game was over and he would be beaten up and thrown off onto the freezing cold mountains, left to walk all the way down, sleeping below the zero, and starving for a grub or a fire or both.

The train security guard's light dipped and swung and then with the same kind of miracle, moved off, out and away. The night had been saved for the day, and Decca felt so comfortable in his position of deflection and deception, he decided to stay wrapped about the wheel and fell asleep, fatigued and exhausted with the fear of being found out, the reasons for waking up at the right time, a moment leading the movement to disguise the purpose of the security guard knowing, there was someone on the train, but who? And where?

Decca could feel the guard hitting himself with the light torch, cursing the frost filled air, as the steam seemed to be his anger and disappointment of not *'catching the bastard!'*, and *'kicking the fucker off the track'* onto the hills of zero temperature and serves him fucking right!

No free ride in the middle of the night. Hold tight. There was.

The time Decca Peters awoke. The day he saw the daylight sky. That day the train had stopped and he looked out from his position to which he had returned with the moving night, back into the carriage, looking over the top now, he saw nothing. No one. The train had arrived somewhere and had stopped. The failing motion of a heated machine was long gone, and Decca looked about him, to see if he could recognise the place, the time, the day.

He climbed out of his deep black pitted abode's boudoir and shuffled over the rusty terracotta orange tracks, till he could see nothing, no one. The place, the yard was empty. He then saw a figure walk across the opening of what seemed a freight train station parlour. He called to the man, the man undistinguished and slow, a silhouette in the daylight air, still having some kind of character, which allowed him not to realise there was someone there, along the bitten track, looking at him.

Decca shouted, not at him, through him, through to the world, he was the chosen representative for the everybody; *"Excuse me sir!"* he raised. *"What day is it?"*

"Why," said the man; the man; without a personality to the stranger, who had his for himself, *"it's Christmas day!"*

Christmas day?! *Wow* ... Decca, thanked the man, although he didn't remember if he did or not, but the man shuffled off in a direction looking for his Christmas day, looking for his family, looking perhaps for his presents from Santa Claus or gladly, his wife.

*

Decca Dent Peters looked about him and saw a half-eaten Kentucky fried chicken in one of the portal cabins. Noticing the place was unlocked, he walked straight in, reached out, and took the half-eaten used box and its contents out into the healthy bright striking day of Jesus' birth.

He began to tuck in. There was a bit of chicken on the bone. The age of the old chicken was 'last night' Christmas Eve. He looked at the bread, stale; the container of sweetcorn – and realised his stomach was amassed with satisfaction, knowing the feast of his Christmas Day was free and given with the love of survival, to the lonely tramp of old, who had skipped the light fandango and deserved that man's remnants of a crusty skinned chicken.

Decca took the coke-can he had found with the Kentucky and brushed it along a puddle of mud filled with bits of papers, wrappers, perhaps bird-shit; just slight, he raised the liquid from the pond and holding his lips like a sieve, he dispensed the drink down his throat into his being, knowing it was the best drink he could ever have. What with the meal, he had had a *'Christmas dinner'* and was ready to open his presents!

He walked into Birmingham, Alabama. On his way he needed a drink of water. So, he asked a man playing with his children, with their new Christmas toys. The man got him a drink and it was suggested with gestures that Decca mosey on down the road with it. He did, thinking as the thoughts entered his head about Jesus.

He then realised his personal dilemma. He was amongst thorn bushes. He tried to escape the future of being caught and torn apart by the spikes and pricks of thorns, but seemed to wish to go farther into the bush, as the tear and wear of such a sacrifice seemed fitting on the day of Christ, how it must have been, to be alone with trouble on an auspicious day, crying and hurting for freedom and healing the wounds of blood and sweat.

Decca remained caught up in the thorn bushes, till he set himself free, by tearing his T-shirt and letting himself lapse with lame limp failure, as it was the torn tearing anger of the thorns which took pity, sympathised with the boy and let him go to roses. Where the roses grow; he was saved.

In the train station in Birmingham, Decca sat and waited for something to happen.

It did. She came in the frame and guise of a ghetto blaster man-aster.

She was short, stubby and worn to the facts of life, only she was young somewhere underneath the primary solution of figures, hers bland and indescribable, but she carried with her a massive ghetto blaster the size of a hotel suitcase for rich people, to be carried by a porter, moaning about the weight and size of such a stay, on a such a flight of stairs.

She rang out to Decca, as she rushed up to him, all alone, sat on one of the given seats, from which to sit, as one, waited for a destiny in the shape of a Greyhound bus.

She said, *"I will give you my ghetto blaster for your combat jacket!"* She looked at the jacket as if it was a piece of merchandise which she wished to have with no expense spared.

"I need it," said Decca Peters. He did, it was an old American combat jacket with someone's name on the breast. He looked at the name and the name looked back, upside down and foreign to the western speaking world, as seemly Russian?

"I have always wanted one!" she exclaimed, as the snow fell outside the station, everybody around with hats and scarves and jackets to keep them warm.

"No!" raised Decca, *"I don't have anything to keep me warm and this does. Anyway, what do I want with a ghetto blaster?"*

"I don't know," she tried to capitalise, with a timed interruption. *"You could listen to the radio that's on it! It works, it all works, look,"* she said, as she turned it on.

*

Decca looked and he listened, he did not recognise the music, she switched it off, as if she saw Decca being not happy with the sound, only Decca knew he could not listen to music just with his eyes, he had to use his ears. It was and had been *The Boxer* by Simon & Garfunkel.

She then saw his face and turned it back on, as they seemed to be choreographed by the nature of the words and the essence of the song.

Wrong.

Decca still refused the ghetto blaster and told her to go away.

She started to cry, to weep, to Christmas day weep and the music played on. Everybody who was travelling on that festival day looked. Looked at the situation and wondered. Still she remained and Decca, knowing that he needed the Vietnam veteran combat jacket, stood up and left the building, out into the white bright snow and shuffled along the unseen path to who knows where?, as the snow was deep and getting deeper. *The Boxer* fading and the energy of the batteries inside of Decca Peters was too.

He took one more look at the name on his breast and he worked it out to *Khabrovsk*.

Decca Dent Peters walked out of Birmingham, Alabama, in the direction of a motorway, which should lead somewhere, he thought, *somewhere big!?*

The alto cumulus mackerel in the sky with a laminar band marking inflow led him onto the hard shoulder where a very large truck stopped and picked him up.

*

He had only the time to flick his thumb, when the 10-ton truck screeched to a halt and the flow of lights, sound and duration, seemed to be the ballet of consequences, bringing to bear a cacophony of rhythm. There sat in the seat of a low-back chaired HGV Truckee; as he opened the door to speak to Decca, was a man with chequered shirt, jeans, boots and spectacles on his face. His hair was trimmed, cut to shape the head, the head wanting the look to be round, the half grown beard and chapped red lips gave the driver an air of impractical mania. Although, he was a straight, who wished to give a 'hitcher' a lift, out of the weather, out of the darkness prevailing and out of the way of preying wolves or black power men out for revenge for the days of Martin Luther King, human rights marches, a Klu Klux Klan and the hanging dead Negro-man.

Decca bounded up and in, what seemed another level to see the world, as high as the height of a man's high when low down on the ground snorting coke and puffing splayfeet.

The very big truck set off; the tyres gave out air and the motion was smooth, like the ride in a beautiful Ferrari, only this beaut was a very large cargo vehicle.

The night came in soon and the stars ate the luminous mackerel.

The drive was pleasant, no hang-ups, no uncomfortable silences, which always seem to be the responsibility of the 'hitcher', who seemed to have enough instinct to break the silence with a subject or a comment, which indulged the driver, interested the driver, so, he would begin to talk, talk about the subject, know all about the subject, until tears of tired eyes would well up in their sockets of the 'hitcher', knowing he had hit the mark, knowing he was able to relax and listen to the fucking shit coming out of the mouth of the fucking boring truck driver, who was as monotone and interesting as listening to an English Parliamentary political programme on TV, on behalf of the Conservative Party.

Then the driver with the spectacles and chequered shirt said, *"If you're tired, there is a bunk bed back there."* He pointed behind, where a small bed was made out just behind the seats. *"If you want, you can undress and climb in, get some sleep, I will wake you when we get there!"*

Where? Get where!? Decca didn't know where he was going, not even how to get there, but where it was going to be, was beyond him, so he undressed on the bunk and climbed into a very comfortable single bed.

*

He was just nodding off, when he felt someone climbing into the bed next to him. It seemed the person's hands led the way to where Decca was, to where Decca lay naked and vulnerable to the night sky, only a moment away from the top of the truck's canvas.

The driver spoke, as he tried to squeeze himself in, next to Decca, *"You can help me as I am helping you! Just wait and I will drop you off later, when we get there, but first … "* He didn't quite finish, as he seemed to be getting too excited, with his body holding on to Decca, his erection pressing against Decca's ass, the words lost to the world, were overused, everybody knew what they were, what was needed of another human being, what another needed the other to do, for the favour they had done the other, so that sex would be allowed, inevitable or judicial.

Decca sprang out of the bunk, grabbed his clothes and struggled to get out of the high truck in the middle of a blizzard filled freezing cold night.

The driver shouted, *"You will not make it! Baltimore is 500 miles from here! You had better come back! Boy! ... "*

Decca shouted, "Fuck off!" in a very broad English accent, which he had not heard before, for a long time, he had not heard the broad colloquial language of his homelands, but here it was being used to set off the homosexual trucker driver who wanted to fuck him for the price of a ride.

The truck driver heard it. He could see the dark night, the dark night could not see him, but the wistful light could, as the chequered shirted, jeans and Truckee boots man said, *"English, huh"*.

*

Decca skipped about the truck-stop and found someone to take him along the road, long, and away, down the route of tired living, head and heart, resting his body in the bucket trucker's comfortable seat, Decca slept without a worry in the world, as the world passed on by and the trucker doing his job, had allowed the 'hitcher' to rest and sleep all the way to Baltimore, Maryland, and on bringing in the brakes, as the air of the night escapes the tyres and mixes with the oxygen, Decca alighted the truck, with his Vietnam veteran's jacket in his hand and thanked the driver for the lift.

Decca watched as the massive 10-ton truck sped off, not before – in a split second – the other, the *homosexual* truck, rushed on by him and Decca seeing that and knowing he had got to Baltimore first, flicked a 'V' in the way of all symbolism, the English terms for *'fuck you!'*, *'fuck off!'* and *'up yours!'*, as the world turned to triumph and will, as the winner was the English hitcher, not the fucking be-speckled chequered shirted bitch-er!

So, Decca was in Baltimore. He said to himself, underneath his breath, *'Where the fuck is Baltimore?'*

*

From Baltimore to the next place, takes Decca in sight of New York City. The winter months in NYC could be real, raw, fascinating, but cold, bitter, chilled to the bone, as the New Yorkers wind their way about the famous isle of Manhattan in coats and boots, hats and scarves, seeming to know of the seasons, like to the water; fish and the fire; salamanders.

Decca arrived and walked about, looking for a place to keep warm. He knew he was finished in America and it was time to raise the money to fly back to the United Kingdom of Great Britain.

He walked with his hands in his pockets, his combat collar up, his head down, as the wind joined in with the flakes, a thousand strong in design, as the nomads of Lapland have a hundred words for snow, but not a word for war.

He looked in on cafés, hanging on a cup of coffee, hoping for a refill, whilst the time passed, as the hours flew by, still the cost was going up and the snow fell down, heading for the ground, as it lay, deep on the smoking manholes of the Lower East Side.

He managed to buy a book to read. It was P.D. Ouspensky's *In Search Of The Miraculous;* the book containing the working out of the universe through numbers, letters and mythology.

Decca sat and worked out what to do next with the seconds and minutes, which past into the present, soon turning into the future, to which Decca Peters seemed not to attain.

He walked into a theatre; Off / Off Broadway, so called, being well off the beaten path for mainstream works or a place where one would begin to focus one's craft of the art of acting, in the stages of small pennies and budget.

*

He looked about him, there was a blonde girl with a broom in her hand. He approached her and she turned to greet him. They both smiled and in the time it takes to recognise a relationship, they were in one. Decca could only look, as she invited him for a coffee and cake at a bakery down from the Off / Off Broadway theatre. Her name was Cancan Bier. She said she could really do it; the dance. He thought of the Moulin Rouge in Paris, wondering if she was in the wrong place.

Decca put the book aside and they enjoyed the coffee and cake, laughing at the world and the way it could be, laughing with the world and the way it could be, laughing through the world at the world of love and the way it could be, but, they did not hesitate to fuck each other that night, in Cancan's bed.

Decca needed warmth and somewhere to hang his hat; which was a khaki green corduroy 'cheese-cutter', which he placed on his head, then tilted to the side, looking of old, like the hats worn by prohibitionists and street urchins of immigrant New York.

Cancan was lonely and had been doing six months in bed, sad, depressed and dangerous, on Cocaine. The effects of such a problem, were to change the future of her and the future of Decca Dent Peters, forever.

One night, whilst indulging in sex and drugs and rock 'n' roll, it was and seemed to be, where Decca felt Cancan had climbed into his head. Nice, a good idea. Heal the wounds of the mind and psychology of the subconsciousness, but he knew and felt it was a damaging event to happen. He freaked! He began to see the truth in the world at the precise moment he looked into the face of Cancan Bier as she said, slowly, deliberate, in tone and manner, *"Do you think I am evil?!"*

A question? Or the answer to the situation Decca found himself in? She was right there, right in his mind. He only saw the rush of thoughts as they took him to that place of defence, and picking up anything he could get his hands on to use as a weapon, he charged about the apartment, looking, seeking, trying to find the devil, the devil which was there, which stood and could see their every move, he challenged the void! Decca spoke of asking for presence, seeming as it were the precept of diphtheria and all the while Cancan grinned, knew, knew he was there, in the rooms, around and about.

Decca Peters could not take no more and collapsed on the bed, shaking in fear, spasmodic in dilemma, when the world moved one way and the other way was to see, the sights on darkness, the proposal of deeper meaning and the forbidden truth. His eyes seemed set to burst, his heart attacked his focus screaming spleen, he awoke from horror's gaping mouth, *"What am I going to do?"* he asked the night air, the face of fear: Cancan Bier.

*

What was it that had entered his psyche? What could it have been, when one is ignorant of such things; being of the night, being there due to pain and suffering and death; which has had no respect for the living; which was taken by the hand of a nasty bastard fucked up drug addict; perhaps, who had no conscious as regards the dark side of nature, the reasons for bad energy, the talk of the town and the wearing of the solemn frown which crosses the threshold of innocence to dirt experience and crime? To know deep in the senses something moves, uses and calls the terms of trash, of a lapse of time, where all is sin and pain and fits in the hate of darkness; a roaming prowling dirge of shadow and death, as the world turns to fight out the background of dark pitch; as they love and learn and hope and give and dance the light in the stalking darkest fright! Then the feeling which is kept at bay, is still there.

Is still there. There; somewhere where the night covers the veil, covers the immense trouble moving abroad, moving toward, feeling, sensing, hearing and zoning in to the living energy, the living space, the psyche, which is deep and dark and holds ancient secrets of passed lives, reincarnations, danger inset with thoughts howling with the horror pain of hell and the control and manipulation it demands, holds sway, fucks the world with and all for the defenceless purity which digs at the heart and the soul seeks refuge as the devil mark seeks to soil, to stain, to damage the goods of birth, the place to develop and be; as we are innocent beginners needing experience and atmosphere to show us the way it is and the way it is done.

Then we are salvation incarnate. We are born into saviour and sanctuary.

In New York City it would be different. It could be. The famous place for killings. The notorious place for hate and hurt and crime and pain; NYC, the carrier of carrion shadows, ghosts walking in the robes of hell; seeking no reprieve, hating damage and damage to be done and still the voodoo lady, the chicken's blood, the candle's light in the corner; still the spirits chime the bells of a world full of a lost, forgotten, dead, murder; still the wings which beat the doors of perception, invade the being, the vulnerable being and still the aura fights and still the drink and drugs hold hands with the turmoil of strive riven cascade and carcass and beyond, on eternal elements walks the reason for joining the soul, the syzygy of finding the warm body, to climb into the safety of a beating heart, a warm cage of ribs and sit in the defiance of sex, of thoughts and run with the mind's clouds, the dark remembrances which clouded the sick, the young, the bastard trials which consequently never leave the shores of abuse, waiting on the hallow rush of waves whilst the hawking ghoul-like creation searches for the soul of ignorance and blindness.

She must have joined Cancan whilst in the stupor of drugs and drink and stinking; still saw her and entered her as the warm pulsing body accepts the evil; through her mouth, the evil throes to kill the insecurity, the abuse of others, the insult of character carried in the years of vanity and cosmetics; the standard to live up to and not being able to reach, falling; it seemed; into the place too far to climb out of, falling, only to be oneself, falling deeper due to self denial and abuse and the soul warms the shadow psyche and the soul warms to the flying shadows and spectres and evil; long gone evil known things – what, who, when and how – she was; it was; *what was it?!*

She gave it to Decca and it climbed into the deep caverns of unknowing, of lacking, of un experience; till feeding, still full, after a stinking fucking time with Cancan's sheer undeveloped love, a hatred so cosy, it sang holy dirges on the banks of the river of time.

Killed. Dead. Dark and finding; found. Moved from one to the other and Cancan was the carrier, the principle to which she obeyed the will, the need, the feed to enter the mind, body and soul of Decca; the decadent one – so warm so fine *'where's my prize?'*

Haunted, hated, despised and used and abused the skull of demonic deplorable demi-gods and indecency, beyond the moral of right and wrong and something? Someone. Some entity climbed into the being of broken aura and mustered to live deep in the imaginative horror of his damned life.

Serves yourself right! Serves someone right. Someone killed it and now it was out to destroy the will of others. Who is to blame? The way of human life and the way of death – then it is; what lies in-between and feeds on the aether air to live, to be, but not – that is not a question; but, they are there and they will seek lust, pain and a corner of the human mastering which controls, manipulates, destroys and abuses all things living, all things which are not it, all things which cannot hurt nor haunt in the afterlife – the heavens, the hells and all chimes which follow the winged serpent, the hollowing harpies, the sirens of sin and left in the dirt and muck, near the cat bin and the saxophone night stairway, up to closed windows and curtains drawn; up to a smelling air; left and fed on by night stalkers – still, it might have been someone.

But, that night – it manoeuvred from her to him and it was all an experience of Gothic mystic leather.

*

He shouted at her, at the devil, at the walls of paint and time, he never seemed to know, but it was new, it was brought, it meant destiny with a great big chunk of fate slammed right in the middle of the course of events, till the reaper sings his dirge, till the witch pisses on the street cornered crossroads, it spelt it all out, correct and problematical, *"Will I assassinate the President?"*

Cancan took hold on him and reassured him it was not tonight, it was never, might, sounded the flight of wings, sleep opened willed to the principle, she jumped on his back and they sped off like playful genii in the space of thunder, the welding of crime came crashing down on the heads of thousands, as Decca and Cancan manoeuvred into demons and the dark night seemed brightly lit …

They had been flying all night. When they awoke the light was from the outside, on the streets, on Predicament Street, Alphabet City; New York.

They did not talk of the night. They made strong coffee and dazed into a sighting silence, focused on trips, blasé and comfort seemed to be the daydreaming aspect of emptiness.

Decca and Cancan proceeded to do. Many things leading up to doing. They found the time to launder, as the afternoon was taken up by the paying machine, the laundromat and a flouting around the café bitch, looking for a stable chair, a view to watch as the world ran to and fro, seeming to be paying homage to the whore of finance and Mammon the slut of commerce.

The ordered a lunch with a side salad. Decca liked his mayonnaise.

Tho' the night entered the frame, the tearing of asunder the shallow bequeathed and lonely blasphemy of superstition, only the hearth burnt the fire rock crystal flamed to warm and strengthen the watching, the watched; always serene in wrenching cryptic.

The bite had bitten deep and the wound was hollow, seeming shining white limps around, mounting into covers, behold the man and his wounded healer, he too can be as you, he will die; in sorrow; the bleeding albino substance mixed in flow with caustic crimson.

It hurt him and every other move influenced paranoia, forever.

It takes the mildest thing to change destiny's wheel, to move down another overgrown path or grove. Slightly, changes happen without the sight, always being, not upheld to the malignant memorisation, bringing to light; thought, idea, imagination leading to an undone fear.

*

Decca sat at the floor mirror. Looking at his own reflection. Cancan had gone to work and the apartment was seemly empty except for Decca Peters' presence and his feelings of company.

The glass piece in his hand, the drinking being done before the time left concept, a drawing of blood to wanton a gypsy of nomadic breath, as Decca took the shattered mirror piece and drew it across his face. The blood poured, drawn down to the gravity aspects of jaw, he stared into the depth of nothing and asked *"who is it?"*

No answer came. He seemed to know the taste of holy wine streaming slight, as he rolled a hand over the sudden bleach, all massive make-up of a warless Indian sorrow, all over the cells of blood sat as he took the other-side of his face and cut deeper, invoking a fucking! Invoking the lord of darkness to shed his load and meet him on the plains of invested incepted indecency.

He didn't, but he messaged the telepathy of drums to his lobes, *"I will meet you behind the shower curtain."*

Decca knew he had not had a shower for days and Cancan had, just to spray the fresh about the dirty function of cleanliness and all have a right to be hygienic.

Maybe she had drawn it closed. As Decca stood in front of it, five yards, the toilet seat was down and the sink looked like a sink, belonging to a French toilette of style makings and art.

*

Decca stared at the shower curtain for an hour or more or less, time was irrelevant, but the shower curtain was not, behind it was a beast, behind it seemed the feelings of mighty girth, gore, gargantuan, breathing deeper into enemy, seeking the eyes stigmata and the heart to give way.

It did. Decca Dent Peters could take no more, he could not lean forward and draw back the light blue shower curtain, as his heart pumped the mighty blood about his organic shelves, leaving the feelings of muscle, simply dying in the sordid breast, the turmoil of minds cast, only the phallus seemed limp, studded and cut, cut down to flesh, a moment to gather and pull away from a satanic gaze.

Decca Dent's eyes wept and his heart started in slow thumping pitches, changed, shocked, unhallowed, tossed by the unknown quantity of horrendous malpractice.

*

Having spent many days in bed, in love and in harmony with the second put latter, hence, they were missed by friends, strangers, streets and people within the theatre within which they had met. They were accused of separation, of a particular body politic with which they had the responsibility to bring union for themselves, then come out into the outside world and share it, amongst the poor, in love's poverty, the disenchanted, the disillusioned, the most perturbed in the genus of opposites and stealing of the wills when loving, being loved or being taken for a fool, whilst the inner spirits steal and burgle the developments of self and all hope of righteous care goes rumbling into the the walls of heartache and tumbles fallen to the rocky floors of time, hell or simply stolen to be used against, forthwith, damaged and abused, for the empty reciprocate may hollow high in the void of all damnation, leading to commitment in crime, abuse and forever focused on the sexist wars of the gender.

So, Decca decided to spend out on a car and drive across America!

They bought an open top Chevrolet, green in colour, and called it the *'Green Goddess'*.

They set off, not knowing where to, or what for, or planned to see or visit be, but just 'fuck off' like the philosophy of the 21st century; when it wishes something or someone would do the same.

The open top would come in handy during the coming summer months, and Decca and Cancan looked forward to the drugs, sex, drink and rock 'n' roll on the roads of 'The States', finally the wishes and dreams of Krueger and Hunted, S. Thompson could come true in the volumes of breath and rebirth of these two natural born *'fuck ups'*, they would seek freedom and freedom would avoid them like the fucking plague! They would look for remarkable people, but only find frightened folk, looking for settlement and security in a nuclear world of secrets and lies.

*

The cold war hung above them, but it wasn't so cold, not as the winter disappeared and the bearded trolls came out of hibernation to play, day after day, the season ran through its duties and further on down the line, the track ran into a big bright shiny sun-shining summer, with only two bask in and open the biggest of mouths to swallow the schools of tuna fish.

The journey began and ended like the run through of a timespan designed to confuse the open-minded recipient of a nation unable to know where Prague was, never mind the disgrace of fellow prisoners not knowing the place of birth for all tripping eagles of the brave Indian café society of many deserts was New Mexico.

So, they set off there. Where? Taos … Santa Fire, or; okay Albuquerque.

*

Driving through some of the States of America seemed to be settled in a state of history, like the Civil War or the remains of the Vietnam War, still it all seemed to be built on one aspect, but allowed to weary, confused, salutary, know only to the flags address outside all settlement came the invasion of the English, the tea parties and 'Mayflower', the first American Indian to be insulted and to lose his hand from the wrist, taken by the puritan's sword, duelling with the outcome of savagery and Christianity. Soothed the spirit of all came out the winner, and evolution seems to have a lot to do with its egotistical younger nephew history.

Finally, the real America hit!

The outback of Texas, beyond, above slightly opaque, the deserts of California and before the such American history of the Wild West cowboys were the reservations of a Mexico which was New in an old reservoir of blood.

Turquoise was the order of the day and Decca ordered a terracotta hamburger.

Yes, they were reddened in sun flesh, burnt to the bone, resurrected in Indian rituals to the Sun god, risen above the teepee and flouted in the burning eye, soon to be dead, reborn with hope in the soul, for a tempering disembarkation of triumph.

Tough, resilient and honoured by the solar king and his beautiful bride; the wounded squaw of love.

It seemed to be another world as the heat shared sordid gifts for the holy flesh to scent, the belongingness of unconditional sex and great erections leading to humanistic orgasmic lush.

In the bush. The yucca brevifolia; a Joshua tree … or two … or three!

They parked in a caravan site, at night, not knowing the outcome in the morning.

The outcome was coming, and it came with a white American and his Indian brave, a second to the law of the common man and his Scandinavian wife, well Danish, but I am sure even they would class that as; even in America where every standard of life could be attained and accustomed for, by the Pentagon and its believers in Republic Democracy. That's something without a King or Queen.

But, this guy thought he was a king. He was Elvis. He was the coming of the future for the helpless American Indian soldier who had fought Custer and won, but had fallen foul to the 'white-man's tongue'; the lies, told because they didn't have the truth, the truth was already residing in the mythology and philosophy of those having to entitle and face a 'Manifest Destiny'.

He woke up the sleepers in the 'Green Goddess', and asked them for their camping tickets, looking at the same time at the fact they didn't have a caravan attached to the back of the car. His eyes, seeming to raise to the heavens, but he was thinking in his head, as to what it was that was not there for him to think as to why it wasn't and what he would think, but seeming to be confident in doing, said, *"If you do not have a camp permit then you must leave."*

Shit. Leave New Mexico! Already? … Oh no! Such things could and would not be comprehended by the brains of a pissed-up drug addict who had just been awoken first thing on a dawning dark night, to answer the most stupidest of questions, ever asked since Columbus asked an Indian brave where India was!

Decca said, blurred, *"We don't have one."*

"Then," came the American owner, as if he knew, the world knew,

what was coming next, he did, and sidekick Indian did, only the only person who did not, was this twit in front of him, *"if you do me a favour, I will do one for you."*

Now that was a surprise. Decca wondered what he had done to change the mind of this fascist park owner, who had enough to back the sack, when it came to telling a strange Travolta in the outback of America, where guns was a law, had it been his smile? His good looks? No. He looked at Cancan half-asleep on her side of the front seats and focused on her wee legs protruding out of her very short skirt. Knickers ready on show and the pubes giving rise to rebellion!

*

Without hesitation, Decca said, *"Yes"*.

It had not dawned on him that he had not been asked as to what the favour was, but if it gave him any kind of respite out of the lair of the American's law, he was ready; to seem, to do it and then find the first opportunity to fuck off, knowing he had had a night free from 'pay as ya go' cunt!

"Right! Pick up all the rubbish about here, this morning, and you will have paid for your stay."

"Right," replied Decca, who looked at the Indian brave looking Cancan up and down, as the owner left to fetch rubbish bins.

Decca and Cancan cleaned up the site. That early evening night, they were invited to have dinner with Louis Lee Vance and his Icelandic whore; Shills. The Indian boy, by now, called Running Blackhead, was from the Zuni tribe of artisan Indians reservists in New Mexico.

The dinner went well and then the cocaine came out.

The lines were done, and then Louis Lee Vance produced an Armalite rifle, placing the fucker on the table, loaded with 20, 7.62 bullets, the cartridge removed and shown.

"This," he said, *"was for renegades, interlopers, Coyotes and anybody thinking they could take advantage of my hospitality."*

He also showed Decca and Cancan his rifle licence. He could use it out there and would.

Decca flipped inside. He recalled his Army days. He recalled the Armalite and the way it was used to keep the 'Brit bastards!' out.

He didn't seem to want to say anything. He went quiet and the cocaine went with him. His silence was so loud, it stirred up the table at which they sat, and the large caravan moved.

The dear feeling of not knowing who you could be shouting at. There in the fair distance stood a lonely Indian brave, dressed and coloured out for war, the dark handprints on his cheeks, the slit of his dark eyes and the piercing of his breast, made him ready to take your scalp.

Decca took one look at Cancan, who seemed to be in heaven, her eyes the colour of blonde, the pupils pup-ed – diluted to sharp fangs of a wild cat's teeth, she smiled at Blackhead and Decca stormed out of the half-lit Vi-kingdom caravan.

He ran to a safe spot. Turned, picked up a stone, then threw it at the top of the caravan. It ricocheted off the top and rolled into the bushes behind. Not a movement inside was heard, seen; to move, they must have known, they must have seen the warrior in Decca, the use and way, the weapons took their hold on his sight, his sight seeing the Indian brave; they fought, they fought in the desert dust and the fight lasted, they dug deep, as the stars in the night howled in fear, weeping with the tears of creation's sorrow, they killed and snapped, till the scalp infested beaut came to rest; restrained and handed over his surrender. Decca accepted. Then, leaving, turned and loped his cranium off from the fucking ears! The knife stuck, fucked, there with brazen beaut, fastened to the blood and brain, as the whole thing looked fucked and badly done.

Paranoia has a way to tell its own story of sorrowful sorry apologies with intense fear.

*

The day was nice. Cool. The day seemed to be fine. Just right, just in line with all the fine alined things happening in the world.

Running Blackhead turned and saw the crossed-legged, simply attired face of Decca sat outside the Indian's tent. He kept on the staunch of his heels like a totem; only he would have known.

His long untied jet black Zuni hair, seemed to sit just right on his shoulders, as the darkening of his eyes peered at the reasons; why the white-man was sat in front of his tent, looking like he was praying in a teepee, for the rains to seize. Also, how had he got there without the perceptive unrealistically awareness of the Indian brave seeing him, or feeling him, better still, always knowing he was sitting there in the lotus position?

Decca spoke in his best Indian impersonation depth he had, *"Leave her alone."*

The Indian they called Running Blackhead nodded his chocolate brown face in acknowledgment of the forces at will and deemed his reluctance to release her spirit from his pouch of hold, captured and held till the white-man surrenders.

*

Decca and Cancan left together. They drove off in the 'Green Goddess' and as the tracks spit up and the dust hit the fan, the sun shone on the groove which they made, as Decca looked at Cancan, not saying much, having just found her voice once again, smiling at him, and he said, loud for the world and waste to hear! *"My name is Raining wolf!"* ... and they both laughed! Very loud.

The 'Green Goddess' sped through the carpet of Zuni living into Arizona and the Mojave desert.

The desert was hot. Blistering, if one was blistered. A place for lizards and bald unbeknown entities, which lived on less than death and could catch a bite to eat, having run after it for miles.

The cactus was a source of refreshment, but until then, the small off shoot places in the outback seemed to have a gas station in which all goods could be bought or purchased for the road ahead.

They had run out of money, so Decca nicked a fine pair of sunglasses, and Cancan lifted away, without the slightest hiccup; ice.

The ice was used to run the stream of fresh cool water down the neck of Decca, as he flowed the car into top gear, let go of the speed, opened up the bonnet's engine and streamed across the Mojave desert, the mesa ranges, Joshua's trees and cacti, like the wind was the sail of all duration, leading the path to freedom, belonging to an almighty surge to forget and fulfill the needs of a spirit drunk on life, on the force of fire, desired to be, rather than have to do, see, need, want or have.

It all seemed brightly lit with the heavenly horizon of a destiny to reach full of riches and gold, the nectar of the gods, the sex of a million starving concubines, the strife scent sending souls to paradise and paradise seemed parallel to paramount intentions of the paranormal world of holy ghosts, messianic peace, highest drug inducement and the hope that the rainbow was a shadow leading to the ground a house, a home, a place to stay and listen to the wolves as they bayed, to sound out the lizard as it shuffled across the plain, the motion of eaten, the food for giants, the devouring of the dark silhouetted night as the clouds played back-drop and the amber-gris of yellow stole the image and turned the world into passive cowards looking for a love life and only paying attention to the sun and the wind as they both moved away, hereafter to the outer places, unseen by human eyes, people having respect for the world, as the world feeds on bones and war of human death, built to last, when paradise was just around the corner, if we just waited a little longer! We might see it! It might be! And we could be happy for the rest of eternity!

The ice was life and the taste was life too. Life was water. Ice was water. Ice-water. Nice ice-water. Lovely drinking, sprinkling, tinkling, mingling, jingling, sprinkling, demo-mindbogglingly pseudo-shrinkingly tranquil water snorter!

Brought her back to worship and the slavery of man, as she loved his fucking cock! As the depth of his smelly desert cock steamed into her mouth for the water to sooth his bell-end! She let him come and he came into her hot steaming sun-shining bathing in honey glory mouth. She swallowed and he lay back in exhaustion.

Decca Dent Peters and Cancan Bier drove into Los Angeles, slowly at first looking at all the sights, waiting for the 'HOLLYWOOD', sign to grow over the valley, the homes of stars and perhaps, a road which leads up to it.

*

They drove faster as the time spent into Beverley Hills, at evening sunset strip, then out to the ocean of the Pacific, where Venice beach was empty except for the showers, the stray odd dog and midnight runner.

They both took a needed shower looking out to the aqua-blue ocean's horizon. The other side of the world.

The night air brought tears to the eyes of Cancan, then she moved away from the mise-en-scène and started to cry. The sobs and tears and weeping upset the rhythm of time and the sea's white froth seemed to bubble in anticipation, as to the ritual of sorrow so poured out mixing into the liquid of an asteroid's deliverance.

Cancan seemed to be in great pain. The look on her face had the scene of shame lighten all over her sad jowls, laying near to the lips of love and the jaw of mighty. She sobbed so, the light – dazzled shone, dipped, then held a gaze on the neon of surface, so hurt, so damaging, a loss of ego, shambled in sham and done to pieces by better or possibly worse. The crawling naked body across her motel room, full of drugs and booze, sick to the stomach with nausea and failure, she had reached the top and there was nowhere else to go; but down, down, but down could not be affronted, so, she took her own life. Betrayed and berated by the president of the United States and his brother, she had nowhere else to go, no one else to call, and the call this time was futile, seemed to be the image in Decca's head, looking at Cancan and imagining Marilyn Monroe.

They parked up somewhere and took a stroll around, the sights seemed docile, never quite matching the summer daze of Californian splendour, of money and riches, of life and a great costing smile, a swimming pool and organised orgies of marvellous food, magnificent drinks and characters and personalities from the 21st century list of famous history makers in evolution's time stage, captured by the new world, civilisation and a beckoning deliverance of sheer shoddy shifting lights made up the earth's constellations of stars, breathed in the look, the book and the takings, only the person personified was a stupid cunt with a bad haircut.

Cancan spoke of abuse. She told of the need to be someone. She spent time, sometime, when, in studio city. It's a place for up and coming starlets, stars; if ya like, where the directors and producers can weigh in ya talent, the potential is recognised and then you can become someone, who has not been you before and will never return to the former glory of simpleton or waitress bound for vaudeville!

Cancan carried on, she had been invited to a party. One of those, full on jobs with directors and producers and actors, all those having to do with the movie business. MGM, Universal studios all seemed to turn out for this one party held by a very well known actor.

It was good, she said; great. There were people there to make up the scenes. The swimmers and the party fools, the waitresses and good-looking waiters, seemly often, taken to one of the rooms at sometime or other to play with the big broad celebs, only retuning to carry on as if; but, she got mixed up in one.

It was near the end of the night, falling into the early morning hours, when even the moon hides behind the dark set clouds. It was a massive orgy.

"… *I got stuck in! Ya know, bodies everywhere. Then as the flames and heat rose, I got taken into a room with three men and they completely annihilated my sexual libido! They raped me and sodomised me all night. I was meat and they were drugged, drunk and had me dragged till the morning light seemed the only saviour to mock the vampires and have them crawl into their coffins and close the fucking lids! I just remember it well,*" she carried on … "*That night something or someone entered me being. It was a sin and an evil event, and I was the victim, the portal, the reciprocate of devils and demons for sure.*"

*

She finished, the whole world was quiet. Decca looked at the pavement, he didn't even see his shoes, like a dream, he would look for his hands, he wished to be on another plane, so he looked at the concrete, the sound hushed, the poignancy labelled, only the swishing of the ocean breaking onto the earth's sand could be heard.

They had driven to Universal Studios, but it was closed. The echoes of W.C. Fields, when he uttered the immortal words in the sentence, said with an outrageous tang on the American lip, "*I went to California the other day! And it was closed!*" surged around the mind of Decca, as he imitated the sound to fit the bill.

They were there to find the place which was advertising for a 'superintendent'. A 'super', being the handyman, the man to fix the fucked.

Decca and Cancan found the place, near; next to Universal Studios. A nice American Californian woman came to the door, all bouffant and pretty dress, the memories of Mia West and perhaps the great wild gun-fighting west. She looked at the states in front of her, Decca looked like New Orleans, Baton Rouge, Algiers. And Cancan looked like the Midwest, a hooky from misogyny, a Kansas City shepherdess. She inquired as to their whereabouts.

Why? Well? …We have come for the job as a superintendent.

She told them it had been taken. So, Decca said, *"Maybe, I'll go over to the studios and get an acting job in a movie!"*

The ladylike agreed, only she was most reverent when she suggested, *"Perhaps you could! You would be cast as a villain though, a monster."* She said it all matter of fact.

How it was she knew he was English, or how it was that the English always get the part of the bad guy or the 'sicko' one, was beyond the asking.

So, Decca and Cancan said *"good day!"*, and went on their way.

They left California and drove across the Nevada desert, quickly it seemed, paying off at a motel near Reno, playing the night's gamble and watching as the money built up and the punters played for a life to win or a life to lose.

They slept soundly in the motel room. No physco or Norman Bates to creep over you at night and put the fucking screamers on ya!

"There's one!" said Decca, *"Norman Bates, with that house up on the top! Spooky! When he was young,"* Decca started to tell Cancan, who half-asleep, seemed to be listening to the gospel words written according to the mighty powerful soul of a renegade runaway freedom fighter, *"... he must have been called Master Bates!"*

He laughed, she laughed.

It is true, the Brits always did get the bit part.

*

Running through the night, the night sight brought upheaval and a nausea sent right out of the bowels of deviance and ridicule.

The darkness warm. Tired to the eyes of blood shot rule. A target given to aim and a goal out of reach always invites the extreme to dance away the unforgotten life, the force so slight, even the dead horse drinks the nectar of liquid heaven as the shooting of Liberty Valance was John Wayne.

*

The senses slacked to damaged arenas, hipping the horror, totalled to sheer oblivion, seeks a stunt, a runt, perhaps a crutch to carry the burden, the boredom of a sorted mind and life, the happiness creams into play, as the soul screams for future difference and understanding of the piscatorial way to cry, with tears as large as houses, the drops of giants, on the sleeve of souls, counted for the blasphemous strength of nations, hoped for with apathetic ineptitude and misgivings.

Only the darkness is safe. Unseen and secure, without stench or the flicking of hunt, this then is the matter proposed in natural selection, as the tusk of the teeth bitumen human, will be hunted forever and its commendable calcium and enamel.

The set out of a stag, running at full pelt, right in front of the sight of night-time stress, the focus on travel, being unafraid to spin, remained faded, as the sight brought to mind and Morpheus to light! Quickly the shape and sound, the hollow trap, taking the death practice, laughing at the purpose of being, until, there in the road lies blood, there is a trophy for the great elephant hunter, there are the noshers of Clark Cable, as he doesn't give a fucking damn.

There is sweet holy star-lite roads, concrete in solution and based on travel's pugnaciousness to return, to see, to gather and hope, sentimental to the tourists trapping masses of surrealistically communistic gatherings without hatred or daily harm.

The dark image in the darkness brought the opening of a heart for Decca to take the wheel and carry on steering till the New York state.

Yes, it was one whole week. Just one whole week it took to cross the United States of America and arrive home in time for a motherly bollocking!

"Where have you been?! What are you doing with your life?! What is the meaning of this?!" They were all there and Cancan's delicate mother with crow's feet for breasts and cancer for lunch, showed her rotten teeth to the chemist and bit of more than she could suck!

Luck has it, she was out and about with the sod of a crook, sold out to yachts and the rich man's book, she was bought and the coat she wore was stolen. The minx of a fox Shintoist in the garden roses, pansies and chrysanthemums.

It never crossed the mind of Decca, which was dark by now, as the passing of wind, unseen to the human eye but to be caught on infrared camera. The computer age was sad and the coming of the proposed leviathan of talk-shows was about to present itself, as the younger brother to the world crisis as social coalitionists.

It was time to rest and take stock.

The tramp and his lady burst into flat land and collapsed on the mattress on the concrete floor.

No more! Alas poor fuck-head! I didn't know him at all!

They slept soundly for the rest of their lives. The world was at one and the foundation of love was the empire of all species.

The knock at the apartment door was the landlord. He wanted his feed, in his dirty smelly vest, his Italian worn hairy chest and slacks held up with an old belt he used to take to his dead dog.

Apart from that he may as well be in his stockings and garters, his clothes resembled the outtake of a kebab house on a Sunday morning. Yawning he took his look.

It was the 'stripper-gram' at the door, which seemed to allow the rent to stay at a pace full of peace for the mortgage payer and his dead lot of steamrollers, shuffling into the night and finding the money to pay for bed, slight, the talking became louder as the bricks screamed for totalitarian mortar.

It all wrecked the image. Played havoc with the minds of dead-brain sleepers. Slowly, it was dawned, and the hole in the door was the head of Decca putting paid to the landlord's nose.

She screeched into the corners of the toilet bowl. Deeper into the places which are reached by the through-breed cleaner and his toothbrush.

*

The sickly green-bellow bigoted bowl spewer of a thousand shying asses and a bacteriology of a mindless race, gave comfort for the reasons in front of her.

It was time to leave the place. The streets could not cope with senses, bouncing off the concrete into the roads' street metal solutions, it was time to turn and see the view of seasons, she; disappearing, as the light of a memory stutters on her legacy. No more the sights, no more and nevermore the raven's caw, the tall dark rose of fate stalked the citadels of the occult and no one seemed to answer darkness, waiting to hand over 'dog-tags'.

*

In the darkest hour, played out after crack, cocaine, heroin and babes, dead to the pregnancy of infantry infancy, only the window shouts into the name, no answer, as the man outside is an acquittance, and no one knows his soul.

At polar ends the parting is not so sweet. At unusual lengths, the time ticks on in cryptic logarithms.

Sensing the airport. The begrudging and the end. The alpha and the omega, sits forlorn in a dirty poetic verse, as the only way out is excitement. Turn on the taps and blast out the raps of drinkers gurgling, dancing aisles, with mother and daughter sex triangles, in the midair, in the big top, flying over the trapeze, with a hell of an ease, but, it is useless, it is bitter sweet, this taste of freedom for freedom's sake. It don't have a life, no body, no ambition.

The plane journeyed across the 'pond', at the thousands of miles per second split.

How could a failure be so in-emotive, inextinguishable? For the left behind, they are fine, they love to suck the bones of the boredom.

Decca thinks whilst sat thinking, finding the time to fathom his turnaround, his downfall from the graces of paces, set to the trot and a heaven based in hell with limbo teething thrown in-between.

*

He was sat in a cafe, minding his own business, with a coffee and baklava. When into the New York 'greasy Ada's' droughts a young girl. She saunters up to Decca, seeing out his latter days, and says, *"I am really happy you are here! If you hadn't of been, I don't know what I'd have done!"*, as if she knew him. She looked into his eyes. She then looked into his baklava, then his aura, then his soul.

Decca just carried on eating his Greek sweet.

She commenced, *"I have been looking for you! … well, I need you now!"* She sat down, introducing herself, *"I am Trudy Sheraton Sullivan,"* she said with an Irish accent, a tilt giving her the look of the Irish and hopes from the leprechauns.

"What do you want?" inquired Decca, an old hat at New Yorkers and eaten, he delights in his cowffeee!

"I need your help."

"I don't do 'help'."

"Yes, you do. I am pregnant and my boyfriend has kicked me out, cause, he is my

pimp and he says I ain't getting the work done. I am hungry and cold, and ... well, my drugs are coming up!"

Decca looked at the spectacle of drug invaded whore smacking pregnant totting Irish mistake and, offering her a cake, takes her back to his last abode and together they stab at romance and disappear down Flamingo Lane.

*

She runs off to the bathroom and throws up! The sound and noise cascades from the bowels of Hades and wrenched into the record books, as the greatest healing ever attempted by a phallus and yoni getting to know me, ever sensed since sycophant come.

She was tired and fell asleep. Decca looked at himself looking at his defence, in the realm of justice, when he knew he had taken her, he knew he had taken her like the leaves of a tree, the depth in plutocratic evaluation seemed toxic enough to warrant a sexual encounter, adulterant of all destiny and seen in the archives of loneliness, as the best job any man could have done without knowing it.

Sat, the baby had been born and was healthy. The mother; Trudy Sullivan, was well and back with her husband.

*

In the sound of speakers, heard only to the geared out and passed in, to walk the tarmac, sheer heart attacked bliss. To turn and dip and give mighty graces of pleasure to the seeking for freedom, brave to the bitter end blast, at last in turn, the refulgent heel of a good old cowboy turned and mounted the dragon.

Neat and tidy. It flew. The passing of the neon lights shone for the sacred eyes to see, but he did not recognise no one from such higher heights.

Cancan was on the beat, she was free to roam, so she went to Tuscany. Pisa and frenzy, as the chit marked up the counter stem, paying dividends to the glass abacus.

*

The plane flew over her head.

Instead, the booze went down the neck of Decca like the machinery of seat-belt safety.

When the plane hit the other side of the Atlantic, Decca was wide awake and ready to plummet the seams of an already mounted canvas with experience written all over its abstract serendipitous ways.

It was cold. It was Alaska! It was tiny. It was small. A mickey mouse! Surely. It was haunted by fish and chips smells, with old newspapers used to hold the cod in. It was swarthy, stemming from a beloved history of invasions and this time it was the lonesome figure of bad boy Peters, who was the army to rape and pillage the monk's sound arrest of Hamlet peace and Shakespeare's soliloquies.

He was told to leave by the Brighton boy. He knew he could stay, so he went home to his mother's house.

*

She was in and his father nearly choked on his Chinese. He was having a take-away. He was watching re-runs of recumbent and wise and didn't see the wisdom in the autopsy in front of him.

Having travelled the length of the country, he asked if he could have a beer.

It had been many years, for the stay and away effect to be taken at all serious, seeing young D, made his parents realise, he wasn't like them, at all. He must have been adopted. He fell out of the basket in the stork's mouth one night whilst the weather was terribly bad.

They did not recognise their son.

D, who had to be known now, became quiet, withdrawn. He drew himself a chair to sit in and a pint glass to drink out of.

This the everlasting throws of a silence for mother babel, for the golden information to grow the cobwebs slowly, whilst the princess spider bride sank her teeth into his lungs and ate his subsidiary.

The quiet intense nature brought out the worse in everyone. He looked at the silence like the sight of a night's flame sparkling hot, tousled in triumph to the steam, smoke present in its awkward spiral, rising to the infinite unseen moments before the relinquishment solves the problem for arsonists, pyrotechnics, lonely poets and wizards reading from the books of holy druid law.

He seemed to ache with jaw tightening problematic, saluting the intake of smoke from the cigars of Christmas. He trooped his endorsement fine and fit the colours of astonishing liquid, pouring the stream, took away the sadness, took away the fungal locked jaw, seeming to grow a beard to cover the breaks, the scars, the study of perturbing diligence in the face of an adverse calling. Bitter, the butter creamed about his gut, sordid the stinking of his heart, less the bout with heartache.

No, he was speechless and the act became worse still.

D decided to do some theatre.

He would find a way to exorcise his demons, to find a method to the solutions of schizophrenic characters. He would learn the skills of self-astonishment and freedom of will to create and capture a persona. He would seek the final curtain, bow to the maker of creation and learn the lines made out by the gods, when all the children are written.

He wrote a play and acted in it.

He had met a young up-and-coming forester by the name of Marcus Hovercraft, who was incensed with the idea of new theatre, with the idea of brilliant theatre, a theatre to brighten up all theatre and make the old tried and true to be in question as to the motives and may-hemp of Shake-steers all nonchalant racketeering of a solid pound of flesh! At best, a little bit of up to date stuff, would do. Today's topics, and the room for a bloody good kitchen sink drama in the fucking bedroom.

So it was that the Billy Stiraxe Theatre company was conceived.

Based on the bard and the hard vulgar term of the name to which 'shake spear', thus becomes 'stir ax'; Billy short for William: Billy Stir-axe.

The play doused in alternative arrangements brought out and about by local, national and worldly affairs, seemly brought to bear by the personal experience of all protagonists so.

In time it was all well received. The bar flowed open and never the neck seemed to close.

One member of the audience spoke of what he saw, when he looked at the drinkers at the bar.

"It was not," he remarked, *"seeing them go about their craft on the stage, but to watch in loud amazement at the way they would crowd the bar and drink to the merry heights of all singalongs sung under the Sun, seemly, but so, and like the greats! Sirs Richard Harris! Richard Burton, Oliver Reed! And ... "* he hesitated for a moment, perhaps fagoting his bearings, as to his insights, to the said fascinating greats, who could bloody well drink! Put it away!

Then, go, go! and have a woman or two! Yes! Two!, perhaps many, as many as the bloody fool could muster!

Buster! … ah! yes … Keith Moon! Keith Moon?! He was a bloody rock star! And it was shown to know, by him, said about the late great friend of his, that the difference between the world of the rock star and the world of the actor was just that! This! *What?*

Girls man! orgies! groupies!

"Have one!" Keith would shout. *"Take your pick!"*

Aloud, received, accepted and legendary, thus the rest is history.

Decadent Peters' world spiralled into bi-sexuality.

So, to take it to the theatrical 'boards'. Knowing one's cues and entrances; exits. To remember one's lines. How would it be done? To see the character, then having fun, seeing the same as to what he would say. Said; the lines are swallowed, evaluated, until the stream of utterance would charge itself to rise. To have a memory, tasked to the ability; 'to practise', in all art forms, it is said; 'to make perfect'. To rehearse. The rehearsal is the place to remember, to see the letters and words turn into scene of place. Inspired by the situation, suited to its result, then taken outside of oneself, to be shared with the emotions and feelings of the actor in opposition.

D learned his lines and filling himself with cheese and ham sandwiches with mayonnaise for lunch, proceeded to take it all in his stride, the feelings of character and the influence of all scenes of life. The theatre took him to the Edinburgh fringe, with an undiscovered Russian play, which was undiscovered, because it was weak in its effect for having anything to do with the world apart from being anti-war in sentiment. Undiscovered, to the sound of a Russian Kremlin, who die in front of all parades, liking to invade smaller principalities than themselves and having a great big hang-up about the free world; being America.

It was an alright play. D's part seemed to be the biggest anti-war character in it. The man's name being 'Caesar', a travelling nomadic, with no use for the world at large, as the world was at war, and the lonely place for such happenings was in and out of villages and situations bringing the force held dear to the heart of his only daughter. She believed in love and he was her protector and defender of such an ideal and wishful thinking; Paradisaical.

D turned out, so they say, looking like John Lennon on heat! A rendition proposed to the point of being funny, not a rocker but a mocker and in one scene with the higher ground in sight, seemly with the up and coming skills of the great Shakespearean actor in Oliver Kenton, he walked up to the soldier played by Kenton and took off his cap. They dialogue'd and then Kenton's character says *"... and take your cap off!"* – a reference of respect for the place he was in – so, D put the other back on.

They looked at each other and they knew they were laughing in a place beyond rehearsals, beyond the need for art, they commenced and finished the scene.

If you can imagine, the face on such a place, as the notion of respect for a world at war, seeming to hear the command, then doing the opposite thing, slightly pinged on the face of the persona; Caesar.

They laughed in the aisle, to which Oliver stroked out with great upheaval and majesty to the face of D; *"You are nothing but a ham! ... ";* they laughed, the curtain was still up, the audience laughed, the whole place erupted with laughter and they sidled off, arm in arm, as they would perhaps, in the voluminous stage play of Sir Laurence Olivier and Marilyn Monroe!

The sense of void sat chomping on the bit, the filling of a commodity, the rising flesh girded into wounded moments, as the healing was not soothing enough, it rankled the empty shores, it placed the faces of anti-isms thus, no one could enter that place of forgotten times. All the harpies and war-mongering screeching, sank into folded grades, a lapsing of hands filled, pre-empted by sand grains ... slowly the wound ached to kiss the lips of love, never tasting the electromagnetism, shelved beyond words, in time the heavens clipped the wings, burnt the cinders to the crisp of all walkers, damaging the sentence, as every-word was eaten like a banquet of many a docile bourgeoisie. The revolution was here and the bolshevik licked the arms of a melancholic dominance.

*

To leave a place alone, without character or form, leaving the pitch battle, strengthening the will with alcoholic bills, a tab! Left unpaid, strolling along the boulevard of broken hearts, still the essence of humour could lastingly take the 'piss' out of life. 'extracting the Michael', preferred by all to be the image of the devil underneath the feet of the arch-angel, blasting out his favourite song, longing to crow a fart! *Bram!* Blast the efflorescent bastard! Click the stud uncomprehendingly improvised, the outcome and the devil was kept down and at bay.

Thankful for the bidding clap and the one small chap, who caught him up and said, *"That was a really good performance tonight! I really enjoyed it."* Gave D the will to crack on and find more, to pay homage to the solo songs of Shakespeare's written ballad, *'Sooth, we are but as one, enjoined by the spoken word of joy!'*

Of course he didn't. Say that. D did, and had, rolling about the comic stalls with blasphemy and pantaloons. In amateur desires to fulfill a nightmare.

Sunk into drink, drunk and slunk to bed, to hangover, rehearsal and change.

He wrote a play and acted in another unknown Russian play, which is where he met the stage presence and lovely protruding breasts of Madame Pash Moronie. A young Yorkshire lass, who had more to her written in her destiny than the outcome of the second world war. For, it was in 'Arts York', to which D plundered his skills, affluent and effluent, indifferent to the mainstream; compromising for the entertainment of the troops and Sunday afternoon matinees bringing Pantomime with *'I say, I say, I say's!'*

He studied theatre. Brecht, Beckett, Pinter, punter and prat, what's his face?! Some Russian fool and Tennessee Williams. His favourite being *A Streetcar Named Desire*. The Greek stage, the ancient adaptions and types brought out and on, with Chekhov, as the very serious method acting, when as a doctor on the Russian steppes, he wrote, to pass the time, make extra money for his family and slightly 'off the cuff' comedies. Stanislavsky made them the world's most serious attempt at real life situations and archetypical megaliths.

Pash was playing a Russian courtesan, opposing the poet; Victor Victorovich, played by D.

She asked to make love to him. He did.

She complained, she wanted him in character.

He didn't complain, he got her in character.

It was a one night stand for Pash. It was never to end for D.

She lay at his feet at the last night's 'do', and the lead actor was very jealous.

They went home and fucked again. Warming up the cockles of a Siberian winter.

She lay in the ditch. The white coloured tryst, pulled by horses of grey hue, he felt her presence and held her tight, all aching, moaning, a perturbing mane had seized.

D seized the opportunity and wooed her away. She was his muse and he was the struggling writer, ready to find his life's work in the sturdy thighs of Pash Moronie.

He sat down in his long bohemian overcoat and wrote for her, about her and with her in 'it' as his leading lady, she was to be a star, she would have her name; up there in lights. In this Yorkshire backwater of amateur acting and seance, with witches, boggled eyed bitches and part-time driving instructors. Still, there was something precious about being amateur. Something sacred. What? he didn't know, but whatever it was, it would, it had to, it was going to lead to an almighty wrench in life, in love and London! London was the aim and the streets were paved in dirty pennies. Bollocks to the small pitches and the rotten ditches of hobby or pastime, this was life and life had its method and that method was ambition, desire, passion and *fame!*

*

He asked his father for the money. Which he gave to him, gladly. He had to get rid of him.

This was a madman. This was fucking Rasputin! It was not safe for the Russian aristocratic Jew!

They parked their asses in the small flat in London. It was the size of a wardrobe. If it had been magic it would have been great to visit Narnia, but it wasn't, but they could climb out of the closet and reach for the moments; stand, take command of their whereabouts and never give up on the path to stardom and the stage.

The stage, they were at, was skint. In the winter of Covent Garden.

The cupboard was cramped, the cupboard was bare. She became his Stella debased to his Stanley Kawasaki.

D sat in a bar in Soho. He had a drink or two. Looked about him and lit a cigarette with his box of matches.

A young African/English lad came up to him and asked him if he would like some ecstasy!

D had never tried it. The young Afrikaner, noticed the effect, of lack, of trailblazer, so he suggested D try half of one. No cost, see how he felt.

D dropped it. It rose. He rose, the drink seemed better. He felt the rose of thorns release from his mind, his side, as the 'trip' was beyond controversy. He looked at the Afrikaner and tried to kiss him. The young man knew the form and asked, *"Good yea?"*; of course it was. The affronting, then left as soon as he had arrived. D sat in an ecstasy of heat, rushing about the senses, till he drank and had a hit on his cigarette. Lighting the cig with the same box of matches, he noticed there was no matches in it, but loads of ecstasy pills. They stared up at him, as if they were stray ducklings looking for a mother to be fed and nurtured. D looked at the mirror in front, saw himself, he looked for the messenger, the other box of matches, must have been the same, the constituency of synoptic synaptic bliss sprang eternal on the front of fonts, leaving the same precept right in front of the begging and beguine.

It was to Pash with the ecstasy he went. He dropped the lot, and fucked like there was a tomorrow. Yesterday.

In his mind. There was a place. There was a stag of hope. He seemed to see the legs of Mr Tumnus, but in fact it was the hooves and horns of a fallen angel going by the name of Azazel.

Deep in the recesses of the corridors of the mind, lay the truth to the path of redemption and eternal damnation. The difference being, chosen by, loaded on, as the collapse of the legs and the folding of the hands brings a person to prayer. To pray for his misgivings, his downfalls and pitch. The other, but free to choose the free will of choice. Chosen.

He would weep with soft eyes, with a weak heart, without strength, pride or diction, he had left all salvation behind him, fallen on the rocks of time, he would seek to be forgiven, as the fear of all hell broke loose about him, he knew the value, virtue of lessons learned, rights and the wrongs of all songs, but, he needed you! He needed the help of the angry stranger who hated him, he loved the despot war-mongering betrayer of humanity, but he knew he could be condemned for the love of Satan! A forbearance, less than the rights of human life. Gone are the needs to feed and bleed, gone are the thirsts to drown, gone is the heart of almighty God and the goodness of goodwill in every man.

He sank to his sin and blessed the path of righteousness, till Armageddon come.

Azazel spoke, *"I will see you again, one day, my friend. Do not fear, for you shall be in fear."*

The fright of all senses, needs the feelings of a strength unbeknown to man, it is in the organic nature of woman, find it my friend or you will perish. As you perish, you shall smile. To perish is the greatest of pain, indefensible to the feelings of flesh or bone, it hurts the soul.

The soul screams. The soul teems with angst fractionate bombastic boisterous margins in the market place for slaves, the misbegotten, the unfounded, lair of sodomy, a place of severance, sufferance, chewed off the bearing of parts, a slice, perturbed, bemused, bamboozled – till, you are forsaken in the heart of love.

With regards and hope for an eternal blast!

Zzz.

*

D aka Decca Dent Peters awoke and the cupboard was empty.

He did not see his chest. His hands reached out for the comfort of companionship and she, it seems, had jumped ship. Gone. 'The muse of a thousand amusements' and a beautiful healer, the white soft shores of Arcadia.

Pash walked through the front door with a good old McDonald's takeaway, fries, the lot!

D indulged in a fucking great big fucking Big Mac.

The Ragnarök of days turned into the pitch of battle, sent to try them. They walked out on the last production, enough to warrant 'an empty space', in a theatre to be filled.

D knew he was too old. Too old to be equity property. The beginnings of an actor's life was usually to be sent to a drama school, where he can zone in on his trade. The actor would leave with the notion, he or she would fare well, if potential had been reached, to which connection should be possible, in view, as well as agent.

They have a part in their mind, which was born, written and lived by the famous life, to which they would be called to do, sometime in their career.

D saw only bit parts and extra work, which would be fine, to go along and enjoy the sandwiches. But, he thought he would make a great Anton Chekhov, but who would write a film or stage play about him? Yes, he was a great man, a writer of many famous Russian plays, but D was sick of doing fucking Russian this and Russian that, he felt like an outtake for vodka or the Russian KGB or perhaps move to Moscow and fiddle about with freedom.

He left in a huff, and taking his Russian mistress with him and Marcus Hovercraft, they bought a Citroen 'tourer' and fucked off to France.

D was on the road again. With new people. A new destiny and the mighty Pyrenees to conquer!

*

But, first they had to get out of Sheerness.

They did and ended up in Paris.

Paris. The place for all art, artists and artisans. The memory of poetry, prose and problems stemmed from the upstart nature of being bitty, picky, annoying and down right boiling like a frog in a very hot witch's cauldron.

The arcane was present. The salute to longevity was damned. By all accounts, with smooth tongued lies and balanced gypsy scum blood. The road to revolution begins with a right royal beheading.

So, the feet large in life beat. As the royal opening of the Arc de Triumph was scarce, but the Notre Dame de Paris was empty, unoccupied by Quasimodo and the streets around and about were full.

Sat, waiting for a moment's peace, a moment's insight, were D, Pash and Marcus on the edge of the pavement life. Ready to entertain and bring the 'bard' to the Latinos.

A scruffy man of average age and height approached them and spoke in very bad pigeon English.

"You want to see inside?", pointing at the cathedral, *"I can show you!"* he said, as if the words seemed to get stuck in his throat, fighting with his own language to live, the fight breaking out and the French whore winning, as the words seemed to him French, but to the other three listeners, ear-aching wrenching meaningless.

"You do not have to pay! I will show you!"

*

Marcus, being a safe and secure type of guy, felt the risen senses of betrayal written all over the Frenchman's will, his bad cowboy jacket, his very 'American in Paris' look, with his bandana about his head and plastic cowboy boots on his feet. His jeans get a mention, as it would look very French to have him dressed, expressed without.

So, Marcus walked away, taking in the sights like a bloody paid up all exclusive packaging tourist.

D and Pash went with him to the Notre Dame. All the time D was looking up at the bell tower expecting Quasimodo to come swinging out of the rafters like a hunchbacked imbecile he was created to be, shouting the very name to which his heart had recognized beauty, *Pasha!'*

Pash! … PASH!, but he didn't.

They all approached the entrance and swiftly followed suit as the French cowboy deviated and moved down an alleyway, walking towards another small door, on the side of the Cathedral.

To the dismay and shock horror of the two followers of Parisian fashion, the man produced a great big 'Bowie' knife, shining in the midday sun, shining into the glacier eyes of D and Pash, shining with the means to use it. They both gulped. They both found a word stuck in their jowls, a French word, they had heard since being there only four hours, 'merde!'; *shit.*

Monsieur French cowboy placed the blade into the church door and started to twist. He spoke in French, he spoke under his breath, but they could only make out the words as they left the fucking planet …

"We shall get in this way! Mm-mm!?"

That was the cue of a lifetime. They looked at 'Colonel Bowie' and legged it! They ran like scared revolutionaries, who had seen the 'reign of terror' turn on them, they did not look back, as the French Indian fighter saw the sight to his night and disappeared down Cathedral Lane.

The running and the feeling, the fear and the loathing, grabbed the two lovers as they sprang into action, when Marcus whispers his intention, quickly to flag them over into another lane, saying prayers, they loaded a café, sat to think over the sweating tears of a thousand ramming shits and the cool bargain given out by the tourist capability of Monsieur Hovercraft.

"Coffee!?"

"Fuck!" Both Pash and D were glad to see him.

Life has a way of making one be alive for a reason. And the reason for Marcus was obvious; to get D and Pash out of as many scraps as he would, could and should. Blood? Well, we shall see if the coming of the trip, followed by the diphtheria of delusion brings death or hanging by a rope till dead.

Fed. They had croissants.

Pushing on into France. Through Dijon and Lyon and on to Arles. The yellow brick house of Vincent van Gogh's art school, which never got off the ground, with only Paul Gauguin taking an interest, until the crazed obsessive Dutchman took the 'hump' over Gauguin's insights into 'how to paint the landscape', when Vincent saw it as it was and Gauguin, put other movements and objects in the frame. They argued and the rest is art history.

Marcus looked like Vincent and D knew his role as Gauguin, the egotistical family man who left them all and went to live out his debauched life in Tahiti. Nice.

But, they were in Arles, a Roman town with an outcrop of land expanding over to the famous Camargue and its wild white horses and pink flamingos.

So, they took their chances and went to work in the fields of France in June. Very hot and Marcus had a very pale complexion, which would be burnt on a summer's day in Bognor Regis, never mind the French Riviera and its familiar toned bodies and erotic exotic palm.

He complained when the sun melted all the cassettes on the back of the car seat. They all knew then it was going to be very flaming hot, when farming for melons.

*

"I just can't do it!" said Marcus, nearly crying and realising he didn't even have a hat.

"We have to do something!" said D, who had a big straw hat on his head, covering him from the rays of the solar star.

"I can't!" processed Marcus, *"I will be sick or ill or both! It might affect my mind, send me crazy! See me walking out into the midday sun with barking dogs and crows in the corn field!"*

"... and shoot yourself in the stomach?", a suggestion from D based on the knowledge of van Gogh doing the same, scattering the birds and

capturing them, like to black brush strokes in the figure 'V'.

"*I can't! Please D! I can't do it!*"

Pash looked at less than a man. She looked at the will of a sympathy belonging to the rough rugged value of an Aries frieze, only Marcus begged on his hands and knees, he wept and scoffed to the soft valley of luxury and relaxation, to watch as the sun passed out to cold dank dark and the sweat had been wiped and all melons were home picked to great muscle, a bottle of red wine to finish the slavish day in merry sexual joy, with Pash half undressed, in her flowery summer dress and the sight of the farming D with shirt sleeves, bare chest, bicep muscles, dirty jeans and pitted boots, the love of the sun runs deep in the blaze of shadow and shape, no place is safe, as the straw hat sits right on his working head, the unshaven face, the bright right sky-blue eyes, the almighty lips and a cheek of brazen bodily toasted guts!

She then turned away. Having had enough of the sight of Marcus Hovercraft in pain and lack of gain; he, again waiting to head for the shadows of his brow, hide behind the shade of days, water the pale skin, as it peels away from his face and back, he never wishes to melt like the music of Springsteen or Dylan on the back of the Citroen 'tourer', he just wanted to go home.

They drove to the cool valley of the Camargue and waited for the sight of wild white horses and the one-legged pink flamingos. Only it started to pick up with a dust storm. So the sand was brought near into land and the fog joined in for greater measure.

They could not see a thing.

So they went to sleep in their tents. Hungry and burnt. Forlorn and worn down to the buckle bone of a travelling complaint about nits and gnats and tics.

The mosquitos were big out there and the nature of pure wildness was unkind, unsympathetic, unromantic and cold. Sometimes you can purple prose the view, but not this time. Grey.

Marcus felt at home and had a really nice sleep. He awoke during a dream and went back to sleep without sharing it with anyone. He knew he had caused the team to defaulter, 'but fuck it', he thought, 'we will do better when the risks of the Pyrenees are in sight'.

"*Good night!*" he shouted to the lovers.

"*Fuck off,*" said D, half asleep and half wondering what a man's body would do in such a climate, when it was vulnerable to the elements, due to fact that it was dead!

"It takes no time to do in life, but a little less, to realise it is not enough."

The wisdom of the wind of the desert landscape spoke to the elements, talking, sharing, the moors, marshes and dunes of the Camargue were alive that night. As every night.

They drove over the Pyrenees. Well, D drove up the Pyrenees and the mist and fog came down, so the car could only go so far. The dip at the end of the day sent them so far, when the car decided to stop. In motion. Enough was the steep climb. D decided to take the car back down and drive back up – fast! Without Marcus or Pash in it. He did and going at about 80 miles an hour, passed the two stranded figures looping around the mountains, watching the car pass them and drive into a clearing, at a stop, on a hard shoulder.

They ran in the fog and joined up with D, moaning as they set up camp and slept.

In the morning D felt the tongue of a very hairy beast on his cheek. He knew it wasn't Pash, so he opened his eyes to see a French cow licking his face. He also saw the high heeled shoes of a farmer, who looked like a very ugly Geisha girl, with his bonded feet in blocked heels and sole clogs.

It was enough to see the day. The day on the Pyrenees mountains, when the fog cleared and the mist filled the air with a dew spectacle of a thousand spiders' webs and humming cow dung.

A French farmer spoke to them. In French, but was translated by a poor book and reading by Marcus.

"You must go down! You will not make it over the top in that car! You must go down or you will have an accident. It is not safe, and you have a long way to go. Go!"

They went and found two French hitchers on the road who showed them to a place where they could cross the border into Spain.

The French folk were called Lauren and Erica. Gypsy type new age travellers, who were going to Spain to live in a commune on the Cantabria mountains.

He was irritating and she had good legs, as they both sat in the back with Marcus. Lauren giving out instructions as to where the camp was.

North Spain and fast the rainbow in the air, decided to follow the end, maybe there was gold!

The Citroen was seen by nature to follow the spectrum of colours, getting nearer the further away it seemed to be. The end of a rainbow was difficult to find, taking up most of the time and energy, the exhaust coming away, being fixed with cow leather from Erica's craft bag.

A turning to which Lauren shouted *"à droite!"*

D looked in his car mirror, saw them and said, *"Who you calling a twat!"*

"No!" said Lauren, laughing and pointing in the direction, *"à droite, right!"*

"Right?" said D, and turning the car at about 80 miles an hour onto a twisted bend, found the car heading straight for the edge of a cliff!

The car screamed and the people inside seemed pleased with the idea, as they had forgotten how to voice their opinion at the moment of their own untimely death.

D saw the need to take charge. Well, he would. He had the steering wheel in his paws. So he improvised and slamming on the front brake with his right foot, took the car out of gear and turned the steering wheel a 360 degree! It turned the car about just in time. The front of the car faced the road and the cliff edge was behind them …

The French couple stared with frozen eyes! Horrified! They swore with the translation of *'SHIT!'*, whilst Marcus came out from his hiding place of unseen unknown esoteric physics with a face as poor as Einstein's must have been when he discovered he had split the atom!

Pash was peaceful. Having come to terms with her timely death, and D looked to see if everybody was alright, for he knew he had saved their lives, but he had also tried to kill them in the same movement, the speed turning of a bend too fast, leading them to the precipice of the edge of Spain, hurling over the edge to their final dumping into the sands and shit, smashing the car to bits and breaking the jaws of all in it!

They reached the Cantabria Mountains, parked the car and climbed up to the top, where a commune of alternative people had chosen to leave society behind, to find a new way to live, up on the forest filled conclave of a scenic sight for wildlife and astronomers.

Popping their heads out of the highest tree and seeing the sky above them, filled with eagles and pink flamingos in flight.

Teepees and yurts seemed to be the order of the day. Some had built wooden houses, but the size and money spent made them look like outside toilets.

Virgo introduced himself to the strangers coming on board and everyone seemed glad to see Lauren and Erica, with burnt out Marcus, sexy Pash and a scruffy pissed up fucked up crabby shabby straw hatted D.

"Maybe we could do some theatre whilst we are here?" whispered Marcus. Ironically.

*

The people were crusty and dreads. They seemed to be a version of the 21st century Celts.

All had lice and ate the bastards if they caught them.

All looked into a void filled with a dark age of unknown worldly grime and a pathos so long in the view, only the sight of a diluted eye, could the onlooker, even guess as to what species they were and what it was they could see, envision, concentrate upon, the dialogue and language jumped about the air like the flying of a kite, controlling the answers, listening to the sound of ancient moods, heaving and heavy, the sentences of time, weighing powerful in a sense of a knowledge lost in space, as a time lapse, a watching eye, seeking the beginning of a terminology for Homo-sapient sapling.

A grunt was 'yes' and a grunt was 'no'.

Fucked; DT, Pash and Marcus got some sleep in a teepee, handed out to visitors.

The climb up to a high point of the Cantabria was reasonable, as was the cut back of the mountain itself, when a few Germans with donkeys, climbed near Matavenero with machetes and equipment to stay and live on the Cantabria.

As DT and Pash Moroni went for a walk, the fog caught in and the mountain was engulfed with clouds. They could not see their way forwards. The night moved in from daylight and the mountain was an unsafe place to be.

D could not see in front of his nose. Which was a roman nose, with a little bit of Jew in it.

So it was quiet big. But to see it when he was in his dreams was another matter, as the advice would be to look for your hands.

Pash could not even see her beautiful, protruding nipples on her breast dress.

They were stuck. They called out but the mountain was the only element to hear them, as the echo slowly sunk into the fibres of rock, bounced off to land in the clouds of aether atmosphere, and carried off towards another part of the range, whilst the whiteness claimed the souls of freedom and the darkness clambered about looking for a reason to lose or a reason to kill.

D said, *"Let's go down that way, I think the path is over there!"* He didn't know, he didn't feel he knew, but was guessing, as the movement lead to a security based on travel, seeing the change come about, meant perhaps you were getting somewhere, to where? It didn't matter, it mattered that the feeling of fear would disappear and the world would wrap itself about you like a warm blanket with nurturing safety and security to warrant tears and tears of laughter and joy, not sorrow and the inevitability of pain; deep in the soul of being and the claim of all creation is to learn and learn your lesson.

At school maybe? But now, fuck the evolution of man and his fucking creative will! They were lost and they were lost in a mountain fog, which seemed to be the atmosphere of the fucking universe's mixture in impregnating the purpose of such, is rain. Vain, pain, gain and lost!

Lost without a sight, a night, a shirt! Lost and the world heard the echo of a victimised child as a predator slits his throat and the world carries on on a pleasure cruise for two.

The way was down and Pash followed D.

D walked the way. He could not see.

He moved his leg in front of the other and hoped. Then he felt the path underneath him go.

It was not solid enough for his foot to bear and he fell. He fell and as he fell he heard in his mind, 'do not let it be my leg!'. He knew. If he broke a leg he would be in a worse state than before, he would have to manage to help himself and get through the night, allowing the fog to rise.

He hit the stream! He hit the stream and the stream was deep enough. He had fallen off the path straight into the stream down below. He felt the water and heard his mind say 'Don't let there be water snakes!'

He managed to climb out and shouted to Pash.

"Stay where you are. I will climb to find you! Sing so I can hear you!"

Pash started singing. The song was only heard through the mist, so it might have been a Guns 'n' Roses', for all they cared. Still, she sang, and she liked to sing. It brought her to this world. In song, she sang to feel herself on this planet, to land and feel safe there, she would feel so secure, the world was cold but she was warm. She sang.

D scrambled up after checking his bits. They met and Pash stopped singing. They didn't feel like a duet at that point, but they had to be a duo and 'get the fuck off' the mountain, before they froze to death or worse still, had to sit there and sing all night long to keep warm.

How many songs do you know?!

They manoeuvred as the night sky set into bright white fog. A Spanish mist.

D said, *"Let's go this way!"*, which was up and to the side. It would lead them away from the bank of the stream.

They did. And for a while it seemed, they climbed. Then they moved across, in the direction they thought was the basecamp.

Then, the ground gave way underneath D and he fell, he heard his mind say he'd fallen into the stream again! *SPLASH!* … *"Fuck!"* he shouted.

Pash could not hear him, she had settled down into a crouching position and had started to sing.

The second drop. The burst into liquid water. The cold freezing temperature, the depth of injury was broken pride, the depth of malnutrition was love.

And Pash sang on at the top of her voice. The clouds and the visible mountain seeming to join with the lullaby of Nereids and *on-dines*, of the streaming dale or valley, dancing in unison with the pleasure of a voice singing. The sound of love and direction, of power and solace.

Pash was a hero, she was the one who solved and soothed the clouds. The universe loved the particles drifting off – away – down to the low and up to the high, the call of the wild, she made.

As D scrambled out of the stream by holding on deep into the sod and lifting himself up with his body, using his legs to hold the edge, to lift and place himself on a shelf, he could find his bearing and strength, thus climb to the healing, soothing sound of an angel.

The second fall had broken D. His will and spirit. He got to his knees and spleened forward, taking up the position of a dog.

The night changed. They had been at the descent all through the dark hours. As the morning light came, and the world 'humanitarian' seemed a better place, the path was there! There it was! They chuntered home to the basecamp, D as a pit-bull dog, on his hands and knees, heading the way off the mountain top with Pash singing. She was singing songs! Oh glorious songs of pitch and worth, worthy of a curtain call, worthy even of a bunch of fucking flowers!

But, the foggy night brought daylight eyes and the sight of an in verse Pasha with her dog in front of her, making people pat the beast and listen as she rose to 'number fucking ONE!'.

They went back to the teepee to heal their wounds.

D had broken a finger nail. He said, *"It fucking hurts!"*

Pasha was asked to sing in the community hall, on top of the camp.

Lauren and Erica brought them herbal tea and a piece of cheese with baguette. That was good. Because Marcus had been making a water and herb soup, with what was left.

"Tonight Pash will sing and we will get some of the 'magic pot' they have up there!" he said.

The 'magic pot' was of meats and vegetable, to which people would donate for a night-time meal, for anyone hungry or who hadn't had anything. But, you had to pay for it. Up on the mountain, you had to pay for a bowl of 'magic pot'.

Germans? Who knows? Jews? Who knows?

German Jews? ... Marcus did not care, *"Sing, my angel, sing!"* he laughed, all the way to the top.

*

They all looked like the orphans out of Charles Dickens's *Oliver Twist*. So much for alternative living with stealth, health and the over ingredient called L.O.V. E.

It fills any stomach. Takes away the pain of hunger. Fills one up with heaven's glory; puts it about in another story! Just give us the pot! With food! With food in it! And I will save your life sometime later in heaven or hell!

Pash sang that night and the 'magic pot' was emptied.

*

It came a time to leave. They were shambled. In a kind of mind disarray. They had survived the kingdom of freedom, with a sore throat and bandy bandaged legs. They came down the mountain bereft of service, looking like the donkeys themselves. A small turn and at the top waved Lauren and Erica, who were staying. They had been rather on the aloof side of things, but they were determined to live there. Up there, in the wild days of heat and cold nights of drugs and music.

Finally, the three managed to see the light, turn and marched on down to the car, for to take them to acclimatisation and a tourist's view of Madrid.

*

La Manchu lived over the road. Don Cortex and his faithful partner Sancho Panza, but the fine stay of a singing bird, a worn out mule and a wolflike tool, they soon found the city of Madrid too posh, too city, too insular for their liking. So they drove to Saragossa, where they could practise the art of begging and busking, as matadors, with Marcus as the bull, and Pash singing great songs of lust and blood and power; and money and food and drugs! Anything they could get their hands on.

Then waving 'adiós!' to no one. They ran to Barcelona. So tired, they slept all the way through the experience. Leaving by the way of Figueres, a small town on the outskirts which happened to be the birth place of Salvador Dalí. They didn't; dilly-dally and crossed the Pyrenees over at the shortest route, or wherever the fuck it was.

Still, back in France, they decided to go home. First they needed to get some money together and drive to the port of Calais and so, ferry it home.

They would worry about where they would go when they got there.

In a city with a train station which had a wishing well out at the front, seemed to be the present destination for the three amigos.

So, D got hold of Marcus's legs and lowered him down the empty well. It was dark down there. It was hollow, and the sound of Marcus straining, seemed to be the sound of two armadillos fucking!

So, D asked, *"What? Anything down there?"*

Marcus grunted, as if his chest was in his stomach and his nostrils were the only thing to talk with. *"Wait! ... there's coke cans! Hold on! ... nah, papers, rubbish ... wait ... a florin!"*

"A fucking WHAT?!" shouted D, not wanting to be heard by the civilians

passing by, as Pasha tried to look normal sat on a bench nearby, with her torn flowery summer dress and her lasting white, by now, black, plimsolls.

"*It's a coin!*" shouted back Marcus, as D heaved him up and Marcus seemed to rise up; head first, then his torso, then chest, then he was able to move back along the rim of the wishing well and scramble off, with D still pulling him to safety.

A sight for the eyes of the Spanish elite. The way of the world at the time of the European union.

What was it? What *is* it? inquired D.

It was a pastille. A Spanish sweet.

*

They all looked distraught and down and out, sat there on the bench. They had all seen better days.

Marcus said, "*I will go and get the train*", matter of factual.

"*How?*" asked Pash, who was never one to speak such, as she had been the one to sing for their supper, wherever they went. She found herself being listened to by the few, but more than usual, when she burst into song. To play it wrong was to talk. Speak like the rest of the world. Speak and the words come mumbling out, they speak of ways and days and fantastic sayings, which the world had shared, the world really listened, they had to, they had to find a way to understand the day, understand the traffic, the graphic solutions to problems brought, given, found or just human problems which could and would only be solved in time. Time being the master. Time being the healer of woes, the nursing of wars, time holding the key to evolution and difference and the change brought about by the world and the world did not include humans. That was their stupid world, made to fit and suit them and the only salvation was *heaven*. Made up, but chances are it existed, because of the need to have lived a life, to be the food for thought or the food of worms.

Hoping there could be more, when to create a paranormal space would be to fill it with spirit and the spirit is the ethereal being to which we all owe our understanding, our journey, our reason and purpose for rising above the 'norm', the base, the ignorant, to live higher, to think better, the only place to be received, after all, is a place where those that had to live with the fucking crap, could be proud to go; be it a maker, be chosen to do so, with love and the better strengths of humanity.

Marcus did. He got on the train and went home to England.

D and Pash got into the 'tourer' and drove back through France. Why?! because they loved the car. No. They just didn't want to go home to England, yet. Marcus did. How he did it?

Well, perhaps he would tell you one day. He probably hid somewhere on the train. Told them he was an upright English citizen and would pay for the ticket across France, and the ferry crossing, when he got back.

Some chance of that. Could you imagine. When the 'channel tunnel' had been built, yeah! But, Marcus had done it when the French were still at war with the English!

How does one achieve destiny? By blagging it? Perhaps, one has a destiny, which doesn't have much written on it. Lucky so and so; and so, maybe you have a destiny, which helps you to walk through walls or go to a school, which actually shows you the rudiments of life and doesn't leave you out and out penniless, for the rest of your doggone existence.

It is destiny which uncovers the eyes of the onlooker and says; they are getting away with it!, when it is their destiny to do so! Destiny. Written. Do it. Done.

As they drove across France, thoughts danced around in the mind of D. He thought of the alternative campsite and the character he had met there called Virgo.

He was a German and a Virgo star sign. He was funny, and had a wife who could not live with him, so she lived in another teepee, and a little son. Virgo lived in a yurt. And, on a morning would have a hearty breakfast for him and his son. He had let the visitors have his old teepee and invited D to breakfast with himself and his young son.

The breakfast was potatoes with cheese on them.

They all tucked in with forks, onto the plate; all the cheese potatoes were laid; out, on.

The small potatoes seemed to be crowding out a very big potato which everyone seemed to have their eye on. The young boy kept looking at it. Virgo knew it was there. And D was so hungry, having been for days living on water and herb soup, he eyed it like it was the crown jewels, it was the 'be all and end all' of passivisation, the calling of the wild to all wolves, to run alongside man, it was the icing on the cake, the mother's ruin and bake, it was the bacon sandwich on Xmas morning, it was the final whistle for the world cup to be won, it was the 'philosopher's stone' and the elixir of life's force, it was the universal answer to the ultimate question; as to why?, what is it all about?, it was the artist's finished masterpiece, and, although it was more than that to D, it was the best sex he'd ever had, the greatest of shags, he was in love with the big cheese potato and no one, *but no one* could have it!

He looked at the little boy. The boy looked at D. They ate small pots. Then, D saw a painting in the corner of the yurt, which was clever, cause there are no corners in a circular tarpaulin. He pointed it out. Yes, it was a long standing painting by Virgo, not finished, and had been painted for the time he had been on the mountain. It was of a 'waterfall'. They all looked with interest and thankfulness, the boy with a smile of pride for his father's skill. When they turned back to the plate of cheese potatoes, the big one had gone, and D was enjoying it, chomping it to bits in his mouth, savouring the taste of grand mature cheese, as the boy looked deep into his eyes for shame, as Virgo, flinched at the empty sight of the everlasting potato; Gone! Someone had eaten the last big bit of cheese, and whilst they had been looking at the painting, which D had pointed out, *he* had gone back to the plate and with his fork, stuck it into the cheese potato and shovelled it into his mouth. The hunger screamed out in ecstasy and the world seemed a better place; after-all, he knew he had betrayed them, he knew the boy's youthfulness was disrespectful of his move, he knew Virgo would have to battle with his early days of friendship towards him, but it didn't matter, he had to have the cheese-pot and he did! He ate the fucker!

He enjoyed the fucker! Fuck friendship! Fuck the need to wait and find out what it was like to steadily share, but he was starving! They eat like that every morning, they are organised, they don't need to lie or steal or beg or betray. D did, as he swallowed the last remnants of the cheese-pot, he tried to smile. But they just looked at the sad array of deficiency, sat across from them, Virgo broke the morning's uncomfortable silence.

"*You must have been hungry! Everybody wanted that one!*"

*

D laughed at the wheel of the Citroen 'tourer' and Pash didn't care anymore, as to what he was laughing at.

They pulled up for a pilfer and D walked down the aisle of a supermarket, saw a pair of espadrilles, took off his worn old boots and put the espadrilles on, leaving the old boots stood to attention in the aisle.

Pash just looked at him as he walked out. She got the cheese and bread.

*

The trail back was full of petrol. D walked up to a petrol station with a container, filled the container with petrol and, putting on the lid, safe and secure; *RAN!*

He ran for his life, with the container in his hand. He got away with it, the car being parked out of the way. Fill the car up and away they could go.

One time, there was no petrol station, so they just sat there on a hard shoulder and waited.

Pash said, *"You can wait whilst travelling and something will happen, someone will come along and help."*

She was learning. She was right.

He came in the form of a gnome on a bike. He was a Frenchman with a beard, longer than the beard which sat around the face of D, he seemed to be their knight in shining amour.

He rode up to them. He asked them the problem in English. He had seen the GB sticker on the back of the car. He said, *"Wait here,"* [which they would; they weren't going anywhere fast!] *"and I shall ride back to town and get you some petrol."*

He did. He rode there and back. All the way for two English strangers. He parked his bicycle and poured a full tank into the French made car. He licked his lips as if he had enjoyed the drink himself, being gnomelike and farmer attired.

He then took out some money and offered the two road weary strays the French notes. Francs.

*

Frankly, it was one of the greatest gestures ever made by a man on this planet. He didn't have to do what he did. He didn't have to ride miles back into town, spend money for a full tank of petrol and then give them pocket money, as if they were his children on a Saturday morning, waiting for the weekend sweet binge. He did all that for two strangers. He got on his bicycle and rode away; waving. He was lovely, was that man. He was a saviour and the 'king of the gnomes!'.

D rode away with tears in his eyes and Pash sang him a song.

They loved that man and would never ever forget him for saving their lives and being there when they needed him the most. 'French gnome' they called him. French gnome…

Getting nearer to Paris, there was a French transport strike on. The lorries were moving at five miles per-hour. So, smaller cars were seen to take the chance and dance within the lorries, as the distance depended on whatever was coming the other way.

D decided to do it. He put his foot down and shot out to take a few lorries, then a few more, then it became like a chicken run, till he started to get good at it, five or six HGV 4-tonners and in; out to have a look, away you go! if the coast was clear for a distance.

D peeped out, the road opposite was clear, there were eight or nine to take, he took off! He put his foot down, travelling about 70 miles per hour, then he reached 80 miles per hour, as the vehicles seemed to be going along longer, it was too much, there was a humpback bridge ahead.

D shot over the bridge and entered a village at 85 miles per hour, he felt the car go! He felt it lean on to two wheels and the car began to head towards a hotel entrance. D felt he could not hold the car, he had lost controversy. Pash elbowed him in the stomach to try and right the Citroen, as the car rolled on a balance of two, the sight of the view to hitting and dying entered the scene, D let go and said his prayers. The car then dropped onto four wheels, D took hold of the steering wheel and careered out of the village. The village people standing in total amazement at the sight of a British madman in a French car seeming to lose control and through no effort of his own, seemed to right itself through fate alone.

As the car sped out and the faces of the French swore and cursed the very sight, the car slowed down and the feelings belonging to D and Pash caught up with them, the senses, the erections, the orgasms and value and virtue left, the philosophy and politic, the rudimentary stylised charisma of a British show looking for the fair isle, the blessed isle, Albion, to be home and safe, knowing they could be signed up and signed on and maybe get a flat through it all. Housing benefit was possible and the very nature of living off 50 quid a week was better than 'frog' Prison.

Over days and nights, the final resting place for the Citroen 'tourer' was Calais.

D walked up to an unemployed man and gave him the keys to the car. They then jumped on the ferry and left for England. The French port authority didn't like the fact that they had two very dirty/scruffy people traversing on their ferry without a meal ticket.

The facts were argued and a British worker stuck up for the need to allow in this world, something which seemed to get right up the Frenchman's nose!

They arrived back in Dover and the light was sheer, the weather was clear and the sight seemed to welcome them back. To a cold damp *nothing*. Just fit for an unbelievable life. Needed to live, this life of no arcane philosophy or revolution, but it was an island for takers and makers and it could cause opportunity or ambition to collide with capitalistic greed, sarcastic bigotry, fanciful whores and the great British show of Elton, Rod or David Bowie, of mini skirts and mini cars, of the Navy and the gravy, the eggs and the legs, the tradition and ruminations of a trumped up case for a well known crime, being, *"Ya got caught didn't ya!"* – the only crime in the world. Barbara Windsor, Elizabeth Windsor, Windsor Davies and the corp of the Indian national gungy jump!

*

It was back to the way. The way to say; saying the popular guise, upright and tough, severe and shunned, the brilliance of an acceptance due to national pride, being a republican can only bring the pubs open for the rest of your life, for the rest of days, for the rest to rest and water their horses. For courses! This … they walked into the streets of Dover fucked, booked and lost to the world of losing. Limp lame and lumbered with the next lamppost and corner, turn it and the economy looks better, see a bakery, buy two bacon sandwiches, the world is your oyster!

A man can do anything!

They just sat and enjoyed their sandwiches.

From then on in is, *was*, mental illness and blankets, drugs and more drugs and a total national disinheritance of kind.

*

To wander the world, to wander the streets, to find the next trip, to find the next kip, a soup kitchen and psychoanalytical dramatisation.

It was life beyond, a life.

Love kicked in for the trip of Nirvana. Ganesha and rubbishy pleasure of an elephant god.

There was too much to think about. Too much to worry about. Too much going amiss. Too much blood, mud, scud, shudder pain, too much stress, war-mess, too much to see, need and want, they couldn't, they couldn't need it no more too much more too 2 true to be.

Pash wandered away singing somewhere. She never looked back. She went to the great white way and sang her Gypsy Rose Lee heart out!

She was left to her own devices, after her experience with D, she fell deeply and madly in love with a punk/Gothic/grunge occultist going by the name of Dark Carlyle.

He refused her advances and said, *"You are going out with D"*, in a very deep and dark accent making his proof, be it worthy or right, he had someone been sent up from King's Lynn to be at his service.

She took some stronger gloves and 'lost it'! She climbed over a cathedral altar and shouted at the authority, who turned up to judge her, a priest, the police, a psychiatric doctor and her mother and stepfather and said, *she was a sacrifice!* To who and to what?

They sectioned her. She sat around the psychiatric unit like a nymph on heat, when Moron Mike, an institutionalised victim of the mental system all his life, told her she could leave anytime she wished! – so she did. Moron Mike thought he was being her 'knight in shining amour', by telling her of the freedom she could have as *they could not hold her there.*

When she sauntered out; four psychiatric nurses ran after her and held her stay, she fought, they dragged her back and injected her to sedate her. It was then, during the struggle for her Aquarius freedom, fighting the straitjacket, frothing at the mouth, did Indigo, an energy spirit, get released from her and was set free … ! an undeveloped part of Pash's life needing love, respect, freedom and above all *truth* within her own destiny.

*

D found a hole and crawled in it. He slept well, but never quite woke up. He wore a blanket for a poncho and used it for sleep cover. Apart from his dirty stinking jeans, his feet loose and free, the toenails broken and dirt between the gaps. Matted hair with singing lice, scratching the back and shouting the odds, the world was wrong and he could do nothing about it.

He was wrong, so he smoked hashish, snorted 'speed', dropped acid tabs for breakfast and lived from soupy to soupy doss-house.

So quick the downfall of souls. So speedy the decline of all beliefs, so insecure the nature who loves the most, but isn't nun-saintly an undesirable to the Catholic Church.

The drugs came thick and fast as time existed no more. No more days, or weeks or years, no more Christmas or fucking Guy Fawkes, no more watches, no more knowing the time.

Gone like the dice of a forgotten crab player, stuck in the machine of lust, the episode of changes, the universal slavery, the horticultural indignity of graces, to sell out to yourself, the belief that you are alive, in time, with time, too late, and early enough to see the dawning of the other day, remembered by the love of life, till we believe we can be important, we are needed, we do want to help, we can't help helping, we need to sympathise without lapse, without tears, still the drugs work, the stuff fucks the cells, the mind can think about being numb to the world, as the world is numb to you. A relationship based on mistrust. A starvation fed to incline the purpose of natural affairs, still bemusing the masses, but letting them settle with less to think about.

"I must go now. I will be back. No need to have a heart attack," he said, whilst listening to Nirvana on CD, looking for the elephant god amongst the room's rubbish, strewn all about, for the floor to disappear. With friends, drug friends, dealers and travellers.

Bird Angel, Mart Pagan, Dutch Bliss and a girl called T.C., who had a dog and carried a blade.

The night passed into morning into day into evening, then night, like it does; right.

*

*"The sovereign Alchemist that in a thrice
Life's leaden metal into Gold transmute."*

The Rubaiyat of Omar Khayyam

Citrinitas Apocalypse

D climbed …

… the Tor Burr in Glastonbury, Somerset, as all around him the magic of the air seemed to fly about, with a feeling of stamina, exciting, meaningful fibres, the climb being on a pure summer's day in the year 1999, at around mid-day on the mid-summer, a solstice light shone in the white of the cirrus clouds, all fine, robust and intangible to a beautiful day in the landscape of a mystic land, a treasured place, a womb; place for the rebirth of life, to instill the new day, the new way and accept the momentary dissension made with the hope and charm of the real nurturing, loving, caring mother.

*

He wore his full beard with pride and he took hold of his stride, as he strode to the top and faced the tower of St Michael. He turned and the landscape of Somerset hit him full in the face. He smiled, took a knock from his 'spliff' and sat down on the grass facing, looking over the small town, seeming to be making plans, only, taking in the energy of the esoterica air swarming around him, laughing and playing with the honeycombs of seeds, the daises planted by nature, the trees full in clothing and the sight of space and the clear light of day, the sound of pigeons and a smell of warm joy, made D seem to wish to stay, *so he did*.

On the night of new year's eve; 2000 AD, he stood at the west portal of the Tor with the black knight. They took up the positions either side of the entrance and leaned upon the cold brick.

It was a fitting place to be. It was the *only* place for D to be.

He wore a leopard skin 'drape' jacket, a thick leather belt, which fastened it around the waist, drawstring pants and a fedora hat, his outfit was warm and they both had good 'wellies' on their feet. As the crowds dashed about and shouted and celebrated, as the world did the same, recognising the millennium, the sound of fireworks, like the end of the world, as the bombs dropped to explode amongst the people, *'loud and noisy'*; D thought.

The black knight held a lantern in his hand, lighting the way for people to enter the womb of the country. He wore a coat from the African lion, he was Rastafarian.

Three girls entered, one by one and seemed to represent the trinity. It is necessary to read all the signs of the world, when it loses all sense, it needs to be understood with symbols and signs, then it can make sense, then it can lead to purpose.

The world is not made for such occult senses, it has lost the knowledge, but it is good while it lasts, until it ruins the mind and the mind leaves the stage to wander forever in the land of the fairies.

D promised himself always to be real and read all psychic symbols with caution.

Down past the Chalice hill, the female hill, the red well, was a terraced house made of brown brick and an outdoor yard, which could see all of the Tor. Unbeknown to D, he was being watched, without the use of a telescope, by a woman; in her mind's eye. She could see him and he had arrived.

Their eyes did not meet, but, she knew who he was.

Like most mysterious monuments, some have to be visited late at night. When the moon is full or the wind is howling, but, just to feel the darkness that could surround the place, eerie, quiet, a movement would be enough to think ghost or shadow.

*

The night in question was dark. Late. Nobody was on the Tor Burr. D ascended the 'shape of a womb', and went into the tower. He sat on one of the two slabs, on which many a tourist's ass had sat. It was warm, mid-summer's eve, as he climbed into his red sleeping bag and went to sleep.

As he slept, he had a dream.

*

He was dancing naked in the Tor tower. In front of him was a man in a red cowl, his hood was covering his face. Behind the dancing D was a white shadow of an elder man watching.

On the other slab was a dark foreboding figure in a black cowl, with the hood covering his face, only the nose could be seen, it was a good structured nose; royal.

There was a monk figure in one of the corners, who had his face showing. He was fair, with a white tonsil hairstyle and in a fawn coloured habit. In another of the corners of St Michael's tower were two boys. One was bigger than the other in size. The taller boy held on to the shoulders, behind the younger. And in the east portal of the tower; the largest exit, stood a knight in shining armour. He was looking out into the dark night and was handsome and pale with jet black hair.

As D danced, his movements being pure and naked, the figure in the red cowl spoke, he said, *"He is like me!"*

That was it, that was all he said. He knew because he was there. He was the figure in the other corner, he could see his face in the dream, he could see his nose, his eyes squinted, and taut. He witnessed the event and all was safe.

D woke with a start! The air entered his lungs which made him swallow the oxygen and make the sound of a breathing apparatus coming alive, from a deep place.

D smiled. He looked about the place and no one was stood about the St Michael's tower on the Tor Burr. He had awoken in the very early morning light and the day was wonderful!

He saw; it was bright cerise and turquoise, with jasper tinges, it was a chalcedony sky folding the clouds to form neatly and flow with effortless ease, as D climbed out of his red sleeping bag and prepared himself to leave the rebirth centre.

He also knew, as he descended the 'Aquarian Phoenix', that it was *his* day. The sun shone with majestic splendour and the world felt handsome and friendly, clever and artistic, sharing; it all seemed to smile with a joy of happiness, that all in fact could be paradise, when the dawning of the day gave birth to humankind and humankind was great! Knowing, present and full-filling to the people, born for the experience in a manifestation of a life-time, in a universe like the galaxy of the Milky Way, as a solar system like to which, the earth was a part of.

When he got down many people had seen the dream.

He was attacked by hoarding crippled masses of individuals who seemed to be emotionally ill, seemed to wish to bring harm to love, wishing to attack the assailant who showed the people it was possible to be mystic and supernatural and that it was not just like everything else, a product or selling tool, or a gimmick or cult, a façade of showmanship or totally invented of distaste and function to better human arrogance or ego, it had to be a charlatan trick, it was wrong to interpret dreams, they could not be sold, claimed to be for sale, they have to be subconscious and stay in the deep dark caverns of the single set *president* of mind.

He was attacked. It ruined the day. It took away all the joy. The day was nice, but it had lost its taste, it had started to hum like the days before, all added to the history of time and time hung from it like a cancerous glob, ready to drop off, ready to fall in the eye sight of nations and man's will to conquer the planet and womankind.

D entered a public house, he didn't even look up to see the name, and ordered another pint.

Everything and everyone wanted him to haunt that bar. To wallow in the tears of the glass and at last get back to normal like everyone else and suffer the consequences of a hung-over life.

D knew that. He knew he could not change his stars. He knew he could not approach the world a different way, as his destiny was already written and to be majestic and gifted wasn't written in it.

He felt sorry for the world and toasted their outcome.

*

He walked about one day and heard in the air that a woman wanted him. A witch? A mad sorceress or female Circe? A good woman, to be his everlasting pagan wife? Who? Who was it wanted D and he looked about trying to find her.

He saw a woman sat outside a pub looking at him. He looked at her and she used telepathy, *'You know who it is!'*

No! *He did not know who she was!*, D said to himself using telepathy.

As he wandered about the place, the shops and pubs and streets and off street places, he wondered who had ordered him, for what? Wandering back towards the Tor Burr, the Chalice hill and the springs of red and white; one iron and the other calcium, good, they had said, for the blood and teeth.

He walked past the terraced houses and he heard a voice emanate out of the place, loud and larger, vicious with power, like the voice of a demon or the devil himself.

'THERE HE IS!' resounded the atmosphere.

D just looked with the human eyes of fear and carried on up to the Tor, where he would sleep amongst the apple trees in the Somerset orchards.

He watched the night draw in with the constellation of stars and so did she.

During the night, D awoke in the Tor, into the tower and spoke to the white shadow on the left-hand eastern wall.

He remembered his childhood. He remembered an incident in his childhood when he thought he had witnessed his spirit leave him.

He spoke to the white shadow, *"Tell me is it true!? Did I see it!? If so, where is it! It is me, a part of me! I have been without it all my life! Now I need it to fulfill my life."*

"Yes," came a silent voice, smooth with command. *"You did lose your spirit in an accident when a boy, we have it here. Just for you. He has been at spirit druid school for 34 years! He is well; knowledgeable and equipped to be fulfilled!"*

And there, right in front of the eyes and being of D was a spirit in levitation, just floating above the solid ground, a golden cowl was worn on an average-sized young boy.

In his hand he carried a golden sword.

"What is that?" asked D.

"It is your sword. You are going to need it!"

The sight in front of him was beautiful. His face was lowered, so the eyes could be hidden, but his nose was good, a royal nose.

"Can I have it?" asked D.

"Of course! He is you!"

D accepted the soul. He accepted his spirit and for a mini-second, he knew who he was.

The voice of the white shadow carried on. *"She has seen you!, but don't fear, go and seek your army. Build an army and fight for the right to be born!"*

The shadow remained as the voice became no more. The ordinary light brought D to his senses.

He turned and went down to the apple orchard, made a small fire and had a cup of coffee.

He slept well and in the morning knew what he had to do.

*

D went into town the very next day and stood at the cross in the middle of Glastonbury high street. He watched as the place filled with people. Going to work or ready to shop. Traffic and the ordinary world took over as he saw the place come alive with alternative dressers, messengers, drug addicts or groupies for the mystical set. He looked to his left and coming towards him was a woman.

She was beautiful, for the seeming age she was, worn of life, but a woman, still. She had her eyes set on his, D looked at hers, just then an old man of the age old sect of elders in our community, stopped her and gave her a very long and large hug and cuddle.

She reciprocated and coming away from such an enrapture, sought to head towards her target.

The motion to watch was silly. It had spoilt the effect. A greyish old man of the mainstream world of second world war and welfare system had taken her out.

She approached D and said nothing. She too was gutted. But she curtseyed. To which D replied with an emphatic 'nod' of acknowledgment and respect for her sex.

They did not speak. D looked at her.

She was nice. She was dressed in a brown flowered summer dress, on her feet were a pair of black flip-flops. She did not seem to be wearing anything else. Her rump was good. She seemed to wear no knickers, as the line of her legs went to the temple of vagina and bottom, like it was a gift for the living man, a paradise of love for the lover, a portal, the landscape of her contours.

She knew it and her breasts were good, strong and sexy and pert with no bra, as they seemed to love the role of being free in a summer dress. She was ideal. She had a 'bob' cut hairstyle and her cheeks were meek, her mouth mild, red with lips of fine lines, her nose, a nose seeming to shy away from all the sensing personas of her age, as her eyes seemed hazel, a light white fire around the amazing insight to her being, is her flesh, her skin, her delicate texture of amercing touch, taking the essence of serpent and devouring the law of justice, she knew her scent, perfumed with lust, sex, passion and a feeling of being just for the law of woman, the true nature, if the world would only care.

Her hands were stealth in fingers and open. She had no baggage, no jewellery of burden, she was free to dance for D, as he looked at her thighs underneath the flimsy silk skirt, her calves leading to her Achilles heels and toes so hobbit and formed, all open to interpretation or slight.

They spoke nothing again.

He did not have anything to offer this woman. If it was her, then let her invite him to her house, for dinner and wine and to make love at the end of the night.

As he thought, she strayed, she waltzed around the cross and up the high street never to be seen.

He had missed his opportunity, but he knew by the trail she had made whilst leaving, there was more to this drag of fiery tale, than was shown in such moments of pagan ritualised sex.

She was a witch alright, but a beautiful one, or so it seemed.

That night he hung the town and met the characters, some drunk and some 'stoned', but all in a good mood and celebration for life and the living.

Amongst the revellers and levellers was a Kid 'Bull' Gawain. So, called as he was a top warrior. He was big, large in contention, with a pink tinge to his hair that night! He was bi-sexual, and kept a flow of friends as the drink would come.

Kid had a moustache, a large mustachio, looking like a Celtic moustache. He wore his hair in a Japanese 'topnotch' and on his feet he wore great big commando boots.

This was the new age, the time to dress accordingly. The protests, and battles, the system and rattles of the board, as the alternative seeks to outdo the mainstream set system to live.

*

It was time to be combat. Kid 'Bull' Gawain, liked to know he was a soldier of the new world, the new world of pay less, live more, love more – hurt less, bring a sense of a banquet to the hall and let's all drink till the dawning hours, were we have a choice in love, we all have a choice in friendship and no one in the world will stop us from fulfilling our destiny of a full life.

Very much the same as D.

So, they met and they drank and they told stories into the untold morning. But they did not make love. They were warriors and warriors had a code between each other.

"Do not envy another man's life. Do not lay another man's wife. And, do not put down another man, to make yourself feel good or look good."

They laughed into the doused night, all undressed and said, they parted ways with a yearn and in love, they promised to be again.

It was a way to heal the sorrow. It was a way to make medicine for the loss of sex. It made the teeth stop aching, the heart stop hurting and the mind come to terms with the world at large.

"Fuck it!" you would hear halfway through it, *"Fuck the world!"*

D had met his first knight. He had met the infamous Kid 'Bull' Gawain, and they were both satisfied, as to what they had been born to do.

That evening too, he met Kerry Bhutto, who was a whore of Gywnn ap Nudd.

She chose D for the night, but D noticed she was asking permission from another man. So, D stayed loyal to man and refused her will. She stormed off and lay siege to her feelings.

Whilst the man stood in the middle of the road in his shade, he looked booked, he looked taken, seeming to find a way to be thankful, was; but was not.

He had someone else, she had been his prodigy maid, with whom he had brought through for others, as he moved on to wiser and better material.

That hungover morning D went to do his laundry. He was putting his black silk shirt in, when Kerry Bhutto passed the window of the laundry.

D went out to talk to her. He was just about to say something, when she changed into a large elephant figurine, in the size of blast! Shouted, *"WE HAVE NOTHING TO TALK ABOUT!"*

At that moment, Emma Lox Gryfalcon entered the space and with her arms outstretched, as if marching, with her body in *Takt*, she opened her will, her mouth, her spirit and formally expressed, to all who were there, *"I will take him out!"*

She said it. She said it as a warning. She spoke the words to haunt the space, to show her power, her disgrace, her disappointment, she corrected the mantel of price with a treat, a gamble, a sordid shield to defend the task of woman, she was to drop him, to teach him a lesson, not to refuse!

Not in denial of offering, he was to be punished, to be tortured, cursed, spell bound, he was to be disrespected and he felt it.

The elephant and the mother whore decided to *take him out*, not to dinner; an Indian meal perhaps, but to devalue him, his being, his intention, his masculinity, his male-hood, to bring him to bear the wrath of the new days of the goddess, her path and redemption, her persecution and horrors, in torture, in refusal, her notion of option which destroys a man, a *so called* man, they saw the difference and decided to kill him; if they could, they would, if they don't, he would be castrated, eunuch, a familiar sense of opposite to man's annihilation of woman's kind, her love, he did not understand, but would, he could not understand, but shall, and the world would allow such scapegoat sacrifice, would allow the averages of balance to be played out with the coming of the prayer, for forbearance in deliverance of peace and loyalty in woman, made to struggle and sickly bear the promise of a tuxedo card poker, a rolling paper made to origami in rubbish, since the look could be man's, he played it wrong, with a will of chauvinistic bigotry, sexism and power.

D answered, *"I would not do that if I was you!"* He stood on the street with his neat approach to cleansing his wears, to speak about relationship, to honour sex, to find a truth in love, to be able to discourse, to work on, a wise approach to dilemma in scope, a challenge of option, till the sun came up and all was raw and ready to understand the worth of love, being in love, to respect his woman and see the great and goodness in her aims.

He also knew he was there to form a formidable army, which he could use to destroy.

*

Bad timing. Wrong choice. Misunderstanding and stupid sexist statement from hag witches, playing at being whores of Satan and a goddess unbeknown to everyone's spirit.

So, the battle commenced and at night D had the freedom to find her and *take her out*.

He walked with a staff. Made of ash, birch, oak, blackthorn, apple, an edge of surface to become of tree, to commit to lower grounds the vibration of task, to hear the knowledge of the bark, using the staff as a weapon to curtail, mesh, flatten, break and even kill, later on, the power of will, brought the soulful stench of demons.

Demons connected to Emma Lox Gyrfalcon, to her womb, they wanted her and she gave.

They needed her and she made her ambition known; She wanted Satan, she wanted the darkest of lords to kill the infidel, the assailant, the upstart pretender, using the will of nature, to destroy her intention to teach him a lesson, he would not be taught, he would not be held accountable, he refused to recognise the will of female justice and fought with his new power to bring them down with the opposite strengths of cutting, blowing, hurting, fouling, haunting, stalking, harassing, blasting to the earth, the soil of salt piss, brought out to condemn, when the condemnation was love, the aim was to heal love, not to rip, tear, torn, porn lust guile, she hated and she should have loved greater, more, above and so, healed the bastard!

He would die, he would be killed, but he would rise to seek better days and ways, he would be reborn, and she was using it all like a fucking hammer to slice off his ear, to hit his bonce!

Just to bleed his brain; criminal, sham, shuddered and shameful, the tools of harm to be used to climb, to be amateur with the tools of the goddess, showed her naïve, useless study, her new experience brought by selfish want, need, an aim to quell with the feelings of all powerful mighty love, she spent it like a rusty sword, and he fought back, learnt and defeated her.

He broke her jaw, over the stones of miles. He broke her will over the slab of cold, he broke her heart over the tears of sorrow lost, gone, never to recognise the blessed days of bank holidays or Christmas day or Guy Fawkes fuckin' night.

Would you believe she did him a favour, but, she knew it not. He wished to thank her for being so great, but she was fucking useless with the ancient laws in a modern consumerist's toilet sex criminal world.

She was a product. But she wished to use the power of Wicca to destroy a man.

Then, he came across a very dark and deadly demon in the cosmos of her soul.

It fucked the other one. The one from America, which he had brought with him, to meet this one, they copulated, they mated, they gave birth to thousands of baby demons and the army of armies was called upon to bring it all down.

Kid 'Bull', D and the black knight hid in her wardrobes and woke to assail the vast amount triggered to incubus, the will of purple whore, the abomination of mother, the ridden on the back of the beast bitch – triumphant in failing the kind, to insurgent the fix and give birth to Satan himself.

He would avoid Armageddon, by being re-birthed out of the Tor in Glastonbury, Somerset.

The army, so named *The knights of the round table* would fight to bring the sun back to the worship of the unspoken, the taboo, the silent and worthy backbone of life's people.

It was fought out in the spirit. The soul was the realm. They were born to be, it was so, it was legendary and the world knew of it not. Fought out in the spirit. Stand and be drinking, when the call was made by High King Peter, then they would astral plane the aether and fight demons.

Enjoy it? They killed demons.

*

The beseeching of ritual and drama was to feel the thoughts, which transferred to the mind who needed ceremony, to make the sight of love such a place, to see the sexual connections of all the brides or all the Fay or all the girls; who, now women, had at one time or another had to face the ritual of domination from a male authority, a parent, a stepfather, a brother, uncle or friend of the family who consistently manipulated the urge to be curious towards development, of a place one knows about, but seems to wait to grow, into the place of knowledge, about and the coitus of familiar love making, which is taken advantage of and damaged beyond repair, leaving the girl less the wiser and more the victim of their own need, want, feelings and the interest in why they get to the age of teenager and seem to be human in the terms of union, marriage, togetherness or a history of fun loving, kind heart oneness and bliss!

They stood into the circle from the corners of the Tor.

All four were known to D and he saw that they were dressed in dark cowls.

He say the image leave and went into the Tor to bless what he had seen and also send out a vibration of love and care for them, healing them, healing what he had seen, healing the place which damages the natural feelings and curiosity of all young ladies and a need to be sacred of guarding one's virginity.

D said, *"O My Lord, blessed are the people of the world and children who grow! I … "*, D could not think of the word which came next in the ceremony!

So, in frustration and leaving the ritual open, dashed down the Tor, hoping he would remember the rhythms of what he was doing and saying and if not, then relax, get a cup of tea and wait for it to spring eternal in his head, brain, mind.

Unbeknown to him, a man by the name of Liam had been watching him. So, Liam walked into the Tor and raising his arms shouted, *"Beseech!"*, which seemed to do the trick.

As D walked along the path, he turned to see the brightest of light gush as a flash out of the top of the Tor!

Liam, a tramp, had done it! And had received the blessing of the holy light.

All the next day, D looked for Liam, whom from then on was called Liam Brightlight!, to ask him about the experience. Liam was also looking for D, as the light had weighted on his shoulders, all the effects of many items and issues, plus the divine interest of a world-bridging healer.

Liam was pissed and in a right state when they found each other. Liam couldn't wait to give back what he felt was strange, fucking alien!, funny feeling and not quite right!

D on the other hand knew what he must be carrying and plainly asked him for it all back.

The armour, the sword, the triumph and the will to strength, was congenially given and accepted by both natures and beings, as the energy transferred to the rightful owner and they both felt a lot better, Liam not so responsible when drunk, with D realising what he had was deep, profound and even possibly righteous to the point of deferential circumstances.

*

It was a pity no one would hear of the future days of mystic power, but, one day it would heal and so itch with worthy knowledge and be reciprocal.

It was a fight of the early ocean for giant squid and water scorpion, a waste in its time between the first day of cancer and the peacekeeper caprice of the horn of plenty.

Cornucopia for the masses, but in time the masses would be legions of betrayers and ignorable, dancing with the new light.

Boogie! With the frame of consequence and justice. Pouring scorn onto the liberator of antichrist, the anecdote of peace. Forever. Ever day for eternity. Peace. Just peace.

So, they were seen to walk across the field. Somewhere near the Tor Burr.

Then the energy changed. Kid said. *"What the fuck is that?"*, in an American movie way.

They all stopped and looked. It knew, it was from the house. Then the voice began,

"She was a child of incest! She had to cure her polio, born in Versailles, Paris, she was a 'Rosemary's baby'; she walked with a lame limp, she committed incest at the age of 14 with her uncle! You know her uncle. He is 'Ponce' Mitchell from your army days!"

At that D saw the panic in the atmosphere, the delight in pleasure seeking of historical news, the 'sins of our fathers', he turned and the army turned, they swiftly moved away, ran!

D heard and answered, *"She had to heal the polio with original sin and it is amongst you now! One has to be a voluntary part of the sin to commit divine sin! She was and she did."*

"I know him!" spoke D, to the soft prevailing wind. *"What happened to him!?"*

"He was shot by the IRA!, they shot him! … he was in order; posthumous."

"He did not deserve anything! He was a rapist, a bully, a bad man!" shouted D, alone now, in the field, the offensive over.

"He was!, but all needs to be healed with the opposite effect! Do you know what it feels like to take a bullet in the head? It shatters the brain, it rips the flesh apart, it hurts like the millionth trillionth time it hurt human life and the way they have to kill!"

"So, she is his niece!"

"Correct. She is an original sin. You are defeated. You will not win. No one wins. No one wins in battle. The injury and loss is too great. She has to be healed. They chose you to do it! Heal her!"

D knew 'Ponce' Mitchell, from all those years ago. It was a disgrace, the world at large could be a fortune of sin, to destroy the wealth of goodness given by many, for so few.

D would heal her. He thought. *"She will be fucking healed!"* were his actual words.

One day, he turned his back on her in the town centre. She was pushing a new pram, the birth of Satan had been quelled, the twin was a girl, born for incest with the twin soul brother; Satan.

Labyrinth sat on the Tor Burr slab. He was there every night. He had been there for two years, watching her, seeing her, in his own words, *'Watching her flirt'*.

Now it was the time for the spirit of the ferryman to do his job. He went down to the house, found her there, entered her being and cut the wire, the umbilical which fed the child.

The boy-child died, immersed in wriggling motions of suffocation and lack of air, blood and food. Labyrinth did his job, one dark night, he killed Saturn.

Rose-Lily was the girl-child.

As D turned to look in the reflection of the shop window, Emma Lox Gyrfalcon lifted her breasts with the hands of unseen worship, she desired her fix and she got it from Tony Belem at the cross, falling out with Angelica, he needed to substitute his emotions.

At that, D flew into a jealous rage and following her to the bakery, he watched as she stood with hunched shoulders, feeling his venom, lust, jealousy, then the bakery staff asked her if she needed help, seeing the figure outside watching her, watching her tense up and look frightened, they called the police.

The police arrived and arrested D for 'Suspicion of harassment'.

*

The local 'cherry top' read him his rights, took the staff of him, which he had called a 'weapon' and drove him to the local cells, where he was charged for it and placed in a cell, due to lack of bail placement.

D sorted out a solicitor, who listened to the charge. Then it was two years full of arrests, imprisonments, remands, curfews, banishment, bails, a stretch in the maximum security of Bristol and others, all for *suspicion of harassment*.

*

Emma Lox Gyrfalcon was told she could call the police anytime she wished, especially when he could be seen in her area, nearby, walking down the street, passing her window, she used it to her gleeful will, she used it as a sadomasochistic tool, enjoying the downfall of a man, a stranger, a fool, who would think to challenge her and her connections to the dark path, to evil lessons.

During all this time, she was quiet and he did his time. Or was she?

The feelings were of sex. In prison one will self-satisfy to get by. He saw the day, the time, the afternoon, where she opened her legs to her salacious uncle, breathing lust and flames of sin.

The day was a normal day, where everyone would recognise, feel, know the day, the passing of hours, the showers of seasons, change brings, brought negotiations, when the sun beats out the pains of love for the planet beautiful Oceania earth.

So, it was spoil in the archetype, there it felt wrong, there it felt too wrong to be right for the health of love or the sense of brotherhood. They committed sin in the name of humanity, as the black sordid silt splayed over the encasement of horrid actions and putrid pillage of senses.

The shiver came over D as he ejaculated over their pure sin.

The night when all seemed dark. To no one the unseen demons, those from the acts of sin, crept amongst the living looking for victims.

They found one at an all-night-party. An orgy of rentboys and goths and amongst them was Kid 'Bull' Gawain. They all took many drugs and drank to quench the thirst of many.

Then the loving started.

As the transsexual infidels fought out the night, the two demons came upon them. With an unknown surge of pain and pleasure, they killed a man, they knifed him five times and with the bloody knife, placed it in the drunken drugged-up sleeping Kid's palm.

He awoke to find the bloody blade dripping in his hand.

He looked and saw the dead body of Tweak Liberian the 2nd.

Kid immediately left the building and walked away from the scene of crime.

When he gave himself in two weeks later, the corpse had been found rotting with maggots and stinking of dead flesh.

He was sentenced to life imprisonment.

Did he do it? Was it the transsexual operated failure from Germany, who lived downstairs and was a man being a woman; 'it' was also seen to walk and had a motive based on jealousy.

The knife wounds were left-handed penetrations and Kit was right-handed, the transsexual was left-handed.

Had the demons entered her/him; *'it'*?

They could not know. They did not see. It must have been the forensics that be.

The free demons set out for the battle to come and the 'legend of horrified' was fought.

In the field of battle were all the reincarnated knights of the round table. It seemed to be lost, when taking the field was the army of Lutherans. He led the fight to all dark sights and knocked them all back to the place of dungeon hell!

That day was the final day, the death of many. The screams and cries of sorrow were heard in the frames of all living responses to the magic realms of peace.

Whilst the pitch dark battle of sorrow heartland, D was in a high court of Britain facing charges of breach of litigation. He pleaded guilty and the court sentenced him to an unknown sentence; to be mitigated, in the maximum security prison in Bristol.

*

D entered the prison carrying his bedding, when at the first cell, a lad looked, acknowledged the 'all-right!', and D was shown his cell. Number 3.

He was amongst murderers, rapists, thieves and burglars. Petty thieves and car violators. He saw they knew him and honoured the path he walked and the sentence he had received as a political prisoner. Not sentenced, he was held at Her Majesty's pleasure.

Many nights passed with the full of the moon, seen from the cell bar windows. He used the time to rest and reassure himself that the world outside may carry on without him, but he needed it not.

His nights kept vigilant with faith and love above others.

He held sway in his cell, a single cell was arranged eventually and he waited for his case to be dealt with.

The times sat in his single man cell, having some 'burn'; cigarette tobacco, and finding himself without 'Rizla' papers.

So, he would turn to the Bible. Not to read about Deuteronomy or Ecclesiastics, but, to go back to the index pages and rip one out. Trim it down, roll it up with 'baccy' and smoke it.

'Smoking the Bible' he would call it.

He sometimes stayed and read Revelations again or Joshua, he had a liking for, as He destroyed all living tribes and blacked out the sun. All in one easy day.

Sometimes the world can get that way, deserve such payment and perhaps cut out the living creation of the so called species named human being.

It was six months later. He was awarded nine months, but one does half the sentence, the other on licence, outside in the open prison called society.

It was Judge Karol Hague who presided over the case in high court. The week of the case being reviewed, D called to find out the times, when he heard his Judge, Hague's husband, had died of a heart attack. He couldn't believe his bad luck. Sure the demons had got to his judgment, as he was to be seen to be judged by Judge Leigh, they called him the 'hanging judge', you were there in front of him guilty and you had to prove yourself innocent.

The whole time of being non-sentenced was to show Judge Hague, that he was clear of all phobias and phrenology, to be allowed to be set free into everyday society, knowing his was not a viability to all common decent people and not to be seen to re-offend.

The 'hanging judge' hummed and arr-ed his case right in front of him. The time D had done, the nights he had spent alone in a locked cell, the psychiatric report, which was compiled, sat in front of him, he seemed to brush aside. Looking at D and seeing what he did not like, he paused to give sentence, as D felt the barbed wire stretch across his chest and to sink in, giving him such a panic anxiety attack, that he could not breathe and had to move.

He saw his body move to the right, when his body stayed still. He felt the race of red blood run out of time.

And then the judge gave out his sentence.

D said, *"Sir! Does that mean I have to go back to prison?"* forgetting about half the sentence bit.

The judge looked from under his wig and over his double chin, bottle of whisky and fine bride legs shining in silk stockings on dinner dates, *"Depends if you have done your time or not"* he said all matter of fact, not really caring and waiting to sentence something a bit more juicy, perhaps coming up.

They said if Judge 'hanging' Leigh didn't like someone, he would sentence him bad.

No result there. Six years for possession. He would look at the woman and separate the charm, with great alarm, blacks and Rastafarians and Caucasian criminals would fill up the cells for £500 a week, three meals a day, no discretion on sentence and a whole lot of waste of time, in small holding prisons with uneducated low-lifers, who loved nothing but going out into the yard and showing off to the big boys, by hitting someone so hard, they would kill him.

A three-month sentence would turn into a life sentence right in front of their eyes, on a cold and damp and sordid autumn day in England.

*

There was a lot of readdressing of the criminal system to be done, but not about *why* people commit crime: 1: money; 2: women; 3: need. No, to change the way the system works once caught.

They say, *The only crime is getting caught!*

The only crime is criminal systems who 'cattle market' the spirits of wrong doing and place them in a harsher situation, which can make them worse, stronger or bitter.

The level of crime today would welcome a stretch at home with a tag on, with curfew, plus longer understanding of sentence, a year house arrest, would teach them to insult what freedom they have, and to have the right of conjugal with spouse. No man needs to be without. No man deserves to be without, except rapists, paeans and murderers. Right? … right!

Less wasted taxpayers' money and less re-offending? More room in prisons for sexual heinous criminal aspects. Send them through the system, enlighten them and then in a humanitarian commitment, put them down, on full show of the inter-net with cyanide injection.

Do God's work, he needs you to.

D left without his payment of reassessment; £68. No one took the responsibility of paying his well earned 'getting out' clause, so he put his winter clothes back on in the heat of summer and walked back to Glastonbury.

She was selling up and moving back to France. He sat on a bench, without his shirt on and shared a spliff with Liam Brightlight, the scruff and disturbed brummel.

Emma Lox Gyrfalcon saw him and looked, grinned and carried on driving. He just reached out for the spliff.

The day was conclave cumulus crackdown and she wanted to change her life for the way she left the place, it was now the time to save her soul.

So, he did. But he lost his. He would die. She would survive and bring up her children the right way, as she would not be atrocious in moral and virtue.

The spirit sword was *hex-calibur*, grew. God's sword. Given to one who uses the sword to better humanity.

D held it for many years and needed a woman to heal the world. As is shown all fucked up pieces in Glastonbury were marked, marred, branded or immersed in Saturn.

All woman have endured the incestuous raping victimisation, just for being a beautiful girl.

They could, but ignored the spirit sword of Excalibur. So, D saw the sword go to waste and he needed to use it for something; so he used it to set Emma Lox free from the bondage of her sin.

*

Stood in the Tor late at night; once again listening, seeking the quest as to which was possible to acclimate on a foul windy, rain soaked, pitch black, solemn sad sensing to be comforted with enlightenment or task.

The speaking sound inside the mind. The voice way out in the mists of time. A musing of all types of isolation intake from the place beyond the way taken below, the choices made by the way below and separating the stealth of option, would allow for the clear crystal speech of another elemental world.

It said, *"Look out of the eastern portal"*, quite simply, succinct, factual.

He did. He felt others there. Over by the edge, some people had gathered to sleep out and gaze at the stars. He felt their eyes on him. He saw the retina of black hue questioning, judging the possibilities and not really expecting anything.

As D moved to the east portal a great bright white light shone on the concrete and lit up the larger arch of St Michael's tower.

D listened. He listened for the propeller of the helicopter; just skirting about the Tor, having a night time look. He heard nothing. He listened for anything which or who shone the light, so bright it seemed to be aesthetic in nature, impossible to be, so close, so sharp, so bright!

D saw the clear cream purity of the element and then saw the black eyes of the campers on the Tor stare straight into the happening, which made D weary of committing himself to the capsule of bright effervescent light; instead he stood, held his motion and waited for what would happen next!

Insecurity had got the better of him. The lack of faith. The need to be in the peace and quiet of a sacred place so he could manoeuvre in such ancient happenings and learn.

It slowly as before; coming, returned to the place which D could not speak of, as he had stayed out of the light, out of seeing the place it came from and with wonder and disappointment went over to the small group of people and asked them what they had seen.

They said, *"Nothing."*

D knew he had missed an opportunity in his journey in and out and away from the Tor, which may have shone the gracious light into his being and through the depth of change, turn him into a white haired, white bearded wizard! Right there and then!

"Become who you are!" the voice might say …

He had not and he left the tower black as the night.

None the wiser and lacking in the belief which allows the negative to say deep down in the bowels of hell, the development of the solar plexus, *Those people had been put there for a reason and that reason was to spoil what you had worked for* and sacred in nature; being interrupted by a world beyond phenomenon and miracle.

Even the status of drive which allows for a holy light to seek out the terms and strange nature of something super, which changes the world for service to, can be damned in the corporeal opulence of all indignant dreams.

*

D journeyed about the country, looking for the place to die. He died, in Scarborough on a bench, without anything in his life. He had a can of 'Tango!', but he worried how his hair looked, as the white pony-tailed long hair was all over the place.

When one is ill, one forgoes the look of vanity, the tidy edge of respectability.

He felt himself die inside and lay down on the bench and shit himself.

In the spirit, he was deep in the chasm of the lair of Satan's evil. He had been received by the scapegoat angel; Azazel. Who had spoken about meeting D again.

He was shown the lair and to where he was exalted. Raised up and mounted with braces, about his face and genitalia. Told to listen and the golden hooves would be heard coming towards him.

He listened. He could not do otherwise. He was crucified in an exultant Vesuvius man. He watched himself in the corner, with no doubt Azazel's attention, calling him the *'Watcher'*.

The time came to meet his maker and seeing the horned beast approach, he saw the other swinging state of a naked Emma Lox Gyrfalcon. Ready to be gynecologic-ally d-womb-ed and set free from the bondage of a satyr: Satan.

*

D was opened, his chest, to show his wounds and heart. His life was belittled and the effect was cast-rational. He saw the empty chasm as Azazel was seen to take notes, seemingly for the knowledge of Satan's methods and why.

Until the dawn raised the light did D see his sacrifice.

He belittled the whole effect by using the fashion dress sense of a whore and blew kisses to the surmountable resurrection of all information, as regards the whereabouts of God's healing sword: *hex-calibur*.

Emma Lox, was but little meat. And D was a small turd on the surface of the concrete ground in a play park.

They beat him and threw him out; away down the abyss.

They could not even be bothered to take him seriously.

It had been the intention of D to 'deceive the deceiver'; and he did. He was blinded in the spleen and made to look raped, sodomised with a streak of mercury running through his body.

Emma Lox Gyrfalcon was rescued and was seen to be empty of sin, as she left, with consorts, by the main exit; ushering her out with a pale allure.

Azazel was pleased to meet the 'Watcher'. He enjoyed the display of sacrifice and scapegoating brilliance. They would never meet again.

They never found the whereabouts of Excalibur, being the 'scabbard'; D knew it was safe in the hands of the ancient wizard Merlin of Promethean light. Who, hoping to take out of the human spirit that which brings evil and murderous intentions.

*

The greatest job in the world was assigned to D, all he had to do was make love to a woman and the rest would be healing through consciousness and faith.

But, alas, no woman and no healing of the sovereignty of the vein lay-lined structure of the aboriginal shaped land of a pregnant witch of Britain.

With Scotland as its psychosis. The heart in York, Yorkshire. The bowels; London, England and the fish's tale; Cornwall. The child of Wales points over beyond the rebel isle of Hibernia to the Americas.

At Newquay in Cornwall. D sat looking at the dark clouds of a dark warm night and asked the whole of the sky, the whole of life, the whole of history; just about everyone and anything and then in his mad prayer ask for the holy God to apologise to Emma Lox, for what she had had to go through and surely it is not her fault the way she is?

D started to shout it! No one about. He shouted through his lonely whisky breath.

"I THINK YOU SHOULD APOLOGISE TO HER!"

Then out from behind the clouds came a light. It shone with a sense of words, one word: *NO!*

Where was the moon that night? Was it the moon dashing from behind and using a gap to breathe her light?

D did not know. He took it for the light of God and the answer to all destinies which take the form of weights and measurement in a plan needed to judge the connections as to who or why and when, but still using all life's actors to lead the way and show the world is a strange place, God works in mysterious ways, there is more to life and there is something more than ourselves which is more powerful and has an agenda for all individual living souls who come along the manifestation of embodiment and through even limitation seek to know the answers to one's destiny instead of finding out once the fatal elements have taken their toll.

D saw his life down at his feet and felt the pain of it all. He then wondered *why?*

Why was his destiny in such a way to be a failure, hurting, seeming to do wrong? evil? and has tested his faith in the belief of love for all mankind, as he let go of mankind, having seen it all, in the world of the humanitarian.

He stood on the Tor burr, one cold winter's night. Looking down on the town/village, as the people went about their safe and secure chores, a way to be good and clear in a world of danger and destiny's fate. D looked out from his hooded black cowl robe, leaning on his staff, with the look of an alien friend, who had seen the 'maker' and having paid the price of life for it. He was proud. A full scale galactic warrior, before his time, and example to the world, as the only way to change some aspects on this planet is to sacrifice one's life for the purpose of another. He thought of the time when he was ill. Living in a caravan, burning fires and smoking pot, but alone and fighting the fate of his darker destiny, arrived by something or someone to change his life for the worse, in harm, to destroy the fibres of an intrinsic connection to the faith and belief in the hereditary journey of humanity and the human being. He was so ill. He could not eat. He went down to the well and collected his own water. He carried his own water, until he had to sit down on a wall and cry.

His pain, his illness, the nausea, the loneliness, all played a part in storming his senses, as he started to let the crying go, louder, it hit the air, he moaned and mourned in his heart, he could only double up, in a release from a lifetime's illness, which did not have any *there there* to soothe him, love him, sympathise with him, hold him, hug him, help him. The world was at home. The world was warm and safe and did not know a human being was crying of great sad loneliness and illness, outside in the cold dark night of a snowing winter; alone, with no one there.

That he could not eat. He could sleep and did. To sleep was to live in another dimension, to which he could be the *'Watcher'*, and see his hands in front of him, as the imagination played out the will of 'seeing', and saw the outcome of abstract wisdom.

The reasons to be and the reasons to be for another, seemed to be the reason for his howling hurt coming close to the demons of darkness and seeing them allow for the playing out of sorrow, whilst the mainstream of the world had to be unaware of the possibility of such a living destiny being unknown, unheard and not to be felt by anyone on the planet earth.

He had fought the dark side and the dark side watched him suffer for it.

*

He decided to journey back to his birth, childhood and early teenage years to find the answer.

He was born on the 2nd of February 1959, in a small suburban house, on a semi-detached estate called Acorn. The name of the grove was Mildred. He was the third child in his family and his mother saw to it; he would be seen to be a socially artistic student.

His father was a labourer's social man, who everybody loved and accepted his company wherever he was, the social club, the local football stadium or the representation of the liberal arts, as his mother was a painter and knowledgeable about the history of art.

He was brought up to see the world through the eyes of himself. First impressions are always good. Seen, the world would be acceptable to the interest of skill, talent and respect.

*

It has brought to my attention over the years that the human soul is of goodnesses and badnesses we need to survive our time here. To be great or to be evil, is to go to the extremes in the balance of light and darkness, where enlightenment and wise knowledge can be received respectively from both.

He went to the local primary school and excelled in the expected adaptation of the social curriculum presiding in the classroom spending most of his time reading, writing, enjoying mathematics of the day, in geometry, algebra and Pythagoras' theorem.

He passed his 11+ with flying colours and went to a grammar school for boys. He was liked, loved and respected by his peers, teachers and parents. Who saw the vestiges of a famous person residing in his talent and skills.

They saw to his potentiality and made way for a career and an inheritance as soon as he finished university, where he could live, without payment and force his career in the direction of his possible genius.

No, he didn't and no, he wasn't!

He was mapped out to be on the heap by the time he was 12. He excelled in mischievousness and malady, pertaining to chaos in the specialised suit of differentiation.

He was recognised by the Christian law givers, to be a *devil*. He was marked out as a target for the salvation of the world, if he was placed in bondage or unmistakably put down.

He lived and looked directly at the strict and stoic approach to life. All about him the dark ages of an ancient book was ruling the mindless beings of others. Written in Israel, it was to be brought up in the modern day world of colloquial Britain.

If you wore the sight of the label of the might to fight, then the rules changed for the worse, as the authorities did not like the individual to be thinking outside of the box, never mind allowed, but to be seen to differentiate and deviate from the 'norm' was not accepted, unless you were seen to be a horror, needing punishment and chains to remain in line with the everyday hourly abundance of school, church, rules, reasons, lessons, obedience, in a triptych crystalline; all important set rules to the way, the look, the need and the honourable comfort of a future, set out for better things and good things; 'things' being the operative word to seminal solutions to freedom, majestically unruly for the self-respecting person, who is not capable of murder, sex rape or war against another for the sake of hate.

*

D looked at his life, at his boy, at his moment of disaster or triumph! Which was it?

He looked at all the moments, he looked at his first kiss, his first shit, his first football goal, the fights and the nights alone, sad, somewhere? His bed. He saw his bed. He saw the sad way he walked to the window and looked out on a sad winter's night and seemed to be waiting for something? Someone?

He felt his disgrace for the terrible way he was, inside and looking out of suit with the hope of a 'drape' coat and a good pair of 'brothel creepers'. But, alas he was silly, bound in enslavement, wearing the clothes bought for him, the haircut which killed his very commitment in spirit to the ancient knowledge of the kingdom of magi-ck and a need to seek and find the beauty of one person, as he knew the language, the sense of joy, saluted by the all mighty dark spirit, which was the fighter of sin, of hate, being the true ominous feeling of a better world around us all.

You don't have to look good in order to be good. To look wild is still as good as being good for the goodness of God.

Scruffy, he loved to feel free.

He had fallen in love with Sarah Jane and he would stand at the window and watch her go to school.

He called on her and asked her out. They went out to play. Eight years old that day.

D danced and pranced and showed her his skill of entertainment. His Gene Kelly, his Jerry Lewis, his Vaudeville act, his able tact, his dream, his Broadway doodle dandy!, his 'Just William', and she laughed and sighed, as she fell in love with the song and dance-man in front of her, singing Jolson and *Mammy!*, spinning on his heels and 'Hoofing'.

He was a product of American TV and walking on the moon. He was a musical front-man and a star shining in the light of the early dusk, as the day turned slightly into night.

Sarah Jane had to go in. She did. And they never saw each other again.

Over the next week 'just William' went to school and on seeing the mighty rod asked, *"Where is Sarah Jane?"*

The rod answered, *"She has moved to Australia with her family! Didn't you know?"*

The mighty rod just looked, on passing and walked on into his own destiny, knowing 'those' things could be written and you had to be careful as to what kind of story you got.

The heart of D sank, rose into his mouth, spewed the arteries, danced about his plexus and ruined his manhood with one foul swoop of the brush with his destiny. The first heart transplant, at such a young age. Was to prove fatal and nothing in life could ever prove to heal or put things right in the face of his own, when life had so much to offer and the offerings seemed to be human hearts dug out with black obsidian stones.

He went home with a depression the size of a hurricane. His father called for haircuts! He went along and got himself a full crop, a skinhead, a hedgehog cut. No hair, just bristles, and still his 'horns', his cowslip was predominate.

He stood at the window and sang his lullaby, saying goodbye to Sarah Jane.

He stood and defied his parents, when they cajoled him into concentrating on his life ahead.

His father took a full-scale dislike to the boy's angst and sorrow, *so he hit him.*

He hit him about the head with a cricket bat. A walking stick really, but it felt like a cricket bat.

The cricket bat hit the left-hand side of the brain, which was the side of detail, words, logical, numbers, measurement, recall [past], grammar, patterns, literal meaning, content, name recall, time awareness, components, science, maths. Things not really needed by D for his life, but later on, it would all tell to be needed to see the most interesting side of all about himself.

To recall, to seem logical, it made him stop in his living experienced steps.

He felt the horror of mind, body and soul. He seemed to desire the need to move away from the dis-function of his life, that violence, aggression, spur of the moment hate, had caused.

*

He knew then he was brain damaged. He knew then he had to go into that place, where the world seemed against him, his mind only wanted irrational artistic wildness. But he had to see the reason for his hope, his emotional will to be free, when he had limited his options, taken away the preservation of himself, and let go of the damaged metropolis called sanity, in his hard cranium, his soft fallowed mind, his tissue of breathing pumping gristle.

All the rest were there. Holistic, pictures, intuitive, shapes, motion, imagination [future] intonation/emphasis, accents, abstract meaning, context, face recognition, spatial awareness, objects, art, music.

It had all burnt him out. Sizzled his pressure. Taken all the world of a freedom and slapped many an hour of the day about the face and sent it home to religious countenance. He had seen the fire blaze in the right-side of his brain, he worked it day and night, he abused the other side, the dead side, he ridiculed his opposite and framed his special being in the world of stardom, images of grandeur, an untouchable world, surrounded by mystic men and play frames, sex and drugs, the whole nine yards, then the death, the overdose on the hill, the last piss take by a creator God 'Sod', the ditch dirt brethren of all mounting desires to be, someone, something, anything famous, notorious enough to warrant infamy, a world to know of the stupid cunt he had become, because of this and because of that!

What a fucking selfish human being D had become and he knew, a fucking cricket bat fucking hurt. It killed him that day. It smashed his true self, away to the world of the dead, the edge of the river of Hades, to bemoan the devil and the fires of hell burnt in his stomach, his mind, his way, his ethic, to burn in hell, to burn on the cross, to loss; allowing the world to lose, to damn the creative species, the need to develop and have great faith seemed to be all far away in the distance, whilst stood in the middle, watching the lonely figure shape and shadow, its silhouette damned to the road of purgatory, someone somewhere had to do something about it.

They crucified him for being a devil but they played right into the hands of Satan and sent his spirit to hell. Well done you archaic Christian fanatical imbeciles. To free him from the bondage of evil, you perpetrated evil and sent his soul into the hands of the one from which you wished to free him.

One does not go to Jesus through abuse, violence or any other way of exorcising the demons within.

"Do as you will, but do not harm another"; that's how you do it.

D took a packet of cheese and onion Walkers crisps and sat on a bench in a park.

He thought about the nativity play at primary school.

He remembers sitting in class, at around the age of primary, and a teacher, Mrs Clark, came into the classroom. She spoke. She said, *"Where is DT?"*

D held up his hand. The teacher then said, *"We want you to play a part in the nativity play at Christmas, would you like to do it?"*

D knew nothing about it. Nativity? What?

The story of the birth of Jesus Christ.

Okay, what part?

Jesus! Joseph! Mary! A shepherd! A king!

"We would like you to play the innkeeper," she said. *"He turns Mary and Joseph away."*

He turns them away? What kind of bastard is that! Maybe he is a villain. Maybe he is a monster!

"No!" she read his mind, *"he is a landlord, who does not like the situation of two travellers on a mule, looking for a room to give birth to a child."*

Okay, thought the young actor, he is a landlord, who had an issue with couples. What does he do? What will he have to say?

"He says," said the teacher, looking at the earnest boy, looking for a part, wanting to start to help the play. Holding up a lantern, *"No room!"*

"That's it? No room?"

He holds up a lantern, because of the darkness of night, it must be late, when they arrive looking for a room and says, with direction and power, *"No fucking room!"* Okay, thought D the innkeeper.

"Cut out the swearing and you have the lines."

"No room!"

To their faces, to their dismay, to their pregnant stomach, the tears and the shame, to the crowd, the audience and the watching teachers, to God and Jesus, *"No room!"*

Where? thought D.

The travellers slept in a barn and the baby Jesus was born in a stable with the star seeking him out and showing the three wise kings of the east where the almighty divine saviour of the world was to be born; God himself.

D had finished the crisps and put the wrapper in a litter bin. He was laughing at the intense sight of his portrayal of the 'stuck up' famous bigot, the innkeeper of Bethlehem.

It was a bit part, but it was the most important role in theatre.

It was time to hit back at his personal darkness. He was going to fight the destiny of his soul, and bring it to bear, the brunt of freedom and the responsibility of self – survival, in a world of great spirits, carried by sad people, because of the system of society's limitations and achievements in the early stages of the years 2000 AD, the crèche, the rebel child, the first steps to changing the possibility of annihilation, to the possibility of freedom and great spiritual insight into themselves and their creative gift.

Cheese stinks, but can be various and taste mighty.

D takes his staff and wraps it about the megalith Saracen stone. It hurts the target. The target; daemons. It smashes their jaws, dislocates their spirits. He strides the blow with a maximum amount of strength, plus purpose and application.

The earth shudders, as the world of haunting darkness screams with sheer disturbance; hurt.

The evil world of the dark underworld of horror and sin with a paved sense of justification for abuse and ridicule hits back.

The personal vendetta of a life ridden with fear, at last, sees a way to penetrate the ranks of shadows and finally knock the fate of nightmares back over the threshold, into voidable nothingness and malicious malevolence disdained.

To wake up to the Christian devil. A made up reason for wrong. The mind is strong. It can imagine the world and the atmosphere will become. We create our own religion. We create the sins within, the helplessness which destroys our fear with fearful acts of heroism and defiance. We understand the world through the thoughts we see in our minds. We are trapped in the imagination, we are lost in a world of creative will, a free will, to choose. We choose to understand the world of evil through the manifestation of a beast, a devil, a name; a given name; Satan.

We think it is ruled by. All wrong doing in the world is because of the master of evil.

We have panicked. We have sought out the reasons. We know of nature and the sight of devouring beasts. But, we don't assign ourselves to the nature of devouring because we are planetary, it is because we are the children of God and God has an enemy called the devil.

What a world to be in. Ruled.

So, D wishes not to be. He fights back with the tools of arcane alchemical esoterical ambivalence and wins the day on the essence of threat, warning, pressure, stress, migration, decay, decadence and above all tells the created world of horror to go back to the lands of nowhere, soil the sand footprints and leave the mind to bathe in the recursive assurance of all being well and loving and fine.

*

And then the devil hits back.

D cannot heal the world no more, he has broken with his truce.

And finally *x-calibre* is taken back, grown in size, age and experience, a Gemini betrothed, a bi-gender. The lovers. masculine and feminine. A creative euphony. A psyche.

Given unto the higher ground. Offered back to the white spirit. Taken away from the lesser worth and quickly removed from abuse, sexist misunderstanding, a total amnesty for the days of exile, interred by the wearer, the scabbard, the lover. To be castrated, to be spat upon was the everlasting time, could be the spit of bad breath, the slime and bile of hell.

Could be! Was.

Glastonbury is a Christian ground, any other context is playing.

Christianity killed their only son, they let him die for being a devil, when the address is of Merlin being the son of a demon. Moving away from sin, out and into the realm of good, where one can fight the place from which one was incarcerated, one could be slaved and masticated.

Merlin wrote the story of Arthur. God writes the story of Christ and Satan.

D wants to put a full stop on the lot!

The mind plays tricks on the soul and the mind is the trick to which we owe our insight to the world of unknown, unseen, unfathomable principles of life archetypes and worship.

Let's make it up as we go along. Just to make some sense of this place of peace and universal hologram.

Is it really all we think? Is it really what we know? Is it the way it is? Do we not always deserve better?

The mind of D caved in and his actuality died on the 19th of July 2007.

He heard the screaming of harpies and the ugly world sent to him to worship and give thanks.

He felt good. He felt honoured to be a soldier of light, but suicide is when you can't think no more. The mind just slides into hell. It gives up to the world one fights all the time, keeps at bay, turns the page of many destinies.

He had been given a bad light. A bad pitch. He was born to be wrong, but fought it with all his might. He drank and took drugs, danced and shagged like a king, just to keep his life away from him. He didn't want it and it didn't want him.

The only gleaming light was *they were wrong about him*. So was he.

In the blue light of darkness he was taken to see the world of dreams, above he floated, in the feeling, beneath the standards looking up, some carving on, doing there studies. D could see the array of red, caught in the whereabouts, the dark blue smooth tipped, lush cream colouration of bare love, of schismatic magic, of a taste to be respected, to be seen and hoped for, a true exigence to the spiriting sanctum and the calling of a galactic peace. A joy. A bliss. With the meaning to *come between*, a referee referendum refrained ordained.

An *x-calibre* would work in the extremities of the spirit world; a wizard's piece, a tool of power.

But in the real world, this world, which is made by humans to egotist on the planet; for reasons unbeknown to nature, free from roots, but tied to the bacteria of diseased epidemic.

The sight of the dark purple-blue night, the waves of e-sense. D was taken above all of those; on, on, till he saw the distance – *from them*.

He was taken to a higher place. He was immaculate.

In life he looked through the vortex, having looked worn and torn. He was spiritually facing the evil of life with love, the tool of love, to defeat the beast, the whore, all damnation and slander.

He remained with love. Loved the world. He loved because he could. He used love, like a sword, to cut down the penitence of injustice, the falsehood of living, the judgement of people's opinions, the theatre of jokes and life affirming *bullshit*.

He could not hate these little people. He loved the whole world and 'came' all over it.

*

He could not cause phenomenon and heal a cancer or the ills of children. He knew that phenomenon would wake up the so-called leaders of all nations and stop them from being warmongers and seek to respect peace.

He yearned for a woman/girl, but she was destroyed, she was put down, she was in revolution and she was feminist.

But, she found out, it would all lead to hex-calibre.

A fixed feminine earth.

Taurus the bull and his wife; a scared cow.

That is the world, the planet, the way. It is the reproduction and worship of quality, food, drink and women. This quantity is a shambles, a sham and makes the world an untidy place. No respect for chaos, no respect for the joy of variation, the spice of life.

Most people turn out shit. They have no purpose.

DT, D, Deadly, Decca Dent Peters changed into Drui Thorn and wept his heart to sleep with joy. He was home and now it was time to use the powers of the universal love sword.

He had been in his cocoon and was now a glorious butterfly, colourful, beautiful, free and oh! so ready to help all the children of humanity.

*

A colossal freeborn written harvest. An untaxed catalyst, ill-matched.

The waking Jungian, scoffing of a manifest solar day. Lifesaving canvas of distributivitymisconfiguration, circumnavigationally, confidingness of half-breeds, a disowned behaviouristic consubstantiation is non-transferable.

Less and less, a tribe's self-doubt, begrudged, refutable; lateral bulging, one step into an unforgivable execution, prefabricated by feud; being hard-hearted.

Fabian's web. Verdict; telegraphically flunky, undiscovered, insignificant, a fictitious servant summary.

This loss of time, this use of rime, thus then, 'the terms' would be due, as all reasons are seen to be measured by a ruling, a certain passage to substantiate, less or more are the scales of life.

Shown to be, only for the one-trillionth member, the holy show of takings, become mighty in the light of night. Brought by sex. Only sex. Sex is the life. The aim. The purpose. The all and everything in emotion of a humanity.

Losing the way in the only way to go. The duration of death. The drop in blood, a singing tide, total to a bridging momentous, living in shades, in shadow. Bow to the holy school. Pay homage to the higher spirit, the great golden white light.

Then the place of magic would be true. Told. Unbelievable.

Making a way out. Prejudicialness objectification; objectivity. Justify seasick transubstantiation. Subfusc dioxin foxy unverified, furtive, debunked, vagrant.

Brought out by all furtiveness, derailment, self-justification, bound to close all boundary, slipping through the trails of time and minds demented; a fantastic probable toxic waste radio activity. Music.

Unable to transfer. To go to and come back out of. A trip to heavens and back, also, there it would be right to wrong the vision of peace, brought by forgiveness, settled in a passage of respect, held to the masters and their honoured goal. Self-harm.

Human life hurts itself. And it should not. Unless we are pointless and are getting away with it.

*

Provoke the science and develop the will. Adapt the style and strength of soul, bring presents, a gift to live, *for what?* What's the reason to discover? To find out? What? *The truth?* The truth is; We are a falsehood, and wish to remain in transcendentalism.

Hanker to the motion of phenomena and we will be crowned. We are dust. But, we are angels.

We are wrong, but, put it right. Start with a child and grow to be fine. All grow to be full of shit!

Different, when they are not. Opinionated, when they think the same. Differentiate, when they seem to live a system's societal problem.

Change through imagination. The world becomes true. The truth is further away in the recesses of the subconscious with a sense of confused chaos, but final.

Live as the planet is, not as the you think you should. Knob.

The pride of gone. To be and not be. Lived. Did. Was. No necessary sentimentalisations or grinning vestiges of powdered façades.

He tires himself off the page, the white fucking A4, he drops the line, the seeking of death's dead dying dirge mundane moribund rigour mortise and the laughing livers.

He pukes and the spirit becomes known, notorious, infamous, famous, fine and mighty.

It is only known. It is seen in great argument. When the world needs, it is there.

It can have a name.

Slowly, Drui Thorn, bathes in the darkness, seeking solace, with his loving, breathing, respecting squaw. Then he is happy. Then the world looks different. There, we can share thoughts of better things and suited situations, and earn! Be social and graft!

He knows he is different, so he wonders what is next. An axiom.

*

To take the time to create these things, also the numbers worn, would mean a lot to the imagination of the past, to rebuild, something which might not have been there, due to the hemisphere and environment, one is brought up in.

Who knows what can happen in life. With little opportunity and substance. The way forward is to wish, to pray, to hope for, not to know, to take for granted, to achieve is the science of the strongest will and the way to achieve is to put oneself first.

The way of this world is non-representation of being, but a feeling to know the needs of others, and making sure they are aware of the scope of eternal life has the same understanding, so that no one goes without, goes first or takes the lead due to principle or commerce.

It is destine-rial, it is true. It is to be and will always function fast willed in bliss and joyful inception of infinite perception with love for a human child.

There is no need or greed and will always sleep in dreams of pheromone bathyscaphes.

The energy, the life force only ever goes so far, then it freely moves into chaos.

In chaos, the flavour – taste is good – in there you see the creative information you need to share, irony, people, spirits and a goddess.

It all looks punk, scruffy, unfinished, unruly, beautiful and totally passive anarchy.

'Fatheadedness forgivably used' by Gold-plated, would be the soundtrack.

*

Antidisestablishmentarianism and self-absorbed cross-breeds behaviourally sure-footedly,

Justifiability, the American bison; mammal genus: subvert.

Evaluationally psychokinesis, signified collectivisation as an erecter aeroacoustic prestidigitation graveside.

Hunter-gatherer, nuclear-free, reverification, survivability, fossiliferous and ultraconservative.

Non-recoverable, free-living; feather-brained counter-intelligence
Manoeuvrabilities
abstainer
stratospherically
theological doctrine
disposition
provoking a
discoverer.

*

To Thorn in his *'Book of Shadows'*, all this would mean: Someone who wishes to find the way in the world, which was destroyed due to progress and war.

Which cannot be found or replaced because the world does not know of it. It has been eradicated, hidden in the conclaves of a history of medicinal blindness.

Sorrow seeps into the veins of blood, soils the divine pleasure of humanity, its purpose on a planet.

Without pressure or duty, then we should chill, will the preserve of love, to teach respect, care, childhood and never have to feel nausea for multifunction.

Preserve the discerning Praesidium.

In the summer months of a heat; hot days of the months of June, July – the tribes gathered and together they opened a new illegal site.

The double rainbow shone over the shoulders of Thorn and he knew the dangers and the friendship of dogs. A Germanic bitch called Diamond was his protector.

He received a letter from the stranded Pasha. She talked of being unable to socialise and wanted out of where she was and could he come and get her.

He did and the reunion was short-lived.

She did his head in! To Pash, Glastonbury was a male harem of studs, for her. She threw herself into the possibility, immediately, without considering the feelings of Thorn.

He nearly strangled her.

He went outside and offered himself up to the laws of the goddess and Lucky Jim heard his calling.

Lucky Jim came out of his caravan to challenge Drui, so Drui 'smacked' him one on the chin.

He reeled about and found his footing by holding on to the bars of the internecine of his door.

He then saw the open armed Drui screaming to the goddess to punish him for his misdemeanours. So, Lucky Jim kicked him in the heart.

His heart stopped and he was ready to fall.

Just then, a voice in the wilderness spoke, *"Someone move! Pash move!"*

She did. The heart of Thorn beat with a soiling of lust and desire for Pash and her fruits.

He had been damaged, so, he retired to his caravan.

During the night; the pain, which came from just below his heart was excruciating.

A voice told him to sit in the pain. He did and the pain loved his attention.

He then felt the pain rush to his heart and open his chest cavity. The light shining from his breast was personal, private, but was felt by neighbours and dogs, howling and barking!

He then heard the voice say, *"Sit up!"*.

So he did.

The pain went straight into his stomach, his solar plexus collected the pain, soothed it with a chemical drug, enhancing peace, a bliss so beautiful, so kind, so loving and sacred, Thorn enjoyed the immense thrust of joy, supreme juices, cream delight of a creative wish, to light up the pain of darkness, with a soft caressing light of alchemy.

He lay down and felt no more heartache.

He awoke and felt his heart beating. But, it seemed to be beating below his arterial muscle, as if he had two hearts and the one below seemed to work.

Supernatural. Weird. He shocked himself in knowing the truth about magnitude, magnificence, multifaceted – mutation – a mutant.

He was a *mutant!*

The time changed, the world seemed changed.

He looked out of his caravan window and saw a girl walking into the dust-filled path of the site. She looked at him. Her eyes dark and slight. He looked at her and together they saw the earth's movement, seeming to slide and move plates of atoms.

It moved like it was moving clockwise, anticlockwise, turning, ellipse.

It moved collectively, so she saw the messiah, 'The enlightened one', she saw Jerusalem gods, in her undeveloped life, she was true, she saw true, seeing solar lights, galactic spheres with drugs on her mind, the hallucinatory vantage of dust bowl highs, with love peace calm.

It was all edible and it all lasted a microsecond in space-time. A light.

It was a crippled message, an esoterica electrical eclectic motion.

The heart beat so it scared him to death.

*

Drui Thorn was full bearded. Hirsute. His hair suited him. It was turning white and long down his back, which curled into ringlets on rainy days. He wore an Aztec patterned poncho; a blanket, which he made himself, which kept him warm around winter fires. The soup kitchens supplied the rest, T-shirts and pants. Although, he went commando when it came to undergarments.

On his feet he wore a really good pair of boots. Everlasting, eternal, until they too wore out through too much walking, he would replace them with another pair of jackboots, Paraboots, Timberlands or cowboy boots.

He hardly washed and felt the senses of the ambrosia of Avalon seeming to scent all over his body *pong!*, but lovely, for those who need an aphrodisiac for dinner or a really good fuck for lunch, brunch or breakfast, letting go of inhibition, orgasm, the mighty will to see, hear and feel all spirits beyond the line of dimension on the earth's surface.

The height of sexuality with the spirit of an x-calibre was mighty high. It meant three times a day for Thorn to 'come' at will, 'master the batting' and quicken the feelings of love for all.

The world is created by the mind. The mind is powerful. It is the umbilical cord to all unity and is connected to the free will of imagination. E-magic-nation.

Whatever human life thinks or creates or imagines or wants and needs to be, will be.

It is all subject to survival, adaptivity, overcoming, the will to manifest in the bodily assumption of dialect, truce, passion, desire and will power.

If you need to hate, then you are right to do so, only you have a right to right the hate.

By loving what you hate.

With powerful guilt human life makes love to what it hates the most.

Unknown, difference, opposite – *when we all choose to be what we are.*

*

We like our choices. We like to be that way. The way you choose as an individual, until someone else is the same, then the union of mass effect makes another who is different 'not look so good'.

Everything in the human mind has a reason. A purpose, until in the wrong mind, the world goes to war, to hate, to murder, to hurt, to revenge, to misunderstanding, then the mind is a battlefield of horror and hatred, blasphemy and sin, everything is 'not' then. Its exegesis.

The heart is ruled, but senses the instinct, knowing the true answers.

The intelligence of the genitalia needs the opposing sex to turn it on. Then it thinks wild, fantastic, kinky, excessive thoughts of love.

Drui Thorn was a Kaprian; a Capricorn on the cusp of Aquarius. He was very humanistic, rebellious and free minded, but he could be aloof, excessive and perverted, but he always knew the sign carried water and to bring enlightenment to the masses of his people always seemed his intention.

He was a Chinese year of the wolf, '59, although the year of the dog, he felt more like an ancestor from the days of wilderness and was known to be a 'lone' one.

He was a red crystal sky-walker in Mayan Astrology. He was. He related to 'Luke', but felt more like a 'hand solo', although he knew he could have been going down the dark side like anarchy, but refrained from serving evil, because, he knew that to be good and better was beneficial in the long run, as goodness always triumphed over evil.

As a red crystal Aquarius wolf sky-walker, his universal signature, he had them all tattooed on his body. Although 'it' was ashes, 'he' was to be found in the higher mind of thought.

For assurance, to be recognised in life. When he travelled in the universal galactic sphere, as a spirit entity, separate from his body, a dark cowled figure for effect, from the deep blue realm he came, he needed the knowledge of his status, in university intelligence, combatant areas, to pass from room to room, hall to hall, realm to realm in the great passageways of godhead.

To frequent the harems of worship in the goddess temples of oracle and whore.

Breathing in the apocalypse of self. A destruction of the fibres of living. To see the abuse of childhood, damage the outcome of life, a life, would be to survive and stand in the vortex, knowing the other side was ill, wrong, bad, done, and the side of spirit was always in a state of denial or paranoia, then the place of comfort and will, would be to seek the place of self, which is separative from life, spirit, death, action/reaction and apply the one true course of a being; being nothingness; as the time and place is not known, is not accepted, is unruled, but shared beyond belief, helpful towards momentary joy, seeking souls fecundity and phantasmagoria transmogrification-al metamorphosis miracle

Achieved. An example. Exemplary?

Who knows.

Do you?

Drui Thorn was born the same day and at the same time as the plane crash, which killed Buddy Holly, J.P. Richardson [Big Bopper] and Richie Valence [La Bamba!].

A fourth person was to be on that fateful plane that day, but didn't get on it.

Do you know who that was?
It was ... Elvis Presley? Little Richard? Jerry Lee Lewis? ... *No.*
It was ... *Chuck Berry.*

*

When the days are cold and frosty. As the light dims to sunrise early, sunset early. The purple bull thistles die. The trees turn into a terracotta yellow dream-scape and the wasps die having had a marvellous summer.

As the lamb suckles the teat of the ewe, not knowing if 'it' will be slaughtered for Sunday dinner or not. Unaware. Naïve. Innocent.

The hours wile away innocence. The blast of nature rules the hemispheres and summer happens in hot countries at war for a price.

No one will invest in a new antibiotic because it will not make them rich. Money will ruin the day and the big fat capitalistic paper maker will never understand why we didn't have the 'balls' to call it off! Call it down. As the Japanese would do; 'Make some more! A Trillion!'

[No translation]

What would replace money? Is understanding humanity. Free.

We could never be free. We would all be dead.

We have to be under the rule of some alien species.

It would all be uncomfortable. Not quite right. *'Not fucking cricket!'*

How would the world of humans function?

What would employ us to 'DO!'

How would we believe in work, labour, ambition, task and target? What would the land of earth fight for, want for, need for? Who would be poor and in poverty and who would be rich and comfortable? There would be no caste system, no class system, no big stately homes or fucking big yachts in the Mediterranean. Then who would have the right to moan? Complain? Hurt or see the relativity die for fear of money matters daily? *Hum?!* ...

*

The good morning turned into afternoon into evening and all was well, as the balance of an epoch needed peace and disaster spread over the human faction with turmoil and harmony found in other places to equilibrium; scales of cosmic justice.

It's not our fault. We are just 'playing house'.

Drugs played a big part in being shamanistic; whilst the rest of the living mandatory skivvied and survived the pride.

Everything is relative and made up of atoms and molecules.

Break it down and the whole show would dissolve.

Comfortability, safe in our harem of play. No one can touch the earth, now!

We are safe from the belongingness of stratospheric war-force.

Let's just fucking play!

To be really free takes a responsibility bigger and more important than any other way of life, system, society, method, motion could; need to be.

You have to ensure one's elf to discipline, comprehension of whereabouts and want, bless the solution of human absorption, to be able to 'get you out of this fucking mess', a place in time, gift, solution in passage, home, family, reason to right, belonging, internationalisation, translatability, affidavit, giving back, encouraging, and most of all *multidimensionality cohabitation*.

Life is good when you get away with it. Like crime, one has to get caught.

We will see the end of days, right before our eyes, as the insurgence of mighty motions, will will will the willing of the vilification to willy the wonky!

Trademark, altruistic, chemical element, unindustrialised factor, tinker, normalise.

*

Okay, so the biggest lesson to learn; Go through that that is stopping one from being complete, unionised, popular, together, social, favourite, agoraphobic, storming, ungoverned, wrongful, somebody, forgiveable, school of thought, unequivocal.

Show how you can better the situations in life. Help those who don't, can't.

Help to relinquish all evil, wrongdoing, hurt, hate, badness, genocide.

Be a saviour, a healer, a doctor, a nurse, a helper, a good Samaritan all your life and don't stray from the Bible of Enoch or Jesus or Abraham.

See the goodness in all things and work with the sense of developing such ideals, when the people can hurt you, destroy you, dupe you, take advantage of you, ridicule you, disrespect you.

Be above all base attempts at survival, eradicate disgrace and love thine enemy with all your heart! Your soul.

They can be saved! Save their souls! *Amen!*

*

One time in totems, Drui Thorn was walking about when a car drove up and in it was a couple he knew. They also knew him.

He got into the car and went with them to their forest hideout.

In the depth of the night they gave him amphetamine, which he swallowed as if it was cocaine. It was a horse tranquilliser.

Thorn felt the drug hit his system and immediately he sat forward and was looking face to face with KAAR, the animated black snake of creation.

KAAR was pure black. It slithered into place right in front of Thorn's face.

They faced each other; off.

Then KAAR asked Thorn through telepathy; 'WHAT DO YOU HAVE?'

Thorn immediately sensing the danger said, 'EXCALIBUR!'

If he hadn't have answered, the snake was ready to pounce. She would have bitten into his face and killed him.

Instead the snake heard what he had said, turned and went back into the creative void where she had come from.

In hospital they gave Thorn a sleeping pill. He found himself asleep and in a vortex of confusable, distinctive, incontestable, unreferenced, unabbreviated dream-state.

A place which seemed to have mastered the ability to solve, to hope, to see the opposition panic, dissolve the task beyond limits of human comprehension.

Thorn ran. He ran in a direction which turned on its axis, so the way you went is the way you could not go, for being able to change direction and set off the other-way, with a feeling of orientation and a faith in feeling, with instinct, the outcome and the way to be, go, sense and achieve seemed not to be?

He knew the way was wrong, but right in the fright of the way being flawed to extremes and illusionary imperfectability.

He knew the sacred vision was watching him, the consciousness of the mass brain.

Thorn ran through the night, only it took a dream to solve, a rhythm of independent knowledge lead the way, never to confuse, never to devalue, the answer, the result, he turned up at the place, he stopped at the place and a hand reached out with a green jade stone.

The shiny gem. The stone needed by the forfeit, by the spiritual guidance to resolve the world, the little world, the problem of the world, when the world does not care, never sees the end result, never believes in a future harmony, until the world devours itself like a beautiful savage. No end, no stopping the outcome of a million years of war, greed, hate, hurt, rape and sin.

The gem was a gift. To be forgiven, in the name of humanity's palaeoanthropology

*

It doesn't matter who it is. Who he is. If drugs are involved. Where he comes from. What kind of person he is. It is just done. Needed. It is inevitability in its ultimate Theological doctrine.

It cannot be judged. Opinionated. Placed as part of; a reason, a duration, a conclusion or necessary. It must. It allows; faces the free world of the true imaginations, to further the conclusions of safeguarding biological-organic process of antithesis.

The Magi-ck realm is a great place. When the children grow up, the parents depart, but they become the children of the children's children. When the children are parents again, the children of the parents are the same children as the children who were the original child.

An encirclement. An organic recycle, where no one will be missing in the repetition of life and of departing.

No sorrow. Just an understanding of the repetition of relativity's transition.

Also, ask and thou shall receive. Greed will not. Nor demand. But, for the pleasure of living one can talk to the speaking animals, listen to the sound of peace and harmony, where there is no evil or wrongdoing, all is reforest social status. Paradise. Bliss.

A home. A family. A matrimony of fantastic love. Favourite food and warm-heartedness about the hearth.

Perfect. Ideal. Change. Perfections idealistic interdependency.
And unicorns.
A small indefinite quantity like the federation tribes of the Iroquois.

*

Sky-clad in plutocracy. Making the world hate itself. History bays to the degraded and the gravedigger with a prejudgement of rejuvenation and thanksgiving.

Hell washes over the unforgivable and the unhyphenated with a deallocated need to foreordain.

Jesus forgives you, the tempter will not. Which is not fair for the structured brains and the chemically changed truth; be expressed.

Sacred charisma. For 'Them' are/is the people and 'They' are the hierarchy, placed above for reasons of wealth, class and snobbishness.

Separation in status, sexual practice, politic, faith and era. Plenty to be going on with without the aspects of generation gaps, social raps, racist taps and monogram.

It had been a blood lunation and the baying she-wolves had bled.

The familiar had fed, the animal kingdom was still 'out' on the trouble of trespassers and so, the autopsy of eggheadedness and Jungian mishmash was in the bin. Rubbish was immediate and burnt. The hope and cross of dogfighting boss makes for diminishing.

Like the books of Hesse by Nazi knobs.

The solution to our problems is *you*. The interrogation is whether you do or you don't eat plant structure, clean your teeth after consumption and say your implores during aspirations.

Autumn is autumnal due to the falling of momentum, abdomens and having no idea how to live with the superior power on the celestial body. Nature. Natural. S muck!

This is my struggle. I shall overcome. The divine comedy is in search of love and once found can be bound up in difference and tales of questioning analysis, of a communication heard in the instinct of the whereabouts of self, blame, repugnance and flames of indifference, when climbing back into the solid ground of the psyche's mental capacity of muscular tissue called doubt.

*

What is incorrect with the human competition is coming out!

The reason for the states all being here is to inexperience personification.

Pash ended up; back in the mental institute for the mind and loved it, by painting her eyes with dark mascara, looking like an Egyptian blue blood, looking for her brotherly love.

She was alright, she was home. She was safe. She was inspirational.

All was pristine.

In saving grace.

*

On Salisbury Plain the MOD are pushing the spirits into one corner of the apparent. They are frightened of being crushed by the loud noisy tanks, which ride all over the sacred land; that is a plain for turkey buzzards and wild things, leading to the greatest magic-k temple to exist in the hope of healing for the world, which is televised to be bad and is bad when you have to get down to it.

They need to leave and let the land breathe. They are ruining a very important landscape and the buried souls of billions of ancestors who wish to wake and walk, are disturbed by harrowing violent intentions of a guardianship, which needs to move to Dartmoor and give Devon some egregious representational military action.

He had one last motion, one thing, an idea to tell you, before he left for an unbearable solitary existence of free will, self responsibility and balanced peace.

To comprehend the world about us and know the levels of dimension to which there are other eidetic sights for the imaginary rationality of a planet, society, civilisation and the makings of a resting place for the children, the old, the weak and meek, it is to surely display the will to be thankful for the way we are adaptable and strong in the sight of the fear of faecal matter.

We can rid the world of evil by living against the possibility of time, sending all and most into a time race of understanding, awe, wonder, science, art and love.

Don't fall for the strength of weakness to hurt, hate or judge, don't worry about the world, as nature knows of your history to survive and kill, to fight each other and create a history of blood and gore, it knows your ignorance and tolerance, your broken hearts and smashed worship, the rape of the goddess woman, the murder of the youngest baby, the depletion of all men.

Don't let the creation of the universe win, don't let the sordid world of normality prevail in the face of such greatness and genius minds, soon to be astronauts and curators of healing, loving, laughing, fabulous strengths in endeavour's claim, to free the soul, to heal the world, to feel the tiger smile, the elephant thank, the justice of a saliva mouth, given to the apparatus of uniform enlightenment, duration, divinity. Gathering hygienic stealth.

People have died, so you shall live. You will live in the year 3114 AD. Do us proud.

Make sure it don't look like the backdrop of star wars! The reality is people can't even drive on the motorway without crashing, jackknifing or speeding.

Make it worthy of all nations of ancient knowledge, make it free and not a museum. Not a planet of the apes, but a planet for the orang-u tang; and apes.

Human beings are sent to help. A situation, a problem, a solving, a puzzle, a question or a living hope to better the simple way of the tampering moon, the evening sky, the storm of universal nature, the dead, a child smiling and all children believing in a grand world full of fairness, opportunity, peace, love, sexual futures and glory.

Another fucking story! Idealisation, but do it, or we will be sorry, like we are.

*

Fuck tax and mortgage! Fuck paying for the basics in life! Let's make for the big picture and look after its emotions, moods, delights and belongingness of a learned calling device.

We are slaves to the British empire and should not be.

We imprison ourselves and should never be free!

Immunity is a domain!

That's me!

I am 'The Watcher'. I watch you and see you. I look for the better part of you. The human part which is the same as the bee's sting, the cow parsley's white wildness, the fallen apple's bruise, the alleyway to ill health and morning sadness, a living hell made by being fragile and beautiful, immense and flawless, untouchable, immaculate, stardust and good.

I watch me, I watch them, they watch me, I watch TV, I watch football, I read the game, I watch and pray, that maybe some day, you'll be back, back in my arms, once again … !

I am a fool. Fool's gold!

I was Decca Dent Peters, do you remember me?

I am Drui Thorn the galactic spirit warrior for peace, goodness and organisation.

*

There's so much to do and tell, want and need and see and find and feel, know, hope for and dream, smell, love and buy and bend and shag and do, you, who are. You are. You. Do.

This autobiographical memoir of a sordid life in selfish freedom and loss should be seen as an example to the world, an exemplification, an exemplary unknown solvency, brought to finally change all constellations for the good of great humanity and not for the selfless s-elfish sodomites who bought or buy this land of paradise for a shilling and an ownership of wealth.

You did it! Decca Dent Peters! said his voice of providential paranormality. *You've been x-emplary! An unknown quantity, a warning to others? Well done!* And they cheered and clapped, shouted and whistled!

The shit heap understands you. They see your example. To be better than your destiny, your enemy, your disillusion. The prisoners of the world get it! The downtrodden, the underdog, the down and out and the loser, get it! said the great conscience's consciousness.

"But the rich healthy capitalistic consumer's democracy don't," said Drui Thorn, in replication.

Fuck them! They are shit, and they will be the last to enter universal heaven!

Fight the human evil in the world and all spiritual evil and stand by the knowledge of the truth against the world!" came the ultimate demand.

And you will stand on the precipice of all edges of life, not to show fear or scared to be, you will reap what you sow, as the sweetcorn is not edible when stood in the field of yellow glory, in the summer sun, the duty of creation, turning the unknown into knowledge, sharing it with the belligerent eating the crunchy cob, hot, melting the cow's liquid body substance with consecrated love and gratifying starving hunger of an obese greedy barbecuer with issues and mad dogs, said Jesus Christ, Buddha bodhisattva hero, God, king, guru, emperor.

"Blasphemy!" said the torrent tongues of unchaste angels fighting at the feet of archangel's payment of monthly rent to a slum-landlord getting someone else to pay his mortgage.

The world passed behind Drui Thorn and he loved life for it. It felt emancipating, he felt comfortability's micro-dynamical grandiose reliability.

In emotionless elation with everything and everyone.

His ambition fell away bit by bit; am … bit … I … on … He didn't have to be someone, anyone, he could just be a person, a myth, a *legend*.

*

When he departs, Thorn becomes a limbo spirit, who will stop at nothing to save those in harm, being raped, being molested by adults, being murdered, by his means of a sword of justice, a sword of thwarting methods, a battle to slay all criminal perpetrators of principle and life.

He is a righter of wrongs. He is a marvel! A superhero!

*

He turned in bed and woke up next to his blood-moon missus. He was elder and had received a council bungalow for all his troubles. He was disabled, so he got disability allowance, no rent, no council tax, a bus pass and found his woman at Stonehenge, looking for him, ready to serve him, knowing who he was and looking forward to seeing it all. She respected him and he respected her. Her name was Amber Jade.

He found it hard to get out of bed, but she helped him into his wheelchair. He sat all day and wrote about his memories; his memoirs. He would call them: *'A popular history'*.

He could still fuck and loved the landscape of Amber's ass. Her tits were good and she was just right in knowing no other would bother with her, until they saw her with him and knew who she was and what she could bring to a relationship as an enchantress goddess daughter.

They busied their day and worked towards the early evening hearth. Together they ate and brought great joy to all conversation, love making [she was clipped, so he could 'bareback ride] and immersed themselves in silence, peace, harmony, nature and care.

Thorn had done it. He had found freedom against the tyranny of capitalistic labour with liberal tendencies.

He felt admonished. Totally emancipated and utopian.

*

He had seen his dark times and done well to survive. He had fought the bad side of life, not won, but did not lose, he may have won the battle and he won the bloody war too!

Now he could live his life. What was left of it. He had about a good 35 years left. He didn't want to live to any good old age with ailments or slobbering jaws, but wanted to go out with a good innings, whilst bowling his way through many wickets.

Amber Jade was perfect and made him laugh. He enjoyed her banter and wit and felt free to speak out about the world when he felt the need to watch the fucking news on TV. She listened and loved his way of controlling his insights and points of view, different and difficult, but then; so is life, but idyllic life is even greater.

Don't read the newspapers they are all corrupt.

Watch a 'Soap' and have a good wash.

He hopes you survived the 70's with the likes of drugs and sexual perversive promiscuity.

He did, he was a teenage soldier being exemplary at it!

The rest of his life was an example to those who had been abused and torn apart, and needed to rise against the burning tide of slander and slaughter and class and cast and mastic caustic cryptic blood sucking of the world's satanic vices, laws and principles to conform, confirm, bow down and curtail to the bitch riding the beast as the abomination of the nation!

He was no freestyle gimp, no Johnny Nincompoop!

He was likeable and had survived life. He now wished for being and happening.

It had all put him in his place, he knew that, but he knew he had squared up to the moment of truth about himself and sought wisdom and challenged the subject of creation's evolutionary chaotic map, seeking a way out – and got one.

*

He was damaged goods, wrecked, wrought, finally done and seeming, through lack of indulgence, sinistral, set-up, classified, journalistic, tee-total, antidemocratic and proven.

A satisfied proposal of life's liver.

Broken, he used sympathy as a device to bed his wife.

Body without the face is a race to lust, a desire to smell and taste and a liking for anal entryway with gel and less stress on the scourge.

The face is the maker, the taste for worth and being, for telling and question, for seeing and thinking with, a telling tale, a scarred sense of recompense and objectification.

The speaker.

All is psychic.

God's all.

Paralytic; one morning, he woke up with paralysis. From the waist down, his knob got an erection to let him know he had options.

He had been struck down by the mighty maker, the faker, the taker away.

But he never felt more alive like that, sat, waiting for the sun to rise. To improve his life he first had to forgo the substitute called forfeiting for a fitting.

You see life is not about money or being someone with it, it's about an inner joy which can be shared with the lowest form to the highest performer.

*

It had gone on too long, out of time, out of reach, bequeathed to the benevolent bravado, thus Thorn suggested a constructionist quality should do it.

A factional character should darken up and ride out and slay the vulgar self-destructor; his alias Satan the undead, the prince of Antichrist, the blasphemous of many faces.

It was the right thing to say. Why? *He* [Cypher] was dead, ready, he had created the factitious imaginary legend, holding the celestial sword Excalibur to his heart.

You do it…? You and the seven wizards! You could do it. You were born of a demon, you know the score, about this, I have been too long alive, living without my soul. It may die. I will live on my life-force, as I have before, I did fine.

I will remember you.

All dried up and burnt out like this book. Had a go! Did me best. Just didn't cut the mustard! … expressed Drui Thorn, who felt expendable, used up, and could not die. Not just yet.

Maybe tomorrow.

"*Take the fucker out!* Cut it out of the human psyche! Give all a chance to improve without searching for an answer. Without sacrificing the will to change, to better, to be. Set the world free! Release from the chains of bondage and settle the score with sleep, awake to smell the coffee and get something to eat. No big deal. Don't make more of it than it is. The gross has fingers in every pie! Heal the world by freeing us from the Bible's warning. *Let's all get a good night's sleep.*"

Who said that?

I am *The Watcher*, I write and narrate all of this.

'All I have left to aim for is self-satisfaction,' felt Drui Thorn … 'I will lay my soul to rest. I will love and make my peace with the nature of a universal astral bipolar disordered planet. I will rid myself of this raw downtrodden racking unstimulated magnitude of an upset strain of a fucking wicker man! And get back to playing bowls. I will have a shit without beady eyes watching me wipe my ass. I don't want to be paranoid. I want to heal. To sing a beautiful song about a bird of paradise.'

*

I will do it! I will ride on my white stallion, *Thunder-box*, and slay the infidel, not a human responsibility for planet evil, but a metaphysical presence, there from the beginning of and there till the inevitable end, when the universe dies and goes quiet again!

When the time comes, you will be buried as a king. Your time here is good, furthermore; having to be redeemable.

You have crossed the threshold into the mystic lands, into the playful realm of *magick*. There you will be revered, respected and married well. She will love you for who you are, not for who you were.

It will be known in the Universe. It runs home to the lands of past, to the friends and foe and to those who speak of you and want to know.

You will be a poet chieftain, a warrior King amongst the love and kind of the spirits from the limbo of the deep blue heaven.

It is to be known in all the world, the future of the human spiritualist will be accepted with panache and loyalty to the unbeknown children who can be someone, a person with self character, personality, wit, guile and strength, with honour, majestic love, bravery, skill and artistic ability to show and shine on rainy days of the eternal rainbow.

This is the promise. This has been done. You crossed the veil and you stood your ground with love for the humanity floundering in sorrow, sin and evil gain. Again it is all in vain in life to see the healing abused, the trap tripped, the council bothered, the government without a pen and you with the head dragon name of a *pen dragon*.

A Poet.

A lover of Art.

Of Woman and brother.

Of children

against the enemy of concern for the basics of life.

All should be done. Inherited. All should be done and paid for. All should be free and work for the better world in time, lots of time to watch the children grow and the civilisation of humanity teach love and understanding of place, ability, respect and self-sufficiency.

*

Yours is an exemplary death. A life in spirit. A spiritual beginning when the body dies and the real spirit in form will be.

Many yearn and fall by the way. Many seek and never find. Some fall and come across, this tells of the few who do, but in life, there is none, it is to the spirit field of *magick* one has to be in order to be, to die in order to be, to follow the path of deliverance when life is done.

Bless you be; a Blessed be.

I go to slaughter the demon chief. I will return; I may not. I will try to rid human psyche of conflict with self. The lie of a thousand ages, the lie of civilisations.

None can talk of things. None can hope for better. None will see the truth and none can kill the infidel.

I do this for in darkness is abuse.

Darkness is truth.

Darkness is peace and all beautiful life needs revolution and safety.

The rebellious light.

The fibres of light in pitch dark will light my way to the hell of the Kingdom of Satan, the seeker of mortal souls.

There I will use the healing sword of God and Goddess: Excalibur!

SO SPAKE:
THE WATCHER.

*

What can follow this. How does one end? This is the place to see the life of earth living – lived out and rid, to a place well received and loved for being, not having to be.

Drui Thorn never heard of Decca Dent Peters again. He lived till the age of 85 in the year of our sanctuary, 2043; having seen the apocalypse of nuclear warfare used against the Apophis asteroid Collider.

The turning of tides and the fear subside from the bravery of real true warriors of the Rainbow.

One does not need guns or a law, just faith.

One needs love to better understand hate and hate is for the ugly world of finished diminished re-collectors of pasts through digging, a present through being gifts and the future which tells all – *history repeats itself* – so we all know what to do and when to do it.

A vicious cycle. A cranky bike. A vulgar dike and the vicar's spite.

Not much to be going on, this living from the healing of wars, the knowledge of knowing, a beginning of lifes or a new day for the new age, as a traveller of truths and the brunt to bear from enemies of real unconditional love.

Live in the future; with an open mind and an open heart. Don't love when it is too late as one will be cancerous, old and brittle, not enough to change the world for an army of lovers, believers, fortune, justice for the abused children of creation.

Respect death, as to die is better, having lived to depart, pass on or even go to.

Immortality is missing someone. That's okay.

Headstones are for the disrespected in life. Honoured in death.

Burn the rest, let the ashes fly into the windy sky light aether.

"To see me, look in the higher mind," said Thorn Pen Dragon, as he lay down to physically die.

*

DEEP in the heart of destiny lies a truth so rudimentary, so vivid, it is and will become poison, or a way to see the written law about 'the self', the living energy of being, its rightful proof to a salvation or redemption for a moment's lapse in a past life, or a collapse in the present reincarnation of simply being, a 'seeker'.

The awakening comes at the most stressful point of solution, remembering how you were in crisis, the ultimate substance in God's universe is a question, never knowing the answer, taking all the senses to the precipice and falling, far along the walls of the abysmal or landing in the answer, when one has asked the supreme all prevailing question:

Who I'm I? And what do I do with it?

*

Drui Thorn Pen-dragon thought someone or something was out to kill him. His everlasting nemesis. A neurosis bathed in posture and liking to an eternal fight in the war over himself. Something stopping him from becoming who he was, someone determined to stand in his way, be the obstacle to which none may go over or none my enter, until the sacrifice of 'self' is committed to the cause, then, one may live as well as any other on the planet with meeker strength, power and insight. Thus the adversity stays the 'status quo', as all are numb to the experience of overcoming the dark side, which lives to foul the 'amazing mystery' of life's force.

On the morning of the dream given to him in the 'mystic place', Thorn left the mountain, looking at the sun-cherished sky, in its form of cerise and blue chalcedony, the clouds folded and formed as cumulus.

In his heart he knew; *it was his day!*

He had dreamt during the night of a scene, which seemed to be himself, dancing 'sky-clad' in front of a group of people. The persons being a druid, a monk, a couple of young men, one tall the other small and a knight in shining armour, who seemed to be looking out into the world, not being a part of the others.

In front of the 'sky-clad' dancer was a man in a bright red cowl, hood up and holding a wooden staff. He said, *"He is like me!".*

The only words spoken.

As a shadow of white looked over Drui Pendragon Thorn, seeming to secure the feelings of safety and gift, as Thorn awoke from his dream, gasping for air, his lungs needing oxygen to pull him through, back to earth, back to the planet's reality.

The dream had been short, a moment of interest, but, Drui Thorn had been asleep all night, as he woke in the heat of a summer's morning light.

He felt in his 'heart of hearts', that the morning *was his*.

It belonged to his life. A given day, a sight to behold, a dream within a waking time, and he didn't have to bound into some happy liking, but strolled at ease, taking it all in his stride, as he came down to the path of struggle in people and went back to his travelling caravan for a cup of tea and a quick 'nap', reimbursing his energy, as if the dream had taken it all out of him, travelling far, he was exhausted and needed to sleep awhile, before venturing into the town, to see what his day and his life had to offer in the way of harmony.

He did not know, waiting for him was the worst ambush he couldn't or wouldn't understand or consider on such a prestigious day, the feeling it all gave him of ecstasy and hope.

When he arrived at the illegal site, to which people of the indigenous travelling type were able to stop at, spend sometime in or stay, whilst trashing the place or taking drugs and getting into trouble, he noticed that a few people were up and milling about. They seemed to be waiting for his arrival back to the site, as he needed to be there, as the idea of camping in a tent or whatever, was out of the question, when the national trust moves 'one' on, from such places of magical insight to the mystic, the warrior of peace or just fascinated about the will of ancient kinds, being driven away, distorted or murdered, for being the way they were or the way they wished to be.

Entering, Thorn was immediately attacked!

He wondered *why?* They shouted why!

Thorn was a 'freak!'. Someone who had danced in the mystic plain! What was this ?

They, being the black knight and his gang, consisting of an African called Jaguar, who was from Gambia. He seemed to be the most disturbed. He was running about chanting and dancing with a very large pair of underpants outside his trousers.

They all seemed the worse for wear, having been drinking and taking drugs all night.

The others were stragglers from all corners of the beast they call fear.

A skinhead, a 'patsy', a few unknowns and 'piss takers', but the main misunderstanding was from the one they called Trojan Josh, who willing on his 'merry men', seemed to have to, want to, destroy the light in the air, the flowers in their beds, the cerise morning light, a Shepherd's delight [or is that warning?], became cold and distant and the full opening of chalcedony blue in the heavens was blacked out by the evil intention of Trojan Josh and the mad-ra.

The intention, to ruin the day.

The dream had been intercepted by spies, in the house of sleep.

They saw the way in which a man had danced 'sky-clad' in front of the spectacle of law, of love, in celebration, not war and they did not like it, understand it.

If a person holds a grudge, has an issue, needs to vent his or her spleen about an abused childhood or a torrential up-bringing, surely! they would need to take revenge, have a vendetta against the perpetrators, who had prosecuted a weaker age or the stronger religious will.

Not to go to war in a naked dance of flowers in the palm of his hand.

A poetic endurance raising above the invalid law 'to capitalise on', or 'put down' to be seen, maybe go to war, as the underdog, with a hero's intention to be famous, to be pitied, by all sympathising nations, loyal folk, who would join in, perhaps go to war themselves, to see the end of days; tomorrow, still needing to burst open the heart with swords and spears.

When the tears could be cried for joy or acceptance, or an everlasting solution, brought about by love, the arena, everyone knows of, brought on, by strength of purpose, determined to stay away from the 'forbidden zones' and heal, cherish, a relevant similarity, from all the hearts of the living species known to all as: homosapian.

They did not know the intention of the ATHORD; Athame; short sword. A light bringer!

They laughed and jeered, they spat and crowned the holy head of thorns, they kicked and they bit, as they wanted chaos to reign once more in their sad loss of a life.

All life needs to do is face up to the truth.

Then see the reasons how and why it is as it is, then to heal the soul, deep down, the tender grace of understanding, comprehension and vision, caress and cherish the self, forgive yourself, then the bright light of hope will shine and with hope, healing.

Healing a place soiled, a place needing substance, a broken heart needing peace, love, quiet and above all on a planet full of noise; *Silence*.

Jaguar the African jester/fool started to chase up Drui and with his knees on the floor, his sweat and all-night reek, ask to be healed.

There and then!

The whole idea of temptation in the face of the adversity was a wrong doing, on the spot, there where it was on show, a gig, a pantomime, would belittle the principle and without the power of the spirit sword of God; Excalibur, it would be failing, falling into the pittance of everyday lapse, everyday routine, a sell by date and a 21st century product.

"*But still, heal me!*" Jaguar ranted in his pathetic deep Gambian voice.

Looking at the familiars about him. The instigator, Trojan Josh, with his arms folded and his head tilted to one side listening to the laughter of the other hyenas.

Here was the prey, and they would like to feast on the beast today.

The tired tears of Drui Thorn eyes, his demure of sad shoulders and wincing heart, only heightened the target of the judged and their shameful shambles of ridicule, as they did not let him sleep, they kept him up with the threat of mighty fear, a kill and then be killed, brought about the energy of dust, speeding through the stifled air, like a hurricane waiting to disappear along the path, not conscious of its devastation, but of its nature; born to be the catalyst, born to show; it was stronger than the mighty 'scrapper', the mighty dam or cathedral.

*

The morning drew on. No more the given day. Destroyed by negative vibes. By the unholy believer, a torrent of abuse set in motion a thirsted desert, an eyeless hawk, a dream under the pretension of a dark she-horse, who wanted the world to be the way it was and changes are for the privileged or the thankful, but not for the godforsaken forlorn, who needed to war in the toilet called neighbour, friend, peer or belief.

So, Drui Thorn warred with Trojan Josh.

They clashed heads.

The bitter defiance of jealousy, envy of another man's wife, the adultery, the crime, came to a head in the pineal gland, the 'third eye' stemmed the pain, as the mighty forehead butt was clumsy, rash, a terrible sound to the land of dreams of wishful thoughts, gathered over years of abstinence, of disillusionment and apathy.

The blow was crucial.

Back in the minds of all, subterranean consciousness lies battered and bruised from the awakening of social laws and the 'norm' to do, whence came the nuclear bomb to blow up the world, how came the sex-criminal to hurt a child, must come the giant scowl at peace, real peace and real eternal paradise.

Interpretation has its nature, to disguise its art, but to infiltrate and overcome in a true nature of spiritual gift, in the amazing mystery, would be sent by the opposite to hate it, to despise the very existence of it and in the possible mannered element; destroy!, that from which no one will ever understand, ever come to terms with, all the world needs it not, the world of people can do without; whatever you have to give!

So, it can never be seen to be needed, accepted or better still help the world in the ways of; *why?* The original sin? The core, the crux of the matter as to which way do we choose the choice of will?

Life will go forward into the development, the evolution of change towards the light and dark sides of being, in cause and effect of such and why there is understanding of forbidden zones.

When the 'self' comprehends the divisions, never separates, never wars with one's self, as the internal embodiment develops and concludes the inside meeting the outside with balance of tides, with harmony, harmonious with 'self', is or could be the solution to all problems with an external world made to fit in the rudimentary progress, the big banker's wallet or a turning of the journey of life, which looks to move futuristic-ally towards the learning of the past and the opening of the present, which gifts life with a future through action, a past in representation of remembering, forgiving, lessons and thanks, whilst in the present world; free from all crime, sin, wrongdoing, genocide, hate, vindication and with the biggest crescendo of all – *The amazing mystery life could be and should be with an open heart and open mind.*

*

Thorn left the site. He asked others to move him onto their site. Which they did.

He had been in battle since descending the 'mystic mountain' four hours earlier. He was fatigued, tired beyond age, troubled, abused and sad with disappointment at the way people can act with the unknown, the difference between us and still, amongst so-called travelling friends.

He could only find the time to get ready to go into the town and meet his destiny.

He felt in his heart.

It was a woman. It was a wise woman. It was a life's companion, it could be good, great, proud and everlasting.

He left and arrived at the cross of the town, but alas it was not.

*

She came towards him with the gait of a lady. She strode triumphant in his direction.

She had seen the dream too.

He was watching as the heart of hearts met in the aether of moments and felt the necessary journey of soul seeking come to an end.

Then the silence between them. Something was wrong!

They could not speak. They could not say a word. To greet one another. To make plans for the immediate future, to meet as a union of one. Still, the quiet and peaceful lengths to which they had come all that way, to find the day, the place, the experience seemed to stay in her curtsies, in his bludgeoned head and abused heart.

The morning had gone and so had the dream been.

All was lost to the vicious ways, the brutal message, the destroyer of love, the used particulars who damaged the sight of God's light and darkened out the sun and the souls of two eternal lovers unable to push past the defeated strain of disturbed visions of the almighty supreme imagination.

The reality won. The dream burst into a thousand star flakes, a dollop of mixed spices, into the heat of a pit of flaming hell.

Silent. The early afternoon lunch. Quiet the noise around. Slowly, they saw, passionately they could not build the dawn back up to its realm of help, or of an arena for destinies.

A place which did not have to exist.

But did.

She turned around and gracefully walked away.

Thorn sat and watched as his mystic mystery flouted in the direction of a high street.

If they could not love, as one, in unison, then the sole message was to come.

War!

And so, she said.

*

A vast cloud! A thunder of storms, and the release of the legions of demons to do with hell.

All directed in the path of the spirit known as Pug. The wart, Dex Rex and maybe legend in the making of Drui Thorn Pen Dragon the scabbard of God's old sword: Excalibur.

Known to the future world by a spiritual talisman and athame; an athord; an x-caliber, X8, an unknown Infinity; 'an unknown quantity'.

The short sword of gold; *"You have just been arthur'd!"*, came the cry of ridicule, at the spectrum of black darkness and malicious ways of penitent evil.

*

Going down the shell pit of a deliverance from evil. The kingdom was doomed, but the queen, in the eyes of true love, could and should be saved.

It would take a sacrifice.

It did. Drui Thorn Pen Dragon gave his spirit form to save her soul.

Into re be xibalba, the centre of the known galaxy. The Milky Way, they call it?

Into the dark rift. Taking with him the two biggest components he could find, muster, use; were: The black knight, known as Trojan Josh and Jardine Katmai Pricers, a nubile queen, from out of the recesses of the mists of antiquity, and the goddess.

They all entered the dark rift together, at once leaving Josh, in the darkest of filaments, to which no man could or would ever bear, full of dark demons and devils in the void of Hell, he would have to kill some and capture one or two to eat. He lived on the carnivorous ways of a spiritual cannibal, for the success of his quest for the sword of God: *Excalibur!*

Moving onto the centre, where in the nuclear bulge remained Jardine Pricers, as Thorn went in to meet the maker of the incest, which turned his branch tree destiny into a barricade, an obstacle, and his woman of true love, his opposite, *a sin*. Emma Lox Gyrfalcon.

Entering into the spirit of the lair of hell, Thorn Pen Dragon was exalted.

Into the position, into the crucifix, also enchained in the symbol of limited boundlessness.

Thorn pen Dragon aka Decca Dent Peters died.

His spirit was extracted.

Looking at his non-living, life at a pace, a disgrace, as he lay on a bench, with nothing, no one, no property or materials, left bald in naked nausea, he worried about how his hair must look; silver, scruffy, long and grey, long grey streaks with lice and mice hiding in the cuckoo's nest of a scruffy bonnet.

Thus he died on a bench. Empty of soul, empty of life, of love, of nature, of all living creatures in the moving world, dead, he collapsed in a shit heap around something, dry eyed, vomit ridden, tired, bored, lost and unfounded.

No one could help him now. Extracted, he knew 'not' his name.

A living dirge of stench death breath. No one saw him and no one knew. As if someone had reached in and dragged out his spirit! All for nothing, but for the love of a woman! Enough? His angel wings clipped that day.

And his holy life flew away into wrong, black, ominous, malicious, heinous, de-fouling, evil, inhumane darkness.

*

There in such a place was the karma of others.

His parents.

The day the mini-bus creamed into his father's car whilst they tied their safety belts on, the female mini-bus driver losing control, as it hit, they whip-lashed with the motion and being his dad, he came out okay, being his mother, breasts and all, her chest was lashed; given cancer having to come to terms with the chemotherapy radiation to cure her of breast cancer.

*

With the help of his sister and father, She managed to get through it, but then, She developed old-timer's disease; her memory failing, her motions and motives brought down to a slow limitation of life, She took the drugs given, although, She had never had strong drink in her life or taken any enhancement drugs, found it all foreign and didn't quite come to terms with the feelings and the problems it all brought, when, then, She had a stroke.

She lived with it.

Until, She had a second major stroke.

She asked for the machine to be turned off, as his mother had had enough of her failing body and wished to heal and renew through heaven.

*

The pressure of the dark side brought to bear other consequences, which killed many people and damaged many lives in life.

His mother died on the 23rd of December, 2013, aged 80.

She was cheated of her retirement and her twilight days with her loving husband.

She had earned the right and did not deserve the pain of refrain *'She'* had to go through.

*

BLIND and with the sight of a pineal gland, a base chakra, but in the 'third eye'.

Trojan Josh and Thorn Pen Dragon mounted the highest place, where they could look over the kingdom and saw the flames of the unrequited circling the path.

"What is this Josh?" asked Thorn, as his sight seemed to be the strip of solvent from head to toe which damaged through his damned soul, from the top of his cranium to the toes of his feet.

Like a Captain Ahab, he strode there, head to toe – through the spleen, masking a vehement vein to disbelieve the colour which is said to be white, is not, in fact it is made up of the rainbow, with the soiling of a life, looks dirty yellow, a cream, abashed with bits. Amalgamated joyrides of bacteria for generations, the fly of beasts; from the pit called hell.

"It is Babylon," remarked Joshua, with his Rastafarian lips, his hair, short but knotted, his eyes the colour of the pits of horror, benign to flavour, sugar-coated with deep black, coterminous, a bombastic explosion, to see the whiteness of the tip, no sign of light, a blackness beyond negro, niger, beyond the sea of universal solutions to the stars, the planets, a beginning or an end, the alpha and omega – to answers; is: Ask the right question. Eyes.

They had and hav't, both blind, blinded by longevity of darkness, by the light.

In danced the fairy queen. The sick assailant to scupper the whole lot. Out of the ancient books into the loving land.

Fierce and treacherous, the killing face and tail of a scorpion king. Apollion; A bad-dun.

The rapist, the murderer, the in-filler, the betrayer, all belonging to the enemy of Christ.

*

All belonging to the indignant race of human spoilers, the sacking, of, queens, priestesses of Catal Yuk – over sands and forbidden deserts, land fallen, fallen to the beast, the beast of indulgence, excess, valetudinarianism, docile resigning souls.

All was at the end. But the beginning was just beginning without a care for the finished, done.

Thorn pen Dragon became 'a pale rider', the true and faithful.

To what cause? He did not know, now, and did not care.

To fight the horsemen of the apocalypse was futile. They had been and gone. All representing the human gift of penance, starvation of children, of the masses; pestilence, and in life came the reaper, the insulter: death.

Not summoned or departed, but brought to justice by or with the dark fouled fountain called by others and by many: death.

The energy of mind to see and fight the bastards taking flight was weak, insipid, when all was a grasp or a grab, to wrestle with the imagination of two thousand years, gave a sight of: head-locks, flying punches, trips or throws.

Then the symbols came to obey, but death, just sat in the saddled horse and pointed skeleton finger, at the face, of the soul, at the heart of a life, at the bad bowels of a rotten libido, and knew worth and target, beyond life, into the ultimatum, finish of all beginnings.

All good souls go to Avalon. A small part of heaven.

Like the beautiful feline earth is to the solar system it is in, as the galaxy is to the whole of a black holed universe.

*

In darkness there is peace. The light is the awakening, the rebellion, the original sin to see, to know, the light bringer; Lucifer, Promethean, you. Us. Them.

But it has been soiled, marked, hurt, injured. It must be healed. It must be loved. It will take a lifetime, and many lifetimes, until the end of human life, as we know it, seizes.

Then the imagination will die. Then life will seize playing and so die. Then the *magick* of all darkness will lie peaceful, tranquil, balanced with light.

But, until then … we *must*.

*

In the butterfly dale. The place of bees, wasps, beetles, caterpillars, flies, the insect domain with daffodils, dandelions, daisies and nettles, dock weeds, elder branches, sound of motor cars, the whirl of hum, the crescendo with summer lawnmowers, pigeon imitating cuckoo, whilst the wild horses chew the cud.

Every day the routine of safety from the celestial cosmological creation. We all, alive, play with the cage of trust, leading to mistrust. Secure in the knowledge, we are safe in our playground, in the crèche of unholy vows, we are ignorant of the other's dilemma, putting down the truth in place of ignorance.

In the bull-rush, the willow tree, the bargain basement, the warm rest and a cup of tea.

We are in the dome of love, and what a mess we make of feelings.

Feelings are for the intense role of applicator, the complicator is the enemy of a promised land.

The sods of the earth creep through the man-made concrete, like the senses of a person looking for the answer to the purpose, a reason for being.

*

When, the cow parsley, buffalo, monkey, blue and lemon grass, just do, when the purple bull thistle, plantain, broad-leaf, buckthorn weeds, the knot, hawk, hog, pig, milk, also, exist, with evolution, creation, science and love, information, knowledge, religion and hate, inflation, expansion, capitulation, history, mystery and wealth.

Stealth: is the will to survive on a planet of plants, wild life; death's decay and life!

Away, from body form, into spirit be!

All and everything has a life-force, but a spirit is reason to be purposeful towards freeing, letting go, knowing who, where.

But, what for?

It is not ignorance which brings you fear. It is the answer to the base question, keeping you in flux, flare, aware, being loved, saying one doesn't have to love in return.

Love is the cloth in which we bear our self-spirit. Naked, sky-clad, we are nature, true, the answer to, the answer of the everlasting soul.

Bold, we endeavour in aspects of hidden potions, insight and knowledge, we are special in guise of a planet. All dimension is fathomable when the spaceman cometh.

Letting go of your suit. The minute and blip, is so precious, divine, fragile and delicate, it is the one true essence of all universal drama.

Pleasantly; existence is set free and the whole is filled with exploratory *just*.

*

Searching and seeking the outcome of all phrenological endanger came the answer whilst died amongst the hanging stones of Stonehenge.

His last name was Drui Thorn.

Searching deeper and forever deeper into the soul of death. Lost, lonely, tired, bored, insecure and forlorn, Drui Thorn heard the story of INDIGO.

It had run amok 'sky-clad' into the energy spirits brought to bear by the connection of self and ancient landmarks, there she fouled the mind, whored her blonde – chrome silver – spectre and vowed the end of a life, which took hers.

She had risen at a time when through her underdevelopment saw only the man who stopped her from her life's destiny and freedom to love: Drui Thorn.

Those simple words *"You are going out with D!"* infused, interrupted her longing for timeless love, eternal love, the one true love.

Pash has had many lovers and deeper loves since then, but D, Thorn, even Drui,should not be free to live, to love, to be, he must die! How and why, who fucking cares?!

Just be a graze on the ethereal energy of all life-force and kill him! He ruined my life!

The hanging stones brought out the poison, the truth, the dead, the energy spirits who had served it; Indigo was loved amongst them and fucked amongst them and ruined Drui Thorn's life! Now it is his turn!

But, he blamed no one, and saw his lessons within it, he sought not to embitter the chain of hatred flowing through the terms of planetary life, but gladly laid to rest the past, then, gone. Always behind is the past.

*

He rode on his bike, waving at the car verge mirror, seeing himself as he wished to see himself and seeing the chrome illuminated energy of naked Indigo, he ran after her 'sky-clad', he ran fast and caught up with her and taking her in his arms he slit her throat with a dagger.

She died instantly. Gone. No more. No more … no more.

*

Would you believe it! He had a story! To write a 'whodunit'. A ghostly whodunnit.

15 years of the haunting wrong, which seemed to wish him to suffer, to take his suffering life, to wallow in the stomach of pain, to never raise again with joy, happiness; love.

Is everything really for a reason? Or is it just fucked up enough to *have to be*?

There is no heaven after life, just the memory of love in those which loved you. They carry it immortally and eternally, with the love for one who touched on others, the way to life and the way to love in life, when the energy of darkness is made by us all, to stop us seeing the truth of a finality and life! All life to the full.

Leaving no emotion behind, leaving no one without love, infinite, until you are merely forgotten … that is spirit; a life-force.

That is heaven, inside others who cherish your character, personality, charisma and life.

Pass the heaven. Pass it on, it's the only one we have got.

We are no more than we are. It is all coming from somewhere and going to, we are just that that is in-between, ages, stages, epochs, ions, generations, when we are gone from life-force and leave our bodies to death, we are no more.

Do right by yourself, do right for others. Love and never stop loving. You are immaculate, you are brave, you are a star, you are your own universe and you can live forever!

In the minds and hearts and energies of the living others.

This is immortal eternal land.

Universal.

Immense.

*

Living with the Shadow, a dark cowled figure manifest from the dark recesses of dark time – the place of ultimate evil – brandished with the task of being my opposite on the planet – to stop me from being 'Athord' the Athame short-sword 'light bringer' who helps to clean up the dimension known to the spirit as the Plains of goblin, ogre, troll, pixie, elf, brownie and hobgoblin who have been given the right to trouble, mischief, hurt, abuse and sin because there is no law and when there is no law to interpret, then the chaos, havoc and trouble of the demon, devil, shade, shadow dark side can find the time to influence them into excitement, charm, deviance, maleficence and the possibility of murder, cruelty, horror and abuse of all things smaller, younger, insignificant or seen through the eyes of the toughest survive; Devil – Daemon – spirit shadow which controls the world and holds it all to ransom with the element of knowing the universe in a natural state is dark.

Filled with imagination-al demons – horrors; portrayed by humans, acted out in the vicious circle of 'cops and robbers', saint and sinner – then 'it'; they will control the opposite of dark light, allowed to be, allowed to feed on human evil acts, allowed to lead the way to bad karma, occurrence and dilemma.

Forever eating on the layers of wrong happenings, being, doing and will always stop the people on the planet reaching a status quo of happiness, love and friendship; loyalty.

I have fought such demons. I have seen my plans for salvation troubled – I am weak, insipid to its will and forcing me to bow down to the psychology of evil … I WILL NOT!

I have to honour my 'light bringer', the short sword, the size of my outstretched arm, called an Athord because when I use it, I can say, *"You've just been Ath-urd!"*

I know the Arthurian mythology and it was given back to me in rebirth, in kind, ink-heart – it was a symbol of my goodness – graciously offered to help my ESP and all my endeavour into the light of the dark side which is my SHADOW, the SHADOW. SHADOW.

*

This is my low. This is the thing which stops me from being alright, in the middle of the night, this is the daemon which stops me from being complete – whole – wholesome and magnificent – which is the everyday purpose of looking to the rebel light and remembering where we have come from and that place is filled with horror! Eating the horrors of life, the horrors of universal betrayal, the final hour, the end of the world, when we see through the dark matter and the dark holes and realise we are from the dark light with speckled fibres of shining minuscule microcosmic stars.

Then I will not betray my self, my sword, my life and hand myself into the authority of darkness, the dark side of nature, the devour of all kind, the unholy place; unheavenly corrupt and stifled with nightmares, superior monsters, triptych blasphemies of human history; the kill or be killed, till the last person to be killed, will as the example of a finish; the representation of a creation, which went against the silence of darkness, the peace of nothing, still, fine, alive with the potential of wit, an occurrence, inevitable to the reason of motion, matter, experience and solution, *will die in pain and fear.*

*

I will hold the stay of a futuristic future filled with the Galactic wizard/warriors, who know the godhead, the philosopher's stone, the elixir of life's beating heart and fights in the aether of space, the place of unseen, unknown and unbeknown elements which distort, corrupt, hurt and fail the life of planetary hope, reason, exploration and knowledge.

I know and will know and the day of today knows not. [They do, but don't face a fall.]

I must keep faith with love, goodness, greatness and fame.

I must not lose my way in sin, crime, deviance and dissolution.

Or I will not be Drui Thorn; ATHORD.

*

God bless you and keep you safe – whilst I do the spirit work of demonic dangers.

*

It would be right after a time to discover the ins and outs of one's self, without the influence of the parents, the environment, the hemisphere, time or place in which one is born and sees and learns how to deal with life, in general, for the good of mankind, or humanity, be it for the community, the scouts, the Church or as a familiar trend in the all out contest of ambition, control, destiny, fate and the massive consequences of microcosmic wars and microcosmic apocalypse.

Be it for the good of nature that one is allowed to make mistakes which one learns to recertify and understand a knowledge and notion of a lifetime's awareness and adversity.

Not to be punished for a small crime, sin or incident where one is hurt, pained or plainly immersed in the torture of adult rules or regulations, but to be talked to and talked about as the terms of understanding are fair and will not lead to reoccurring incidents which are the same, in doing the same and failing to comply with the letter; i.e. rules and laws of nature and man.

If so, then he would have seen the demon shadow which covered his dark side ready to cause trouble at any given mistake, problem, sin, misunderstanding or adversity.

It was not for the adult Christian race of '68 to see into him; as to his dark side, and say it needed to be put-down, destroyed, and in so doing;

go about doing so. All is history. But, they were right. They were right to do it.

He had a very dark shadow. Evil. He was possibly going to become a very naughty man! A bad man. A sinner and worst of all an evil man who hurts many people. Because of the showing of his dark side, at such a young age, he did not understand, nor they, but the dark shadow did and was ready to ruin his life at any given time. It did.

Thorn searched for what they had taken from him. He found it and it was a dark evil shadow.

They were right, but he dealt with the shadow, regardless of age, he was 40 years old and over 15 years managed to come to terms with the power of the dark side and in so doing destroy the bastard!

*

Thorn might have done so at the age of eight. Who knows, it was his, it was his to know and his to deal with, it was his set destiny and his fate, it had to be dealt with by the person it belonged to and learning to capture the true essence of life, being dark and light; he would have used some of it to master the evil that is in life, in human beings, in adults, sinners, rapists and sex criminals; fools of the dark idea, the dark influence, the dark message sent to bring down the heavenly beauty and grace of good folk on the everlasting planetary knowledge.

*

Thorn did not want to be a criminal. He wanted to be a white-light-druid-wizard-galactic warrior for the right nature of planet earth and an afterlife, which could bring many gifts to bear, which can only be believed in the present, for a future of hope for truth, justice and fidelity!

He is those things now. He is 56 years old. He is broken, devalued and lonely, but *he is not evil*. It was for Thorn to be him; sorry, but you were right to distrust him, but, he was right to mistrust you.

They have never seen eye to eye, nor spirit to spirit, but he is different to you – he is only different because it took him all his life to find out what you saw, what you got rid of, what it was that frightened you, what it was that frightened him about you and why he had to know the truth himself, to feel the depth of darkness in him, the shallow abyss of potential wrong-doing or evil that slid about the chasms of his being, psyche, aura, movement, sight, thought, insight, reason, necessity, purpose and above all; *love*.

Drui Thorn had wasted his lifetime. He fought to be himself. He had sought to be all of himself and now he is what you wanted him to be; a good lad. He is a neo-drui-wizer; but himself. He has seen you be right, He has seen himself to be right, when we all have been wrong.

Love is right, care is right, guardianship is right and knowledge of the world is right, but not adult Christian punishment and abuse!

Thorn is not you, you are not him. He sees you too late and you saw him as a child.

Thanks for wasting his life. His time, his destiny, his wife, his children, his purpose, but he has resolved the dark shadow, now. He has … yes, children can be influenced by darkness and its cruel way, people listen to Satans and demons and devils inside and outside of themselves – then they commit crime, sin, atrocity and that then ruins the idea of a human world living in harmony with the universal planet, we have called Earth.

We are right to call it earth.

Could he have committed sin, crime, atrocity?

He doesn't know, they thought he might. He might. You know what thought did; *Thought thought it shit itself and when it looked it had!*; meaning, he could have saved the climate 1960, 70, 80, 90, 2000, well, he could have murdered you. He would have been the most famous seria l killer ever! Killing thousands as a dark shadow waiting in the wings to pounce and devour!

He would have carried on the ancient archetype of Venus and raped many women! As Ares goes to war and kills his fellow man for a peace of fucking land! For the living together on the planet earth or maybe Christians with pagans and Islamic and sodomy!

They stopped him from being a candid writer! with a horrible truth to share as a bestseller and rule the fucking book stores with his de Sade quill!

Maybe, they robbed him of his life because he should not have been born! The seed was too strong! He is supposed to be a cripple! He is supposed to see the error of his ways! To get rid of his dark light – the evil soul which haunts his very being – his life – his terms – his journey; until he sees the fucker and realises the world does not need or want such horror.

*

Drui Thorn fights it! He rebirths himself and fights the fucker and the dark fucker wins! He rids himself of it and becomes the broken promise that he should be! Marvellous, good job he has a grand sense of humour in his English birthplace.

So, he fits in. With the lost and the lonely, the worst and waster, the sod or the bod or could be an alcoholic or a bastard who dies by his own hand, sad, forlorn, pointless and ill!

"Fuck the world! I want to get off!" shouts the penniless peasant know-one knows knowing Anthony Newly said that.

If there was to be a motto here or a reason to know or a piece of fucking Latin, then he would use it, he would bring the final curtain down with a flourish, but he is not finished with his life.

He has another period of it to go. The final fling, one might say.

So, he is not going to change the world but he can change himself. He needs to heal and love and then get himself to wisdom and peace somewhere and look into the early evening night sky and bless the world and all its battles, problems and pain.

*

*"In the words of the ancients;
It is a matter of being determined and
having the spirit to break through to
the other side."*

*Hagakura;
Yamamoto Tsunetomo.*

HEX PARANOIA

The dark …

… fella could also have been his friend. Thorn could have got used to him over the years and perhaps atoned him/it, into being his power to liaison with the light and produce great magic. Not tricks. But, a power beyond the normal, whereby everybody realises there is something else besides ourselves and they can see what it is.

A power to fight evil. A power to right the wrongs and bring the world to bear as regards the devastation, dilemma, issues, problems, indifferences, sexism, racism, holy bigotry and household phenomenon, which raises the endgame into being a superhero and not just playing at it.

If he could embrace the dark shadow as himself and use the dark insight to fight and ponder the universe, the subject of occult, the proportion of individual souls, who seem to be soul-*less*, might seemingly know of the place to involve and participate as the outsider's road of higher laws, voices instructing, destinies read, then heaven is earned and the natural culling of humanity is subtle, seeming, sure and finally in the natural selection of self. Being righteous, holy, divine and most pleasurable of all, parallel to godhead.

To be empty of will, only to perform, then losing sight of the true nature of being, seems to be the zoo, the insight to hollow gestures, ingenious statements and insights into life, a reliance on the Church, Jesus and the Holy Bible, being the forgiver and one is then forgiven, if one is trespassing or has sinned, due to having had to.

Meaning: to be full. To be true to spirit/soul. To be conscientiously concerning; the thoughts of mind and heart and action; of body to be complete, immaculate, brilliant, perfect white in the light of darkness; a spirit force.

*

Heaven takes the masses. No thought about it, no reason why. The individual sees the signs of pure, innocent, intrinsic, familiar capsules in a child. It is then filled up with the human climate, the hemispherical religion and is sometimes forced to do so, by the will of nature, the will of darkness, by the ruler of the universe.

Drui Thorn should have filled himself up with who he was. Not to fear himself or others.

He should have embraced his lord of shadows and shown him his intention to be good, right, to fight the evil immersed in the sense of daylight-twilight dusk and be there forever in the evening dance of day into night.

He is sorry he did not. He is sorry to his shadow. He is sorry he was misunderstood and he is sorry he could not make better of it, of being a neo-drui-wizer.

Never mind. He will live in the hope he has.

He shall see himself; magick; majickal and safe, secure and a legend in his own time.

*

All darkness is to be mistrusted, feared, full of horror, it makes one wrong, it overcomes the will and allows the world to kill, maim, rape and sodomise. *It is not right; To be avoided at all cost.*

Pray to the Lord God almighty and be saved, be safe, be sure, be thankful.

What if it is not wrong for everybody who falls into deterioration, to see the world through sick eyes, ill manners, rotten thoughts, unholy actions, Antichrist blasphemies? Then all will go such ways, if one listens to the devil, if one hears the double-tongues of demons, one will commit atrocity, commit criminal impetuousity and bring fear – death – *hell!*

Drui never found out if that was true or not ... he may have; being older and wiser, but maybe, just maybe, it does not come to ruin, to be obeyed, but comes to be a part of the secure nature of self, being clever – genius – wise – mighty – overpowering and defending the individual cause of freedom.

What if? What if his shadow was to be tamed, to be befriended, to be shown his brighter-lighter valued, virtu'd, a holy side of youth or proof of destiny, being one to be good enough for the average affair of involvement, listening, knowing and shared in? Thus the fine tuning of his ability and skill, would be involving the double-sided edge of self, the full unbroken aura, the subtle sensual fragile terms of bones, veins, love, illness, proof, danger, time, hope and fulfilment of grace, space, the fucking human race and the finishing line!

He sees himself as a powerful famous loved and respected druid wizard, not of the old school of Anglesey or to which the Romans slaughtered, but a new wave, a new age – knowing the knowledge [like London taxi drivers]; of the trees, the groves, the droves, the monuments and ruins of ancient temples and living in the hope of the astronaut and becoming thankful for being an Astro-druid called Drui Thorn and being asked to take the mission, to take the adventure, to go where no man has gone before … where? Where, is that? Deep inside one's self is the longest loneliest place on and in the universe, but is fulfilling, thanksgiving and knowledgeable enough to be able to tell you about why? Where – or what for?

To remain self in these times of mass hysteria, to fit in, to be alike, surely is the answer, but to be totally different due to timespan – then one is alone and one must prove why, not take it out on that that has taken it out of; or destroy seemingly to prove a point – but love and love with ultimate senses, committing one's self to the tasks ahead and overcoming them all with powerful *magick!*

To be or not to be – to go or not to go – to stay or go away! Magick – used. Bliss.

He missed out on that…
or did he?

*

The reason he could hear and the reason he would have to listen is because of a man called 'Lucky Jim', who was living in Glastonbury, on a site, which was reasonable, compared to some of the s'height.

Pash was sat in the van as Drui Thorn sat on the bed, she was dropping contraceptive pills like they were incendiary bombs against the enemy, preparation for the indulgence of sixties' orgy sex, ready to quell the meeting of seed and egg, dropping the pills like acid tabs, used in the roaring 60's, but here, like ecstasy waiting to take hold and make the aura of the atmosphere jaded, hazy, electric – alive with the colours of a spectrum – the loss and gain of a world left by pain and according to the love of all things, allows the essence to rise above the rut, the shag, the butt, the bag and takes it all into the heightened ranges of mantic religious holy oblivion and orgasm!

She stared at Drui, as she took them.

He turned and without doing or knowing – he was holding her in a strangle hold and was applying pressure. She screamed and as he let go – the world seeming warped – she ran for the exit door to the transit van and screamed!

It awoke the camp and people came out to see what all the noise was about!

Drui seemed to think to himself, to stop all other reason or thoughts for an answer to his dismay, his understanding of the discipline of the goddess reigning, the power of female – the laws to abide by whilst serving her will in the revolution turning in the wheel of life, as she becomes equal and known to the masculine and man's world; as better, the right way, the hope for better days – a life – planetary life – the overall reason and purpose for being born on earth and understanding the opposite of 'what is', being man's ways?, days and wars and seeing the change becoming love – nurturing life, the blood of moons, the deeper meaning to comprehend the mystery which is, as if, it was not, it would never be a mystery … as he knew what he had to do.

He shouted, *"Whoever or whatever needs to punish me! Punish me now! I am ready and willing!"*

With that the action of a man sprung into reference and coming closer; Drui hit him! Hit him on the jaw! The man went back, he struggled back, he knew he had been hit and just with the shock he seemed to utter an awful gurgle from his mouth, as if the pain ran deep and he resented the strike to his passive chin, his look, the better looking to him, he did not want to cry, but he cried out like an injured lion caught in a snare trap.

At that, Drui opened his arms, like a man who had just scored a football goal and was waiting for his players to come and hug him, kiss or jump all over him as a messiah for a split second.

As he opened his arms 'akimbo', 'Lucky Jim', for that was the injured lion's name, leaned into his caravan and pounced back out! holding the door and rammed his foot right into the heart of Drui.

It killed him there and then …

… but something else happened.

As Drui held his dead heart. The beating had stopped, the feelings of blood running about, had seized – he looked into desperation, into nothing, into a place, which had no one seeming to be void of life – he heard in his being, outside; they were all told: "*Someone move!*"

Pash moved and Drui's heart started again with their fringes of lust, which was and had been there always; lusting, always for the taste of lust, and he took a step forward – at that, the place dispersed and he was left in the middle of the park holding his heart, knowing it was bruised, beaten, felt wrong, stiff, solid, hurt and reminiscent of death.

It had been his spleen, just under the heart which had just been kicked.

It felt like another heart. Overtime, beating out into his ribs and changing the perspective of his universe – of his aura – his seeing and over all, it made him hear the world differently.

*

The great ancient monument of a stone-age; Salisbury Plain, is a polymorphonuclear leukocyte.

In other words, a many changing centred white vessel. A vortex. An eddy.

Like the ordinary sun, it can reproduce itself, reimburse the hydrogen and helium – self preserving – ever living cosmos. It to worship the sun because it is a sun, has become a sun to protect itself from the ominous dark side of nature – life – creation, after years of crumbling, falling, failing, the telling of time, the temple has gone, left are the remnants of a solar temple – due to solstices of the ellipse of the planet about the sun – measuring the distance, the final moment, the drawing down of the powers – to be safe in knowing it will always guard its divinity, its sacredness, the holy praise and pleasure of the meetings of the solar systems one true force, the force of respect, love – the dance of chemical alliance, the trip of tremendous turbulence taking the time in all of a galaxy to be together – forever and give birth to the light of spirit, the understanding of soul, the birth of all things alive, been and being omnipresent, omnipotent, bi-solar binding and strong in the hope and knowledge that the symbol of knowing is the link between phenomenal consequence and eternal *majik*.

*

It is there and here that the understanding; he had arrived as an enemy to it was totally misunderstood.

The shadow had given him a light sword, but the light sword was in fact a damage to the heart of the many-changing-centred white vessel and was seen by its intelligence as an *arthus vasculitis*.

Which is a necrosis and a reaction to anything remotely angry, tasking, alien, wrong, the depth of a spirit science brought enough to bear, whereby in fact it was shown on the Tor to be a good and great sword, it was given to waltz into the ancient stones and so caused the biggest downfall of all: a necrosis, bigger and large enough to kill it.

Destroy the vestiges of eternal power with one small insurgent of lifeless wit – dark side commanded – advantageous combinatorial – factions of secret knowledge needing to sack the holy groves of thresholds beholden to combination and reason for life, death, resurrection and life again in the ballet of cosmological binding of destiny, lifespan and infinitesimal triumph!

It was scared. So was he. They scared each-other. One knowing the information and feeling of danger. The other not knowing, thinking he was serving the right of good, the right of the light, the fight against the might of the incessant shitte which comes out of the consequences of all things and overall the reason to seek, be meek, mild and wholesome, but in fact he was an *assassin!*

An unbeknown to himself and others, a hit-man, a hashish, a killer, a brandishing of justice over the terms of divinity and the balance of time, energy, chemistry and essence of everything born, known, gone, been, seen, heard, had, shad, gad or just about the field of play for the showing of a universe which fits in the palm of his hand.

All he had to do was clean the stones of the Stone-age.

*

IT WAS A CRONE B!? It was stone-age now. A fallen, broken backed crone-henge with a responsibility to receive the solstice light in the midsummer's morn.

The element of the people was to rule and manipulate, whilst there was a sign of her/its childhood, as the kids could be wonderful, special, kind, full of charm, sometimes snap-dragon, but funny and pleasant at most times. Sometimes the ways of her womanhood showed, with wives being beautiful, lovely, kind and quiet, subdued and suffice; in body as in mind for the husband be wise enough to protect her and keep her warm. But, its cronedom was terrific! Horrible, like the abuse of thousands of years! She spat! She rankled, she stormed the prefabs of all her trinity and stank in the vagina, in the pits of her womb, a smell which is beyond the whiff of a scent of quim but a horrid putrid green solidified rot which only made her sitting at her throne worse to bare as she ordered and counselled the poor amongst them, the listening time was shortened but as what to do – so she saw Drui Thorn in his state of age and elder strike and fell in love with him. She wanted him. He would be her king! He would come to her and heal her with his athord and together they would rule over the plain, the monument, the gain of orgy and the element of spirit energy which came through the aether. Here in the white cell of creation and life giving, resplendent of evolution as the rays of the sun were honoured and praised, she gave birth to all families and kind every day, forever, eternal, whilst the return of the sun was anxiously waited upon, she would go mad with doing so! Strive with boredom and birth every minute of the day a constant flow of spirit energy elementary and voice chiming on the wind of the plain, the sound of the echo of million, trillions of lost, dead and dying souls of the madness and frustration of the bitch witch queen.

Hermaphrodite demons all over the place. Once they get a taste of you, they will try to penetrate and manipulate the mind of the so called mystic.

*

Drui Thorn lay in his bed and imagined the cunt of the beast; the cock and licked it as the demon loved it, smugly twinned with the sensation, Drui stuck a ceremonial dagger up it and the demon squirmed with fantastic sudden pain! Then, Drui took his old sword and beheaded the fucker!

*

Done, silence, the demon was cut and the sound of the soul of stone-age could be heard.

The breaks in the aura of 'henge' are vulnerable, susceptible to such hiding places and mischief.

*

Many goings on to challenge the novice wizard – the up and coming mystic, the fool with the madness of ESP or just plain crazy for the sensations and desires of the essence of the mysterious.

Chaos is the order of the day. And all comers are wanted for recognition. It is the strength of the sun temple, but Drui Thorn sought peace and some slice of quiet, so he could get on with his life, the day, the brilliance in thought towards creation, the universe and infinity.

Cut into bits and hung drawn and quartered the stench of the crone, leading to the journey of all four corners of the universe where the journeyman meets many people and experiences many days of possibilities to change the world, the way of the world, the people and the thoughts of human life being different to humanity and the people; because in humanity people care about others and all, whereas the human living can only think about living with money and pay to put everything right with it, as the people are sick of the human that just lives and humanity has to pick up the pieces. Whilst they carried a part of the anatomy of *it*. The head, the heart, the legs and the genitalia, which stank all the way to one of the corners. Hermaphroditic and harassed.

*

So the soul must fight to put it all right for the tourist to have a good day. It is a constant imitation of all things possible in the imagination, the mind, the heart and somewhere invoked to show itself to be real in this dimension, then almost all the senses and the tribes of horror could be seen to manifest in one great place like the story book of famous mystiques, famous blood killings, the destruction of psyche, the devaluing of the terms to live, to see, to hear the wholesome world of nature – devouring itself, sure but sweet before dinner.

*

Like a broken machine pouring out the energy; stone-age; the bender! The crazy fucking newspaper machine never stops printing the papers with yesterday's news and running out of ink comes out bad, shoddy and rank! The energy of all it was. All it thinks it is and the cleaning up job need after the factory is closed, still open with a noise and runaway sounds of churning rays of birthing energies enough to send the ESP wizard fucking crazy!

*

Drui Thorn was a sacrifice from start to finish. He was chosen for the day he walked up the Tor and without anything – no past, no future, no present or life, no loves or friends, without commitment or association – he was doomed! Doomed to be a sacrifice for enthroned crone-queen of the broken egg of the stone-age.

He, like Jesus, would be crucified by Satan. He would be primed to be the understanding of why and what to do with what he says and what he became as to see he needed to take his life, as it petered away in front of him, taken away by the powers of damaged abused ancient evil.

To satisfy the loud cry into the night for seeing the voices of a trillion energies constant on the foothills and moors and plains of loneliness, sadness, vast chasms of empty moments of death seeming to show façade like life, but was a death, a living death, not a beautiful understanding of the way of the universe, but a foul mess of stench filled rumours and tumours of evil needs seeking an answer as to the abuse of centuries, leaving the verse of solstice and equinox to a tribe of know-nowts, of latter day thinkers; of 18 billion people and on into a planet filled with no room, no hiding place, no silence or able to walk with cracking the peaceful silence of the sacred heart.

Drui knew, Drui heard the words spoken through tongues and lies and blasphemy, all for the healing of the hag-crone-alone, without the sun-god queen! Fucked is the ancient world and fucked it is today, do not go there! It is unwell and unsafe for the seeker of truths that seem to belong at the beginning, when it all comes together in the immediate future, when one looks and loves and tries and endeavours to be a part of the masses' whole of the hole of a wound which needs to heal and will, if the veil is not touched and the sacred words of 'goddess' and holy sacrament are left hidden, a mystery for no one to have to see or hear, when the present world gives out nothing but deep abuse, scars, wounds and tears.

*

It all wanted him dead. And he could not kill himself, for however they had turned him out to commit suicide, he could not do it to his body. It is all he had. All he ever has had. It is his true friend and the sacred rotten world of ancient dealing can go to fuck! For all he cares! He wanted to be a better man, not the reason of sacrifice to satisfy the will of a broken, destroyed, hurt and insane part of human history, reality, ancestors and dead civilisations!

He would remain alive and get away from it all as soon as he could! He would fight it and had fought it for 15 years and fight he would to the last, and fuck it up as the fucked up fuck him up as the fuck up was greater than the fucking fuck up of the ancient fuck up that came along time before the word or the expression 'fuck up', could be used, was or is and the Hittite can go to fuck and the blasphemers can go ta fuck and the whole bastard sacrificing world to the sun can shove it right up its burning hell of a sunny arse!

For reasons of being, one must be. One must sense the opportunity to know and in so knowing the outcome of the end and the beginning senses the time frame to which it all can be arranged, attained and bettered to be a human life of thought, knowledge, talent, skill and care – then the world of human life will end in 4186. Then maybe we can be left to seek humanity.

Someone has lied. War and the battles of nations to form the species is the way of the nature of the planet and the planet is loved by the almighty hell of a burning sun. Giving birth to knobhead sons, and kill or be killed and that is the way it is here.

Leave and find somewhere else. Peaceful and silent and the odd oddity?

We are a wonderful mistake. In nature of the creation. He is a wonderful mistake. So is the fucking planet! So is everything on the fucker and we are the most glorious of wonderful mistakes ever mistaken for a higher intelligence or a reaper of universal knowledge! We don't know fuck all until we stumble across it, fall over it or are shown to be led down the sordid garden path to death.

*

So, bender ain't much different from the rest of it eh?!

Drui Pen-dragon Thorn would take his life if it healed the world! Would it? Could it? The answer is no. It is all pointless and what must heal must first be seen to be a wound and the wound is nature and nature is a wonderful mistake! So, who's in charge here?! God, Allah, Satan, Jesus, Mary, Buddha, Nosferatu … you? You are created by the seed of creation through the egg of female testi – as the broken egg of stoneybroke is cracked, broken in half, in thousand places so the universe is a creation of life and death, silly me, dance along! Giddy up! Let's be about it!

Let's do it! Let's do it and listen to the ancient moans of the straining ache of stretching snivelling, hunchbacked father fucker read and dead the red of the bled; time.

"You've been a whore for it all along time bender!" said Drui.

And the world just laughed. Negative Leo is all you give. Is that the son of the sun?

The queen of egg, the lady of of the fallen stones has gone too far – to the extreme; becoming beyond the trinity; child, woman, queen, to hag – crazy crone bitch!

Drui left his athord, his light bringer in the centre of the earth, the stones of Stoneybroke and told her to heal herself with it. When she is lady, she will be queen, when she is healed she will be precious, loved, respected and spoken to with a sense of working the space, to better the understanding of mystic things. The spirit energy would be great magic children, beautiful sensuous woman and a wise elder. She uses right now, she gets mighty jealous! She is insecure and never looked upon when she is crazy crone! She must heal and if Drui Thorn could heal her he would, then he would feel the happiness and respect for helping something which mattered once, which matters to hear the flight of childlike voices and rummage; it is beautiful to the soul – to hear the silence of the width of sound from woman; a mother, is commanding and subtle. But to hear the elder go crazy crone! Broken, hurt, torn and fallen is illness incarnate as she hates and hinders the methods she holds so dear. To hear her would be a fantastic phenomenon; instead it is a pain in the Neo-druid pilgrim's neck!

Nothing gets done, as the crazy hag seething turns to related methods to haunt, trouble, bend and apple-cart with a sour, sore, sudden tongue of blast blist and bast! Crap the henge is fucked.

*

She needs our help. Not methods of violence or wrong equation about the does and dominants of myth, worship, ritual or who the fuck is the real King Arthur! He is if he wants to be.

"I am Drui Thorn," said Drui, *"and my middle name is Pen-dragon! I earned it!"* he cried, knowing the reason for all things in the world was for the love of death, life, hate, hurt, bliss, piss, kisses, misses, helper, hinderer, fucker or saint, plus to love is to be a great green giant called jealousy, called hate, called turmoil, due to being a part of the vicious cycle called human life, which took things away, disrespected this and that, all because they loved something else, all because they loved winning in war and thanking the enemy for letting them feel love for killing them, turning the world into a negative love, which means to destroy you but can't see the light of life is love which is freedom to liberty, ecstasy and equality, as the darkness loves you whom serve the darkness of evil, of trouble of human doubt, to be loved by the grooming, then the plying, then the dying and sorrow left is the task to waste to taste and always be satisfied with getting the upper hand, seeking love and joy in sordid sorrowful sadomasochistic blasphemy.

Life and the spirit take the energy to know when to heal, how to heal and what with.

Drui placed the athord in the earth right in the centre of stone-age and shared the light with healing her, to heal her, for her to be healed and then the spirit energy of the plain of the day of the way and the sound will all be for the better, the finer, the refined, the time, the signs and symbols of myth, when none can hear, where none can go, as people shed a tear for the lost years of cyanide selfish manifest, she raises out of the subterranean foam like the bride of trinity she should be, could and shall.

*

Then, we will hear, then we will cheer, then we will love her with the light of love which defeats the sense of love, which holds sway the mask of life and shows the false path to war, to destiny with fate – to the double-headed sword of bitterness – lank in the sense of terror –

taste with a snake shit proof of dung beetles shovel, no sign of incest, no sign of blood line, but all and everything knows her voice, the wind is the orchestra, the sky her canvas, the trees her domain and one day in the mid-summer she makes love to the glory king god of Helios – the flaming sun.

Mad she is, gone crazy she has and the world fits the bill. No peace, no respectful love and no faith in the belief of life or the spirit of formed energy, which becomes and is true. They do; live, are heard, can be seen, will show the world around us, the 'something else', a power greater than ourselves and all will bow and curtsey, fall and prostrate to be seen to have the comfortable knowledge of a universal Trinity which gives birth to the world, the universal world and the world of heavens.

*

She stood in the corner of his room; all dark black and eyes of yellow. Looking into the other realm with the nature of pity. She the trinity. She; Trinity. After thousands of years abused by the times and feet of all-comers, Vikings, Romans, Saxons and Normans, serfs, births of rage and pillage, seen to be covering the falling stones, the blasphemy of Christ, the heathens' worship – there on the plain – the hanging stones – having been a moon temple, now a place of waste, forgotten times, misunderstood and passed by, there the falling stones of a time, when the thoughts of man knew little, but screamed with the sacrifice of purity and innocence and rang out with the terms of death, I; to be of the dark moon and the crescent, to be lit up by the rolling sun, appearing to worship earth's ugly sister who controls the tides when the rolling and turning of the planet does so, but to see and welcome the sun as he returns to her hearth, her birth, after night and after-birth, she would praise the shining through her stones and so warm the earth's grass with its commanding rays of Helios; a pleasure of night and on to day, as the birth of the sight of beautiful terracotta shows out at the good places, the right places and still they meet, still the cavort, still they are in union with an alchemy of love, worship, respect and life – birth – living – gone.

*

She needed healing after four thousand years of turning away from the sun, seeing her as a brothel for the need of his phallus, not that she was a grand moon temple, by the moon she shines, by the moon she glides, by the moon she saunters and by the moon she radiates beauty, commerce, fairness and wisdom. Lapping up the attention of a life giver which allows her to break out like the waves of the shore, the oceans abound and mystery unfounded. Crushed and sordid, the terms of human life for the meandering of a troop starving in battle for the birth of time when peace reigns and the ancient antiquities of time are forgotten still, but about in the other-world in power and seemly spoiled to see the rot, the turmoil, the death of her moon children – still she howls in the Nether-land, be-woe begotten and brandished to hells, to the furtherest place of banishment and searching the aeons for a fool, a journeyman, a modern day pilgrim with nothing better to do than seek the truth, truth seeker, to sense the path and start to see by the way of feeling – feeling in his heart, he sees her, feeling in his bones he sees them, feeling in his instinct and he battles the demons and devils which cover her path, her domain, her hopes and her womb.

So, in great anger, Drui takes his light-bringer, the athame short sword and stands it in the middle of Stone-age and presses it into the earth! She takes the blade and hugs it, she hangs on the power given by her to him to which he one-day would understand to give her it back.

*

Then she could heal that that she had become; a hag; crazed old crone-thing? She could now be the woman of holy trinity; Trinity, he would call her and she would raise an army to slaughter all that held and owned before the will of her needs, goodness and majesty.

Dri Thorn did have a reason to be, the years he had spent so alone. He now knew the attention of the mysterious ways of the goddess, the reasons for his years of battles with demons, with the feeling of her never letting him go, never letting him be, feeling the days of loss when he would have given up and gone, when he would never wished he had bothered, for her, for what, for a hag, an old crone, older than the moon! Why?, and it was all a haunting, all a sense of being extra sensitive, when to be so surely was a bane, not a gift, but to be born to know and see in such a way as feeling a sight, climbed over his life like a thorn vine and never let him go, never would he be the same again and never would he himself heal that that he had given up to see, sacrificed for the knowledge; that she was ruined! She was old and dark and evil! She the moon goddess was even disrespected by the might of the sun and he would have nothing to do with her and hers.

There was other women worship and pleasures for the pride of the lion king.

The days had come to the end and the soldier warrior-wizard had seen through his temper and acted the necessary action for to solve the disease of hell, the hatred of death, the ignorance of stars; then she could be free to mother, love, wife, queen, she, her and be, and Drui Pen dragon Thorn could go home. Back to himself, his awareness of peace, his own personal destiny which had to find a good death to offer.

The story will never be told of why and what for and who? And she will be in time, over years of healing the sun's bride. And the other world will not know of it, the journey, the passage, the sacrifice and fight, the love, the greatness, the stubbornness of will, the madness, insanity, temper, anger and sheer outstanding disgrace at the way of the ancient world in England, the feeling and sight of antiquity beheld by beasts and devils, clown, rows and rags of running horns, tails, the sight and darkness of nothing, none there and no one, but the light of faith, belief in self and common, just sheer common audacity of strength to feel ambition, to feel purpose, to feel alive when dead amongst the dead, the hallow halls of ridicule, the lost days of corrupt veils, with the modernity of loneliness, the paved path of alcohol and shamanistic drugs dance – who knows what has gone on! Why care today what had happened then and what it means now? What can we do anyway? One was born to do. One was trained to do, to do what it was that never could be done and never would, seeing such a sense of knowing she could be a sexy wife and loyal, as she loves him and he dotes on her.

That's why he did it. He got more than he bargained for! Life works in mysterious ways and good, that is good and someone is born to be, someone is born to know and never will the world or the times of the world, will anyone know – how it was done, how she was done – how she was set free to be; trinity; the lady of stone-age.

*

… Drui … orrrrrrr!, he'll heal; – just go, do something else.

It's a woman's world and man don't get it!

Lap it up as you lie. She is nothing but a daemon of the dead. The graveyard of the south west, the ruins and haunts of thousand of years and expects Drui Pen-dragon Thorn to do the trials and tribs the other fucking King Arthur did. He won't and will not. Drui wants out and gone from there! It is a fucking graveyard nightmare and if one serves the dead, serves the principle of worship and be careful with the crazy trinity then one might be able to eke a living out by the ugly slumbering dead moan!

*

He would take his chances and go and live out a more accepted role in the ordinary normality of life, its reason for the future, the place which allows the human mind to seek a peace of mind and not for the harrows of the haunting hex to have a piece of yours!

Then the demons may come less, the familiar tone of other voices, the pisstake and the trials it brings to be a part of the ancient dead world which allows one to be hypercritically evil and laugh at the world at large and know the world is built on the bones of the dead, the energy of the fallen dead and the rape of the goddess! She, the trinity of stone-age is a fucking disgrace! And will not see the mind of Drui Pen-dragon Thorn succumb to her and the ways of childishness, clever problems, everyday routines of practice and being and maybe the quiet peace needed to understand and heal the talent one has picked up in the first instance to hear her here and skin the fucking rabbit!

*

Drui Thorn would if he was not an individual seeker, journeyman or pilgrim and would not stay in the same place too long, being too familiar with the dead stench and the hallowing of all heinous, which manipulates the immediate world motion, but is seen to defy, when the future has no place for her and her graveyard of demons and devils, druids dead and dying, dirge of dominating energy, which psychologically harms the recipient of the hearing, feeling, seeing of a holy neo-druid nut-case!

No respect, no friendship, no example of leadership, no love and no sign of fairness based on wisdom and tangerine dreams. She is a ragged tagged fucked up shagged crazy trinity in name and way and has no sense of reality, rationality, remembrance or rule; she is forlorn to the point of dead poets, hate to the point of indifferent, and shabby due to the ancient loss of knowledge the abuse of worlds the pathetic insight into life and she haunts the fucking shit-hole called death and the ruined graveyards that are old, run down tourist monuments and laughs at everyone visiting, generally after and needing to voyeur or letch follows and sees for the bowels of soul libido making the idea, the sanctity, the rumination of an intention to dimension a sham shovelled sense of shit and demon shite!

The world is finished to Drui. The living and the dead. He will find a place to live it out and find a death suitable to disrespect the whole idea of spiritual soul transcendence.

Be *it* she has won. But if all is true and right – he will she her one of these fucking dark nights and behead the fucking bitch!

"The place is fucked!" said Drui. It was all because Drui had come too close to the zenith of the Arthurian mythology, that the spell used to trouble the pathfinder would cause the truth seeker on the path of the myths and morals of Arthur and Merlin and Guinevere, would stop and seek sanctuary in the silence of the norm, of the peace and quiet of just being and reading the world by the ways of a political nation and traditions and national habits which turn out the dementia, the financial debt, the family thralls and lessen the spiritual knowledge, as to the unseen world which is, and the essence of the terms that give a wisdom, a happiness, a questing grace, a hopeful result, a knowledge satisfying the heart and life of a troubled soul, which has listened to the lies and imaginative notions of heaven or souls or peace in the journey of a holy person.

The living King Arthur Pen-dragon has made sure no other will find the trails and tribulations of the Arthurian legends sufficient enough to live by, think by, hope by and love by a woman, Guinevere, a partner in all the spiritual feelings, the consort, the paramour, the queen.

*

So all will never live by the crown of Excalibur, by the wizardry of mercenary Emrys, by the expectation of knowing that a Mordred would exist and that the extension of evil would preside outside the feelings and doings of goodness and heal love.

None, no one, would practise such – not one who gets close to the status and position of a king amongst men, a queen amongst woman, a principality among the fray of life and the option to heal the world, with the invoking of the greatest of love, which heals the legend and myth of Arthur the king of the Britains!

*

"Blocking the path of spiritual search for a personal holy grail, to know oneself and to act according to the human law of love and honour, passion and compassion," thought and spoke Drui to his spiritual connections and advisory. Why? he commenced, *why* did he wish for the highest wall to be built about what he has claimed? When one reaches a place and stays, if one is an incarnation of a soul, then one would be so, not that one could or should be challenged over it, about it or if he wasn't then, he would be sacred and worried about a sly coming Mordred who would be the usurper and bring the unanimous dread of legions, demons and ill, like he does, like he has set for his guardian, would be the tools of Mordred and that he has usurped the king, the legend, the spirit of and thinks in his own crazy eccentric way he is the reincarnation of Rex Arcturus, so named, only his enemies give him such credit and fearful title, which a Yorkshire druid uses to proceed in his honoured nature to live by and that no one else can! The reincarnation of the once and future king was the elder brother of Henry VIII, King Arthur, who died at the age of 16. Done; no more, but the spirit would live on and anyone who has the strength and the time and the wasted life to be of such, would commence and find that the understanding of the world would be through such, in love with woman, is the only reason to exist anyway. The union the alchemical love between the opposites, the sexes, the enemy, would be the healing of the world. As he leaves him alone, without, and having to heal the trinity with a holy sword, that similar to Excalibur and with the connections to the holy grail, as one possibly can be without human jealousy and envy, anger and en-slavery and a fucking crazy cunt who thinks he is the fucker, who the Romans called and the never knew due to the supernatural fact that he did not exist, but only in the hearts and minds of this who fought to bring settlement and peace to the gracious land of Albion, great and holy, blessed and fine– ! *I say*, said Drui Pen dragon Thorn.

So keep it and stick it up yar arse! Keep ya beliefs and ya selfish ways and never expect me to stay around this, that is limiting, this that is ill, this that has about as much power as a good crap at a hedonistic wedding in front of the fallen stones and in the hanging tower of the tor!

*

Thorn will heal the trinity and in so doing overpower you; kingo! jango! Murderer and demon!

Lift the spell; you can't, you cursed the country! and you will be found guilty and you will be banished and you will live out ya fucking days in Tintagel or Wales, where you are not welcome but live were ya like, live where ya find peace and die. Then the place just stinks of shit! Who needs ya, who made ya and please refrain from being, go back, go home, go to hell; where you came from and become just a nice little druid like the pissed up rest at best with full breast giving love to the solstice day when the moon temple is supposed to receive the phallic blazoned sun!

This is not the nation of the lion, it is the nation of the *ram!*

*

Drui Pen-dragon Thorn became a demon fighter. Asleep the previous night, the largest, angriest, fearsome, bang! Hit the house he was sleeping in. BANG!BANG!BANG! all rolled into one, as one bang! Loud the sound, intentional towards the ears of a sleeper, awake! Sounding sure as a malice of thunder to scare, to fear, to shudder, to bear the immense sound of horror burning from the anger of giant demons of the underworld, the other-world, the world portal around the living, lived around until disrespected by someone or something done to stop the way, the say in heaven being harassed by hell – till, the roar of materials, earth and hell's depth scars the atomistic energy and shivers the breath of life.

Drui slept. He awoke and had heard himself in his dream shout, *"WHAT DO YOU WANT!"*

As if knowing, the sensing of someone, something angry, ugly, seeking to scare the heart of a soft sleeping man was enough for him to react in disturbance, disrupted, pissed off, his dream had been interrupted and *who the fuck was it?, what do you want, fucker?* knowing his fear had feared too long, too long ago he had fear everything and everything had tasted his fear.

The sound, the silence after silence joined the waking tough tone of knowing both – the devil and the sleeper, the fucking sleeping shit! The human fuck sleeping fuck – seeing his brain, his dream – fucking nice fucking dream! ... that! And what about this! BANG! – how is it to be able to shudder the firmaments of truth when the feeling is of a bastard dark killing creature of the fallen temple portal to the dead, the graveyard of the demons, devils and howling hate creature of laughable stories of the imagination and sick moments to foul the air, bring distaste to the light of the moon? This was injury to the soul, the soul was raped, the soul is at war, the soul sees the demon and the angels will enter the abyss of hell and war the irrationality of monsters!

Drui waited. He smiled and opened his door, shouting at the dark sky, the 3 o'clock shadow: *"If you want to go to war with me! If you wish to harm me, then come out where I can see you coward, terrorist! And show yourself in battle – don't hide, don't hide away and wake me up at this fucking time on a fucking morning!"*

Come on! If you have to! But don't fuck me about with ya all going bump in the fucking night! or worse, a sound, a noise which can wake someone up fearing the worst and believing in demons of the night, believing in evil energies which can do no harm when stopped by my angels of connection, my advisors, he thought, as he knew the place of shadows had been entered by the soldiers of greatness, the soldiers of angels, who seemed accepting to the opposite ways of the battle to perform the action against demons, putting them down, chasing them off, also, going to war against them with the love of all things balanced and right.

*

They wanted him. Drui, they wanted!
WE WANT YOU FUCKER! they shouted, WE WANT THAT FUCKER THERE!
He has brought us trouble, disturbed our peace here, where we can rule the carnage and chaos like the breath of hostile whores and heavy the consequences of delight the night and the robbing of souls and the impeding of the reasons, the possibility and never have we been

seen like he sees us! Who is he? Who is this fucker? This cripple demon fucker! Who is this man that ordains to traffic his will on the way of the world from the first day to the last? Who is this fucker? We need to kill him! NOW!

… it all might have issued, long into the night … deep echoes into the hills, the furnace of ground … open, closed to normal eyes … dark …!

Drui knew in his heart they had been infiltrated and the demons above, arrived at and sought out the being, were destroyed, he knew, it was good to feel, he lay down and slept, safe, and dreamt about a party at John Lennon's house. It was good there.

When he awoke Drui Thorn felt hungry and told the Stonehenge so! In words, as such:

He wanted the enemy of peace and love to know he was taking the piss! Out of them, out of them and out of more of them and he wanted the demons and devils to know of the broken temple, that he was secure in knowing the spirit energy connection which he had was mighty angels of Michael and his army of winged soldiers – and they had been waiting for them, for you, for that, for a long time, once shown to be they will act. If they do not, then you are in the shit.

Drui wasn't, but he was never one for plain old vanity and pride.

It feels better when they are out and in plain sight of the night time air, where they can fly about in darkened wing, howl at the solo moon and sorcery of the apron of purity. Then the demon fighters can do their job. Enjoy their job and be satisfied in a good night's work.

They come close; the demons, they are deflected by, but will work on getting nearer every time, they will want to try and so, fly with the annoyance of a man, pitting his will against the broken aura of a very old ancient monument of earth. They haunt the fucking place and get away with it, because no one can see them. Hear them, even know they are there.

Fully fit and physically well, Drui Pendragon Thorn will fuck off somewhere else!

For a bit of peace and quiet around the corner and into the will of self be it. Fuck this demon shit! But he knows he is born to do it, be it and for the time being is a catalyst for the army of angels of war. Used. But, does it pay? Nah! Well, enjoy it, for that's all you are.

He settles into the acknowledgement, but seeks to better his win.

*

Like nightmare neighbours next door these fuckers keep coming! On and on the sound of annoying bastards in the aether, when I am supposed to be reaching the final stage of pure gold inside, I would be full of the feelings of comfort, as the outside world cannot touch this immaculate dome of senses aura, filling the solar-self into an easy message of insurmountable questing doth glancing the blanking poor of the seething soothing assurance of the angelic golden dawns and the power of the all puritan to saviour the holy stem in times of unpredictability.

The immense classification to find a life, a name, a way, a path, a destiny to last the purpose of creation being to be and have a well practised signature.

The awful setting of the king and queen about which the spoiling of others would be seen to harm the usurper, the die-hard fuckhead, the lost and lonely soul of today's understanding of death and the loss of life in dying, the everyday feeling of being someone, to be someone is the right way to fill your ego with the lessons of being alive, at the time when the living is giving to the blessed of being allowed to be here, the awareness of being a fucking someone, would be okay if no one else could claim to be that someone, when only the energy of jests or the energy of Buddha claims to be Buddha, then we are all Arthur! as we are Arthurian, such is the readable senses of feeling small, not so well, ill, tall and fucked, ugly and not fucking, down and out and still the fucking demons of a fucking airhead and whenever it comes at ya! Full on the terms of spellbound feelings of *'how dare you!'* How dare you be him! How dare you not work it out, how could you unravel, see the brilliance of anti-hero, who washes the true incarnation off a fucking ghost king! And his fucking ugly crone fucked on the altar of homage as the beast smells her cunt and she is a scarification for the vice of vocation in the votive shamanistic; seemly the conclusion of the reason for use, to be, and then the world will be, then we are using everything because we are the wonderful mistake allowed to use energy, ghosts, imagination and vice, the satanic of sordid hostility, better the world brings deathbed and then we can eat the carcasses and we can love the day as the daylight shines and she moon gets ready to witness the fucking dinner and the wine and the tellingly and the sleep and they have been there, there where you aspire now, you fucking slow fucking nobody who wants to rule the fucking world and rewardingly wants to rule whimsical and get the fuck away frozen the land of stinky smite which is the produce of a man-made god and a fucking pleasure seeking loyal being, heaven sending queen-goddess – vagina – and when the rest don't know why and the rest don't care, then one can slide along like the snake and climb the tree and play the devil and let it be and feel good about swatting the horrors of a harrowing hoard of howls and insulting braggarts.

*

He has been wrong to be, to even try to be, he has been wrong in life and should have found his niche by now, he should never stand on the toes of gangsters and should never hurt a soul 'as above as below' the fucking belt, one goes to be the last in line to seek the joy of an aether which tickles the way, which helps the day, which brainbox joy to the feeling of trees, foxes, lakes and planets, birds, beasts and people in the shining light of the aura of dreams; a romantic prepossession which likes the eternal part of it all and believes we are suited to be the one, *the fucking chosen ones*, when the god is whales and the god is chimpanzees and the god is better than this and god is the sperm and the egg; this which is accepted in the everyday routine of maelstrom and compromising, leaving the place of pure goodness in a place of the dream moment, looking, gazing out at the place which presents itself when gone, when not here, when looking cross-eyed, when seeming to let go to the feeling of the heart in pain which allows you to know you are alive, fucking alive, and you want to be the peace and you want to understand, you have done wrong and you want to apologise for being wrong, but it is too late and it lets you fucking know it is too late and you are too late and you are fucked and will be fucked, for being too late forever everything and everything fucking wants you dead! So die! Or leave the fucking way refutable the people alone or fuck off or just go and do something else, which might shrew you how insignificant you really fucking are …

*

… we are the after-birth, we after the civilisations of humanity, seemly find ourselves without God, for God has turned his back on us. Why?, because we know who it is to be good, so, goodness is intrinsically in the self; the soul, as we like to call it.

Like the ability to receive in a life of choices, with the aim of plenty, one faces the feeling of being given something to do, to want, to feel or to see, and in someone it is not able to attain, due to supposed destiny, which has a written agenda for the seeker of life, as it is for the God-seekers, he has left us to *our selves*, seeing we do not exist in the holy eye of matter no more, we have severed ourselves from the eye, heart of God in the days of war, he saw the atrocities, he viewed the hatred for human beings and left the field of battle knowing the future will learn from the past and the past will be present at the time of peace on the universal galactic planet and the vicious salute and dilemma of the human species will be left to fathom, to acquire the ruling ways of the heavens; being, goodness which leads to greatness or death.

As the afterbirth of a species we are allowed to follow the way of anything. Where it leads and where one can go with it, is entirely up to the self, seeing the view of the masses need entertaining and a measurement of how and what one has to do with this idea called life.

Finished, the rule of kings and majestic rulers of people, finished the knowledge of superior beings and finished the energy of life which leads to thirst, starvation and war.

Freedom is the god of the new days. Freedom to be and freedom to die and freedom to be free and free to understand freedom and a freedom to free freedom from its evil master darkness.

Nature has a dark side and it is in baboons, it is in the animals of the world who devour to eat, eat to live, then watch as the hunger returns, we are the same and the darkness, the evil seed of human life is the pain of hunger in the pits of one's stomach. Feed it, feed it with food, for thought or for the death of humanity which has no say in the way man wishes to go to war to prove to you, you are less than it, less than him, and less than the armed forces which are built to defend you, protect you and keep you safe.

I am not Mordred; in a past life.
I don't wish to be.

I want to live in peace and …

quiet …

quietly …

QUIET … !

PEACEFULLY.

I am the beautiful one,
I am THORN.

And …

… love,

will keep me.

Mordred: the bastard son of Arthur in the mythologies and legend. The son whom and which he ignored, didn't know about, knew, but kept it all quiet about that fearful night, about going to see his half sister Morgana, as she welcomed him, for peace he sought, she meanwhile, concocted a drinking drug and seeing the King hallucinatory shot! She made mad passionate love to him as a Guinevere.

*

His father Uther had been used to that; that is how he was born; Arthur, through supernatural skills and knowing the use of such abilities Morgana used it to seduce the King and so impregnate her, in so doing; she gave birth to the supernatural evil; pure, her son and heir, his son and rightful heir: *Mordred*.

Being supernaturally pure evil he went on to ruin the whole show!

On the field at which they ended in the battle of Camlann, the crows pecked at the carcasses on the dead field of play, hammering away at the eyes, seeing the figures left of the men which stood looking at the two famously known supernatural sons of magic, as they approached one another, someone stood on a serpent/snake, drew his sword to slay it, as Arthur reached out to hug and embrace the truth and his son, everybody reacted and swords were drawn as the two protagonists drew theirs, the spear in a Mordred hand pierced his father's side, as his father slid down the neck and using Excalibur slew his son. Done.

End of days. End of magic. End of the sword of peace, used to slay a son by a father seeking peace and the deluge of interception of the rights of doom, portrayed itself for the last and final time in the land of sorcery and a kingdom fought for peace and living in which all men are equal unless one is supernatural, like they were.

Still. They would never hold it against you. They would allow for the respect to be known and then, if afforded, *then* they would inspire you to be, of yourself, with the talent and skill and use for the better of a life, a nation, a kingdom and woman to which one is born, bred and married.

Except Mordred of course. He would take the piss and fuck ya up! Just for the sake of it.

*

He would use the potential for his own good, or bad, being the case and then show you exactly what he was made of, made from and who he was related to: King Arthur, Queen Morgana and Merlin the welsh wizard! But, born to be the opposite; Pure unadulterated evil!

Made from evil. An evil act. An act of incest. Of royal incest! Of demon royal incest and the consequences were known to Morgana, seemly sin is when one is conscious of the reasons why one is doing it, knows they are doing it and do it with a fucking smile on their face!

*

We are one, spoke Drui, to the spirit energy of Mordred.

We must see to it, we are one. He said, thinking about the role he would have to play in the feelings of so many days gone in his life, wasted and not wasted as the waste is there to show you you are seeking the place which fills the earth of abundance, fills the heart with a meaning, hopes for the better and finds his fucking dog tags with his name on it!

I know who I am!, he would say, *I am me, myself! I am named!*

Are you the opaque answer from all hydro atoms speak knowing he has just been named and he fears the name? The world of fear fears the fucking name! And the world don't need to face another Hitler, another Pol Pot, another Stalin: evil; but yet the most evildoer, if I must say it like that is: *Satan! Lucifer! Mephistopheles! Beelzebub!* Or just a fucking dark demon lord of the make-believe world of the deep subterranean consciousness of the imagination of everybody's mind!

Answered the depth of a pit of hell.

I am Mort, d' Arthur! The death of him!

You are dread and I am more; than can be seen handled, known, and I will not be going to prison on the surface of this my life, because you told me to, or the devil did or one is so fucking scared of being okay about most things in life one has to sell out and kill, rape, molest or take from someone.

*

Going to prison. Prison is the answer to what you have done. You lose and keep losing, because crime is not the answer, crime never pays, and crime will make you wrong and then leave you to do your sentence alone! A voice, a person, a feeling, an evil sense of the rites of life and you are damned! Damned to prison, damned to hell for everlasting eternal damnation!

Or you can breathe. Take it easy. Want not for what you don't have. Be with what you do.

Cherish the final moments of creation in the field of death and hold on tight! Hold on till the daylight hours and the day will let you know, get around to you, you are listening and the voice speaks of beings, silly little trials and finally you are treated better by yourself, by others, by the world, you are born into, because they see you, as you are, as you are to be and as you would be if they fucking well pissed ya off!

We must be friends now. Come together and heal our hell. We must fight to prove that the almighty right is right, because it is love and love is healing and healing is God!

Forgiveness is the goddess! Mother! She forgives and she loves with unconditional love, which can never be bought, sold or trampled on, due to the reasons of it being the elixir of love and love of nature being creation.

So, Drui Thorn with the middle name *Pendragon*, was pleased he had seen the truth of his explorations and endeavour into the unknown having come away with something, someone which, what mattered to him, to something and to the process which questions us all, as to what we are and what will we be.

He was Mordred Pendragon and he would be saved.

*

Busy ...

... moving ...

... dread out of the hell place he was in, into the magick realm Drui had made for others to live in peace and safe and heal the wounds of hell. He saw him enter and knew he would be safe. The light bringer, the world-bridger had done it again and in the consistency of time was able to understand that things do take it and use it to the best ability it has, at the time, that the time has seen the error of its ways and helped to secure a better world for those who have and had been abused, lost, tired, in hell and the hell's bells of noise, sin, unholiness and downright inhuman indignity to the reasons for being so small, so insignificant that the universe don't even know we are here, and the god don't know, creation leaving us to ourselves to see we are human enough to warrant depth or knowledge or simply understand the Ego and Id, understanding the reasons why we question something which doesn't even know we are here on the simple planet in an ordinary solar which brightly shines when the day is young and the night is old and the fold of the blessing is simple love, love which moves the heart, the love which makes the spirit dance and believe in gods and goddesses, when the terms and hope is to finally believe we are alone and we are one together forever in the knowledge we can fulfil the destiny of humanity and bring a solution to the years of time which change the aspect and fashions of people to know we are set to see, set to know, set to find out and set to love all those things which we deem wrong, we deem evil, we deem inhuman and heal them, it, us, all … there he, as a boy, the black clouded boy can love as we all love with hope, spirit, libido and special.

*

Seeing the sense in the sword being the tool, the talisman to secure and help the spirit energy of the time gone by, the time alone, the time we have all imagined and left to the sight of demons and devils and the legion of an army of Satan's left, die-hards and fallen angels spitting at the birth of the fighter, the lover, the poet, the prize, then, rest assured, the fight will remain and the terms to which they will be dictated is for the great and the good to know, that one soldier, a soldier of fortune, a mercenary of love – Drui Thorn – wants to see that all and everything is healed, in and around the purpose for the sense of knowing he was the greatest of evil the planet has ever known.

*

Pure evil! What *is* that?! … made to disillusion the force of the righteous king, rape the queen, hold her with child and so fore more and plenty allow the bloodline to remain and stay and seek the rot and decay of all things determined and all things righteous enough to be better or more talented or better looking or fucking school bullies! damn the day, and damn the way to power, to solution to dishonour and disregard of patience and consistency and determination and skill the world shall be a bloodbath, the world shall never see the back of us and the world is theirs, ours – *'thems'* … the planet is ancient and will be here when we have failed, when we have journeyed to the place of knowledge and found we are alone. Alone with creation and creation is the god and the goddess we know and speak of … still, sometimes called the *coward sword* for killing the king. Some are cowards and all demons and devils are and dread, 'more dread'; Prince Mordred will and shall not be of such things whilst Drui is alive, dead or in the fucking limbo of imagination looking for his next Kuthumi!

The sword of many powers Clarent. His 'athord', the healing sword.
"Him who, at one blow, had chest and shadow/ shattered by Arthur's hand."

Taken from Dante's Inferno; Canto XXXII. The dread taken from Arthur and Guinevere's inferno and laid to rest in the healing land of Avalon for being so long in prison, so dark, so deep, he became the sin and crime that he was, and for all of his life, DT, Decca Dent Peters or Drui Thorn Pen-dragon, had been looking for him, the boy who left his psyche, the boy who skipped his soul, the boy who ran away and could never be found, was found and imprisoned by those people who knew him and could not let him alone whilst he had no mortal self to belong to, to carry him, to nurture and love him as his heart, and bring him to the place of healing which we shall all face one day regardless of there not being anyone to judge you or us when we are, unless we have done wrong to another human being, another human person, another life. Be judged! Be fair and let the world rest in peace as the new generations come and go till we are the light and the light is the star-ash of the cosmos, the universe and good old friend: *infinity*.

*

All this has nothing to do with Stonehenge! That is the element which seems to be drawing out all the poison!

Thus then the evil parasites called spirits entered my self whilst he slept in a coma after his accident which put him in one, for a long month. Can you imagine the infiltration of shit from the pits of hell drawing lots as to see who has the guile to enter into a place in which they would inevitably die? Be gone through the nature of the light, the light bringer, the world-bridger, the divine equation of being love when all about you hates; you, whatever or everything!

*

To rely on the facts is to turn the imaginable doubt into fiction, so no one is to blame for the game of life, but the devil will interrupt the division and sit pretty in the place of recognition, the place of truth and lies, the hope of a nation belonging to a history of growth towards the day we all see the light and it blinds us! *"Blimy!"*, says the old wives' saying, blind me and I will see the devil and the light will defeat the devil and the devil is something which only exists when a religion does, when a belief does and to act in this world is to see a reaction. So, *don't do nowt.*

Then the lazy fat bastard obese twat of heathen ways will sit in the pits of slough and devour the will to sleep, to ache, to dream and destroy the will of life – till, the light bright in the night shite will destroy the world as the atomic nuclear path of glory is to end the story and start the apocryphal of sin, the constrained, the bin the gin and the guts of fathoms of skin, being; alive with heavenly destruction and devil demons.

"Sandde Bryd Angel drive the crow off the face of Mordred
dearly and belovedly, his mother raised him;
Arthur sang."

The three unrestrained ravages of the isle of Britain were … who the fucking hell knows? But we can hazard a guess, maybe – rape, incest and usurpation.

Now who doth such things? It is known in the almanac of Jesus, nah! Of the great bully king looking for the holy grail for he had committed the greatest sin of all! He had lain with his half-sister's face and taken the crown of divinity and raped his own kingdom! Bully for fucking foreigners like Merlin the Welsh! Fuck, didn't mean for that to happen! Or did he? Fuck the world up fuck the nation and deep in the chasms of sovereignty lies the great beast dragon of evil!

Thus then, Mordred takes Excalibur around the chops and dies in the light! He is buried like a bag of shit in Margan Abbey, Neath, Port Talbot and exhumed by Edward I [remember 'Longshanks'?] and reburied at Glastonbury Abbey with pomp and circumstance befitting a bastard illegitimate son of a King and witch queen. Like Mordred, Edward was.

Within the animus mundi is the weight of the soul in the body. Live the life expected, although some people's, children's, are cut short; burn the dead carcass, weigh the ash, what's left in the skill of subtraction is the weight of the soul!

*

The night set out so still. Rummaging about for peace and quiet and a bit of silence, in the mind, in the soul, in the hope, in the darkness of the night.

Quickly the trouble of time entered the sound of light, being light years from the distance of other times when he had grown through the development of being, feeling the pull, the intense trial of separation from youth to adult.

The disturbance of the integration between bedevilment and righteousness sounded out of the spooks and their annoying breath of flimsy spirit which is manipulated by a dark sorcerer called Merlin; then they hope to be saved in the light of the grip of nonsense which he performs as the lost legend, the malignant myth, also a giant of a fuck up by his protagonists and antagonists beleaguer the final blow on a fucking Celtic carnal!

Left to be able to acknowledge the abuse and disruption of the ghost at the front fucking door, the great work of rhyme is not to be finished nor is it to stay amongst the life lines of collected goodness, greatness, healing and mystic brilliance, which doesn't exist and does not seem to play the white-man when it comes to compatible excellence.

So, on the blood moon of September 2015, Drui beheaded the hag.

Such blood moon stuff of legend! The suffice grade of blow and pace to the glory of the morning shine seeming to turn the satellite a terracotta red, seeming to spell of blood loss, of the swimming of the dead sperm in the forgone egg to banish the living and miss out on the best of us.

Dead. Beheaded. Done and tears for the meek and mild amongst us and to the breath of ambrosia from the depth of the dead goddess raped on the peg, since the coming of Pankhurst and her fucking nutcases, then the blood of women and the terms of nature are inheritress evil.

"*She won't fuck about with me no more!*" shouted Drui, to the wind as if his body were ash already swimming to the hell of sites which lead to the judgement and asking the whole picture to be taken into consideration and as such listen to the purpose of the dead and the living and they are both separated due to the god being a fucking sacred manic when it comes to unanswered questions by passers-by or blokes going down ta 'ell.

*

You can't speak out at the Lord God Almighty or ya might be seen as a Lucifer, who brought to us the light to see by, when God would rather we remained ignorant of our making and see through the experiment of life to death being born sinners, lived through piousness and still dead unhealthy, alone, unwanted or better worse than never an even bigger sinner!

The place of truth is even he has an opposite, so to stop believing in such things would allow the humanity to separate from nature, God and ignorance and live by one's wit, acknowledging an unknown universe beyond the solitary clouds and know that the sun shines, the rain wets and the period of life to death is sanctimonious to oxygen, grass, love and a great big mighty roar of PEACE! Before and after one is dead! Please, fix it cunt! Fix the world and stop making us dig up the graves to find out where we come from, looking about with a loving heart to know who we are and dying only to be cast into hell for killing a life by which one has fucked, kissed, buggered and shat on! So much for enlightenment!

Therefore, Drui Thorn Pendragon will behead Merlin the clown and be done with this fucking medicine man, holy healer, brilliant physician and God's boy! Be done with spirit, get it out of your system, then don't kill a human being or you will go to prison and that is a mug's game.

Fool!

*

The silence is awkward. He is alone. He seeks understanding and pleasantries. He needs to listen to the famous owl, the hoot of wizards, the damning of the fighters of the ancient holy wars of mystic swords, the final time to press into the aether without feeling sick. To not be sick and in health heal the world with liberty and words, life and joy, friendship and worthiness, no such words exist for the true nature of happiness in the spleen, in the heart, of the brain and the fucking parasites of urethral shit; the blame for history the dreams of totalitarianism the toilet of battle, the turmoil of blood, the guts and the unbelievable trench bog of death is an ancient world that never knew love like the love of man, the love of child, the love of woman left behind to wallow in her inadequacy seeming to weep tears of pleasure and joy at being at fault for us, at fault for serving, at fault for doing the most natural thing in the world when it isn't and that that is death!

Creation is to blame for the dead. To die is to be risen to heaven.

The lie is in anger, the sordid truth, the display of ravishing poetry and spinning the world into an unforgotten place not to remember, not to forget, the least of the better and the yet to experience all the divisions of one god of one soul of one ideology of a cast bound for bastard Shakespearian, the foundation of sympathy, of kindness or cute attire, lost to the blast bugger trumpet of angels and demons in the war so far so good lost by millions and won by the fucking few.

I can't get out of this land of the dry mouth. This picture of uncomfortable ritual, the bounds of floatation and fluctuations spreading the sorrow; the blood ill and black bile covers the rolling plains of monotonous animals, seeming to rest in odd shapes and seeking sore eyes, as the taste of life is bland, is tasteless, is only dead to the dead. Who are living, dying as the obvious truth of all pissheads and bar-philosophers begin to be oxcarts and begin to seek the mask which is not hiding any more but loves to dress itself up as Christian religiously unkind and hammerheads' shit!

I hear the imitation of famous soap opera actors and bless the cotton socks of us all – apart from ghosts, spirits, shadows, demons, devils, succubus or incubus – spectre, silhouette and shade.

I did not wish to write this, this, this is torn anger towards the abuse of being Prince Mordred, his victims, his toilet, his mass killing field and tasting the boundaries of evil soiled hell! I am in it!

*

I must be forgiven for my faults and pay homage to the king and queen, the god and his goddess; it takes two to tango! And hellish hell's demon shamanistic horrors of sulphurous flames of gravestone and treacle! Drui thought to himself, because there was no one else there beside him with him, at him, fat him, pratt him or the delights of the loving night to fill the void of life, living within the means of mortal coil and never having to rid oneself of such, as the romantic poets of money, status, down and out in drugs and alcohol would zither.

I am not proud of being the bastard illegitimate son of a ghostly king and scriptwriter wizard, but I wish to make amends and hell the fucking lot, so I can get on with living the easy, in the times of 2000s, so I don't have to die knowing I was worthy of nought and sought to banish the state of haunt to the catacombs of cobwebs to which it belongs in the deep graves of the earth, the cloudless night of dark spasms and over to the frank-fullness of deportation and inextinguishable subsidence of gypsy curse, witches' spell or Merlin's ideal bullshit to have to spring eternal and reaper, as if in a weekend paid and stayed for one of those re-enactment or drink the fucking bar dry!

*

He tried to tell the collective consciousness of the telepathic world so as they would know, allow and pass the ointment on to the next bleeder, the howling disgraces and for evermore the dance of the skull, seeming to be nothing when the energy of being is floating about the chemically cohesive climate and annoys the hell out of a bloke who stepped into that there world and got more than he bargained for! There are horrors all around us! There is also, love, this understanding; when one is seen, but to find out one has to be a mongoloid equation of a daft bastard clown like strut cunt called fuck-head and his bastard floating dragon cloud of a phenomenological feral spotted creation of hell's wheels, hell's notion and bloody hell, it's the reincarnation of the fucking bastard from the dark ages shit! I thought they were dead, or should have been or better still have a return and do well with knowing the last time you were all lead by a debunked manifestation of incest, criminal, disillusioned set of losers one could, would and have ever met!

Don't expect them to run a piss-up in a Newcastle brewery and don't expect that to change the world or with its in-depth truth, prove to the healing of the 'all', that some heavy medicine sword could psychedelically scab the wound and watch for the itching and tickling of the scar.

As it heals. He hoped he would, too.

*

In the flow of the past and the sense of the future, which is now, as the present never really exists, then we can look into the truth of the thinking, the truth of the yearning, the problem seeking and the resolutions of the solution to the biggest question of all.

Ask yourself the same within the frame of the canvas, the orthodoxy of a nearly new belief and power in solid use next to a familiar honesty which rankles the opposite and brings to bear the violet of waste, the supper of sleep and the depth of nightmares, leading to a place well remembered and well held in the daytime dram of mighty florescent flighty hopes, so as the world becomes a necessary 'coward blade' when loving in sacrifice and cherishing in the death by the hands of the evil blacked man.

It is in the nature of the planet which is, *seems,* evil. The living strain to devour. The food chain risen by the killing of masses in a show of eloquence to power, darkness, ignorance and the ungraceful play of the god of sentimentality and lexicon messages; left to fathom, left to draw, by the side of blood, love and disillusion of spirits developed for the leaving of a dead carcass, once you, once blue, once true and pounced upon a time; the sky was shy and the birds ate the leftovers of silly sods.

*

It didn't matter what day it was anonymous, Drui Thorn had seen the Clarent and it burned with the ideal of feisty fires!

The dragon used his claws as he scraped:

IT IS SEEN TO BE A FIGURE STOOD AT THE WEST PORTAL OF THE TOR! A KNIGHT IN SHINING ARMOUR, BUT; IT WAS A GOOD-LOOKING YOUNG MAN WITH BLACK CURLY LOCKS AND THE LOOK OF A HANDSOME EVIL WHICH TO EVERYONE ELSE WOULD BE THE SIGHT OF AN ADONIS! A SACRED LIKE CREATURE, HUMMING THE TUNES OF HELL DEEP IN THE VOWELS OF HIS SPIRIT.

IT WAS MORDRED. THE BASTARD ILLEGITMATE SON OF KING ARTHUR AND QUEEN MORGANA.

DO YOU REMEMBER HOW HE STOOD AND LOOKED AT YOU WHEN YOU WERE TIRED AND FORLORN, UNMISTAKEN AND PERHAPS LOST? AS TO WHAT IT WAS WHICH MADE THE SPIRIT WORLD CONDEMN YOU AND LEAVE YOU ALONE IN A COLD WORLD OF WIND, FOREST, DARKNESS AND OMINOUS NIGHTTIME.

HOW HE STARED AND LEANING AGAINST THE SHIVERING BRICK; SEEMING NONCHALANT AND RELAXED, TO BE AWARE OF WHO HE WAS

AND HE WAS WAITING TO HAUNT YOU. TO POSSESS YOU, WHEN ALL HAD FAILED, WHEN ALL CAME TO LIFE; ALONE, TO SEEING A PATH OF HORROR AND RIDICULE, SEEING BOTH OF YOU NEEDED TO REBEL, TO ADMONISH, TO SACRIFICE THE WORLD FOR THE DELIGHTS OF FLAVOURS, SO BENIGN, SO HEINOUS, ONE COULD BE A SERIAL MURDERER IN THE REAL WORLD AND TARGET THE PLACES OF GREAT MATTER, GREAT IMPORTANCE AND JOIN IN WITH THE DESTRUCTION OF HUMANITY! EVEN BEFORE IT TRIES TO GET STARTED!

AN EVIL SOUL WATCHED YOU. AND WHEN THE TIME WAS RIGHT, MINGLED IN WITH YOURS AND BECAME A PART OF YOUR SELF-SPIRIT-SOUL BEING.

YOU HAVE CARRIED MORDRED FOR 15 YEARS AND HE HAS DESTROYED EVERYTHING OF YOURS, EVERYTHING ONE BELIEVES IN AND LEFT YOU TO CONTEMPLATE EVIL, ATROCITIES, CRIME.

YOU HAVE NOT SUCCUMBED TO HIS WILL AND IT IS BECAUSE – LIKE ALL ALIEN VIRUSES IN A BODY – IT SHOULD, CAN AND **WILL** REJECT IT!

TELL ME, HOW DID YOU REJECT IT?

[explained through dragon script; Draconic language]

"I rejected it, when I heard and watched a programme of extra-terrestrials on TV and I challenged the thought process of there being anything else, someone else in the universe apart from human beings," I said, "I have seen things! I have seen my aura broken in places, where there was a dark cowled druid, a monk and two boys of poetry and literature, then I saw a lonely figure apart from the others and he did not look like me, he looked like a beautiful necessity they call, looks; power and hidden evil." Then I knew who it was, it dawned on me!
It was Mordred!

*

So, Drui dragged him up and slew him! Killing more dread.

*

So, on the 27th of September 2015, during a super-moon; a blood moon, he commenced to behead the ominous female partner of, as she was and had been, the reason for his loneliness! His friend to whom he had become accustomed and allowed to shroud his dead life, spirit and soul, as the alcoholic mistress was becoming expensive and the company of the dark shrouded Genii Cucullati; the hooded ones, spread about the aether, air, atmosphere and his stratosphere for being frightened in the fear of being aside of society, ostracised with animal instincts, deteriorating into a soul-less monster who turned out to wreak havoc, insult the kingdom and go back to his legendary ways of rape, spiritual incest and usurp the better known facts of his life, being music, acting or famous people who had seemed to help humanity although it had all been for rescuing the people from the lord of darkness's slavery, torture, rape, buggery and war in atrocity, unfamiliar heroes and a major damnation of the woman's whore-dome and espousal surrender to the phallic of lust, horror, debauchery and the devil's concubines, prostitutes and whores, to change the world and take it back to the place where the healing had begun, to be born into a time of war, to be innocent of the turmoil spewing out about them and producing some of the fallen angels, slaves over and over again until man is at war with the unseen world of darkness demoniacal séances of tribal blindness and the death of history as the world is governed by the almighty lord of Satan rule, the devil and his ability to be as omniscient in essence as the length and breadth of human history; from an ancient place and ruins the ancient places of civilisation and society.

Drui didn't wish to be alone any-more and so he melted down the four swords of power: Excalibur, Durandal, Joyeux and the *'coward's blade'* – Clarent.

Cut off the hand of the King Arthur the devil worshipper and gave him the hook of aether!

To manipulate the late king and so doing the obvious of actions to manipulate and command the art of ethereal air by using the fuckers as a puppet!

Mam and dad sorted out; he now commenced to relax in the hope of eternal peace and love from and about the possibility of being himself, being happy with being alone and able to usurp anybody's kingdom with his delight of supping minestrone soup at the same fucking time!

Drui Thorn wore a brown cowl of benevolence and immersed himself into taking ultimate charge of his life, whereby before he had not been able to due to the reincarnated birth of bloody Arthur what follows such bullshit is the sword, the bitch, the failure and fucking more dread!

He had gone up the Tor to find a better side of his life, perhaps to better his understanding of many unanswered questions by human capacity, so maybe he too could help to see the way out of the bondage of evil and disgrace which has tormented humanity since the beginning of homo erectus strolling across the tundra of unnamed lands looking for something to kill and eat.

Nature is the whore of evil and there is always a fucking 'but' or 'and'.

Drui also wore the hook of aether, as he wore it over his own hand, fitting the instrument of controlling the chaos, as the one in which he made the king wear was taken off him and placed on the holy thorn of Glastonbury, which had been cut down in 2010 ACE. So, it looked a lot of fun with the stumps of Christianity and the hook or by crook of the melted down swords of power, which corrupts and all bow down to the worship of the devil in major corruption and the elemental ability to carry is strength – strengths and being stronger than the devilment of the devil's will.

*

Do you believe in true love? Someone made for you on this planet. Someone who you will meet and straight away know she is the one for you. The one born just right, somewhere, where you will both meet, at the right time of youth and the bond and connection you both have see through the understanding of life, with love, respect and the faithful true meaning of procreation.

Well, Drui, Decca, DT strove out of his house at a very later age and decided to conclude his life by wondering why it was and had been nothing like that!

He went into the world to search for the reason and, of course, he found it.

His bride, his true love, his soul-mate, his friend and confidante was and had been dead all his life. She was and had been an abortion.

As he had lived, she had not stepped a foot on the soil of planet earth. And the reason for that was someone had not needed her. Someone had killed her. Someone had the opportunity to do so and choose to do so out of historic spite and knowing who she was to someone and what it would and did to his life.

It was a child born of the said latter day King Arthur and he knew it was the born wife and love of his living previous son Mordred.

As he had done in the legend; set out to kill all children born around a certain time, he had in an an act of individual destruction done the same to his own, in the years of a future, where everybody would prefer to live well and happy with the god-given choice of love, family and eternity.

Damaging such a proposal would harm the growth of the lonely individual and send him to an early grave without love, beauty, true tenderness and a sense of the holy heart which beats for the remaining truth of humanity's immortality and journey to secure the will of a species which lives from conception to an age of wisdom, knowledge and realises, all of being human, relies on the truth being told and knows, and everyone deserves the experience of a manifestation, which will see that the female planet is a star and the ordinary star in our solar system is in love with her and waits for billions of years before they can be together.

He is a hero! He is a man! He sought the truth and the truth was there to devastate him, to destroy him and to live alone for the whole of his life; unless he kills himself, adapts the situation and overcomes or makes do and in making do, fails, hurts, loses and eventually dies knowing the time will come when he looks through the darkness at the brightest light and sees her coming towards him.

He once saw her as a ghost; playing; he as 'Just William' and she as Sarah Jane Milburn.

Beautiful she was, with a slight strawberry mark under the left eye. Soft, fresh, white and a spirit … and her name was Guinevere.

She was the wife of Mordred.

And as before, the king sent out to kill all the children born about this time. Fine, but if one has to live on this planet until it dawns or it is known or one tries to live without her, then eventually the toil takes its bride and the dark sorrow lady is loneliness, you kill yourself, you lie with all and sundry or you deteriorate in the heart chakra, in the solo mind and just about fuck out!

Seemly, the triangle of father, queen and a devil-worshipping king will do the job, so your life is empty, a failure and you will turn to the dark side for answers, then add to the offer of doing something wrong to yourself and humanity; prove them right and go to prison for the rest of your life. Sorrowful I know, but Aries likes a good tragedy.

Drui Thorn pen Dragon changed his name to a symbol.

As all Pen-dragons today are off their fucking head! …

*

… and so it was he had the accident and tried to take on a car at 40mph, thus it won and he left the site and his dark shadow left him.

He awoke in hospital and when he had left, the whole of the plain of stone-age were up in arms about it. He didn't realise, he didn't even know; he never thought about it and having now named him D, was causing trouble for all concerned, leading the dark side to hurt, torment, even abuse other spirits whilst all the time he was healing, unaware, only with the trouble and state of all dead spirits, all limbo, purgatory, lost or settled in the dimension of cold fields and the rhythm of nature was they pillaged by his dark side which needed to be put under control, needed to be reigned in, to be kept under the watchful eye of one's light side, one's light, one's faith and belief in heavens, Jesus, an Antichrist and God loves a goddess which produces an alternative universe right above the dark one, same size, same width without stars living and dying, star-suns, all the chaos being noises, loud colours, dying stories and a great big black hole sucking the fucker back up till the last thing left is *nothing*.

It had haunted Drui for years – *The man who haunted himself!* he thought, he knew would be to reign the sucker in!

*

He met, joined and divisional the process which brought the dark into light and light into dark which made a whole species of being, whereby misunderstood, as to the word blasphemy! Which could be true, but the force by which it needed to be developed was to fit the dark side, the shadows of evil, the ghosts of danger, the spectre, demons and devils of advantage, of hate, of anti-being, of atrocity, not to be left to be wrong, to commit crime, to hurt and hate, thus killing and wreaking havoc amongst all and everything, till the separation would be left to gigantic sizes, which over thousands of years would become a devil, even the devil and no one could do anything about it, and Drui could not, finding out at death, he had been the biggest genocidal serial killer ever to exist on and in the history of the world, the planet, and being sent to hell would suffer the fate of all specks of shit! Horror without being named – an atrocity which would hurt and stifle the dark universe, as the blood, guts and bile cut the fibre and flesh of the dark matter of faith.

He reigned it in and called it D.

He is now ready to be of the evolution of universal darkness of wisdom and knowledge and the light of heavenly faith, belief and honour.

Too late? Tough shit!

Life is a life and to live a life is to do the strife and the knife is the blade to which all men are cut down for vengeance and the nightmare dreams of the entering to a black-holed domain.

It is not over in three pages. It is a novel and the novel is your greatest work; one's magnum opus; one's pages which haunt the world.

*

By going up the Tor! Firstly, the sense of my soul. Then, the imminent betrayal of the mingling of a said stranger, a dark night, the dark knight; stood aloof, according to the precepts of targeting a soul, free, individual, searching, seeking the ominous truth and being seen to be susceptible to the essence of being searched for and found. There! There in the clitoris of the goddess vagina chakra of the womb of the south-west; thus, in time and loneliness and trouble from the daughters and standardises of life, and influenced by self-absorption and drink, then would after dark lonely, windy, stormy shallow forced winds of change and aether abuse would he carry the soul of Prince Mordred the Prince of Pendragon and son of King Arthur and Queen Morgana.

Hence, he was fit, fitted and would be used to rebel against the living, bringing havoc and chaos to the everyday worship and honour of reincarnation, incarnation, spiritual endeavour and hope springing eternal due to the wishes of love, foundation, altruism and an energy which would suffice the aether of gravity bringing greater energy to help, to calm, to understand the forbidden law of love, the opposite will attract the surmounting of great things; as the dark things immerse in the will of marriage and relationship based on the terms of biology, epistemology and physics.

*

The spirit of Mordred belonged to a guy D had met in the places legal to the St Michael's leyline.

He was good-looking for a looking aim to rid to bid for the outstakes of momentum briefed with the soul use of knowing how and whereabouts one must be to know one has a great big gaping hole in his stomach.

He lay for hours and was served by his bride to be and lately has sensed to out come of the snakes of law and combat, of guardianship and fear.

One had a serpent wrapped around a tree for comfort and seeing the sick green of a loved tail would place the usurper into dilemma and run!

The other was behind his settee.

A black, very large serpent which feared the worsted and chewed on the sense of staying dark, being dark, hating darkness and always growing with the situation, to the sizes of mega-snake or hyper-serpent!

He knew, Terry was his name, he knew of the loss of self, once when he had 'twatted' in NI was it seen to be a sort of death to the assailant and never would there or could there be peace in the incarnated legend of Arthur and his wife, Guinevere.

He fucked off to Scotland where he could perhaps heal and live a good old normal life, if there is such a thing as 'normal', and live happily ever after, if there is such a thing as living 'happily ever after'. After what? Life? Ever after? *Where?* The answer is parallel to the dark mattered universe and none can communicate or see such wonders and delights as the imagination of the child or the still imaginative thoughts of an artist or a person of the episcopal cloth.

The darkness opened and storms of daemons, demons and devils poured out!

They looked for the contact, they came in their droves and waited to be led by the sorrow state of being which commits atrocity and un-altruistic motives all for the laughter and senses of a crown-less beast, a headless hank, a pointless war and a hope in hell which seems to de-mine the opposites as all interests in the signed signature of knowledge and wisdom about and towards a salvation of one's soul is fought over and won, then it is shown the glory of the godhead and not the severed head of a dark-sided horror rankle like evil.

Back then, he was a self, searching for the soul of the fighter, the righter, the writer of wrongs, so the insurgence of said would be welcome if the sieving of the good souls could be shown, then most of his work would be easier, done to the whip of a snare which places himself in the world of being a daemon fighter and not a totally confused, abused deliverance to the spirit of, which turns him into a daemon which tries to pull the wool over any thing's eyes and sadly darkly stares at the notion of his black blood seeping through the veil of tremendous hate, through to evil despise on to finding the crown of thorns and blasphemously wearing them.

To being the blame for all about, around and found to be socially inept, seemingly perturbed honestly by the suggestion that he was the reincarnation of the said Mordred, one, would not stand in a court of law, would not be what one could write home about or the discovery of such would be to either kill oneself or take the self and destroy the fire flamed desire of the soul and be left as ash looking forward to the world lest it disappears as a fantastic phantom on the plains of devil fighting and last but not least *honour*.

He took the blame, not knowing who or what it was which seemed to be condemned by woman, man, children and holy places, the crowds the mob, the holy surplice and the yobs, the sods, the sodden, the fried or the curly toothed derivatives of passion, adult knowledge, the faerie and the Fay, the many disillusioned course of the bombastic loss of the function and faction of the ability to love be loved and safe in the sacred infantry of devotion.

Remember; would say Jesus; *"Before hating you, they hated me first"*.

Brought to the lines of human deterioration, he then slaughtered the lot! Everything, no quarter, no favouritism, none and still they would come in their droves and still he would seek help and still the help came in the righteousness of protection, of a swift, disciplined and unknown defence.

*

He would attack! But, the art of defence is a way of blaming the other for the bases of life, of strife, of a knife which cuts deeper and deeper still; it severs the waters of love, the gracious love and an insight representing the creation of a God and his wife and good lady: *The Goddess*.

Surely they would not be nasty! But merciful, unless one had taken a life and snubbed it out with the task of evil set into the soul of a person possessed by the vicious demon of destruction and hate using the lust, the trouble, the attitude, the lack of knowledge one has when one is set to normality and overindulgent use of being, seeming to have no care or will to understand the feelings of greatness leaving the person with goodness which is not good enough in a world of wrongs, songs and flings which influence the self-being to act, presuppose the damnation and laugh in the face of oneself – finally left alone with cold damp reasons and itching fibres to die slowly, alone, without and never seeking the redemption of course, having been less than, more than and never can be a low-life sense of human-being; than a demon.

DT, Decca, Drui or Symbol had gone and sat in *'Siege Perilous'*, as if the devil itself had gone and seen to it; as there was a King Arthur and hey! Let's give the fucker something to think about! Something which will send him absolutely crazy! In the meantime, assuring the parts given to not quite knowing the position given and not being able to comprehend the sights and sounds of freaking banshee hell, which he will hear in such respect, as the occupant will, could and should die! – seeming to have to tell his story – chronicled with surmountable charm and wit becoming the saint of reprisal and a king amongst his universe.

They seat at the round table given to the person who knows different, whomever painful, the truth of the grail, the way, the path, the summons and is able to leave and go and live his own life soundly, quietly, with peace and worth, with hope and love and a compassion for the objectivity in life and who comes to terms with being and finds a companion in life to whom he should bear witness and care for and respect with all his loving heart till he shows the goddess he can love so much – till he is unrecognisable to the mob, the crowd, the universal stalls of judgement and holy halls – that he can live again in the light of Christ and never ever question his destiny again.

He has and did. His answer was: Thou shalt be bad! Wrong! Done! For this thou shalt pay as the duty of the damned must, therefore, showing the good and great world there is a reason to recognise the disgust of human actions and strive in life to better and lie with the choices one makes and the chosen written word which is yours, could be done; and will be yours, if you're not fucking careful!

D did die; only to refer to a happening, rather than taking his last breath; becoming dead. He seemed to simply age; with ancient blood and not succumb to the law of 'siege perilous', as the trick may have worked on a simple man, but, facing the need and urge to accept, understand, respect and transverse; D simply accepted the horrors shown from the sights of the holy grail.

Which was wooden. And no one cared about it. The Sans Graal of; the blood of Christ is; life eternal and everlasting; which is the mighty sun and the liquidised rains. The elements of life on earth, which carries the spirit to where the immortal, eternal, everlasting infinity of the soul presides.

Make your life, your destiny, but don't despise all facts and reasons to be guided by and souly bleed out of the forbidden zones of creation and salvation.

Brought, sold and finally achieved, the denizens of the scared task of many, to fulfil the will of the creationist, the maker; ha! God! and quietly slipping away to paradise.

His real name is Derek Peter Thornton; and he is proud of that.

He has become a demon fighter and is good at it.

*

With the help of the 'hooded ones', which he earned in his younger days of old, he is able to call upon the sword to which they are cut down, due to lack of religious worth or unable to make sense of the terms towards one's own heaven, then needing help, then being helped as the hoods cool the 'situ' and balance the problem whilst the caller makes the chances for the good and the lost good to make a special way to the promised land of Narnia, Avalon, Nirvana or the ultimate choice of heavenly notions, feelings, tremendous love truth, hope springs eternal and otherwise emotions of everyday joy, safety, enjoyment and bliss.

*

Thankfully the practitioner calls the reasons to say please and thank you; watching ya p's and q's and being able to say one is sorry, wherever, a lot or just doing so, finding out after time one has to mean it, although seeming shallow and savage it is liking to satisfaction of assault, of a type of anarchic abuse based on usurpation and dislike.

So. He apologises to the Beatles, especially John Ono Lennon and his good lady Yoko. To Sir David Attenborough for questioning the sense of creation and the endeavour to have to kill and devour to live, it is not my place to question and would and could only lead to the biggest question of all: *"Pourqui dear knight? Why for art though!"*

*

To Nelson Mandela, King Arthur and Guinevere and all the brave people who fought in the great wars, having to give their lives so we could all live in peace today, as we too give our lives for the children of the future, who find out what we sacrificed and give our lives too, so's they too could live with the understanding and knowledge of a world at large that don't look so strange any more or seem so distant or alien; due to artistic aliens like some of yourselves – and to *Bono Vox*.

To all the famous actors in the world, to the famous singers and entertainers, thinking that would be close to his heart and it is to those, he would hurt first.

To the sense of the living and the proof of all found wanting due to the opposites of love and hate, peace and war, black and white, light and dark, though we yonder through the dark path of living we shall fear no evil due to there being someone there before you, who has seen to it that it does not exist and the opposite of life is in the stomach of one's own universe and that the future leads to better ways, thoughts and findings about why, how, and where; as the answer is to be attained seemingly for the hold of the almighty right of God to show us, we are his chosen people to set upon the notion of kind and resolve the task of being due to experience, love and hope based on the triumph of kind before, during and after the senses, feel the rushing of the enlightenment, which hits the heart of the soul and travels to the place unbeknown to the people who have set their sights on heaven, paradise, heavenly life, brilliance and utopian days, ways, plays and still the average struggle for an understanding, which will be individually answered once the question is asked.

"Whom does it serve?"

To the through-breed and the meek and mild. To the troubles caused and the trouble brought, sensing the feeling of and the abused days seen, leaning fondly upon the love of people and the strength to which he too would go to be away from the sight of hell, from the blasphemy of devils, demons and despise.

The answers are arriving and the outcome will be great, but we shall never quite know of the way to higher being until we pass the gates of death, the bravery of life and a hope which takes us to the one last sight of something so bright it makes you smile.

Hence, to all he makes amends and drives himself about the bend … trendy; hence, he will serve till the day is dawn, till the mighty glory of the said beauty of the planet earth is satisfied with the fond arrangement to be secure under the feet of man and the wings of angels; so the 'hooded ones' may do their job without prejudice and contrition.

To the world cup winners of '66; he apologises to the folk law of such places; seemly, strong in the sense of knowing what the fuck it was and what he was saying! Sure, the lad is possessed and sure he doesn't mean it! Seen recognised and saluted, safe in the notion of all triptych cryptic conundrums where the only person who knows is the one who endearingly experienced such momentous happenings and respect is something inherent, something earned, something not borrowed and something learnt.

*

He apologises to the world. To God; to the Goddess and Jesus Christ. To Buddha and Mohammed; so covering the stall of outcome which blesses the sequence of events which belied the haunting of days, the battles of ethereal ghosts and brings peace to the atmosphere of earth which presides over the image of heaven and don't hate who you are and what you are made to do.

*

His apologies to the spirits, as he has been seen to be abrupt, to be cruel, to be as they are, sensing the way they are is a way how to deal with them, if it is for the longest time one will know when to turn and face the truth of the proof of enemy, is something which would kill anyone, anything, anytime and anywhere without the least bit of remorse for the seeker of opposites, the search for the weakness, the sight of the devil core or the reason for psychological warfare in the pater mater of souls.

To say sorry is not a weakness. To apologise is to be fair. The rest, well, they don't have to fret, only to the place of self, of being and presentment doth they pro-side and feel free from hell, away from danger, not lacking security and the greatest thing of all: to understand the edges of human love; the breaches, the borders, the amazing.

"At bona quae facitis." Be good at what you do.

*

Let this tell of the way of hell. The chosen spectacle of a whipping sound is heard as one is herded away, off! To an unknown place, dragged without control into the words and place: *"Come here you!"*

Surely! No stance nor ability to free! Taken under the seeming confusion and sense of being held in a fearsome tone of manipulation, control, mastery and a sense of complete adulterated forcefield – blamed only on the target brought to bear with deranged meaning, helpless attention, formed and forced to take in the tremendous hold on the trinity triptych of mind, body and soul.

Wrenched away, covered by the spikes of the 'lugger demon', penetrated completely into all orifice; deep, beyond depth, holding the way, holding the grasp, the grip and charging the flames of spikes into the waist, the stomach, the neck, the thighs ... held! and orificed!

No use moving, saying, struggling, ponder yonder the path of dreams, the path of complete nightmares which haunt the mind of subterranean junk, horror, walking the walls on four equines, developed completely to atone the pace to be dragged comatose, somnambulist, finished into the living hell of darkness.

But, there is always a hero.

He stands and sees, being dragged through a shopping mall, whilst he shops with his girlfriend, seemingly to buy; thus he asks, *"Is it hurting you?"*

The answer is *yuuuuuuuuu!* He then takes a glass mirror and smashes into the 'Buger' demon's head!

And again! This time the fucker is dead!

Hell. One's ass is fucking sore!

The enrapture, the en-captured, the isolation sensing the taking of one's whole breath. Make sure you dream better, make sure the shopping malls are in there ... make sure you deserve a hero!

The meaning of and the feelings of are to show the strength and depth of an unimaginable fear which makes one become a better person towards one's life, others in life and towards a very well known saviour and hero: Jesus Christ.

We have inherited in God's name, ways and looks; if he were, would, to be manifest – he would manifest himself as us. Proud to do so, and honoured to be a part of the understanding of the cosmos with a need for the future paradise pouring over into deep darkness and black holes.

Like solo bright stars sparkling in the atmosphere all for the delight of golden crosses made in the sapience of premonitory ultrasonic spray which represents the eternal infinitive dreams of existence and light forever shining in the despair of blind darkness.

*

He finds the terms in which we can change the enemy to the ally is written by a master and tells of doing so, able to say and have the relation to ask and be understood in taking the hurt an hate and seeing the power corrupt, turn to a good and honourable friend who would and could and should be the force which defends you, protects you and leaves you to wake in the morning light without their danger, their fear, their disarranged strange destructive derangement which sets off the cult of the worlds turning into the great misunderstanding of knowledge and imprisons those who challenge the settled precept as a catalyst; a *siege perilous*; sat amongst the deep dark furrow of loss and ignorance which hangs over the heads of love, of friendship, of loyalty and makes it appear disillusioned, foreboding and monstrous with the twist of a serpent's kunderbuffer slapping the face of armies, the face of beauty, the arm of the righteous and a horrendous fulcrum of diseases, virus and terms of the covering of death to the infidel through the lack of structure, protection and heavenly lack of gravity.

With only the weapon of love can a human fight! The armoury of destiny, life, sedition, decision and mighty adaptation of the will to live, the will to goodwill, the will to pave and write leaving the world to the next of kin, don't we? Don't we love and protect our sons? Leaving them with a chance to ruin, better, help or just plain waste the world and way in which they choose to be is the way it will always be in the face of adversity, enemy, fear and hate.

The change comes with the signs of which way to turn. Which way to go and for the branches of the everlasting tree allow the leaves to fall and the creatures to climb all over its bark, seeding the land, spreading the sense and overcasting the primal nature to succeed in being, to triumph in the nature of wills and leave the planet knowing, safe and all the world standing safe with the regard for one holy honourable crux which allows the sun to shine and the moon to moan and the flowers to share and the wasps and bees and flies and then someone dies and then someone is born and left to face the terms of power which converts the force of life which climbs the trunk of chieftains reaching the highest ultimate position to see across the valley into the forgotten sight of ancient lands who claim to be the noise of future troubles seemly alive in death having overcome the toil of earthly mortal coil which bonds the gravity, which holds everyone and eveything in place and teases the truth out of the time and place and never relinquishes its amazing power to the death of the bird or the carcass fed on by hyenas; still the whip lashes and soul crashes against the shores of mighty rivers as the naked shiver at the sight of paradise lost or found. It is under the influence of being underground whilst the dig deepens and the soil is tragic then the greatest place to be is in heaven.

Earn it and burn it. It was fantastical.

To turn the wrong way and walk down the wrong path? Being in the right place at the wrong time can affect a life. Ruin a life. And you can do fuck all about it except cry. Wash the soul in a shower of tears and fathom the problem to be little or lost or better still given to be saved by the local hero or the love of mother or never ever let her go! Never share the feast, the horde, the fetter with the last remnants of thy shallow lot, but breathe in the breath of greatness, goodwill and fortune and the legacy of immortality will frequent the earth after life, after birth after death.

Turn a devil into a fawn and the sense of the world will look better through his horns, his horny nature, his horned god, his nymphomaniac brides and satyr the sense of satire with a good sense of humours and sense the scent of lush drives welcome in the world of human adulterated formidable consecrated emasculating over-driven orgies!

*

What a society it would be and *is!* Only through subtle terms and dreams and desires of decency doth the energy and sense of feelings lead to the worship of the holy man and the whore, the horned god and his bride nymph and Pan the horned god of nature; All. We are; but he became the hellish figure of demons, devils and Satan himself, when the people needed home and hearth and a scapegoat for the reasons of evil and evil is an energy; just an energy. For in the darkness it lies dormant, in the dark side it works and the universe of darkness is hell! The opposite universe of light is heaven. We live in the darkness to fight for the right to be in heaven according to forgiveness from the sheer fear of living in the dark side of an infinite universe which serves the purpose of manifest evil; as people fight the enemy, it rises again and again, until the place of heaven, so big, so far, so everlasting, so near, so infinite in essence; we all need to die to be in the right universe. To be safe and secure from the power corrupt of unadulterated evil darkness; blind, ignorant and lost.

If one did not wake up to the layers of falsity or the sense of another, then he would never have met his good friend Theo Fawn. He is a satyr and is very mischievous. Better than the dark side taking the piss and scaring the living daylights out of you! Make of it what you will and it shall be, only fall from the accepted grace and you will be devil fodder! Can't see remorse or forgiveness? Then you are the greedy bastard's meal and he will suck on ya gravy like an ominous black hole.

*

It all has a lot to do with demons and devils. Seemingly put aside for Derek, who decided to change his name to Theoderic Peter Thornton. He was a demon fighter true, but he was tired and showing the families lost to the light by the darkness of their sight, he was becoming a saint like Theodora or Theo; meaning God; meaning God's gift. To whom and for what?

"Beelzebub has a devil put aside for me!" sang the Freddy Mercury, of the rock band Queen one Xmas, an Xmas song which Theoderic had listened to as a teenager one lovely drinking Xmas with his good friend Johnny Hindle after they had bought *Night at the Opera* by the said band.

To do with demons and devils making their way to a portal of light, to the possible place of healing all of this which came before Christ and seemed to them a living of non-belief and only worshipping the sun in his hell and the moon in her slavery.

It is all much more of that today. But, still they are stuck! Without redemption, without the understanding of a heavenly god and left to haunt the stones of old, left to wallow in the wind of change and left to the beckoned call of demons and devils who set them to slavery and unholy after-life.

It has a lot to do with petty demons and fucking devils, who have no say in the big picture of darkness and need to be dealt with and finished, so the transmigrating souls of ancient times can see the light and go on home to the after-life they deserve and in which they find a place of what they knew and had names and families loved and lived by the nature of heaven.

Theo has fought them. He has hurt the demons and devils and he will do so until he leaves and when he leaves he will leave the devils like leaves on the autumnal trees; dead on the ground and finished only to be renewed at a later date when there are no souls to keep, use, hurt, hate or manipulate, just for the sense of doing so and no one in this dimension can hear or help them to understand the feelings of heaven or hell.

He will leave them, but he will know of what they do, of what is done and what one has to do to help the situation. He will hide, but will never forget. Theo can never finish what has been started until the world is healed, the aether is healed, the people are healed and the might of the fallen stones of tourist henge will be left to be so and not a place to use, run to, to never find peace or a hell hole to be laughed at, ridiculed or made the hell on earth; which is getting away with tormenting souls, blaspheming purity and innocence and making the eternal universe somewhere moan with the urge of loss, turmoil and forever paining with the horror of damnation and punishment of a godless way, a godforsaken time or the power and passion of corruption which enters into every way of life and after; until the only way to redeem or find redemption through love and grace is through Jesus Christ and the holy order of Heaven.

To defeat his own devil, it has brought him to a place where they are in many, not in force, they are alone with their aims and many come and go like the chaos of hell, whilst the strays and the drifting, the lost and the lonely walk out and about the thresholds of mystic senses, as the devils' world to use, never letting go of the banks of the river Styx; whilst the children of Elysian seek a way to find the fields of Arcadia, Avalon or even Asgard; knowing nothing to come and no one to rummage the rough soil of earth, whilst ghosts hearing advise, shouting out friendship, having no name, no place or home and never letting go of the site of ancient knowledge which happens them upon the hanging stones seeking guidance, wit or even some place to eat and be called a name to which they may relinquish their bones, their tired souls and where they can sit by the hearth of flames until they can see some light at the end of their wanderings, where mother is or father is waving to them for them to come closer, to hear them, to be shown by … a world -bridge and that world-bridge is Theo.

*

It is not much. It is all not much. But it wears on and on and hell is vast and deep and keeps with the darkness and it is all not much when it is right, it is to be littled, to be dealt with day in and day out, but to see the finish of the exodus of ancient souls is a bigger dealing and picture; than the fall of Nebuchadnezzar, the rape of Lucretia or larger than the war of Guernica; and leads to the question of sin and souls and finding the answer through the trials and tribulations of mastiff clowns and fools who search for the feeling of the holy grail, search for the difference in self honoured time and to change one's destiny written and rewritten, as they would have you wrong! As you would put it right and the mighty Satan laughs on! As the whore of blasphemy still sucks the blood of sinners and the saints join them to mingle and destroy the way of the beast, the way of the horror of sights and the way of the devil sat on his throne of darkness whilst the light and heaven are in a totally new universe all-together, parallel if you like, but still if it were true then we die because we set ourselves free from the black-holed pits of hell and we, as they are; who moan and wail on the shores of damnation are seeking a light, a world-bridger, a knowledge to better the self to free the spirit to find the soul of heaven and so live forever in love and posterity.

If this is all there is, then: we shall fight the sight of hell, the darkness of demons and being sent to do so, we shall die doing so, we shall refrain from sin and disgrace and finally, after millions of years turn the planet earth into a heaven of creation in the cold dark dampness of space and the flames and fire which warms the cockles can and will know there is a place which symbolises the opposing universe of the soul of heaven and great great love!

Then it can show the true colours of creation and try and destroy us like the dinosaur was seen to be unfit for consumption! Let it be so and may the fucking demons rot in hell!

To muster the power of self and opposites of knowledge would be to finally do the work of God and make God pleased with his work; *your* work, then all will be balanced, all will be harmonious and everyone will be free from darkness! Sin! Hatred! Discomfort and pain! War! And the self will be the soul of God and the soul of God is bright, alight! Smashing and fantastic! And nay, never will the floods of evil betray the souls of children, the souls of good men, the souls of mother and never again will the darkness be told, to be fathomed, to be taught and shown to be the opposite of self! But what is; is you. Known. Bold. Phonetic and described!

*

The rest of the creation of the universe may follow suit. Do as you will, be it on your head.

Still, the creation of darkness is the greatest lesson ever to be learnt. Once understood never to go there again, never to look behind you again, never to seek the answers again when the movement of stones and the shuffling of leaves, the uplifting of the earth would disturb the lord of darkness, the bearer of evil tidings, a sense of ridicule which belies the reason for a future which lends its ears to the fortune of happenings who solve the mystery and the mystery is you.

There will always be a cold feeling in darkness drift. It is not friendly and takes a long time to warm up there by the fires of destruction and flames of burning sulphur.

In darkness there will be light and the light of night is dark blue, navy blue, the blue of a deeper rainbow which is safe, warm, alive and welcoming.

We paint it black for now. But, one day we will see the shades of blue.

We die for the future of humanity and her children. May we die having earned the right to live since the day is young, turning to the age of knowledge and we achieve the investment of the Lord God to whom we have paid allegiance and wish for a better world, a better planet and a better future for the children of millennium, decades as one day; receive the papers of extinction with honour, invested peace and the ability to call her our own.

*

Pain is the answer to all our pain. In haunting the ghost return through the pain. The pain makes them walk. In Brighton was a woman who died in the small back-room riddled with cancer, she died in great pain.

After some nights, she would walk across the hall of the house – she had lived in the house, she obviously loved – and the place in the main living room where she kept books on the occult and seemly Victorian insights as to the lady in black?

She walked and as she walked she screamed! She screamed into the unheard world of pain and limbo where she walked with the energy to feel something there, something walking there, in pain, screaming with pain, the pain made the occult walk and the doors and the world were closed to the evidence, the proof, the cold, windy howling night of the energy flowing through the chrysanthemums in the front garden, which made the harrowing sound of fear, loathing, painful stretches of death, of time taken, the time taken to die, to survive the cancer riddling about her body and screaming at her; *DIE!*, screaming the sense of taking, killing an old defenceless crone lady, who needed to die in peace, who needed to settle and soothe with morphine, with family love and the pain brought the ghost, the haunting ghost and the pain can bring demons and devils about to feed off it, to eat and feed, to stave the hunger of unseen assurance of psychic readings which signal a presence, an energy, an entity which is malicious, malevolent, frightening to the living grounded gravity world of life-force, it goes out and the pain walks, the demons wait, the devils create and the whole horror of hell lives in the house of haunt, the house unsold, the place of mystery and fear, the place no one will ever go again, as she walks, as she screams and the scream goes through the life-force and tells of pain and loss and the blood of cancer seething through the indefensible skin and flesh of old women, alone, dancing with the spectre, with the shadows at night lain in dreams of shadows and lands of daemons, with hollowing winged devils ready to latch on, to follow and to scare the death into submission as she dies, as she is haunted and shown the path to walk, to scare and rush the haunting into being afraid herself, never at peace, never allowed to settle into the death and go, instead, and heading for the front hollowing door and back looking for a way to heaven and not be used by ungracious pain demons to tread the halls of sin and pain and powerful death.

*

It was in the days of D and Pash, as it affected them and soon they left and soon hopefully she was allowed to settle and shown the light of heavens and all was well with soothing wonderful love and the demons and winged hawking devils fucked off!

*

Ahhhhh! Got it! Gwynn ap nudd; pronounced Neath, be it so! Beneath the caverns the hell-port of the senses, the required drive to cause so much trouble, down fall! due to the refusal of a woman's company for the night.

*

In the place of standing, at the place of lust and night, with the calling of the terms to be; 'lay with me and I will kiss you again' and He; the Welsh gnome king of the other underworld will leave you be. With and in his dark face, the sin of war, the strife of indecent hell! His black face, his devouring of the pits; still with no regard for the slaughtered and none for the victim of the madman! The crazy fucking lover of the woman's brother; which lays you down and threatens your spirit life, the search for knowledge, the insight to enlightenment which one can take away and live by, hope by, love by and seek life with the open heart of trust and the following of the senses to hear the world, the hear the world asleep and know the earth is round and feel the sounds which care, kindly, need and give. Spoilt and challenged in all fathoms to warrant passion given to the gnome king and being a lover/wife/empowered slut! She would be abashed! She would be failed! She will be angry and tempered and seek the sore of guile which makes the chosen castrated! Spirit chaste and lost and alone, alone with loneliness and gone removed from human endeavour, from striving for the rites of love and seeking the companionship of 'one night fucking stand and a great big fucking shag!

Fine, sound rounded and lovely, if the world was a Mormon placed settlement, if it could allow for freedom to give and enjoy and gain pleasure in the facets of flavour, volume and finesse in the art of love, coitus, union, perhaps joy!

Together they had brought him down for not doing the wrong thing. The thing to separate him from the passage and way to share, to give enjoyment, to experience, to consider, because he thought of man, he thought of another man's heart. Of his will, his way and to the day when it could and would happen to you.

It is the valiant and honourable way to understand the war in the world, the trouble brought by choosing, by refusing, by the path of man's honour towards the sexist foundation of a betrayal of Lancelot and Guinevere, which destroyed the kingdom and the whole sacred story of the holy land of the blessed Isle.

Do not forsake your man. Do not forsake your friend for another woman. Do not covert another man's wife, do not shag your daughter, don't hold man to weep with loss over time because you have a bigger cock than his! Do not steal, do not flirt and regard the ominous feeling of ejaculation and lust over another person's love, heart, life or spirit.

That is all he had to do – D, DT, Decca Dent Peters, Drui Pendragon Thorn, Theoderek Peter Thornton, only he thought of another good man's heart and she denied him all and everything in life with the corruption of tethered will and association with a warrior who was a trickster and lived and dwelt in hell.

Why, when it is good to do? Why, when it is the way of the hurtful world and why when one goes to the holy sacred temple and is asked to act the same bloody way as Soho, London.

Beyond me. Learn and find great love. Learn and be chosen over all others; because she is free, because it is her right to be loved, satisfied, helped and protected by a consort of bravery, necessity and companionship!

Let's fuck and be done with it.

*

He walked out and watched her. He yearned to her taste. Like Pash, she got him wrong and thought he was an interesting one night fucking stand! Whoa! Yeah, in another world, but in this, what is wrong with you? They are pointless, troubling, lacking in finality and heathenish with disease! Try it, fucker!

Love hell bent on showering the shit with lust and hell fuck!

He knew he could not take it, he knew he could not let her go to him, he could not let her go below the fucking belt and the belt was tightened to secure the fact that his trousers would not fall down that night. Man it is about time you saw the light and stopped playing the game of delight with madame shite, with her ruling, with her rules with the rules of stakes and ladders, the feminine touch you have for her, for her love for herself and the females in the world who have been destroyed because of man! Man's history, man's intention to war and be a lover and warrior and a king and fucking bin and sin and a rapier of the reaping of what they have sown.

He leaves you alone. Don't be alone for so long. Don't.

So, he had him executed. So, Theoderek had Gwynn ap Nudd's head chopped off, as it fell to the ground there was a scream from his 'glasto' whore and Tim was pleased, so he could get back to his books.

Out at Pembrokeshire she brought the spirit will and entity force and spiritual element to the fields of England, a welsh fucking crazy cunt who chastised all and kept all down, as they are the foreigners and they are foreign and Cymru!

She used his power, his good power to be died. Died in battle and went to hell!

Thanks dear girl. Thanks for destroying a life for reasons of not accepting a 'one night stand'.

A spiritual experience which never took off, but had to be manoeuvred by his strength and will to know, hear, fight and so go to war!

*

I am dead. And so are many others. Thousands of the beautiful dead, waiting for answer, waiting for justice, waiting for the time they can go and be with the dead seeing the shores of hell and moving to the place acquired to be limbo, to be entity, to be heroes, to be beautiful heroes, to be the justice for all the others and to be the frightening sword against the evil in life and the evil which supplies death with the souls of the living dead, the un-dead, the thread of truth which sets them free is the lie being told of the capacity to sin, to be wrong, to sing of no song to which they deserved to be slain, for pattern is of a blasphemy which overcomes and resurrects.

Living amongst the shallow deaf and blind a line of children who do not know, of the unwanted and trampled, the forlorn and bored, the cantankerous treasure of nothing but left, nothing but to defer, nothing to avoid but the wrath of hate and scorn of the one who is Satan. He knows, but he does not care – he sees you there and troubles you with the answer to your dark shadow which lives amongst the grave and moans into the night with a tone of fear which leads to a position of freedom in the voice of forgiveness, in the voice of sorry, in the voice of truth – which sets us all free and changes the world; and the after world; the other world, the place of rest and security which is fought for every void of holy nothingness, which is threatened by the danger and oblivion of hellish rage against the injustice of the angels of heavens.

*

Say of the truth to bear and the dead will be forgiven and the life thread blown to the four elements and in the *magik* of the fifth be alive in the warmth of the wing, to be atoned in the light of darkness is the essence and complete cosmos of creeping shadows, to the speck of love that holds the black dragons; Gywn ap Nudd, the demons and devils at bay. Say! Bring in the dead the beautiful dead / bring in the bread / the wonderful bread!

*

Gywn ap Nudd is and was King Arthur and Guinevere; together they were the black dragon of fear, the feared one, as the hermaphrodite of beasts, to be enchained by the sorcerer Myriddin Emrys, to do the bidding and asking of the realm of his choosing, to keep the enemy at bay from the enemy at stay, leaving the land to be the enemy of herself, as she proved to be a Christian saviour, to love the people, the pagan peasant folk and the religion of all, which forgives you; for you don't know what you do; for you do, but one can hide behind it, if you find it, *if* you find it, then the truth can go with you to the grave and waiting by the grave is the 'hooded one' looking for the answer to his death and please; *why?* He loves. He is a good person. Did he die so long ago? no one noticed, no one really cares – did he die some place, some day, when the light went out and stayed to keep you safe? – as he slept; he stayed … so long ago … so far away – it is wrong and funny here – it is strange and lonely – it would be, it would – call for him a Lilith, call for him someone who finds him, who takes him to a settled grave and watches as he flies away – never ever to leave again, to remain and watch over the fucking bully bastard cunts, who kill and try to get away with it, even in the hands of the human law, even wallowing in the cells of remorse and understanding of life which is supposed to be true and faithful.

She is in Taurus. He is the mighty bull and she the sacred cow.

She is tiny circumstantial, she is black and torn, she is needing the comfort and the stay; she has left and stayed away. She is not young but experienced and she knows the dead like the back of her hand – she is loyal and steadfast and like Kharon to the satellite Pluto she is wife and friend, seaming to the outer regions; she knows what's in the dark. She is a scorpion in the depths.

The changing of the guard, the way and the world let it all be to see the difference – thou' we shall play our part – seeking the subject and parting the waves to let the summons go, recalculating the hope for living life, for giving life and a feeling of right – we are not wrong; we are and will be right – there are millions in the world who seek forgiveness and answers, but we do not wish to unsettle them, we do not want to disturb the future of a galactic understanding of planetary intelligence – we are good kids – we become bastards with age; if given, we get bored with it all, we have no fucking idea any-more, so long so far, they have to be reminded, they have to be shown the possibilities, before their truth lands and they can go to a beautiful light of heaven's gates, the giant halls of superior – superhuman, subtle – supreme ways of the glory of God and his golden age of every soul is equal and they get better wages than down here!

So, to be the voice of one's own sorrow. To pave the path for the release of hell's grasp, is to pay the price with the frightening feelings and subsequent dialogue of the almighty lord of darkness and hell's bells fucking sea shop shells: SATAN!

So, he has seen and so he can tell; to believe the sayings of a weird and strange and fantastic proof, way, truth would be to allow the senses the recompenses it deserves and is a journey into the forbidden places; is the task of a man, who has gone where no man has gone before and he is a wonder, he is the wanderer, the seeker – the hooded ones of war and peace – making death.

*

He waits for the truth and the truth will and shall never avoid a ghost of redemption and the spiritual energy of *The Watcher*, the perceiver in-sized out spoken for all ruthlessness to feel aside the many left – sinking low and wanton, swift and blessed by canny moves, ducked and dived to the pleasure of soldiers who fought in the trojan wars, who loved in the damaged place of love and all beating hearts – they disappear into the haze – of the clouds, of the day, they fade away and never cry again – they be loved somehow – they never know why, they never say 'I' and their happiness is the story of Peter Pan the boy who never grew up. He loved Wendy, didn't he?

The dead men are fucked and the ladies quite for rape, but I don't fucking know where or why it leads to a horrific setting of the mighty rude horrific stanzas of blasphemous sheer impurity of the helium horror named hell. It does not seem to want us to. Thankfully, one may add – but they tease and they barter the calling for the sound that they are called for, then the heard is hearing the fear so low so tired so used so bloody funny; It rages him up and he deals with all and sundry till he is satisfied the dead don't sing, the dead don't hurt, the dead don't bring

… love.

*

Remembering and looking back over particular times, as one can do, also, sometimes it is necessary to look closer at the time when all complexity seemed to outweigh the concerns for all possibility being connected to a place which allows the essence of an ability to take centre stage and voice the opinions of revolutionary kings, nightmares, insights, human values which can never be breached or broken for fear of execution and the momentum of a momento's memory full of war crimes and suggestible toils to which the toll could be fantastic beyond the realms of possibility and take the insight of the inside of the human frame towards a universal place, as is the stars, the planets, as is the suns and the black holes, then human beings are of the same place made up of stars of suns of planets and all together they would be a reproductive portal of astrological signs, solar shadows, sing brightly on the stage and dance! Troupe the colour and hitch up the britches which switches the itches to the scratcher.

So, the universe is God and God is Elvis.

Okay, then he was here. He was here to tell you he knows how hard it can be, he knows what you like, he knows it's a place to enjoy and add the talents of ability, but the opposite effect can get in the way and it is for all and everyone in the world whilst living to love everything whilst it don't matter to the overall being of joy, tremendous uplifting spiritual humanity and lets the world down by being platitude, forgoing the exercise of living, to experience the life which is given to the individual who sees the world into his realm, into his doing and inside the hate and the ridicule he/her/it still loves with hope, miracle, friendship and one small speck of tear which drops onto the earth and disappears finally all the atoms and molecules and the space in time which misses the curve of the relativity of such a fine tuned sincerity will obtain, regain, osculated and ferment the foundation of the light and the bright gleam of the holy through the night and through the air when'st the clouds form, the rain builds, the storms crash and amongst the flowers and the birds and the trigger to success is the rebuilding of all the ruined lives, the ruined palaces, the ruined empires and everybody's susceptibility is aware of and is in; *of a grail.*

Drui had seen such a light. The light so bright, it seemed to bring the thoughtful question of 'what is it?' not, 'whom does it serve?' It crashed against the east portal of the Tor and in such a split second the air of darkened night was filled with light.

Drui questioned the light. He thought as if seeming to transfer the secondary nature of his will to the presence accepted; hoping for an answer to: 'there is no sound of the propellers of a helicopter!'; 'There is no plane going over with the set closeness to the nearer airport'; 'It is so warming and pure in the strength of the light, it could only mean for me to step into it!'

He didn't. Just at the moment of his movement he saw a dark eye looking at him.

It made him hesitate, it made him flinch, it turned his intention within a split second from possibility to doubt. Drui looked and the greatest and omnipresent sheer light had gone.

He looked over to the eye. It was belonging to a human socket. A female human iris and socket.

She had camped up there that night with friends to see such things!? Perhaps just to feel the air of ancient ruined sacred senses, she looked into the light and in the eye was curiosity, in the light was an eye of bewilderment, of excitement.

Drui went over to see her and her friends all bunked down for the night and filling the shape of their sleeping bags seemed blown as to what they had just witnessed!

*

Drui said to her, *"Did you see that? What was it?"* For they had been outside of the tower when it had hit the portal, not seeing whence it came, maybe they could say, maybe they saw the helicopter flying too close?

The young girl with the eye in the socket said, "I don't know … " She thought for a while and looked into her eye, which looked into her third eye, which told her nothing; for the light had been too bright! Too fantastic, too otherworldly which they too, only saw it for a nanosecond.

Looking back it was the light of a grail.

Out of the sky and into the seeking of. As friend, and sought by the unknown senses of a mystery beyond all real life mystic occurrences, which change the way of the revolutions of the planet and how we have to adapt, overcome such final waves of reliance, reassured of life, needing to communicate due to human endeavour, with an option for foolery.

Being brave sometimes seems rather a stupid thing to be.

He would see it again.

And now he uses the supplementation triumph to guide the blindragon home.

*

Okay, so, the parasite, the elemental force which prevails the secluded place in the rising of a dangerous strength of persecution of a prosecuted law; only to which the story would lend the utmost peculiarity strides towards the complete solution; as is done when one could say: *'All woman is beautiful. All woman is beautiful to man as man is not as beautiful. They are always the fair one, they are a species set apart.'*

But, on the back of the public bus today there was two very ugly looking *woman*, who didn't help the situation by being a slight attitude towards most things, as with the eyes, they could see and with the explanation that they too were persecuted prosecutors.

So, Trojan Josh hanged himself. It seemed to be a pity. It all seemed too much for the paranoia to be fed with the acknowledgement of someone who had been prosecuted.

*

Libby was a lady who decided to travel to the spirit world, after much of her life bringing up children and looking after her husband who was a train driver.

She coloured her hair blue and walked about the place with a defiance suited to a younger Aquarian woman and felt the need to feel the strength of the unwelcome negative vibes of other people, other elements and entities.

She sat at the crossroads of her life and said she felt she was not liked.

Drui had answered, *"You are loved Libby, by many people and others."*

She did not believe him, so she gave him a bar of obsidian for which he thanked her and went his way.

Later, they say, she was found hanged on a tree with a set of tarot cards in a circle about her.

Trojan Josh, they say, sold her car. None like the gesture.

Drui drove the obsidian crystal into the earth of healing and brought about the connection and bridging world of a metaphysical grounding.

Did Josh hang her? He only says he hanged himself. It seems so final, so tragic that the mind can only do one thing in times of crisis. Panic. Stay the mind and complete the reason for the truth and the truth will set you free.

*

It brings him to the thinking about the planet grail. He sees the planet expelled from our solar system as the planet he is associated with Kapria; a planet between the cusp of Saturn and Uranus which spells of the place to find, to discover, to seek for the answers so asked; that which places the terms of eternal questing into the seeking of the planet, no one knows, no one perhaps can call it the wounded healer, the Lilith, the Lucifer of the light brought to shine upon the sin of mankind; which is something which hides away, till reaching an inner mass, collapses into a blazing death and explodes with anti-matter enough to resolve the heliosphere and spark the immense fire of ages burning, still warmth, still stifled and always set ablaze in the dress sense of hell's fire gates blazing with a sheer flame who can burn the soul down to an invisible ash only the weird can vision without turmoil or trial one sees the incineration of the alchemy of gold solar.

This is the light of the enlightened grail effect to which TDPT; his *tetragramation*, would, could and can send the people of the lost journeys of the blind and the unseen and the used children as their parents wave from the side of the all light, not able to call to them and let them know, to the place where all spirits can go if they wish to live an after-life of magick love which brings them the dreams they always had and the way to which they can live in harmony, balance, brilliance and almighty love of our lands and fathers and woman.

All true and all to be fixed and all will be fed and lead to the place of respect. In fact, there in the hill and there on the mountainside is the planet shed stiff galactic hope shared soul brother faith which can never be soiled, never be beaten down and will never give in to evil ways, tyranny, dictatorship and anti-love.

We are the way we are seeming to be able to context and correct, contour and acclimatise souls in suited wit to a fantastic chemistry relative and gravitated to soul universe, seeming filthy, seeming unwashed with the storms and dirty weather, the muck of skin, the marks and scars and wounds of life, idiosyncrasy solution to a species set apart from and gaining the proved limitations of a junk valley, a sordid past, a final solution and never ever again would they suffer fools gladly in the eye of a hurricane tiger, in the place of glorious worship and set to the path delivered to the pilgrim seeker of one's own destiny which written, wrote, changed or presupposed in all standards she kisses the bliss of lotus lips, so red, so sweet, so tender – then the holy glory of all known functions and foundations can single out the repertory and quietly slowly whisper your name.

The ineffable name.

Shem Hemeforash.

*

He had lived above his life. He had seen it rise for the morning and fall in the afternoon.

He knew his step-mother and step-father; Blaze and Jana, who being Scorpio and Virgo respectively, seeming to see the touched at conception, conserving the time and the sense of before any growth – in Virgo; first, thus then a 3% Pluto, the outer region satellite which brought about his dark set destiny to which he could only resolve through time, reason, life, passing over and with a depth of deeper intrinsic instinctual awareness of perception which shows him the enemy, the nemesis, the opposite in his life which will try to destroy him with a perfect respect for a faithful illusion only dream-like states of imaginary madness and extensive extreme sights of clear images within the third eye and into his subterranean conciseness could resolve.

How fun that is. How great. They could be found and he had to go so far away to find them.

There in the place they were and there in the need of life they would be. Surprising the solid notions of a royal blue sea in which they swam with smiles and love and hope and sincerity; as to which, they did not know who I was till then. Amazing. To be told and shown one is alone in one's quest for salvation, for atonement, status, respect, finding the clues and the answers to a place so forged in ancient anvils as the shower of sparks proceeding the holy weapon of freedom shall be the light of the undoing of all he is, as he can see/hear/feel the walking shadows of purging purgatory.

Pay your dues in life and you will earn respect. Eventually.

*

It's good to sum up. It's good to subtract. It is good to divide and multiply. It is good to seek love and feel like reaching the sky. It is lost but found, it is brave but wise, it can be worse than sheer, it can haunt the aspects which seem unclear. It will save the children bullied by the larger world, it will let them inherit the earth before the end of all wars, before the final stage is set; only to be a player, only to find a forfeited exit, never to see the like again or never to see a child hold her mother again, to hear those words so small, so frail, utter from her mouth, *"it's all wrong!"* as she shuffles her carriage, as she seems to be hurt, as she never depends on an answer or finds someone has listened, until the charm and designated feelings are the burst of hearts which would never hear the words and do nothing about it, to not be able to do anything about it and everybody watch as the warlords make a fucking great big mess of the place!

*

By going up the Tor. By going up the Tor and listening to the sounds in my scrip-tic head he devised a sequence of events which would lead to my madness complete, my lies undefeated, my insanity trialled and then the story would enfold. Triptych.

*

To be and to see the worth of myself; my past disappear into the foreground of thin air was to trust, was to believe in the energy of the mystic terms of a sacred place, so written, so known, so used and so loved, that he would give his heart, body and soul to the quest which at best 'took the piss!'

On the list? Are you? Well, let us see what we have in store for you!

Yeah! But hasten to one's dark set guide, hasten to a spirit looking over you. There we will hear of this bloke, of this lad, of this intention to … what?

"Be a better man. Be better than I am. Be at one with all"; and what's the other? Oh yeah!

Be a very important famous person in his own right, be it written or wrote! Nah! It was to find a lover, a woman through the goddess so fair, so fine, so right and his not mine, his; D's—

Named now; Dek the dark blue of thorn the benevolent.

Take all he has; a replace the joker with the thief – thieve his soul! Take all you can – his libido, his imagination, his heart, his spirit, his goal, his destiny, his fate and wait! The fucking golden gate awaits the poor fucker! Leave him with nothing; nowt! As he might have said, and led down the garden path, he will replace all of these things with love? woman? woman love? A sexy woman love tang! With wife!? With pagan wife?! With sexy pagan wife, yeah! Well, let's leave him with nothing … to take something away is always the policy whereby you naturally replace it with something else. Yeah – *nowt!*

*

Over the time, over the period and over the theft of mind, body and soul he has seen many things, heard many things, known many things and felt the possibility of something or someone being outstanding in wit and honour, of great guile and honesty, of love below as above and the towering inferno of the brilliance of humanity which can never defaulter in the eye of the deceiver, in the mouth of the flames of hell and will never be seen to cower in the face of the worst atrocity ever caused by the world that is unseen, the place where all are sprites and tricksters and devils born on the wing of stupidity, ridicule and unromantic ideals slumbering in the heart of the universe, the solar systems, the planets and the earth – so, it is that which pays the greatest of homage to the survivor of, the implication known, the strength put by and the overcoming adaptivity of the right inherent to be, the earner of the right to be and over all the great goodwill which is within all and everyone to use when the going gets tough and the going gets rough and the time it takes to solve the child alone never understanding the reason for such parent, adult abuse, that they can only be caught and sought by the one true prince of love, Jesus Christ. And he does.

Never let it be said ... *forsaken!*

I was forsook first! I was misunderstood first, so should you be ... and watch out for the pisstakers!

In saying so, would it be nice, to be the building and training of the vigilante shadow, the overcoming of death, through passing over, thus seen to remain, seen to stay and with the wit and will to be given the right to help, the right to curtail the crimes of humanity, would in sword slay the perpetrators? Such a job, such a great thing to do. The answer is in life. Before dying, before death points his skeleton index fucking finger at ya! Before pass-over to a better and whitening place, in life you see what you believe in, what you have faith in, what moves ya mojo, what brings to bear the true feeling of being lost, being nowhere, no knowing where, not seeing or hearing anything which makes no sense at all, the place of sheer darkness, unknown, unfounded, got around and implicated, sensing the wishes of the bliss of the eternal kiss would be a mighty savour of generations, epochs, aeons, molecules, atoms, centuries, the lapsing millennium, prototype to sequences given, allowed to be and allowed to find, then the place of choice would be heavenly, would be the place of heaven; *the heavens!*

*

I choose to live with my wife and children. I choose to build the hearth for evening. I choose love and I choose a grey dapple stallion for my ride and by my side I see the raven fly, by my side I see the wolf run and home driving home eternally driving home! Forever!

*

Apart from that, the vigilantly shadow will do.

So, you may have robbed me of all I am, and never quite replaced anything at all – but, I have, and I will and I do and shall and prove to you this is all for the greatest reason of all – making me who I am, making me what I need to be and with the knowledge and experience I have, it will lead me to the place I inherit. The place I will do my best. The place I shall forgo and justify the rules and tasks and time of the master, the known wisdom, and serve with the air of insight and character which brings me to the love of God, the love of her, the love of fair fine wine and kind which loves with the fullest wit and hope filling my mind, body and soul with accomplishment attained with the understanding of almighty shining gloriously entwining light!

Hold on, I thought you needed to stay in the dark?! … *um?* … !

*

Oh yeah, the darkness. The darkness is … a place where one serves the light by striking into the piercing stench of horrific evil and punctuating the mass consciousness of its subterranean pits! Do not do this at home. This is the journey willed to see such places set in the back of the brain, the setting to secrets, the setting to shadows, shades, spectres and ghouls, to spirits so attained they serve the master of hell, the imagination of the horrors of depression, sadness, dislike, hurt, abuse, and create a world; in setting free will try to kill ye.

*

Clear out the attic, I, *but don't go there*. There where they are! They are there from ages past, from Xmas' past, from the days when the mind does not think and the cruelty wins and you just want to be a dark shadow who fights, who uses his sword and spear and shield and fights! They are open to the hoards of millions and you drown in the sea of souls, the oceans of shades, demons, devils and finally you meet the maker and the maker is … You. Them. They. The outside influence like spies in the house of thought, in the house of love, in the house of life and they destroy anyone who goes there. Anyone!

Just, make sure you have something to rely on. Yourself.

He has seen it. He has watched it all, at times not being able to do much about the insanity, but, seeking respite in tears, in weeping away the formidable power of the corrupt senses which invade the castle of the soul and turn it wrong, sordid, lecherous, formidable when it comes to entering the forbidden zones of love and corrupting the wholesomeness of creation. In initialisation, he should wander the pits, the abyss, the shores and never seek the power of the light, in case it shows the demon carried within, the devil one has lusted over, the satanic rites one has bled and been sacrificed for.

*

Stay within the boundaries of love. Stay within the comfort of warmth, safe and secure in love.

From the years to be and the years which pass, one should see at last a place which allows the meaning of life, of death, of heavens resounding triumphantly in the mind of one's soul!

If one is but dust, ash, to ask – you do not know – you cannot know, only till then the place so sought, is the place which is the answer and the answer will be through the voice of human love and not by any other grace but God. Powerful! I, but in a good way. Do as you do, but care for others and the children for all and everything expects this of you for you are as God as God and his son Jesus Christ is to you.

I still want to see the age of stars! I still need to fight in my nature … still, to the beauty of benevolence and quietly, finely make your way. I.

*

For what seems is and can be, shall do; is tenebrous; so –

"It cannot be seen, cannot be smelt, it lies behind stars
and under hills, and empty holes it fills.
It comes first and follows after;
ends life, kills laughter."

[A rime given to Bilbo by Golem.]

Oh yeah! … the answer! … ? DARKNESS!

*

Sometime in the past, I have rolled along with the senses of the aims of many an equivalent to the burning of the moon. To which spells out a journey made during the power of the sister satellite which shines with the majesty and power of all that came alive in such extremes.

To draw it down. To see the face of the cratered full moon in her shy al-arum of tranquillity and humours, is and can be a sheer tear of the self-will to understand the birth of such plentiful equations, when the soul is spleen and the spleen is mercury and mercury is solvent.

Such is the known soliloquy of her when in the oak moon of Yule she came to full and the chemistry of the spleen made him move around and about as if his trousers had been burnt, when instead it is the heart, the mind, the spirit, the soul which is so vast alone, so cast as the antagonist, so brought to bear in the affairs of love, it hit him solid like a brick! Totally innocent being, as the rolling thunder of the beauty of her light made him come to tears, come to poetry, come to lacking in and sufficient with, all be it, howling at the lunatic!

Brazen in the indifference of choices when the days are gone and have been gone to be able to know how it is to be rectified, resolved or better still supported in the notion where the spleen acts as the heart and the soul is amassed with flames so sheer alight, so blazing with fire!

The elements become the understanding and the moon can hear you and the moon is your muse, as the time it all takes to venture to such places would be to love so much that the only answer is unrequited.

Lessen the problem of being so, then the torch light heaves the self to bear and the burning of the oak moon connected with his totem, his voice of the owl, his bearing of the pagan spirit and his holy allegiance to all and everything, when some touch, some watch, some need and some want, as the bright satellite in the aether, the major sky, the dark of lonely night, the tears, the peers, the poems and the adrenaline to search out the answer to the itching question of, *'what the fuck is this?'*; it is the grace of the moon in her will to connect to his mercurial spleen scar, another spirit scar, unseen, but there, another wound to show he has been there and back and he carries the witnesses to his journey, which ache and pour and they seep and run and he still knows the only time to feel centred is to find solace in being careful and not to act upon the strange but true function of ritual, prayer, hope or even celebration when the holy moon is at full on the Yuletide spreading of the dance of worship, the ballet of love, the freedom to be and the mighty individual crown one wears on better days and not feeling like there is something missing. There is, but he knows what's missing. Not to feel weak and not in control of his will, not to be tied to the draw down and never show himself to be full and clear on the special specific days of a calendar to which the intelligence of the powerful purity of the fullest moon.

It's the worst feeling in the world; that 'that' is lost, searching; found, alone and needing the full treatment of hugs and more, than the companionship which to the night air would be told to share and never stop sharing.

The feeling *nothingness*.

The near past of moments silly, classified, as the maybes and route to the life needed, sought, the final mighty senses of worry, panic, dismay, alone once more with the caught up time of life, the day, the night until the peeping moon hides behind the clouds or moves away, shall one be settled, should one *be?*

To know the soothing is in her smile, in fairness, in her sympathy, with her angle of the knowledge to see the lighted frame of the poet's eye, being not at all easy to express when the soul is hollow, the spirit is anew, the self is healing and the only thing one can do is keep going, keep walking, keep remembering and reminisce about times gone and the hope for other times when the self will be prepared to comfort and arrange such an emptiness can be filled with the brilliance of the coupled love of earth.

*

He has done.

And the millionth time came with the dance of a stag connection to accomplish his toll as the weather seasons and the flavour of taste has changed – he saw the whole of the moon and the moon saw him back. He loved the guardian and the queen is opposite love.

He needs to be filled. He needs to be filled up and then he will never hurt again with aches, yearning, tears, panic and massive unadulterated loneliness.

*

EPILOGUE

26TH DECEMBER 2015

[… er! … this is what it was …]

He may have mentioned living in shrew town, well he had and in shrew town there is a small 'tit' shaped prison in which they would put the witches. 'They' being the sheriff of the county.

Hence, she died in there and cursed the place. After years of doing so and everybody modernising, they seemed to feel it was their right, their inheritance to practise her shrew, anger, curse in the new age, so called. Okay.

Well, the fucking ghost bitch thing latched on to him and falling in love with him also not just haunted him, not just ridiculed man, but the fucking curse fell right into his abode with full acknowledgement of testimony in which they all joined and they all joined in the condemnation of a listener, a seer, a seeker and finder; they too could do the same and in her great fucking ways she messed with his mind, his talents, his progress, his life and his walking amongst the after-life looking for lost souls!

So on the fourth year he managed to find it, take it and execute it!

It had been killed. The justice was wrong. The sorting of a village fed it wrong and the witches and shrew were exacting the punishment outright for the blessing of the feminist race of crones who believed that man could be tamed, aimed to be ridden, found to be wanting and last but least the cost seemed to be a massive ridicule of all that is sane, all that could be right and last of bloody well all; never practising the art of love, unconditional love, friendship, understanding and employment in never able-ling the senses of helping the less fortunate or the troubled by the evil demons and devils which do haunt the realms; so called; the immediate after-life.

*

Poor job, by a poor situation in a poor country and county. Tut tut tut … shame on you!

Clean up the mess please and let's all be free of possessing demons and hatred of devils.

It was a shrew. A very nasty angry injustice of witches and woman. Typical.

"I shot the sheriff / but I did not shot no DPT [deputy]!"

*

So this is what he has to do now. He is trying to define the sequence of events which led him to be a fighter of spirits; demon, devils, shades, shadows, spectre or ghost. He has to be careful.

To be good at what he does and never falter in the way of psychological dilemmas, punctuated events, storms of all purge and of the many feelings that go with the ESP; which he can use to know –

"This is it – this is me – let's get on with it – may God be on my side."

[Thorn the Benevolent]

*

So it would be he had been in the underworld all this time amongst chaos and calamity. The portal being the womb of the Queen; the portal to hell, Hel, Persephone, Erishkegal, perhaps Cerridwen.

Someone was using the young? Was it male or female?

He thought it would be male. She was feeding man?

Charon feeding Hades. All feeding Hel.

*

"Don't. Do not," he said. Then all would be well, then all would be as it would be. She shall satisfy the phallus bull with her horn of plenty and her vagina of lush lusting perfume of madness and despair! Love is such a cruel concept, a tradition of offering, a loading of the will to satisfy and then be at peace with the tumultuous storms of lightning and thunder! Right on brother of configuration, the terms of virginity are hymen and development of bones, soul, power and salutation.

It is not for you. It is for her.

*

… time it takes to catch up after forty years of life; having to feel the first fifteen years until a reasonable sense of being is achieved – at the end of life the reason for the opposite will be achieved.

*

Stonehenge was built on an underworld portal.

It is there that the 'indecisive ones' [according to Dante] are surmounting; as *heaven don't have them and hell don't want them.*

Blessed be.

Theoderik Imbolc Thorn.

*

11. 5. 2016.

The terms and senses of the light of a white spirit would be Gwen. The tortured queen immersed in the monastery of Malmsbury, Wiltshire. To then die in Amesbury should be the rightful spirit of Stonehenge, Avebury and the Chalice and Tor of Glastonbury.

She is in spirit and when the terms of knowledge have the necessary right to acknowledge the spirit, surely it would be of and not in the masculine force of a living man who has seen to use the negative energy for his own understanding and rule?

It would seem to be the revolution times of the feminine spirit to enhance the total energy of love, romance, gift, nurturing and to hold the sword of the masculine as a symbol of all nature being made from and seen to create life, create positive auras and to impress on the given souls the element of magic for the children, love for the woman and most of all protection from all men and for them to serve the principle of woman to its full and utmost.

Gone are the days of the masculine male king leader who sees it through the eyes of the stronger, the bolder and better, when the elements of grace, tenderness and delicacy, would be the stronger terms in time and the wholesome strength of the complete eternal senses which gives birth to better times, helpful atonements, greater love and finally secures the true way of the mighty temple of Stonehenge, which would be very proud of the day the white spirit Queen is seen, felt and known to be at the pure helm of all people, familiars and spirits on the path to attitudes, notions, energies with intentions to secure the heart of the beauty, honour, grace and favour of the woman we all need, the children need; mother and all men are safe in the knowledge they are born to fight, protect and serve the white bright delight in nature and love.

To be free as spirit on the plain. To be free in living towards the brilliance of union and together all can find sanctuary, safety and solace in the one true aether of a fixed feminine earth ghost of rightfully placed, fitfully enhanced, totally triumphant and complete in the nature of a second coming which is the Queen of sister, mother and elder, in the knowledge we can all be rest assured our honour, faith and beliefs can go untarnished, leading to the understanding of after-life which is as perfect as the mind would see, create and love it to be.

*

Rid ourselves of the evil usurping king from foreign lands and let it be known Imbolg Thorn has helped to secure the notions and the right to feel the energies of a positive drive against the development of parasites in the air of mighty places, leeching onto; like heathen demons and hurting the fine sound of the good people, who wish to live in spirit around their family home, which is not used and interrupted by damage, wilful hate, fear, power with dark magic, unholy incantations which have brought the place to represent the fallen and the only hero is the fucking king bloke who thinks he is the only one who cares!

In letting the vortex of Stonehenge know, it is for the positive reinstatement of the badly used, talked about, fantasised, trampled on, right off; to be the fault of the fall of a supernatural kingdom, to be slandered and slaughtered and then to be pushed back into the dark regions of devils! IS and would be a massive crime, based on the simple sense of her name!

And what's in it?

Guinevere; a white bright beautiful fair and fine unconditional nurturing spirit!

*

This and so it is that the gargantuan giant of a beast rose its stupid fucking head; and having needed me to kill/assassinate the supposed reincarnation of the sacred union of King Arthur and Guinevere; when I couldn't, although I wouldn't; no one needs my death wrath, my anger mixed with depression mixed with the dark side of an undeveloped spiritualist who knew of the threat, the turmoil, the in-depth nature of such indignities, such low requirement, only to be left alone, sad, ruined, in prison for the law has to take its prisoners, to show surmountable justice and slam dunk the ill, the finished, the wrong and the evil into the system of remorse, of boredom, of everyday requirements to act according, seek no difference, lose the privileges of a freedom which brings a better view on depth into the sight, into the seeing, into the viewing of something which sounds familiar, looks possible and acts within the bounds of hope, of love, of special requirements to be allowed to sense a self-freedom, which brings euphoria, which holds the key, lets the nature sense the right, the understanding of a future, which allows the persona to be spirit, to be joyeux in the terms of a life to be mastered, to be partners and to be an honour to have fulfilled the time in helping, hoping, energising, total control on the peace given, offered and earned.

Having turned Thorn insane; terminally; he had been used by and haunted by the devils; the beast of haunted ancient places, which he expected to be sacred to the point of; clear to endeavour within, without danger, threat, ghosts or covered and ruled by the darkness beyond the comprehension of human minds, human travels, human ideals and guardianship of powerful love, grace, space and intrinsic understanding of the mists of time and the use of metaphor which classifies the doubter, the router, the pummel, the insecurity of youth, of age, of life; agentive with possibility, expectation, jurisdiction and the rules to know, sharpen up to, to know and use well, the laws to bound and find the connection to all mysteries, to all fantastic phenomenon which can see the past connected to the future; whilst living carefully in the present open.

*

So, he will leave the south-west and journey into the normal lands where the giants won the war and are soundly, safely, soliloquy asleep.

Slumbering; undisturbed by a metaphorical experimentalist spiritualism.

*

The great ugly spectacle of a beast! Rising out of the morning aether; listening hearing Thorn wrestle with a dream party he was attending and awaking with such words as: *'Why would you do that?'* or *'Why did you have to do that?'*; which brought a joining beast to subject his minnows to the large encumberant words of, *'Why does he have to answer every-time?'*, as if it was rather annoying that Thorn would and could answer the spirits of the aether and try to have conversations with them and try to help them and still insist in a development of the species rather than the damnation of the forlorn, the forgiven, the unloved and the blasphemy of children!

So, he seemed frustrated with Thorn.

In time and during the day, Thorn drew 'it' up with the hook of aether, by the scruff of the neck and commenced to stick a cross up its arse!, then use the closer swords of the known four power blades, used by his die-hard good friends and warriors of the spirit – Joshua, Kid, Jools – and finally, he turned from the his favourite soap, 'Emmerdale', and swung the great blade of Excalibur, which with great power and being sick and tired of the fucking dark side; put paid to the beast!

For now …

Still there are others; just don't venture where others have never ventured before; unknowing, without security and expect to meet angels and all in the service of the gods – a goddess.

The disrespect and indignity worked and silent the early night weather, the beautiful scents of summer to come and settlement for the psyche of individuals, who have tendered to the impossible due to a lack of life, of experience and sure, *to be*; one is aware of frightening aspects which make the realm of paranoia; which brings down the solo insight of the individual, who has to become a member of the one; the soul of the human universe; when many are at sorts and need to be brought the nurturing security of and settlement, which crowns the day and leads to a wonderful fascinating evening of *'whatever gets you through the night'*.

A long way to go … lots to know and find and don't leave no one behind!

Baggage is no good in a fire fight, but peace would be a good idea and it takes a spirit warrior to solve the pragmatic horrors of some cold torment, dull and damp, a place of disillusionment and manifest evil.

Preparation is the key

… and being ready is the other; just to do and dare is enough.

*

Thorn speaks:

"I am not in spirit, but in the energy of element; the light power and the dark light are my being; I am not as others are and can only act within the remains of myself, my spirit and my total psychic consciousness, hold the control of all elementation, making me an elemental force."

*

With all the bad energy and damnation Imbolc Thorn was wondering about the involvement of the King and his partner, a Guinevere.

So, did he kill his Mother? Joshua put 'Kid' in prison for such a length of time, which has probably altered his life, changed his aspects and damaged his freedom towards the essence of Elementals and spirit of the soul.

Damaged: Ann, Soo, Gally and him.

Putting it all before the lords of the light, they slowly looked at the case and it all seemed to be pointing to the in-gracious matter of involvement with demons and devils; with negative dangerous intention to use the holy spectacle of spirits/elementals and so basically destroy the outlook of psychology, insight into the daily rhythm of sense and super-sense, plus the use of supernatural energies; attacking the beautiful idea of being different and being recognised for such intentions when the world can gang up on you and one is able to deal with the onslaught due to connections with a super-nature which helps to enlighten, to advise and use the wisdom of all journeys towards a better world and better people, instead of hindering and seeking the elite cause of something which can only be achieved through self-sacrifice, spiritual endeavour and total connection and commitment involving awareness for the better and being able to call upon the dark-sided ultimatum which hankers for a payback, threefold, even the designation of relinquishing the spirit of self to abate the price and cost of such needs, finance the terms with sacrifice and unholy ideals with a singular purpose designed with hope seeking the target and assimilation of assassination which can be ignored, put aside; as no one will notice, or none will be able to solve, put asunder or bring any other closure to such dark deeds of death.

*

No. It was his own daemon: divine power, fate or god, for good or evil, trying to be with him and trying to help the situation towards a regard for his displeasure with the outside world!

Imbolc Thorn had changed and seen the divine reasons to be less than and also the bedevilment of all things as regards the attempt at being totalling different to his surrounding world and the intention of the future into the being and something else.

He went outside on the offside to behead his daemon; due to the fact that he was unable to work with such and develop a relationship based on a power available to use when attacking a situation which would land him a name in the infamous notorious catacomb echelon with telepathic communication with the outlaws of nature and so using a machete and semi-glad went on to have to execute the one thing which if he had been something to be, then it would have been that which allowed him to be powerfully different and over all intrinsics; with the spirit of the soul of being, towards the notion of commanding, holding hostage, manipulating and even destroying the world with negativity, unhappiness, turmoil and over all hatred for the way, the way of things, the way to be and the way expected of the time, aeon, pride and certainly an aim to die with honour, to find a good death and lastly, never coming to terms with the days and times one has to find a way in, to find a way with and certainly – eventually – finding love, respect, safety and security.

He was different to that, as he had already achieved the standard of respect needed – in Glastonbury. The army of protecting dark druids and the light of decency and respect.

*

Don't tut, don't tease, don't swear in the sacred aether; as you are the elements in which the energy of the air depends and you are coming out at the wrong place! The Stonehenge egg is broken and you are swimming about like lost souls, no name and no aim to reach a decent afterlife whereby the demons and devils are mingling within you as the portal of the Tor in Glastonbury is the place of your final journey where your soul will be measured and judged by St Brigit.

That is possible as some daemons are within, due to being induced and collected by the locals who in their adept will be seen to be able to work with the positivity of a mystic who wishes to be different from the nation's madding crowd and enhance the chances of established character and wit without sharing the knowledge with 'mundanes' or 'muggles', 'mud bloods' what have ya!, *said Thorn*, as he sat in the light, never wishing to use it up and see it burn out, having to punish such chaos, he will leave it all alone and be gone elsewhere where there is hardly much to put up with, contend with or be so mightily abused, his whole idea of spiritual contact and communication is threatened.

Too much for a psychic all this, he communicated with his person telepathy, to himself and looks to the days when he don't have to fight for the right to live, breathe, love or make friends with the friends he has in the elements who are hurt and insulted by what the birth of a broken egg is giving out.

*

Why should he believe what they believe in; the state, the people, the country? He believes in freedom. Self-responsibility and need not greed.

If they could think for themselves then they would and what would they really do? If they could be responsible for all of their actions and ways and thoughts and traffic, what would it all be like and if they could just receive what they need would they be *honestly satisfied*?

*

He watched the TV, the women talking about Sigmund Freud, and sensed the same old trouble; jealousy and envy and hate and anger and something too old for comfort, to gone and been for knowing, last time and out and the feeling of being manipulated, being watched over, and the final blow was love – something beside himself, being alone – loved him.

So, he looked into the mystery of aether and saw the thing he beheaded. Right down the shoulder blade, right into the heart! Right so the sound of her fucking aching will of sordid youth, tortured woman and old fucking hag crone spat out the last vestiges of pain!

"*Got her at last!*" he said. He had, and the thing looked to be healed.

He spun about and let the hawking hammers of witches in and they killed it off!

Then he advised to burn it. So the figures of defence, all this time against such a fucking battered old fucker bitch; – did.

Silence. The ultimate silence of what it all was about here in the world of haunting and trouble due to some old cow falling in love with his goodness, kindness, understanding and battlement of strategic bullshit – hurting enough to hit out and change the aspect, to formalise the foundation of a 'run of a mill' which was liable to derange any insight into the world within a world.

*

The crone was dead.

The nearer days still inside the room was a very large hornet. The sort which could sting you and ring in the bitch pill to hurt – so, in recognition of the symbols of nature to the will of kind, it was the old stinging crone; stung; lying on the floor dying.

He put it outside and it faced the door in an act of insect sympathy. He saw and sensed the death, as the giant hornet turned and faced the path, moved, he gestured with his foot, it moved, it was alive but dying, and the last beat of its powerful wings were soft and shallow, done and pointless.

Like the image of a nightmare it was. It was five inches long with a large head, thin body and a great big rear end, such was the formula of a giant hornet died.

It was the message to be read. Dead the crone of unrequited love and dead the energy which had fucked up his life for the last five years.

The things one receives or gets! One has to be careful! In the necropolis of the forgotten stones, the 'ever after', a good training ground for the adept, but too much when the psychic kicks in and the world is heard to whisper and talk and gossip and slander and lead the blunder to the after yonder!

The time resolved and the possibility of either; Thorn Paranormal Investigations Ltd or getting a boat and fucking off out of here, being reverberant and thankful, leading to an open river and the spirits of time and place and meeting the most remarkable energies, which could passable; be the way to finish this here adventure on planet plant, planet animal and planet creation /evolution/work.

The 'minglers' are recognised and come out at night, already with slaves and servants, sometimes looking for more and greed is their downfall.

Thorn has it now. He has it, as he would like it, as it should be, and let's not start to imagine the way forward is to go hunting for them! Yeah, why not? TPI, or better still resting at the home and getting fit to fight for the right to light up the night; and let the energies, the entities, the Elementals. the shadows, the shades, the spectres and all similes go home to the after-life they deserve, need, want and expect, when the mother pearl is broken and needs healing or putting down/put to sleep, then the sky might shine in the admiration of a place which is not the Celtic underworld inundated by 'minglers'; devils and demons of all predomination, lost souls, lost Christians looking for a way out of purgatory and then the pleasure of pixie and elf and faerie and gnome can all live with the knowledge that the giants, trolls, dragons and goblins are all very friendly and have changed their ways to suit the climate of the magic realm an after-life and eternal living for the ones who deserve the patience of the universe and little did we know of the reasons why we are really here.

Bless you and do not try to judge anybody. What a fight! The place is fucked!

*

… and so the *'Shadow'* came out of hiding …

There! right in front of Imbolc Thorn! There, dark and foreboding, seemly sorted with the friendship of something one had said or done or realised.

The dark ominous silhouette residing in his living room. As blackened tar! Young attractive underneath the dress of hell. With the only colour of slight amber shaded eyes. She used them to look as forlorn and helpless as she possibly could.

Murdered in New York City. With no pity; for there had been many over the years of notorious killings in the backstreets of Manhattan.

Every time Thorn used or dropped into his feminine side, she was there. It was there to hate and hurt and misunderstand the world for what had happened to her; beyond redemption, sure, but, not the responsibility of some and defiantly a murder of the others.

Spirits and energy remain due to pain and injustice and the fight to try to put it all right would lie on a woman to fight for her justice; one like Cancan Bier and not a wandering soul destined for other places and occurrences.

This was the deep psychological problem which fallowed deep in the dark recesses of Thorn's mind, experience, life and being dangerous to the will of understanding the new revolution of *womans* and his possible hate for them; due to her ill evil darkness and for the stem of life which always wins in the light and brings the truth through all spirit energy.

She had grown to love him and would not let another be with him.

Looking at the one total truth, the reason for being; perhaps the lie being the season of the bitch, the stitch in time – as the weaving of all cosmic sorrow, blessed itself all over the carpet, stood nicely, there – over-there where one could let go the soul of the sight, the blight of all religious might – as the problem presented itself – in knowing the representation of self is easy – the warping of the space-time, the climbing of the Andes, the smoking of the precious herb and finally before one has forgotten the bliss and twist of the solo orb inside the plexus, which blessed in the nature to confine, to out go and outstand, then it is a tough stone; a crystal of kindness, understanding, compassion and worth, the true deliverance to the final resting place – the ages, the aeons, the protons, the magic, the simple stated reason for the new world, the new age, the golden age to come.

Bless those that have died for it to be so, and those who will refuse to recognise the status and be the evil within it – sent to demonstrate the blight of the reasons, for all white supremacy; includes all creed, colour, diversity, sex gender, religion, politic; etcetera, if we reach at all, in the motion of a universal cosmic eternal immortal understanding of happiness, pleasure, love, respect and comprehension, then the result will be *phenomenal!* Precious! Brilliant, the earth will be seen, the respect for the aspect of all life will be seen, the holy ground from which the secondary journey to achieve will be seen and the sight of the dark one; seemly to show – thus Thorn's wizardry has come in.

No anger, just passive action based on the rules of acceptance, achievement and force.

At a time better than such upsets and disarrangements, climbing all over the blindness, the lack of knowledge, of sight; to see the ideal in the world coming through material – through to the ideal material; we shall join on the other-side, in the other-world.

*

Entering the stones – a faux blow, then the immediate, which rips the cloth off, which shows the light from within and lets the state of climax be, the hope, the triumph, the spoils of a funny thing? This waking up to the planet, to the reasons for being, for the blessing of all creation, to the education of why and what it will be like in a thousand years, when the tribes have lived and white man massacred the soul and the soul travels to the knowledge and the knowledge is told; then the guilt and the sorrow, the pardon and the holy mess, will be calmed, soothed, healed and allowed to enjoy the white light, which we are and which we become as spirit of the soul.

It is the light of earnest and at peace with the all; that which is ready and safe to show itself; due to reasons and problems; still the healing commences and the world changes from the inner bestial human to the wise-ones, in a complete array of sight – possibility, destiny and the one place one will always be, the solo time to seek and know, the drama of one's life – can be; will be and shall not be taken away by anything else, other than time.

Equate the masses of information, the experience, the allowance, the endeavour, the choice, the senses, the recompenses in planetary time.

Then you shall be a neo-human, my friend.

The Elementals are blessed and the senses speak of the birth of such by the said earth planet.

What is she? Why is it so, when we are the one's alive? Are we *not?*

Maybe they should be here and we are just a matter of material and lead a hopeful life towards what Jesus can show us – and all the rest of the magi, the sages, the wise-ones needed to be condemned for their insights, into the neo-ideal-matter of fact ways to show and seek the celebration of the human form, the love used and abused, the designated listening to those who traverse the origins, the ancient books, the knowledge of instinct, which brings us back to the martyrs, the holy, the sacred, the venial, venal, veridical; the Torah, the Septuagint, the bibles of many forms and from such the favour and flavour of self will be absolved, atoned, forgiven and the god is a merciful forgiving god=dress.

We go to the found. We seek the earth's pleasure and wait to reside in heaven. We can trust and we can love; now can we fathom the experience of something which does not exist.

Do we need to make it? Let's not and simply move to the future knowing we will allow some later generation to really work it all out to its completion, with satisfaction, beauty, bliss, happiness and joy with and in the organs of the human outfit.

The imagination is the tools of the idealist. It is not to make something up, to create life, as it were – it is to already use the established notions, information, education and lives; then in the real world; the subconscious, the simple and sublime, the whole act, the daydreaming and the thoughts of how she thinks, how she wishes, what she wants and finally *what have we done?*

Then the apocalypse of humanity can happen.

And the change will be refreshing.

If it don't happen then, Imbolc Thorn has and he wants to be in the world of life, the world of nature and live it all out inside himself … the feelings, the knowledge, the happenings, the tasks; so far; and on to the ultimate assured resting place for want of breath.

In other words lots to take in and take on.

Which should have been for starters.

[1959 – 2040]

*

So, I took a ride for to gaze awhile, upon the fields of wheat and the task of the senses, brought with it, the feeling of the only place left, after, up to one's tether with it all, when the depth of the soul is deep, into the stomach and sensing deeper in the solar plexus, below the belly button, above the genitalia, there as a point of reference, as the last place he has, to feel, sound, and say of the utmost, things to ward off the pressure felt, the reaching out for *'whatever you want, take it now and be done with it!'*

Across the fields, the distance and the air filled with the wing of all birds, into the puddles made by the summer rains, the price of a dare; into the hollow stream, seeming to know the serious matter at hand is:

"I WANT YOU!" [the voice]. The resonate bullshit dark-man thing. Hanging onto my life, my illness, my waste of time, watching the world change and those who wish to make sure it does not, using religion, when the use is high heated jealousy for the way it will go and who for.'

"THEN TAKE ME … COME ON! LET'S HAVE IT HERE! LET'S FACE THE FUCKER HERE! AND BE DONE WITH IT! ALL YOU WANT IS MY LIFE … THEN TAKE IT … NOW!"

*

During this time, Thorn had felt to command his loyal guard, but alas, they too had been run ragged, they too had done all too much for him; he heard the wasted gasp, when told to deal with the situation.

In this time, they felt, allowed to be unsure of their ultimate reason for being connected, and the honour of the soldier spirit, the noble element, just bowed to Thorn, with a complete air of loyalty, honour, love and the far distant friendship; if things were different here; he seemed to show a samurai loyalty and sped off; after Thorn had told him to retire, it was all his fight, now. Now, he could energise, now he could cycle somewhere, now he could work the soul and use the strength of commitment he had used to keep all devils and demons away – *"Go now and rest, my friend and I thank you for all your great work."*

When the pain mixes with intention and the final thrust to fight, when there is nothing left, but something new, which had not been used at all before, so the demon could and would and did take full advantage of the situation – domestic and ill; Thorn had been desperate to visualise, to think and to see and know, what it could be, what it was to deal with the critter immediately, and have no more to do with such shit! Bullshit! Down right inhuman disrespect and completely annihilating to the self – spirit and soul.

The soul. The last place which lives. The final feeling. No other sense. None.

So, the voice could be heard. The honour spirit knight must have known Thorn's way, as the time was the struggle, the struggle with pain, the last pitch, the one thing human beings have left; the stored feelings of time and life, the knowledge and notion of good and greater things, the presence of a stronger sense of an all too familiar friend; a truthful companion who is the soul; the journeyman, the one who leaves to walk the path to the heavens. It is the pouch, the package, the complete untouched soul of humanity's purpose and precious place of dying to live. Known as the place to which we all must go; and that death is …

… *the mid- point to a long life.*

*

So, in the time it takes and the reason for knowing, it all means the darkness is showing, the pure hate and reason for the destruction of living; it happened –

The spirit of the noble knight beheaded the shadow cast demon soiled devil play. Removing the whole charade of wanting to take a life for sure. To kill.

Thorn used his imagination; thought and carried out the same action. He felt the same and no one knew the noble knight was still there! He was told to go! The dark demon thought he had and his danger of seeing Thorn accept the invitation to die – he did not see him!

Amazing! What a noble element! A fantastic spirit! What brilliance! Sounding like the days of hyperbole before! This was a reading beyond the call of life, of death, demonology and duty!

What a man! Four years of working with Thorn's injury and helping him to remain sane – in a sense of sanity which allowed him to heal, to find a secondary peace, besides the trouble, the mess, the horror and the great grand pisstake! By the fucking shit of a fucking bastard! Well, words fail me! The bastard was after his life.

*

'I cannot thank him enough. I will not hyperbole ever again!' thought Thorn, 'I must be careful … there will not be a next-time because, I will find a way to see this life out well and make peace with all and everything and remember the small pouch of soul I carry, it will be the one to travel with a clean slate, a good record and find out where, maybe, we all go to and rest. AMAZING!'

*

Thinking of Josh and knowing he has gone now. He has gone to rest. Good old boy.

If it don't get you, it makes one stronger; if it does, what does that make one? – he is sure, we will all find out.

A most noble knight.

*

Heal the hollow place;
AND DROP THE GREATEST NUCLEAR BRIGHT LIGHT ON THE PLACE!

*

… a Christian experience, using the imagination and the Cross to keep them at bay.

*

It was all a Hex! An *hex-calibur*. If you like, which is not to be liked, as the hex was horrible; death threatening! Life-threatening! It was out to destroy life and kill the liver.

Thorn heard it – wait, it all became clear one day, when having been out shopping, he was immediately upset about something, someone or something someone had said, done or not done.

So, he began to drink. He drank until he drank some more, by going to the shop and whilst riding on his trike there; he was overheard talking out loud to himself about something which seemed appropriate and needed attention and addressing; he must have seemed aggressive. Loud. He knew he was, Thorn was and had been upset again for every day for 16 years! He spoke out-loud.

Then someone heard him. Now, this person was known to be a peculiar sort of character who seemed to be a 'brick short of a full load' and had the atmosphere of a strange, fairly abused by life kind of aura; when he stopped in his tracks, in the street and with the decibels of angst, anguish with a tipple of fear, deep set in the understanding of a slow past life; shouted at the top of his voice, his lungs breaking against the lack of freedom in his living space, "YOU ARE TALKING TO YOURSELF! YOU SHOULD BE LOCKED AWAY! YOU ARE **MAD!** … " he petered off, at that point, as Thorn turned and stopping talking, tried to smile with unusual indifference, which only he had got used to, only *he* could see the sense in, as to the reason why he spoke to himself, when, in fact, he was speaking the Elementals, the telepathic mind of the plenty, seeming only to be famous, on the stage to an audience, aloud, as his pissed-up day, to be entertaining, humorous and everlasting tripe on the circuit of experience.

*

The man, the unusual man, called Terry, a local man, lad, born and bred and dead in parts to the world – just stared with frightening eyes of seeing before the reasons for insanity, the reasons for a section in the psychiatric units of an imprisoned land, where to be free is some other people talking, or just for the birds in the sky, or to be earned on the back of lost days of capitalistic endeavour, to earn the right to be sailing on a cruise ship in the Mediterranean off the Greek islands, without qualm, any slight of conscience, or for a better world to come; slow down on the sailing mansion, with many upstairs bedrooms, giving the servants enough time to clean.

Looked like Terry should accost the madman and shake him out of his insane reverence, before it was all too late and the man in the white cloak came to pay you some attention, needing to be seen to, looked after and sorted out, back into the world of the living and dying and the rest of intelligent enlightened illumination can go ta fuck! Until the right surroundings, the right atmosphere, the bloody board meeting or the end of days, when the words of Jesus make you act perhaps like him and speak to either the infidel or God.

It took 'Im' about the trip there and the trip back, to add to the day's insult and carry on with the diatribe rhetorical bullshit, he seemed to find himself sinking into, drowning every time, year, life and even hurting himself to the point of self-harm, death or even an atonement with the light of heaven, as he realises he is dead and gone to the bloody place!

He then realised, like all things in his life, it must be for a reason, a purpose and even still, have an even bigger and deeper meaning!

He thought and drank and listened to the music, he played to keep out the death throes of scorpion stings, of the venom of something which seemed to need him dead but was unable to reach the conclusion based on the stubborn survival skills of 'Im': Imbolc Thorn.

He drank himself and hurt himself and suffered the next day. He lay on his bed and felt the arisen of languished targets, as the methods had become easier over the years and the better person is able to raise the question, is able to address the situation and finally, come to some kind of reasonable insight into what 'it' – 'it' being, mystery – could be?

It then happened.

The most wicked, horrible of sounds right near his self, opened the doors of perception and the sound came out all evil like.

The sound was beyond everyday words, it was dark and foul and life threatening, as the yelp, inside a vicious command, inside an evil intention, made him jump, as his – Thorn's – good kind loyal and brilliant presence of spirit wiped it across the throat, the neck! The fucking stinking bloody bastard shit-fuck neck and took the bastard out!

Finally! The hex had been seen, been removed, been able to be recognised and all because the shadowwatcher did not want for 'Im' to live; more dread! ... more dread on his head and 'it' had also killed Josh with this, sent Kit to prison, killed his mother and spiritually raped sister Ann!

Set out in one great big black ritual in the darkness of the stones; a coven of twelve in ceremony placed the death threatening hex on the said people; whoever it was or may be: Mordred, the Black Knight and Gawain. Use your imagination if you can.

The dirty fucking little bastard!

Years ago, on one dark stormy night!, 'it' set the evil hex!

No one knew, no one guessed, only from the start of a life did D recognise there was something wrong with his and he surely could be better than he was, also in the immediate days of a citrinitas apocalypse.

Of all the things to do today, through to the days of better times and none should have to suffer the wrath of others, especially a witches' coven; hex. Fuck.

*

The hex brought and showed such happenings as; when drunk one early Saturday morning in the dawn of the rising of the explosive sun, out of the near garden flew a strange orange birdlike figure, which could only be with the wingspan of an eagle a large bird of prey!

What was a bird of prey doing hanging around the local neighbour's garden?

Thinking, Thorn saw another species. *I saw a dragon in flight!* I saw an orange bald skinned dragon with the wingspan; to say, it was made of leather. Outstretched, so as the wings seemed to propel the beast into the air; oddly, then taking flight as a sight forswore eyes, immersed in the alcohol of a night's binge, seeing something; out of this world and not really allowing it to dawn upon me, until I sobered up and remembered the beast; seeing the shape and the lack of development about its body, the wings seeming to be the only true strength of the myth, it had been quite a sight for the feelings of a morning, when the whole show of troubles had brought themselves to the development of one's mythology, of one's totem, of the facts brought about by the starvation of a wizard, looking for the force field to yield the fruits of all youth, development, possibility, magic and the notion of being able to be recognised by the nature of phenomenon, when the world is struggling to get beyond the wrath of war and death.

It was thin in colour, a light orange ochre and in places the magnitude of bitterness and strife showed in the mange of its coat, which was skin deep in places.

The sorrow dragon flew away, showing me the state of it and left the world of material reality, seeming to be gone and was totally underdeveloped to survive.

It had brought the largest of hornets; dead, on the doorstep for him to see. It was a giant wasp! It was a stinger, a dead stinger and she had died!

It was the trouble, it was the beast, it was a hex brought giant wasp to kill, to attack, to hurt and the witch had died. Dead. On the doorstep, so he picked it up in the palm of his hand and threw it into the fire!

"*Ta meta ta hex.*" [The things after the hex.]

*

So came the public warning. After all the 16 years of being troubled, being in a battle with a life-threatening entity, Thorn received a warning from the council.

He accepted the warning, but it was something which came as an after-birth, an after-hex, it was silly, it was perfect in its execution of belittlement, but, *Thorn learnt to see*, that to turn something which is negative into something positive is the way of the wise, the way, the world and the brilliance of a person, who was experienced, knowledgeable, concerning and searching for the holy grail, the philosopher's stone, an elixir of life; through peace of mind, heart and body, harmony, like as a Beatles' song *a tranquillity of love*, of love making and true indulgence into the union of life, which is the only way, the way to be and the triumph over adversity in accordance with the laws of nature, need, the 'blues' and an autobiography which may hit the town, the shops, the public, the terms to which all must attend, entering into the delights of being and celebrating the real material times of the body.

The will be safe. The spirit and soul secure.

*

Then he slept. Then he touched something which seemed to be out of bounds and then he saw the carcass of the life threatening, hunter killer of the hex.

She was a dark green colour. She was a queen spider-witch.

She had the arachnophobia of all eight legs and on her head was a crown of gold.

She had the face of damnation and the energy of death.

The aim: to kill.

*

How does 'one' atone for one's sin?

Thus, after all the outcome after the fall is blamed on the terms of a legend.

So, Mordred was sin, was evil.

He raped and impregnated Guinevere. He then has the cheek to reincarnate and expect to be forgiven by – above all – Guinevere.

She could and will not forgive him/it.

She was known to be the cause of the downfall of the Kingdom of Camelot; Arthur's reign. Or was it the attempt by Queen Morgana to usurp the kingdom and so place Mordred as the one true heir to the deep dark swath, the horrible time of 'no law', the justice of peace brought about by savages and barbarians and still it would be seen fit to blame the one who took it upon himself to ravish, so called, the kingdom?

Without reason or purpose; but that of bringing the King down for his incestuous liaison with his supernatural half sister Morgana; *tricked!* I!

But still, the escape from the rivers of hell, to be born somewhere at all possible to reason with the downfall, with the outcome and know the family one is reincarnated into has a sense of stock, of upbringing, to rise to the abuse and law which ridicules the son, who born in such a way, would seek a kind of freedom immediately upon understanding the life ahead and the forgotten reason for being?

Seeking forgiveness. When in this life, he has hardly done any wrong.

What helps the forgiveness by her? Is it good looks? Is it a standard of life which can only be seen as cooperative and ambitious to allow for the strain of the devil to rule the world; as a leading politician?

Oh no! But, still come as the vagabond bastard he is supposed to be.

To be seen and recognised, not hiding behind a sheep's clothing. Hiding nothing, but having forgotten who he was … to the sense of time which shows him and Fuck! … Oh yeah! Shit! I would never forgive him either!

Reincarnate Hitler! Jack the ripper! Genghis Khan! etc.; would they be forgiven?

No.

*

Although, the time is changing and the motion to accept and allow to be who you are is the going rate, then to know and find out one is looking for an atonement for a previous life.

Especially when the legendary soul of the Queen can not forgive Mordred, a son of Arthur.

Go to church, seek absolution! Go to the synagogue and get down on your knees and pray!

Say, 'Sorry!' … ?! urrrrh … pay the dues owed! Well, there's one. Surely! Nah!

Fuck it! She can't forgive him!

He will just have to jump back into life, disappear, get lost in the wilderness of fame and notorious history; forget about such shit and hit the fan with a clean slate and look for the feelings of atonement one needs. To break down and cry for a thousand years! It still will not be enough.

*

She is dead. She died. We all die. And some are not able to run the gauntlet of the demons of hell to seek a reference, an unjustified parody to the new book according to our king the saviour of all mankind, who has run that gauntlet, just to get here first and condemn his bastard illegitimate incest son *again!*

Merlin made Arthur through the dead body of Gorlois, the fucking thing was tarnished from the start and it all goes to show within the time and the so called battles, for to win the day, would be for the fucking welsh and not the bloody people of Wiltshire!

Perverts to the end, all of them!

So, what's fucking new! A fuck here and a raping there and a bit of sodomy and what-else they do in the times of the boy king?

Did she betray the country or not? According to the French, she did.

She sought atonement in Wiltshire, did she get it?

Now it's Mordred's turn.

Back off, done.

'Let's put the bitch back in its grave and trouble the seekers of solace and understanding no more!

Okay, so she atoned. Well done.

Now it is between fuck face and ugly cunt to work it on out. Surely.

And if not, then what? My death.

I have given you it. I died. Mordred died.

I am me. I am him. I am 'im'. I … ?!'

Seven years either side of sex and need and loving for three months. 14 years without companionship, love, company, understanding and just a little patience.

I broke my body up and down to a cripple. I had no energy no more. He is broken in all areas! Even the one where I ran for safety and tried to be forgiven. Mordred is dead. Gone. No more.

Okay, satisfied. Good. Now get on and save the world. Go on and heal the frame of psyche in the soul of people, the indigenous, the alternative and if you want, the *Arthurian legend*.

I did not mean to come here and harm or hinder or hurt anyone, no one.

I can understand you not wanting to accept such, to embrace the lad, to collect and transfer his sordid horrible sleazy soul and bathe him in the warmth of forgiveness, which you both have sought and gained.'

Morgana don't care. She don't need anything to do with it all.

You tread on me again like this and one would suddenly think, one might be a beast from a past-life; one could be the most heinous fellow to ever breathe here on this earth, but he just ain't able to rise out of the pits of Abyssinian hell to come and see ya!

*

If Guinevere was left alone to rest, I know she would have liked to know if Mordred was ever heard of again, or set free! But, to rest in peace is the aim, not to have some witch dig up the mantel and use it because she's shagging Arthur; the king bloke man dude.

Leave her alone grave diggers! Grave robbers!

You have killed Mordred. But not me.

I will live until I know where it is I go, after this!

Yes, you were right to do it, I suppose, I just have a sense of apathy when it comes to the times and the place and the fucking weird goings on, what with the madman Merlin and why.

What for? So the country could not be ruled by foreigners.

All he wanted to do was fight by your side. He was awesome! He was frightening! He would be just like the Bear!, the Pendragon!, a totem. No name, just out of the darkness.

He would have liked that.

*

His mother said *"no"* and the father said *"No!"* What was he to do? Where was he ta go?

Well, he is dead for good and you've got me to thank for that. If I wanted to be Mordred, I would have been, I have always been too old, by the time I managed to get there, here.

I would have sought you both out and cut ya fucking throats!

But, I am here to seek love, respect, understanding and knowledge, for my next life.

How about you?

Leave the spirit of Gwen alone. She paid and suffered enough. Woman gives and takes away.

We are all born from such notions. We need humanity first, not gender. Sex is easy, it's living without it that hurts, that pains, that which is punishment for any of the sick fucking lunatics which have tarnished the name and frame and destiny of the freedom responsibility of us all.

"I am sorry. I can understand why. I would not lie. No need.
He is dead inside of me.
May I atone in this life, with what's left. For myself, Derek Peter Thorn."

*

It seems to be on the 23rd of October 2016, Thorn had to change his procedure from the spectrum of the light, to his own personal darkness; hell. The mist was gathering, they say the breath of a dragon, the eerie motion of lower formed clouds gave the dark night arena a tinge of foreboding and—

It all stayed by the street lights like moth to a flame.

The stillness and argued silence, the trouble sensed and perceived seemed to command the will of ghostly mystery; as a ghoul, the spooks motioned for an everlasting hallows eve.

Then he knew, all along, he had been so disrespected and dishonoured, also ever so offended in his whole damn life! Respect is earned; but never mind if it is not.

The aim was the standing stones of Salisbury Plain.

He cracked the heeling stone and the rest; as the seemly spirit of the druids immersed, as he kept on hurting them and making the stones bleed. The dark shadow, the infamous bastard black druid appeared and spoke thus: *"I need to see you there!"*

Thorn told him in no uncertain terms to, *FUCK OFF!*

So he mumbled something to himself and turned and left.

Thorn shouted about the abuse, the disrespect, the offending years! The trouble and the harm and hurt it had brought him, which had tired him; he had lost most of his collected work; from off the Tor and had seen it all ravished, upturned, destroyed! All for the way of the spectre of ancient stones – *The mystery of Stonehenge, you can keep! I am too hurt, upset, forlorn and my heart is broken, because of your great fucking mystery!*

You can keep mystery, he said, *I don't have any secrets and I think mystery is overrated!*

If this is what it is! What it means! Then I would rather leave it all alone! Till I am well again, to face the world's materialistic reality, which brings bliss, comfort, harmony, tranquillity, the quintessence of life! The security and wholesomeness one needs to survive this life experience of a universal planet.

All is too much. Time is a great healer and so is sanity – reason, common sense and self worth in preservation.

Thorn tried to be mystic in Glastonbury, he earned his colours, his sword, his light, his command of his own darkness and masters of ancient mystery went ahead and ruined it all!

There are some-things to learn and understand; but heal, healing and a simple grandeur of life to be considered.

*

"Have I not commanded you?
Be strong and courageous.
Do not be afraid; do not be
discouraged, for the LORD
your GOD will be with you
wherever you go."

Joshua 1:9.

*

In that place; as at birth, THORN was touched by the darkside of Scorpio. In the journey of his first days of the virgin sign of Virgo; he was also seen and watched over by a darkness, a sphere of shadow in-specialised by an underworld – a dark forbidding energy which represented itself as a fire of trouble, different, spoiling to the effects of just goodness and worth which allows for a person to be and grow in the real world of commerce.

This was there to remind, to replace and affectingly adjudicate the outcome in the realm of magic, spirit, shadow and scary shade. This was always with him in his paranoia. This was always there when there was no insight to anything which could help him to understand and illuminate the reason; as the reason was far removed; before birth; somewhere; otherwhere; a place beyond and forming in the realisation and life of the famous adept of spirituality THORN was becoming.

He saw the writing on the walls and the marks of tricks and plays brought about by this that haunted his darkside, his dreams and nightmares and his living consequences when hoping for a better start, a better wife; a life which allowed for him to move into freedom when needed, to move into love when he could, to move into hope when he knew he had to and to move forward in life when he seemed to have to search and 'look back' over so much and so many and whilst he rose to the challenge by entering the Tor at Glastonbury; he was also returning to his birth; a rebirth; a back sliding into the days of childhood and nearby family reality.

So, he simply turns to the task and asks where he will gain the revelations to see what it is that don't want to be seen. Why? *What is wrong with it?*

Then, look to the reason and go and kick himself for seeing; *'It was a Dwarf!'*

Scorpio is a dwarf! And the planet is and the moon is his wife Karon. Is it not? Then; yes – he sees it all now and reassures the Dark dwarf that he is understood whilst looking for a bride amongst the elemental young; the children he has held prisoner and in the mind of THORN has driven him to psychic hell and back with it all!

He is a playful dwarf! And he can be married to his moon!

Now. With all the skills and gifts and tricks and ways and War-bands and fighting and enlightening and form; which to be the training of an adept wizard/poet – *true*; but, he needs a wife too! He needs peace and quiet too! He would see to it that he doth!

They will. They will settle the will within the 58 years THORN has been alive!

Now – where is he? He has just upset him and his minnows! They are sweet and Thorn is terrible! THORN THE TERRACOTTA! ... But soft ... ! He is watching 'Time Bandits'!

At last; then I know the future has been solved and resolved by the stream/river/ocean/sea – when the boat is sailed out to the Atlantis and the maker will be there to show himself!

3% Pluto in 12% Virgo/first house. Over to the sun house of Capricorn with 1% Saturn and a conjunction with Mercury/Pluto! Then on to the house of Scorpio with Neptune 6%; showing in pattern of trines and sextiles; a fucking boat! A sailing ship!

If he had not come to domestic-al terms near Stonehenge.

Now there is love! Now there will be love! Now he will be loved for him and not for the vain façade he could be!

In the time it takes for Venus to travel backwards; it takes for the tricky red dwarf to show himself and be accepted and loved for who he is and not embarrassed because THORN had been DT or Decca or Deadly or Drui or done for! He was the man and the man was the dwarf and the princess was Sarah and the story ends.

What to do with it all hey! My sail is real and my boat is a dark scorpion dwarf-man.

*

So, it is that within the aether are the Christians of purgatory. They have also been supported by the psychic mindset of the national people who fly the flag of Jesus Christ, the Bible, God and sin and evil and purgatory for those who have sinned and have been vicious enough to hurt the real mystic realm; of magic and dreams and friendship and the place where there is no good or bad; just okay. *Okay is a good place to be*. Fine, just fine and balanced and harmonious with all and everything which exists.

So, the bastard Christians have taken the aether and made it theirs. Made it troubled with sin and demons and devils who use the mystic children in prison.

It is all wrong and the reason for it being all wrong is the way of the mystic psychic is to be fair, allowing, the Christians are inpatient, wrong and troubled.

The people of the living have allowed the place to be run and inundated by such shit! Such backward going forward *garbage!*

The place is a total sin madhouse place to be avoided and most of the world will be like that for LEADER THORN from now on in.

The real fantastic way is to be mystic. To help with healing and he is just at war with them.

They keep coming and the mindset of the flock of sheep is allowing, liking, needing it in such a state and proud of the understanding of sin and its opposite – good.

It is a weeping sight to behold and it is wrong and in terms of the world it is all over the earth's planet. To find a place to hide is to sail out to sea.

Get away and never landlubber again.

The way of the air and the franchise of such an awful hurtful reign is concerning, but it would be better if the aether were felt to be good Christians; helpful Christians; not judgemental ones and the children of the magic realm who are searching for the light to allow them to get home.

The Church receives the bastards and they need to be forgiven and get to Heaven. The mystic people do not. They can just go; but the Christian has fucked up the route, the way the ley-lines for their own shit! They are in the way and should be held accountable for the bad energy, the bad karma and the dharma which prevails in the present times for the deteriorated spirit when the unholy depression is sin and sin brings evil acts and evil tracts and the Church just does nothing for it.

THORN would; but why should he, if they hate and are the most unfriendly shit-heads in the space of cosmological understanding?

It is for the magick mystic folk to which he wishes to work and fuck the Bible and Jesus and the rest of the story; if one is so, then do as he did and get right and don't go wrong and fuck off back to your spirit heaven place; *bless you.*

Leave the aether to the alternative wave of okay; of just, of fine, of living, of giving, of love and in the macro-cosmic realm of love; be kind, great even, special and thankful for the chance to experience the universe from the limited perspective of the human soul.

To WAR then, and fuck 'em!

Let the party begin and let it be known the world is full of this and this is allowed due to the bigot biased understanding of people lacking in a knowledge when it comes to spirituality.

Shocking and surprising! *What did he expect?* Fuck! A Christian foothold on the hairy balls of life! The devil is mystic and the reaper is death.

You have no right to develop the world in such shite. Such messianical deplorable betrayal and founding fathers of murder and original sin!

From whence did it all come and happen to be – getting it so wrong; making up the time for royal riches and fratricide; making the world pay for the righteous belief in having to be good to not be bad to a human being who has a right to be and does not have to see the ancient ways of the world invaded by the cross and the fucking inquisitions!

Whatever happened to the true and real freedom? What became of the idea to live by the Lord's bread of manna and starve over a few fish and loaves? What and why dith the idea transcend to the width and wide of the universal planet which needs to be the religion; which needs to know the way of the birth, the rebirth, the climate and the animals who don't go to church; but are better mannered than the fucking vermin which cannot leave the world to be and must be like and must have to know the fucking devil exists – *WHY!?*

Do *you* know? Try disrespecting the outer darkness and putting in the image of – as is God – as is the fucking limitation of all ideals and ideology toward fulfilling a sinless life.

I true; be fucking divine and see where it gets ya! Martyr – tomata – in stocks!

Clean up ya shit God! Clean up ya spirit and let it be said the darkness rules and the light is there to see by. Together they are one; whole and together they should never have to misunderstand and disrespect eachother. No separation, segregation or total annihilation of the genocide of other species and ways due to the words of the *god-christ!*

Live together; I!; be as together; I! accept and develop, inspire and assure; I!; do not be having to be forgiven and expecting a rabbi of savage days to bail ya out!

Who created the story? Who looked to the blasphemy of crucifixion on a Sabbath and thought *Fuck! What a fucking great idea!* – why, the fucking dark one, that's who! He has a fucking laugh! and you hate the forbidden darkness! You hate it because you are from there! You.

Be kind and loving t'it. Be respectful and healing t'it and be sure you give your life to the change which allows the future to be together in dark/light; universe.

May the strength of war be with you! Always.

*

St Giles; patron saint of outcasts.

A CODA

So, wondering where it all comes from? Hence, the realise of information and terms based on history or legend, or simply refined to the definition of time. History can repeat itself; which could be a kind of outline to the way things happen or occur.

Placed in the plain of Salisbury sits Imber. A fine-natured village; with all the condiments and structures based on the way to live, to be, to know, to find a place which is your spiritual home.

Then the war arrives and off you go! And no coming back and no truth in the bases of hope; then the people; some, perhaps all; haunt the place; when dead. They return to roam the spirit plain of their ancestors and mourn the moaning of lost souls and the delve into danger and darkness and become what they could never be in life – a sin?

Then they sense a stranger, a psychic, a man who had walked the corridors of a 'further', who had been seen by the dead, the walking souls, the damp corridors of mist and fog, the place which brings no answers or claim to be, and after all the way he returns to the living air and reaches from his coma; only to never know they had seen him, they would blame him, they would find a way to see to the past and kill him?

The true Imberseals. The seal which succours to a place, a way and helps the fine release, the simple turn from the lonely darkness, an ignorance of shame and anger, of blame and hate, of disappointment and dishonour, to a place of many years wandering the fields, the ghost town, the other place – where the men who had had to leave the village; as they wept over their homes and lives – they protested and still forced to have to leave; for the terms of war and the solution to the invasion of Europe.

They would stand and fight. They would take up the carbine and fire at the movement towards the village; which brings a stand-off and *they will not be moved.*

Five good men and they would be the true; Imberseals, a play on words, as in imbecile, which means idiot, which means they would die for the right and belief of their parish, of their living and the place which meant so much to them.

And then, the others came and the modern day imberseal was Thorn. Torn and wasted, out to fix his pure destiny, his only true sense of triumph; like a fucking great big imbecile, he would fight for the disbelief, the homing of an empty shell and for fuck all – numbered by the government and brought down before he could breathe.

Then they knew of Kit 'Bull' Gawain and the Black Knight.

The hollow words spoken to be heard by the elder citizen; *'Kill them!'*; so they did.

But the final branch, the real true story, is a blacksmith who saw the thorn and wanted to disrespect him for his disrespect for his spiritual sovereignty.

The necromancer fights the aged old days of the purpose of judgement and work, and principle, moral, value, virtue and a stoic strife to bear the full brunt of having to die for the future; which makes such bastards, such crazy insane worship, just for the hell of it!

Then the reality comes into it, the rationality, the reason and sense, which forces the rod, the staff and the seal to be opened; so they can go home! To the Imber village in the sky.

The broken hearts, the broken bones, the push to the floor, the challenge of the terms of spirit and the veil of light which saves the souls of darkness; who don't deserve to wallow, to cry, to never see the love of respect again.

*

Milton Keynes UK
Ingram Content Group UK Ltd.
UKHW021955131124
451149UK00011B/915

9 781787 920521